The Rise of Common-Sense Conservatism

The Rise of Common-Sense Conservatism

The American Right and the Reinvention of the Scottish Enlightenment

ANTTI LEPISTÖ

The University of Chicago Press
Chicago and London

Publication of this book has been aided by a grant from the Meijer Foundation Fund.

The University of Chicago Press, Chicago 60637
The University of Chicago Press, Ltd., London
© 2021 by The University of Chicago
Published 2021
Printed in the United States of America

30 29 28 27 26 25 24 23 22 21   1 2 3 4 5

ISBN-13: 978-0-226-77404-6 (cloth)
ISBN-13: 978-0-226-77418-3 (e-book)
DOI: https://doi.org/10.7208/chicago/9780226774183.001.0001

Library of Congress Cataloging-in-Publication Data

Names: Lepistö, Antti, author.
Title: The rise of common-sense conservatism : the American right and the
    reinvention of the Scottish enlightenment / Antti Lepistö.
Description: Chicago : University of Chicago Press, 2021. | Includes bibliographical
    references and index.
Identifiers: LCCN 2020036090 | ISBN 9780226774046 (cloth) | ISBN 9780226774183 (ebook)
Subjects: LCSH: Conservatism—United States—History—20th century. |
    Culture conflict—United States—History—20th century. | Ethics—United States. |
    Common sense.
Classification: LCC JC573.2.U6 L46 2021 | DDC 320.520973—dc23
LC record available at https://lccn.loc.gov/2020036090

Contents

Speaking for the People in Culture Wars–Era America

Whatever happened to common sense? The question haunted Irving Kristol as the year 1984 was dawning. Already well known as the leading voice of the neoconservative movement, Kristol decided to tackle the issue in his first monthly column in the *Wall Street Journal* that year. It was a short essay, one of dozens that he wrote for the paper between the early 1970s and late 1990s. Yet this essay captured particularly well a dilemma that increasingly troubled Kristol and his fellow neoconservatives in the decades after the 1960s cultural upheaval: What, if anything, counted as "common sense" in an age that was burdened by a deep cultural divide and conflict between liberal and conservative Americans over profound issues of morality and national identity—a war "for the soul of America," as candidate Patrick Buchanan later put it in his widely noted "culture wars" speech at the 1992 Republican National Convention?[1]

Coming to the mid-1980s, it was a common perception that the period known as "the sixties" had contributed to a fracturing of American culture, and what had appeared as a relatively stable national culture in the postwar years seemed to be turning into ethical chaos. Were there any beliefs or principles left, Kristol was now asking himself, that would unite all Americans after the nation had witnessed the popularization of the counterculture and the rise of the identity-based movements of the New Left? Indeed, what happened to common sense in an age that saw Americans battling over the meaning of Americanness itself as the nation was becoming plagued by angry disputes over education, family values, and entertainment—as well as race, crime, and poverty—at times intermingling with loftier academic debates over the meaning of truth, beauty, and the Western canon?

Such questions confronting the neoconservatives in the culture wars era did not leave the group's leading voice without answers. In Kristol's telling, common sense in 1980s America had been obscured by the "tyranny of ideas." "The intellectual historian of the future," Kristol explained in the early Reagan years, "looking back on the past half century of American experience, will surely be struck by [this] phenomenon. . . . It is a tyranny exercised by academic, quasi-academic and pseudo-academic ideas over the common sense embodied in the practical reason of traditional wisdom." Yet "sooner or later," Kristol assured, "reality will have the last word." Take the issue of child-rearing, Kristol suggested. It was just one of the many topics that had recently become "a source of anxiety and controversy," and for no good reason at all. "What can possibly be mysterious about child rearing?" the journalist and widely acknowledged "godfather" of neoconservatism asked. Questioning the very idea of a deep-rooted cultural fracturing of the nation, he appealed to the moral intuitions shared by all Americans: "We all know, without ever having read a book, the difference between caring parents and uncaring parents. We even know, by virtue of our common sense, the difference between sensible parents and silly parents. Such gross discriminations are intuitively available to us all, and they are quite sufficient for purposes of child rearing."[2]

Kristol's 1984 essay followed the logic that characterized the neoconservative contribution to the various culture wars clashes of the 1980s and 1990s, including those over abortion and gay marriage, education and multiculturalism, and welfare, race, and crime. At the time, a prominent group of neoconservative intellectuals led by Kristol provided an intellectual revolution in conservative thought by embracing the "common sense" or, alternatively, the "moral sense" or "moral sentiments" of "ordinary people," going against cultural and intellectual liberal elites and their espousal of cultural diversity, welfare statism, and moral ideals that seemingly suited the zeitgeist. Traditionally, conservative intellectuals, including many neoconservatives, had been extremely nervous about popular rule, demagogy, and the dangers of a mob mentality. Kristol, for one, in the late 1960s and early 1970s, had been troubled by the pleasure-seeking "urban civilization" that in the United States was "becom[ing] everyman's culture," arguing that the American people were "more and more behaving like a collection of mobs."[3] Yet in the final two decades of the century, he and other neoconservatives came to argue that the culture and morality of the very same people were not the problems but rather the solutions to a crisis created by the elites. How did this striking neoconservative turn from a manifest mistrust of "mobs" toward a full-fledged common-sense populism come about?

To understand how and why the neoconservatives introduced to American political discourse a figure of the virtuous "common man" and thus significantly contributed to the late twentieth century's rise of right-wing populism, one must move past the usual suspects of neoconservatism's key intellectual influences—the antimodernist and elitist philosophy of Leo Strauss and the powerful anti-Stalinism of Leon Trotsky—and reorient the scholarly focus from the famously hawkish post-1970s "neocon" foreign policy thinking to the neoconservative culture wars. Indeed, the (neo)conservative average man who lives on in the favored language of twenty-first century's populist conservatism—including the rhetoric of candidate and then President Donald Trump—was born out of neoconservatism's intense engagement with the culture wars and the contentious question of emotion in moral and political judgment and social policy.

More particularly, the willingness of neoconservative culture warriors to speak for the assumedly unerring American common man—their embrace of a populist epistemology—was a result of a serious engagement with, and reinvention of, the Scottish Enlightenment philosophies of "common sense," the "moral sense," and "moral sentiments." Famously, in the eighteenth century, thinkers such as Francis Hutcheson, David Hume, Adam Smith, and Thomas Reid had contributed to the emergence of naturalistic, secular ethics by arguing that all humans—not only sophisticated individuals—were capable of distinguishing between right and wrong because of certain inherent characteristics of human nature. Hutcheson, the father of the Scottish Enlightenment, traced this human capacity for moral judgment to what he called the natural "moral sense," while Smith spoke in more sociological terms of "moral sentiments" and Reid of "common sense."[4] Two centuries later, beginning with Kristol's 1976 essay "Adam Smith and the Spirit of Capitalism" and continuing in texts such as political scientist James Q. Wilson's *The Moral Sense* (1993) and political theorist Francis Fukuyama's "How to Re-moralize America" (1999), the neoconservatives delved deep into Scottish moral philosophy and refashioned it into a durable, demotic figure of thought: the appropriately Americanized figure of the common man whose natural moral sense was the best available guide to key culture wars issues such as abortion, crime, and welfare dependency. Reinventing the Scottish intellectual tradition, neoconservative intellectuals turned it into a weapon against the supposed authority of American liberal elites, higher education, and social reformist policies.

The moral philosophy of the Scottish Enlightenment has been previously overlooked as a significant intellectual and conceptual resource for neoconservative culture wars thought.[5] While it is generally believed among scholars that neoconservative intellectuals molded America's intellectual and political landscape rather profoundly in the 1970s, 1980s, and 1990s, and while much scholarship exists on the neoconservatives' famously hawkish foreign policy—antidétente and intervention in Central America and the Near East—the neoconservatives' contribution to the culture wars of the 1980s and 1990s has remained a more open question.[6] According to the prevailing picture, the largely secular neoconservative movement responded to the perceived decline of midcentury bourgeois moral culture and the alleged threats of multiculturalism and relativism by highlighting the social and moral goods resulting from a restrengthening religiosity.[7] As one often-cited study puts it, it was "the consideration of . . . moral truths enforced by religious attachment that composed the last great project of neoconservatism [i.e., the culture wars of the 1980s and 1990s]."[8] Others have agreed that "religion in the public square was the neoconservatives' remedy to [the] values problem."[9] Still others who choose to emphasize the influence of Leo Strauss on neoconservative thinkers insist that neoconservatism as a movement was characterized by an elitist Straussian world view that distinguished between responsible elites and an unreliable public whose impulses needed to be restrained by a conventional morality that could easily be grasped and passed on to the next generation.[10] Due to the neoconservatives' arguments about religion's healthy social impact, and because of the end of the Cold War and the disappearance of an external threat, it has been claimed that neoconservatism was absorbed into the broader religiously inspired conservative movement—or even "lay fallow" or lost its purpose—in the 1990s before the movement's turn toward an aggressive Middle East policy at the turn of the century.[11]

Neoconservatism, this book argues, neither lay fallow nor lost its purpose in the culture wars era of the 1980s and 1990s; rather, many leading neoconservative theorists were or became heavily involved in the culture war, which they understood as an extremely important and consequential battle to define "Americanness" in the liberalizing, increasingly multicultural society of the late twentieth century. This cultural struggle over *what it means to be an American* climaxed in the 1980s and 1990s, and many leading neoconservative writers did their best to influence its outcome. The neoconservative response to this elemental cultural question about the idea of America was to formulate a new conservative conception of "the average American's" moral perception of the world. In an age of growing political polarization and the liberal elite's strengthening multiculturalist ethos, they sought to piece the national culture back together by invoking a deep-rooted moral philosophical idea—that ordinary people share an instinctive sense of right and wrong—as a source of unerring moral wisdom and the foundation on which a common American identity and a social and moral order could be based. At a time when ruling conceptions of American values were seriously challenged, key theorists of the neoconservative movement invoked this natural "moral sense" and some of its variants, especially "moral sentiments" and "common sense," as essentially conservative instruments: they were shields from a dangerous moral relativism and perceived moral decline and a means to define in conservative terms what it means to be an ethical American citizen. In doing so, the neoconservatives employed, in a culture wars context, a vocabulary that derived from Hutcheson, Smith, and Reid, one that had been used for conformist purposes already in eighteenth-century Europe and America.[12]

Four eminent neoconservative theorists—Irving Kristol, James Q. Wilson, Francis Fukuyama, and historian Gertrude Himmelfarb—were the ones who, in the last quarter of the twentieth century, most consistently reworked the neoconservative moral and political language along the lines of previous moral sentimentalist philosophers: namely, Smith and others who contributed to the eighteenth-century intellectual flourish that Kristol called the "Anglo-Scottish Enlightenment."[13] These neoconservative writers recurrently affirmed both their high opinion of the ordinary citizen and their admiration for the supposedly morally egalitarian Scottish philosophers.[14] The guidelines for this line of neoconservative thought were most clearly formulated in 1983 when Kristol stated that the "self-imposed assignment" of neoconservatism was "to explain to the American people why they are right, and to the intellectuals why they are wrong."[15] With the benefit of hindsight, Kristol's assertion can be seen as the neoconservative manifesto for the culture wars of the 1980s and 1990s. Exploring and reinterpreting older ideas on the moral sense and moral sentiments first generated by the Scottish thinkers were a way for the neoconservatives to explain to "the American people" why they were right in the context of cultural debates over the family, crime, race, poverty, and multiculturalism.

What is much less well known than Kristol's 1983 neoconservative—and populist—manifesto is that it was brought into effect during the 1990s by Wilson, one of Kristol's closest friends, in his works *Moral Judgment* (1997), *Moral Intuitions* (2000), and most notably, *The Moral Sense* (1993). In *The Moral Sense*, the "pivotal problem" was, in Wilson's own words, "the moral sense of the average person versus the moral relativism of many intellectuals."[16] Related to this scheme, Wilson set for himself, in private, an "intellectual task" "to rehabilitate the scientific, evolutionary [and] philos[ophical] status of [shared moral] emotions" and urged American decision-makers to formulate policies on crime, family, abortion, and gay marriage in a way that took into account the moral sentiments of ordinary Americans.[17] Kristol's wife, Himmelfarb, for her part, spent a significant part of the 1990s and early 2000s studying the British Enlightenment and its key idea of the moral sense, which, according to her, made the eighteenth-century British moral philosophers "respectful of the common man" and provided a cornerstone for an individualist social ethic from which contemporary Americans had much to learn.[18] Similarly, Fukuyama, a second-generation neoconservative thinker and world-renowned author of *The End of History and the Last Man* (1992), confirmed in his late 1990s works that "the 'moral sense' is put there by nature," and he proceeded from there to make an argument about the proper way to "re-moralize" America.[19] Significantly, then, all four of these renowned neoconservative theorists and culture warriors agreed at the height of the late twentieth-century American Kulturkampf that an ordinary citizen's moral sense, or intuition, ought to be taken seriously in public affairs. Accordingly, Wilson concluded in 1996 that "the neoconservative temperament has come to assign an increasingly high value to [the] beliefs [of the average American] and to interpret social problems and government policy in light of their implications."[20]

Not coincidentally, the neoconservatives introduced the Americanized, conservative version of the moral everyman during the mid-1970s economic crisis at about the same time as the Republican Party, in historian Jefferson Cowie's words, started to capitalize on the "postwar drift of the idea of 'worker' from a materially based to a culturally based concept." Starting with Nixon at the turn of the 1970s and followed by Reagan ten years later, Republicans persuaded the white working class to abandon the Democratic New Deal coalition by making use of popular resentments against the 1960s left-wing movements, the counterculture, and the black poor. This realignment of American politics laid the ground for the culture war that was perhaps an inescapable result of the massive cultural contradictions of the 1960s.[21] Inspired by the African American, women's, and gay rights movements, many Americans in the late twentieth century began to approach cultural diversity in an increasingly open manner, while liberal Supreme Court rulings on abortion, affirmative action, desegregation busing, and school prayer forced Americans to readjust their behavior and rethink their country.

For many Americans, especially those in the religious heartland and among the white working class, however, such developments entailed compromises to their most deeply held values and cultural status. The neoconservative appeals to the moral sense, moral sentiments, and common sense of ordinary Americans are best seen as efforts to provide consensual boundaries for debate and to legitimate moral views that were assumed to be widely held among working- and middle-class whites.[22] While the eighteenth-century British (mostly Scottish) moralists had invoked the moral sense and moral sentiments to help secularize ethics and common sense to respond to the new diversity of opinion in the wake of the Glorious Revolution, the neoconservatives used this vocabulary to rationalize middle American positions—real or imagined—on many culture wars issues from gay marriage to crime and punishment.[23] In the hands of neoconservative theorists, the moral sense idea and its many variants gained a new political function as a response to the question of how to hold American society together in the aftermath of the 1960s cultural upheaval and the rise of an increasingly open and multicultural society that allegedly contributed to such worsening social problems as broken families, crime, and poverty.

At the heart of neoconservative culture wars discourse was, then, a populist logic and an epistemology that claimed that moral truth came from the average American's instinctive capacity to perceive the world in moral terms. Much like the eighteenth-century educated avatars of common sense, whose actions historian Sophia Rosenfeld describes in her work *Common Sense: A Political History*, neoconservative intellectuals invoked the moral sense and moral sentiments to depoliticize the public sphere, to supplant legitimate intellectual conflict with a made-up moral consensus at a time of perceived moral chaos.[24] In neoconservative hands, all three of these eighteenth-century concepts were used not only to give new validity to the judgments of the so-called average American but to encourage the exclusion of liberal experts, intellectuals, and journalists, as well as the urban black "underclass"—those whose moral views allegedly did *not* embody the shared moral sense or common sense but were better described as either nonsense or amoralism. Similarly, in neoconservative hands, as in all populist rhetoric, "the people" was a moral category rather than a sociological one so that the reference was not to all people but to those segments of the population—working- and middle-class whites—who assumedly shared the neoconservatives' views on the need for traditional family values, severe punishments for criminals (especially the criminal underclass), and the bourgeois values of hard work, self-control, personal responsibility, and individual merit.[25]

By concentrating on these underexplored topics—neoconservatism's intellectual roots in the Scottish Enlightenment and the specific forms of moral populism that developed in the historical and intellectual context of the culture wars—this book aims to broaden and, in part, revise the prevailing understanding of the "neoconservative moment" that stretches from the 1970s to the American invasion of Iraq in 2003. The scholarship on early neoconservatism of the 1970s has focused on neoconservative ideas about the unintended consequences of (liberal) social policy as well as on the neoconservatives' punitive criminal policy, implying that such ideas both helped conservatives rise to political power in the 1980s and inspired Republican and Democratic welfare and criminal policy in the 1980s and 1990s.[26] Much of the academic study of neoconservatism in the 1980s and 1990s, however, concentrates on the movement's foreign policy ideas about the "Vietnam syndrome," "benevolent empire," and transformation of the Middle East, which received much support from the White House around the time of the US invasion of Iraq in 2003.[27] The present book readjusts this picture of the evolution of neoconservative thought by highlighting the importance of the culture wars of the 1980s and 1990s for the neoconservatives and by showing how their efforts to speak for "the people," together with their reinvention of Scottish moral philosophy, contributed to the rise of right-wing populism, whose political potential and cultural impact was understood by many Americans only after Donald Trump launched his 2016 presidential campaign in the summer of 2015. Neoconservative intellectuals of the late twentieth century must be seen not merely as foreign policy hawks and analysts of the unintended consequences of liberal social policy but as shapers of the Scottish intellectual tradition—common-sense populists in a fractured post-1960s America.

For those international relations scholars and other writers whose understanding of neoconservatism relies heavily on the movement's foreign policy discourse, the idea that neoconservatism paved the way for Trump-era right-wing populism may sound perplexing. After all, the neoconservatives' interventionist foreign policy—including the George W. Bush administration's ideas about spreading democracy around the globe by the means of military power—is expressly *elite*-driven, and the rise of Trumpian populism could be understood as involving the supplanting of neoconservative interventionism by "America First" isolationism. Similarly, those scholars and writers who perceive a "Straussian" emphasis on the importance of intellectual elites, high virtues, and gentlemanly education as the main philosophical foundation of the neoconservative movement are likely to see a sharp break between neoconservatism and Trumpian populism rather than a continuation from the former right-wing tradition to the latter.

Neoconservatism undeniably involves important "elitist" strains—the interventionist neoconservative foreign policy discourse being the most important of them. In this sense, neoconservatism seems to fit an image of the American conservative tradition in which conservative intellectuals and right-wing populists stand in opposing camps. Such a view has been expressed by scholars such as Rick Perlstein, historian of American conservatism, who argued in a much-discussed *New York Times* article in April 2017 that he and his colleagues had failed to anticipate the rise of Trump's populist politics because they had spent too much time studying conservative intellectuals and other "polite subjects." Historians had failed, since they had played down "the sheer bloodcurdling hysteria" and ugly racism of many conservatives and "organized mobs." In order to make sense of Trump, Perlstein suggested, future historians, instead of exploring (merely) conservative intellectuals, "need . . . to study conservative history's political surrealists and intellectual embarrassments, its con artists and tribunes of white rage" and risk "being impolite."[28]

Contrary to Perlstein's premises, this book hopes to show that the conservative intellectual movement *is* very much part of the story of the rise of right-wing populism in late twentieth-century America and, consequently, the rise of Trump. After all, neoconservative intellectuals, well before Trump, suggested that *they* were the voice of America's ordinary men and women and argued that popular "sentiments" and "common sense" were reliable guides in many culture wars issues. Inasmuch as Trump in his campaign, and then as president, posed as an expert in common sense and popular moral instincts, he resorted to a language that had been used in American public debate for decades by neoconservative intellectuals.[29] Indeed, by consistently presenting the so-called common man's intuitive, conservative response to public affairs as a helpful approach to America's gravest and often complicated concerns, neoconservative culture warriors of the 1980s and 1990s did much to lay the ground for a culture in which politicians might successfully use similar language for political gain. Significantly, this populist logic—including the neoconservative average man as an idea—was born out of the neoconservatives' intense engagement with the culture wars rather than foreign policy.

As for the elitist "Straussianism," the main flaw in the argument about neoconservatism as a uniform Straussian endeavor is, quite simply, that Strauss was an insignificant, or even incomprehensible, thinker for numerous key neoconservative thinkers and social scientists—including many first-generation intellectual architects such as Wilson, Nathan Glazer, Norman Podhoretz, and Daniel Bell.[30] A denial of the accuracy of the most sweeping claims about Strauss's critical influence on neoconservatism, of course, is not to say that Strauss was insignificant for *every* neoconservative writer; on the contrary, Strauss was a more or less important source of inspiration for some, like Kristol and especially Fukuyama, at some points in their careers, as will be shown later.[31] Yet while some neoconservatives acknowledged the significance of Strauss for their intellectual development, the elitism and cultural pessimism of the Straussians were not the dominant elements in neoconservative culture wars discourse. Rather, the leading thinkers of the neoconservative movement who regularly contributed to the *Public Interest* and *Commentary* and did the most to shape the neoconservative approach to the culture wars—especially Wilson, Kristol, and Himmelfarb—looked to the tradition of Scottish philosophy to craft a positive portrayal of the moral capacities of "ordinary people" as a source of moral wisdom against the relativist and statist views of liberal intellectuals and policy makers.

The Ordinary American as a Neoconservative
Concept and Moral Authority

Significantly, populist language and concepts such as common sense were not exclusively "owned" by neoconservative theorists during the culture wars of the 1980s and 1990s. Texts by other conservative writers, such as Christopher Lasch, Wendell Berry, William Bennett, and Charles Murray, testify that there was a broader intellectual engagement with "the people" and their moral and political sentiments—typically, the "common sense" of "the American people"—at the time when "the dominant tendency [in social thought] of the age," according to intellectual historian Daniel Rodgers's celebrated book *Age of Fracture*, "was toward disaggregation," and "imagined collectivities" allegedly "shrank."[32] In many cases, the imagined collectivities, after all, may have been wider, deeper, and more tightly connected to the people's emotions than many students of late twentieth-century thought have fully acknowledged.

Bennett, for one, was convinced in the 1990s that "Americans," after having long submitted to the authority of elites, were "regaining the confidence to express publicly the common sense sentiments they hold privately."[33] Bennett, the conservative writer and former secretary of education (1985–88), felt that such a restoration of common sense was especially needed in the education system and in response to America's drug problem. While the current education establishment merely offered common-sense-defying excuses for not promoting a core curriculum—Bennett's pet project—the "vast majority of U.S. parents realize[d] that some things are more important to know than others, and c[ould] agree on what most of those things are."[34] Similarly, America's battle against drugs, according to Bennett, who was also the director of the Office of National Drug Control Policy under George H. W. Bush, required "restoring common sense and, more important, common moral sense about the drug problem." In Bennett's conservative lexicon, common moral sense meant "recognizing the primary importance of those things contemporary liberalism has sought to undervalue: law enforcement, individual responsibility, and reducing the supply of drugs on our streets."[35]

In a parallel way, Lasch, in the mid-1990s, called for a new way of thinking about moral obligation, "one that locates moral obligation neither in the state nor in the market but in 'common sense, ordinary emotions, and everyday life.'" The prominent conservative-leaning historian admitted that America's social problems could not "be solved simply by taking account of 'what Americans believe,'" but this was "certainly a step in the right direction." The notion of common sense, in Lasch's use, served as a defense of the traditional family: it allegedly told "us that children need both fathers and mothers, that they are devastated by divorce, and that they do not flourish in day care centers."[36] The problem of the left was precisely that it "no longer stands for common sense" and thus "finds itself increasingly unable to converse with ordinary people in their common language."[37]

Another well-known common-sense conservative of the era was Berry, the writer and environmental activist for whom the notion of common sense was a rhetorical device to defend local communities and ecological ways of living against the modern embrace of material progress and economic growth—liberal ideas and goals that in his view led to the destruction of the diversity of local forms. Berry's "common sense," unlike that of Lasch or Bennett, was thus an antimaterialist concept; as he explained in 2003, it "tells us . . . that economy and ecology are ultimately the same, just as economy and community are ultimately the same; ultimately, people cannot expect to prosper by doing damage to the land and to human communities." "A lot of us," Berry insisted, "could now agree to that general statement."[38]

Finally, continuing with the conservative language of popular sentiments, Murray maintained in his widely read 1984 book *Losing Ground: American Social Policy, 1950–1980* that "social policy since 1964" had "ignored" key "popular wisdoms" and for *this* reason had "created much of the mess we are in [i.e., growing poverty and violence despite an active welfare state]." "Popular wisdom," in the libertarian political scientist's idiom, alluded to three supposedly widely held beliefs about human nature: that "people respond to incentives and disincentives," "people are not inherently hard working or moral," and "people must be held responsible for their actions."[39] Murray's appeal to "popular wisdom" served an antiwelfare state agenda, and it was thus a far cry from Berry's ecologically relevant idea of common sense, yet both represent a wider conservative engagement with "the people's" nonexpert sentiments that supposedly cast doubt on liberal nonsense.[40]

Ordinary Americans, as feeling subjects, made frequent appearances in the literature of the contemporary cultural left too. They were especially visible in the field of cultural studies, which emerged as a fashionable research area in the United States in the 1980s and 1990s while celebrating popular taste and everyday life against experts, bureaucrats, and elitists. As Catherine Liu has shown in her *American Idyll: Academic Antielitism as Cultural Critique*, "academic populists" of the era—many of whom were cultural studies scholars—"imagined a world of ordinary people with popular tastes and deep passions who, as fans and amateurs, could finally create a culture of their own that eluded the experts."[41] A prominent figure among such scholars was Lawrence Grossberg, who wished to "overcome the cultural and political elitism which condemned popular culture to be little more than the site of ideological manipulation and capitalist production." Grossberg, like an increasing number of cultural studies scholars at the time, was convinced "of the importance of passion (affect) in contemporary life," arguing that the source of popular culture's "power" could "be identified with its place in people's affective lives."[42] This had been shown already by writers such as John Fiske, who argued in his 1989 book *Understanding Popular Culture* that ordinary people with popular tastes were "attempting to evade or resist the disciplinary, controlling forces of the power-bloc" by wearing old-looking, ragged jeans, for example, and thus were "working to open up spaces within which progressiveness can work."[43]

What, then, was distinctive about the *neoconservative* embrace of populist language in the context of this wider academic engagement with "ordinary people" as well as popular emotions and taste in the 1980s and 1990s? In short, neoconservatism, unlike any other intellectual movement of the era, undertook the task of creating a new moral language that was based on a distinguished tradition of Western moral philosophy and that could help restore cultural and moral cohesion at a time when the meaning of American identity was intensely debated. This unique neoconservative orientation toward both moral philosophy and the culture wars conflict over the idea of America manifested as a populist reinvention of "Anglo-Scottish" moral thought. Characteristically, their goal was to create a plausible moral philosophical equivalent to contemporary populism by systematically using the moral ideas of Smith, Hume, and Hutcheson as the resources that they reworked into conservative commentary on hot-button issues such as race, crime, and welfare dependency. In contrast to other conservative thinkers such as Murray—who reminded policy makers of the "popular wisdom" that "people are not inherently hard working or moral"—neoconservatives such as Wilson and Kristol emphasized that the majority of people *were* instinctively ethical judgment makers, and unlike Berry, they invoked common sense to validate certain judgments about cultural and moral rather than ecological issues. Indeed, much of what was original in the neoconservative language of popular sentiments—when compared to Lasch's or Bennett's but also religious conservatives' or "paleoconservatives'" nativist idiom—*was* original because the neoconservatives drew from the allegedly "democratic" Anglo-Scottish moral sentimentalist ideas and adjusted them to fit the context of the contemporary American culture wars.[44]

What the neoconservatives took from or, at any rate, greatly admired in the Scottish thinkers was the basic belief—in Himmelfarb's words—"in a 'moral sense' that was presumed to be if not innate in the human mind (as Shaftesbury and Francis Hutcheson thought), then so entrenched in the human sensibility, in the form of sympathy or fellow-feeling (as Adam Smith and David Hume had it), as to have the same compelling force as innate ideas."[45] Tellingly, however, Himmelfarb and other neoconservatives did not show a similar appreciation of ordinary people's *aesthetic* sense as Hutcheson and other Scottish thinkers had done.[46] While the neoconservatives paid homage to the conservative *moral* judgments of ordinary Americans, they still tended to prefer high aesthetic culture—Mozart and fine French wines—over American pop culture and Budweiser.[47] It was an ordinary American's moral sense, not their aesthetic sense, that the neoconservatives wished to mobilize in the culture wars. Needless to say, here the neoconservative perspective radically differed from that of Grossberg or Fiske, who celebrated popular aesthetic taste—TV game shows and ripped jeans—for its rebellious potential.

The neoconservatives also reworked the Scottish sentimentalist tradition into a neoconservative sensibility by stressing the fragility of what they called the ordinary people's moral sense in the face of the countless moral hazards of modern American society. The neoconservatives suggested, explicitly or implicitly, that American moral and social order rested on the rather delicate moral sense, or common sense, of ordinary people, and in doing so, they fused Scottish moral philosophy with a conservative understanding of civilization as fragile, easily disrupted, and in need of protection by every new generation. While the neoconservatives thus were *shapers* of the Scottish tradition rather than being shaped *by* it, important aspects of the neoconservative culture wars discourse were nonetheless familiar from earlier eras, for, as Rosenfeld argues, "common sense generally only comes out of the shadows and draws attention to itself at moments of perceived crisis or collapsing consensus."[48] The culture wars era of the 1980s and 1990s *was* an era of perceived (moral) crisis amid a deeply polarized cultural environment, even if the nation at large was not as divided as were the political and cultural elites.[49]

Significantly, the neoconservatives were correct in pointing out that many of their fellow Americans were displeased with various post-1960s cultural developments, such as affirmative action, the breakup of families, and the increasingly sophisticated "expert" efforts to explain rather than judge the actions of criminals. Yet it is no less true that the moral sentiments of the American public were always more diverse than the neoconservatives suggested: greater tolerance and openness to new ideas and behavioral patterns relating to homosexuality, premarital sex, and divorce, for example, spread quite rapidly in the final decades of the century.[50] Moreover, since Smith or Hume never portrayed "the people"—to say nothing of the (white) working class—as the infallible source of truth or systematically attacked elitism, the neoconservatives' borrowing from them clearly was a reinvention of the Scottish tradition in populist terms. Indeed, for the neoconservatives, Scottish concepts and ideas were instruments in a political battle whose terms were set by the emergence of post-1960s liberalism.

From a post-2016 perspective, in light of the countless references to the "posttruth" era that were heard in the aftermath of the "Brexit" referendum and Donald Trump's election as president of the United States that year, neoconservative intellectuals' celebration of the average citizen's nonexpert moral sentiments as the best guides to public affairs is striking. *Posttruth* was Oxford Dictionaries' international word of the year in 2016, and it describes a situation "in which objective facts are less influential in shaping public opinion than appeals to emotion and personal belief."[51] Whether one finds it substantiated that the role of facts in shaping public opinion really was significantly reduced immediately following the election of Trump compared to earlier eras, it is certainly the case that many neoconservative intellectuals did much, well before the Trump era, to present ordinary Americans' *intuitive* response to public affairs as a helpful approach to America's gravest concerns. Insofar as the neoconservatives simultaneously encouraged doubts about inherent biases among all establishment sources of information or expertise, they helped produce a posttruth moment that ultimately undermines efforts to find common ground.[52] In short, the neoconservative works on common sense, the moral sense, and moral sentiments provided a language with which to discuss the opposition between the average American's morally pure gut feelings and out-of-touch academic abstractions as well as shared Americanness and the hazards of identity politics.

The issues of populism, popular emotions, and identity politics became extremely topical immediately following the 2016 election, which inspired responses from self-proclaimed liberals who wished to replace post-1960s "identity liberalism" with "a common feeling among Americans" or argued for "a new language of inclusive patriotism."[53] The history of the neoconservative culture wars offers evidence of the prospective difficulties involved in—but not of the redundancy of—such efforts at national integration, as it explains how the neoconservatives' self-imposed assignment to intellectualize, and speak for, ordinary Americans' gut feelings ultimately turned into an exclusionary form of white identity politics.[54] Indeed, the history of the neoconservative culture wars testifies to the fact that the location of "ordinary" Americanness is, as literary scholar Sally Robinson puts it, "a site of struggle over the meaning of normativity, in political and cultural terms."[55]

Neoconservatives and Populist Persuasion

I do not claim that Kristol, Wilson, Himmelfarb, and Fukuyama were populists in the same way that they were neoconservatives. Rather, my approach is similar to that of historian Michael Kazin in his book *The Populist Persuasion: An American History*, which is to say that I will analyze how Kristol and others employed populist language as a "flexible mode of persuasion" to convince other Americans "to join their side or to endorse their views on particular issues" (Kazin himself does not discuss neoconservatism in his book).[56]

By defining populism more carefully than earlier students of neoconservatism have done, it is possible here to be more judicious than previous works have been about *when*, if ever, particular neoconservative writers incorporated elements of populism into their moral and political rhetoric. I suggest that the neoconservative attack on liberal cultural and political elites—what the neoconservatives called the "new class"—in the 1970s should be understood as a form of anti-intellectualism, or antielitism, but it should not be equated with populism. This is because populism, as a form of persuasion, depends on a very distinct idea of "the people"—namely, that one part of the sum total of actual citizens (the "common" or "real" people) is a noble assemblage and an unerring source of wisdom.[57] Moreover, populist speakers always introduce themselves as the true representatives of an idealized people.[58] This kind of moral and political language came to be used by neoconservative writers only in the 1980s and 1990s, *after* Kristol in 1983 proclaimed that it was "the self-imposed assignment of neoconservatism to explain to the American people why they are right, and to the intellectuals why they are wrong."[59]

The neoconservatives thus invoked common sense and the moral sense to *build up* a moral-political consensus in the United States by suggesting that such a consensus *already* existed among "the people." By redefining the original eighteenth-century ideas of the moral sense, moral sentiments, and common sense and by giving them a new moral content with relevance to contemporary culture wars issues, they turned the language of the Scottish philosophers into a form of white identity politics.[60] This kind of rejection of moral or cultural pluralism in the name of a supposedly concerted "people" is understood in this study as a key feature of populism.[61] Populism famously divides society into opposing camps (the elites, ordinary people, and—characteristic of right-wing populism—racial minorities), even as it claims to speak for the whole nation (i.e., the people).[62]

The Neoconservative Culture Wars

There are of course many ways to conceptualize American intellectual history in the late twentieth century. One is to speak of a culture wars era, like sociologist James Davison Hunter does in his classic 1991 work *Culture Wars: The Struggle to Define America*. A different, but likewise useful, conceptualization is the one introduced by Rodgers in his widely acclaimed *Age of Fracture*. Rodgers refers to the last quarter of the century as the "age of fracture," since he thinks that basically all Americans, from the 1970s onward, came to think about social reality in smaller and smaller units—namely, that "the terms that had dominated post–World War II intellectual life began to fracture. One heard less about society, history, and power and more about individuals, contingency, and choice." New notions of "flexible and instantly acting markets" appeared, "identities became fluid and elective," and notions of power "thinned out and receded."[63] Rodgers's book can be read as implicitly suggesting that the moral and cultural quarrels between liberal and conservative Americans known as the culture wars were not as consequential for American thought and culture as were the general fracturing and destabilization of the categories that had been used by virtually all Americans to describe and make sense of the social reality around them. Clearly, Rodgers's "fracture" thesis captures something germane to the general feel of the twentieth century's last two or three decades in the United States. Yet at the same time, the fracture metaphor downplays the increasing appeals to "the people," especially on the political right, as a response to such cultural and conceptual fracture. For this and other reasons, I have chosen to use the "culture wars" metaphor, which emphasizes moral and cultural conflicts between large ideological collectives, throughout this study.

The most obvious reason for the focus on culture wars is that neoconservative writers themselves often used the culture wars metaphor and clearly meant many of their published texts to serve as contributions to what they perceived as potentially very consequential battles between liberals and conservatives over American values and identity. In many of their commentaries on culture wars issues, neoconservative writers identified a large, multidimensional, power-hungry liberal elite as their opponent. This group was the key social and cultural force whose growing power to influence—and corrupt—certain conventional American ways of thought and conduct ought to be resisted. Neoconservative intellectuals, like many other late twentieth-century Americans, tended to view their country as deeply polarized between liberals and conservatives, even if—as noted—the country at large was not as polarized as was the political class.

Most importantly, it is reasonable to use the culture wars metaphor to discuss neoconservative thought in what Rodgers calls the age of fracture, since the fracturing of American culture itself was the major moral and political concern of neoconservative thinkers. As intellectual historian Andrew Hartman points out, conservative thinkers of the final three decades of the century, including the neoconservatives, perceived cultural fracture as ethical chaos.[64] The attempts by neoconservatives and traditionalists to resist cultural fracture or to piece the national culture back together typically tended to inspire a passionate response from liberals who celebrated cultural diversity.[65] The culture wars metaphor, then, highlights the fact that the neoconservatives, traditionalist conservatives, and left-liberals fiercely fought over whether their country, as it was fracturing culturally in the twentieth century's final two decades, was also becoming increasingly immoral—as most neoconservatives and traditionalists suggested—or just transforming or becoming more tolerant, as most liberals thought. In this context, the neoconservatives' idea of the common man with a natural moral sense came to authorize many moral predicates of contemporary conservatism as intuitively *and* collectively right.[66]

While the long arch of the culture wars stretches from the 1960s to the 2000s (at least to 9/11 and the subsequent War on Terror, perhaps all the way to the "Trump era" and beyond; see epilogue), this book sets the focus on what may be referred to as the "high" period of the culture wars of the 1980s and 1990s. This high culture wars era was a time of neoconservatism's serious intellectual reconstruction, and it provided a critical context for many key neoconservative thinkers' populist turn. Most of the neoconservative texts dealing with the "moral sense" or "moral sentiments" of ordinary citizens were written in the fifteen-year period between the late 1980s and the first years of the new millennium.

A significant stimulus for the extremely heated cultural conflicts of the late 1980s and the 1990s was provided by philosopher Allan Bloom's unlikely bestseller *The Closing of the American Mind* (1987), which claimed, in Strauss's footsteps, that the United States as a modern country was declining morally and culturally due to its closed-minded liberal "openness," which Bloom saw as a threat to free society, since it undermined the intellectual and moral commitments upon which free societies were based.[67] However, for many social science–oriented neoconservatives—particularly for academics such as Wilson, Fukuyama, and Himmelfarb but also for journalists such as Kristol—an equally or more important stimulus for reflections on the moral condition of the nation was sociological evidence on the fate of family life, crime rates, neighborhoods, communities, and trust.[68] Wilson and Kristol, in particular, were among the first to publicly point out that many social statistics on such issues that became available in the 1970s, 1980s, and 1990s gave a disturbing image of the evolution of their home country's social and moral order—a development for which the liberal elites, according to the neoconservative view, bore a responsibility. Correspondingly, after the mid-1990s, neoconservative writers began noting that social statistics relating to family life, crime, and other issues were once again showing signs of improvement, indicating that the post-1960s era of cultural "decline"—or what neoconservatives perceived as such—was coming to a close. Thus in the late 1990s, the neoconservatives had to revise their moral message (as will be shown in chapter 6).[69]

Did the neoconservative culture wars, then, come to an end with the improving social statistics—or "remoralization"—at the turn of the century? Himmelfarb explicitly denied this in 2006. She insisted that "the culture wars are not over; they are only in abeyance." The neoconservative historian admitted that the culture war had taken "an interesting turn" in the sense that many combatants on both sides were "declaring victory and, in doing so, pronouncing the culture war over and done with." Himmelfarb found this "odd" at a time when abortion, gay marriage, and euthanasia (the Terri Schiavo case), among other issues, had "inflamed tempers and exacerbated the divisions between liberals and conservatives, Democrats and Republicans." Himmelfarb, like many of her coideologues in the early 2000s, held that conservatives had been successful in "the war over one sense of culture, that measured by the indices of crime, violence, illegitimacy, and the like" but admitted that they were "losing the other war, the war over the popular culture—losing it by default, by sheer, willful inattention."[70] What follows focuses on the former side of the culture wars, the one in which the (neo)conservatives, in Himmelfarb's subjective estimate, had been effective and successful.[71]

The six chapters of this book detail the way in which neoconservatives developed a new epistemology and moral theory by reinventing the Scottish philosophical tradition in populist terms and then applied this epistemology to particular social institutions and perceived problems arising out of post-1960s liberalism: the restoration of "family values," crime, poverty and urban social dysfunction, continuing racial inequality, and multiculturalist relativism. Instead of simply asking what policy preferences neoconservative intellectuals held, the chapters aim to make sense of the conceptual universe in which Kristol and others operated and the ways in which key terms— *common sense, ordinary Americans, the moral sense, underclass,* and so on— offer a window into a particular shared intellectual and policy outlook.

Chapter 1 asks how and when the neoconservative common man with a natural moral sense entered political discourse and, in doing so, examines the evolution of neoconservative thought from the future neoconservatives' "social engineering" approach of the Great Society years to the demanding "civic republican" moral vocabulary that characterized their response to the New Left in the late 1960s and early 1970s and finally to the Scottish-informed moral populism of the Reagan, George H. W. Bush, and Clinton years. While the first chapter analyzes Kristol's and Himmelfarb's readings of Scottish moral thought, chapter 2 shows how Wilson, perhaps the most distinguished neoconservative social scientist, continued his coideologues' Scottish theme and how he aimed to raise the status of popular moral sentiments in American public debate. Wilson's defense of popular moral emotions against social science in the 1990s was a complete rejection of the future neoconservatives' mid-1960s mission to offer relevant social scientific data to America's liberal, technocratic decision-makers.

Chapter 3 details how Kristol and Wilson appealed to the moral sentiments of the American people to define the boundaries of acceptable—not only "moral" but also "democratic" and properly "American"—discourse in family-related issues, such as child-raising, moral education, gay marriage, and abortion. Chapter 4 turns to the racial and class dimensions of neoconservative thought. It asks whether neoconservatism, or the variety of neoconservative thought that claimed to speak for ordinary Americans, was a form of white backlash—and if it was, how and to what degree. The chapter sheds light on neoconservative thought on race by exploring how Wilson's and Himmelfarb's seemingly "color-blind" talk of moral sentiments of ordinary Americans linked to, or contrasted with, their conceptions of the poverty-stricken, criminal black underclass residing in the inner cities. Chapter 5 continues on the theme of race by analyzing how Wilson drew on—and distanced himself from—Smith's ideas on moral sentiments and the punishment of wrongdoers in his writing on crime and criminal justice during the 1990s tough-on-crime frenzy.

The final chapter studies the evolution of Fukuyama's moral and civic thought from the late 1980s to the early 2000s, charting his intellectual journey between two poles of neoconservative thought—namely, Straussian cultural pessimism and the guarded optimism of Scottish-inspired moral sentimentalism. Toward the end of the chapter, a discussion on Fukuyama's late 1990s work on the natural moral sense and "spontaneous order" extends into an analysis of the relevant links and notable differences between neoconservatism and "neoliberalism," two conflicting yet intertwined ideologies of the late twentieth century. Neoliberalism's principal intellectual proponents (such as Milton Friedman and Friedrich von Hayek), like the neoconservatives, claimed Smith's legacy, yet the notable differences in the reception of Smith, I suggest, reveal essential aspects of the nature of these two mentalities.

Finally, the epilogue asks whether the neoconservative program of explaining to ordinary Americans why they were right included some helpful building blocks for a truly unifying national vision that transcends identity attachments and provides something in the way of a shared glue of "we-ness" in a fractured American society.

The Coming of the Neoconservative Common Man

The idea of a shared human foundation for distinguishing between good and bad, right and wrong, was widely held among moral philosophers in eighteenth-century Britain. As the neoconservatives often explained to their late twentieth-century readers, British Enlightenment thinkers from the third Earl of Shaftesbury and Francis Hutcheson to Adam Smith and Thomas Reid "attributed to all men the same natural quality, the 'moral sense' and 'common sense' that defined them as human beings, as moral creatures within the same moral community."[1] What the neoconservatives never properly explained to their readers was that the notions of the moral sense and especially common sense—an outgrowth of moral sense theory—had become in eighteenth-century Britain cornerstones of a moral and political campaign that stemmed from the uncertain position of virtue and truth in the modern world. It is useful to begin our story in early modern London and Aberdeen, for the early political history of these ideas gives us important clues as to why the neoconservatives found the moral ideas and concepts of the Scottish thinkers useful for their own purposes in the context of the American culture wars. Such a beginning also sheds light on the various different possibilities of political usage offered by this moral language.

As Sophia Rosenfeld argues in her insightful work *Common Sense: A Political History*, the idea of a shared human capacity for practical and moral judgment is typically invoked as an authority when other forms of legitimacy are in crisis. Rosenfeld's study deals with appeals to the plain wisdom of ordinary people in various eighteenth-century locations ranging from London and Aberdeen to Amsterdam, Philadelphia, and Paris, but she begins her narrative in early eighteenth-century Britain, where "a problem emerged to which common sense would soon seem to be the answer. That was how to hold a heterogeneous society together with a minimum of force." That such a problem emerged in Britain was mainly due to the liberation of censorship laws in 1695, the new freedom of the press, and consequently, the growing diversity of opinion. Within this new discursive environment in the aftermath of the Glorious Revolution, political writers strived to find a way to attain an elemental level of social and intellectual cooperation and help bring about a common culture. A pioneering role was played by Shaftesbury, a cosmopolitan aesthete and Whig essayist, who postulated an innate "sensus communis" and put forward the first rather casual theory of the "moral sense"—a "sense of right and wrong." As Shaftesbury conceived it, this sense made possible reliable judgments and basic agreements about ethical and aesthetic issues.[2]

The full flowering of common-sense thought, however, took place a few decades later in the small Scottish city of Aberdeen. There, in the 1760s and 1770s, a small group of moderate Presbyterian academics and ministers who felt anxious about recent developments in philosophical skepticism—most famously, Reid—began to rework Shaftesbury's and Hutcheson's moral sense theory. Behind Reid's and his fellow Aberdonians' uneasiness was, in particular, David Hume's epistemological skepticism, which cast doubt on the independent existence of the material world and, in the words of Reid, left "no ground to believe any one thing rather than its contrary."[3] To respond to Hume and to thwart what they saw as a disturbing trend toward uncertainty and doubt, Reid and other Aberdonians, such as the moralist and philosopher James Beattie, embarked on a project that was, in Rosenfeld's words, an effort to "discover nothing less than grounds for validating what one believes, indeed seems to know in some instinctive way, as the truth, and for reaffirming (middle-class, Christian) community norms in the process."[4]

As part of this moral project, Reid wrote the key texts of what later became known as the Scottish Common Sense School, which expanded the range of Shaftesbury's and Hutcheson's moral sense theory to cover not only conceptions of good and evil but judgments of truth and falsehood as well. For Reid and other midcentury Aberdonians, the notion of common sense—whether understood as a common-sense *capacity* or common-sense *principles*—provided a shared foundation for distinguishing between truth and untruth, good and bad, beauty and ugliness, and therefore it also offered a means to promote a sense of community.[5] Such eighteenth-century British discussions on common sense that were sparked by the new freedom of expression and expanded as a response to modern epistemological skepticism, Rosenfeld argues, have had far-reaching consequences for Western democratic and populist discourse, for they gave rise to a new *social type*—the educated spokesperson for the truths already understood by commoners.[6]

While the actions of Reid and his fellow Aberdonian academics and ministers offer an example of how Scottish common-sense intuitionism worked in the service of an essentially conservative moral project, the common-sense idea soon came to be used also to legitimize the expression of political dissent. The best-known radical proponent of common sense is undoubtedly Thomas Paine, an English-born American revolutionary who used this idea in his provocative and extremely popular 1776 pamphlet *Common Sense*. While Paine followed the tenets of mid-eighteenth-century British moral intuitionism in the sense that he wrote about the natural human capacity for an instinctive and irrefutable form of perception and judgment, he, unlike Reid and his fellow moderate Presbyterian academics and ministers in Scotland, employed the notion of common sense to *undermine* the ruling conceptions of the day. Reid and Beattie had used the common-sense idea to defend their conservative Christian outlook, but in Paine's hands, common sense became a defense of ideas that were *not* commonly held at the time that he wrote his famous pamphlet—that is, American independence and the idea that America should be a republic. Paine's idea, then, was that by using common sense, the mass of people could find true knowledge, which, in turn, would enable them to "begin the world over again."[7]

The larger point that emerges from this eighteenth-century political history of the common-sense idea is, then, that the shared human capacity for moral judgment was invoked by both radical and conformist writers to further their own personal political causes. This holds true with American thinkers too. Indeed, it was not Paine's radical reading of common sense that eventually became the most lasting interpretation of Scottish moralism in America. More typical was American educators' moderate interpretation of both Hutcheson's moral sense theory and Reid's notion of common sense. They became highly influential in American universities for over a hundred years until the first modern research universities were established in the country in the 1870s and 1880s. In the academy, Scottish moral intuitionism provided the language with which American educators could teach the cultivation of character and a good republic without resorting to divisive theological and denominational claims. As social ethicist and theologian Gary Dorrien puts it, Scottish common-sense intuitionism "serviced the need of a broad moral philosophy that was not owned exclusively by any theological or ideological party."[8]

Even though the impact of Scottish moralism on American political thought and intellectual life declined in the late nineteenth and early twentieth centuries, a sort of renaissance occurred concurrently with the rise of the culture wars in the post-1960s decades. That is to say, at the same time that neoconservatism was emerging as a new conservative sensibility in the 1970s, eighteenth-century Scottish moral thought and especially the Scottish thinkers' impact on American political thought were emerging as much-debated topics in American academia. The Scottish Enlightenment was in fact becoming at the time a deeply political affair in the United States in the context of a debate about the American Revolution.

Much of this polemic around the Scottish Enlightenment had to do with the work of historians, including journalist-historian Garry Wills, who published in 1978 a much-debated book *Inventing America: Jefferson's Declaration of Independence.* In it, Wills offered the startling thesis that the eighteenth-century Scottish moral philosophy of Hutcheson, Reid, and others contained the key to the American Revolution, at least via Thomas Jefferson's actions. Wills's argument was, in short, that Scottish moral philosophy, as a kind of protocommunitarianism, was a more important inspiration than Locke's individualism for Jefferson's Declaration of Independence. As Wills pointed out, the Scottish thinkers had argued, first of all, that humans were naturally sociable and benevolent to all in some measure and to their family, acquaintances, and compatriots in particular. Inspired by this kind of belief in natural social cohesion within compact societies, Jefferson had defended a measure of social homogeneity that would make strong coercive actions by the state unnecessary. Moreover, the Scottish thinkers, Wills noted, had understood "all men" to be equal, or nearly equal, in their mental powers and moral faculties, while a shared "moral sense" was understood by the Scottish thinkers to be "man's highest faculty." This, in turn, had inspired Jefferson's notions of "all men" being "created equal" and possessing "inalienable rights."[9] In late 1970s America, the Scottish moral ideas were thus associated with a communitarian political agenda.[10]

While Wills's left-of-center interpretation of the Scottish moral sense and common-sense theories is well known, it is much less well understood why and how neoconservative thinkers, at about the same time, began to harness the same Scottish moral ideas for their own purposes in the context of the culture wars. As we will see, Smith and other thinkers associated with the "Anglo-Scottish Enlightenment" captured the neoconservative imagination during the economic slump of the mid-1970s, pulling neoconservatives by Irving Kristol's lead to rethink their previously skeptical attitudes toward the American common man, his nonexpert sentiments, and populism. To understand this intellectual development, one must first get a sense of the neoconservatives' initial skepticism toward the man in the street in the formative "civic republican" years of the movement in the late 1960s and early 1970s.

The Rise of Neoconservatism and the Idea of
Democratic Decadence

As is well known, the roots of the neoconservative movement date back to 1930s New York. This story has been told in several books, and there is no need to go through the events in detail here. Suffice to note that Kristol, Daniel Bell, Nathan Glazer, Seymour Martin Lipset, and other notables associated with the neoconservative movement came to know the life of the mind as young anti-Stalinist socialists in the famous Alcove No. 1 in the cafeteria of the City College of New York (CCNY). There, these Jewish Trotskyists learned to wage ideological warfare as they battled against the communist students of Alcove No. 2. In this world of student clubs, everyone engaged in a life of endless political debates and read the works of Marx, Engels, Rosa Luxemburg, and Sidney Hook (who was the first American to put forward a comprehensive interpretation of Marx), as well as the *Partisan Review* and the *New International*. Along the way, these future neoconservatives blended into a group of thinkers that became known as the New York intellectuals.[11]

While the anti-Stalinist, intellectually combative CCNY experience of Kristol, Bell, and others certainly contributed to the political origins of the neoconservative movement, most neoconservatives were not former Trotskyists. To understand the movement's origins, it is thus most important to see that when "neoconservatism" was born in the late 1960s—that is, when the label was given to the movement by outsiders—the scholars and intellectuals associated with the movement thought of themselves as (Cold War) liberals.[12] The core tenets of this form of liberalism were anticommunism and the effective containment of the Soviets abroad and democratic and social progress at home. During the heyday of Cold War liberalism in the 1950s, liberalism could include a considerable amount of conservatism in its agenda, as liberals strived to differentiate themselves from the leftists that advocated fundamental change. On the other hand, a leftist wing developed inside liberalism, particularly toward the late 1950s when some liberals wanted to proceed faster than others toward desegregation and civil rights and when intellectuals such as Arthur Schlesinger and John Kenneth Galbraith insisted on moving toward a new kind of "qualitative" liberalism that would focus on dignity, identity, and self-fulfillment instead of economic issues.[13] Cold War liberalism ultimately disintegrated under the pressure of such left-liberal and leftist ideas, while some of the intellectuals who remained largely loyal to the midcentury's centrist liberalism eventually came to be known as neoconservatives. This group included the ex-Trotskyists who had traveled to the political center during the Second World War and early Cold War and others who had been liberals from the start (e.g., Daniel Patrick Moynihan and James Q. Wilson).

While the events of the Cold War surely were a foundational experience for the future neoconservatives, it was the launching of the great social programs of President Lyndon B. Johnson's Great Society in the mid-1960s that became *the* major turning point in the evolution of the movement. These events provoked Kristol and his old CCNY friend Bell to start a magazine to study the greatly expanding public sector and contemporary social policy. The editors launched their magazine, the *Public Interest*, in 1965 in the spirit of Cold War liberalism and its preoccupation with technical expertise, consensus, compromise, and pluralism (symbolized by Bell's 1960 book *The End of Ideology: On the Exhaustion of Political Ideas in the Fifties*).

At a time when government by experts and scientists—a technocratic ethos—was largely accepted as the norm, Kristol and Bell aimed to offer relevant sociological and urban studies data to all kinds of elites: bureaucrats, decision-makers, professors, thinkers, journalists, and activists. To achieve this goal, Kristol and Bell gathered around their magazine a relatively large number of social scientists and other writers who could contribute sociological, nonideological, perhaps even somewhat "dull" articles that would merely report "the truth about a matter under public discussion." As Bell and Kristol explained in their editorial to the first number, they wished to help their readers know what they were talking about when discussing issues such as "Paradoxes of American Poverty," "Where Welfare Falls Short," or "The Professionalization of Reform" (article titles from the first issue).[14] Thus at the time of its founding and for the first years of its existence, the *Public Interest* was considered moderately liberal. Among the regular writers at this point were ex-Trotskyists Bell (a sociologist), Kristol (a journalist), and Glazer (a sociologist), as well as social scientists Daniel Patrick Moynihan and James Q. Wilson.

Although the *Public Interest* was launched as a social science–based, nonpartisan magazine in 1965, it did not take long until the group united around Kristol and Bell's magazine came to have serious doubts about the idea that social science alone could help them solve America's gravest social problems, such as poverty, inequality, and crime. The group's intellectual development in the subsequent years can be, and has been, described as a turn from social science to moral and political philosophy.[15] While some historians of neoconservatism highlight the diversity of viewpoints existing within the movement in the following years and discuss key thinkers individually, others argue that a shared neoconservative moral-political vision emerged in the late 1960s and early 1970s. Typically, scholars in the latter category refer to this moral and political vision as a version of "republican" thought. According to Mark Gerson, for example, the republican line of neoconservative thought—he calls it "the neoconservative vision"—began to emerge among the intellectuals united around the *Public Interest* when they "realized that their models and those of government planners presupposed a rational individual who wants to partake in the bourgeois culture of hard work, individual achievement, close families, and educational advancement. . . . Rational policy analysis was predicated on a population with similar values and goals."[16]

While Gerson stresses the point more emphatically than others, he is not the only scholar who identifies an essential "republican" element in 1970s neoconservatism. Historian Kevin Mattson, for example, notes that Kristol, "the most prominent figure in the neoconservative movement," advocated in his contemporary essays "'republican' language (small-r) about the common good and the need for civic virtue."[17] Moreover, neoconservatives themselves have written about the rather quick transition from the original "social engineering" approach of the *Public Interest* to a mode that emphasized "values" and "virtue." Glazer wrote in the final issue of the magazine, forty years after its launching, the following:

> What astonishes me in glancing over those early issues was how soon the simple notion that science and research could guide us in domestic social policy became complicated, how rapidly this theme was reduced to a much smaller place than originally expected, how early the themes that were shortly to be dubbed "neoconservative" emerged. Managing social problems was harder than we thought; people and society were more complicated than we thought. . . . We began to realize that our successes in shaping a better and more harmonious society, if there were to be any, were more dependent on a fund of traditional orientations, "values," or, if you will, "virtues," than any social science or "social engineering" approach.[18]

The neoconservative insistence on the need for shared values or virtues typically meant values that middle-class whites recognized as their own in postwar America: personal responsibility, hard work, delayed gratification, and individual merit.[19] While Kristol and others at times called for self-improvement and sacrifice to the common good explicitly in the name of "republicanism" (an issue discussed later in this chapter), they often conflated private or bourgeois virtue with classical civic virtue. Nonetheless, whether they spoke of private virtue such as delayed gratification or of ("republican") sacrifice for the common good, neoconservative virtue talk in the early 1970s sounded dour and demanding. The key neoconservative theme at the time was that the social programs designed by Great Society social engineers (which targeted poor Americans) would not work unless the people first committed themselves to certain basic bourgeois virtues, such as a willingness to work and an ability to delay gratification. An important corollary of this idea was that if these bourgeois virtues did not exist, they had to be encouraged by the government. Or, at a minimum, the decision-makers needed to make sure that the welfare state itself would not unintentionally demoralize citizens.

Kristol spread the word not only in the *Public Interest* but elsewhere as well—for example, in his *Atlantic Monthly* piece "The Best of Intentions, the Worst of Results," in which he argued that "a liberal and compassionate social policy has bred all sorts of unanticipated and perverse consequences." This had probably occurred in relation to the African American family, Kristol insisted, since "as many poor black families are breaking up *after* they get on welfare as before they got on. . . . What we can now see is that the existence of a liberal welfare program might itself have been responsible, to a significant extent, for this family disorganization [since it robs the head of the household of *his* economic function]."[20] Kristol also assumed more generally that a more generous welfare state would create more dependency. He and other *Public Interest* intellectuals told their readers that the welfare state could, despite the best of intentions, demoralize citizens by diminishing their willingness to work and by creating incentives for having children out of wedlock. It was inevitable, then, that Kristol and Bell's magazine soon came to be known for its deep skepticism of liberal reform.[21]

Kristol's assessment of the welfare state reflects the fact that the neoconservatives lost their prior confidence in social engineering and moved toward a demanding insistence on bourgeois and civic virtue in the late 1960s as they gained evermore insight into the unintended consequences of supposedly well-planned government actions. Yet the *Public Interest* group's emerging moral and political philosophy was also inspired by the group's more foundational observations about American society and their fellow citizens as well as about themselves as (political) personalities and thinkers. Their observations about themselves as political personas were provoked not so much by anything related to the Great Society but by the expansion of the student rebellion and the continuing rise of the New Left and the counterculture in the late 1960s. As the New Left leader Theodore Roszak explained in a *Nation* article in 1968, the counterculture was "the effort to discover new types of community, new family patterns, new sexual mores, new kinds of livelihood, new aesthetic forms, new personal identities on the far side of power politics, the bourgeois home, and the Protestant work ethic."[22] The identity-based movements of the New Left—that is, Black Power, feminist, and gay liberation movements—in turn challenged the contemporary consensus-oriented liberal political culture by demanding civil rights and by highlighting distinct group identity and various "values issues," as well as by arguing that students and minorities had replaced the working class as the new revolutionary class.[23]

For the *Public Interest* intellectuals, the growing power of these left-wing movements was a truly profound experience in the sense that it forced the group to assess their own value system. As Kristol notes in his memoir essay, the student rebellion and the rise of the counterculture, "with its messianic expectations and its apocalyptic fears," was the moment when the contributors to the *Public Interest* discovered that they were conservative-bent "bourgeois types," "but by habit and instinct rather than reflection." "This shock of recognition was to have profound consequences," Kristol writes, since now they "had to decide what [they] were for, and why."[24]

For our purposes—being interested especially in the emergence of a populist logic in neoconservative discourse—it is especially important to note that the neoconservative criticism of the New Left was in part an anti-intellectualist or antielitist endeavor. In increasing measure, Kristol and his friends analyzed the 1960s social movements as seedbeds of a new kind of liberal intelligentsia or knowledge industry. This resulted in the emergence of the neoconservative "new class" theory. The concept of the new class has a long pedigree, and it had been used in the midcentury by leftist writers such as the Yugoslavian dissident Milovan Djilas, who had argued in his book *The New Class: An Analysis of the Communist System* (1957) that the communist new class, or bureaucracy, in the Soviet Union and Eastern Europe "did not come to power to *complete* a new economic order but to *establish* its own and, in so doing, to establish its power over society [with the premise that they alone know the laws which govern society]."[25] The neoconservatives took Djilas's concept and used it, together with the literary critic Lionel Trilling's concept of the "adversary culture," to explain the anti-American turn among their home country's intellectual elites in the universities, media, arts, and some parts of government.[26]

For some historians of neoconservatism, the fact that this kind of anti-intellectualist or antielitist rhetoric was on the rise within the neoconservative movement in the 1970s appears to be enough to justify the claim that there was a *populist* aspect to the movement as well at this point. That is, 1970s neoconservatism has been described as a version both of the demanding republican virtue tradition *and* of populism, which by definition does not ask any kind of sacrifice from the people.[27] This confusion is, I think, partly due to the fact that too little attention has been paid to the *evolution* of neoconservative thought (*from* "republicanism" *to* more populist ideas).[28] Moreover, populism is almost never defined by students of neoconservatism. What is needed is a more careful analysis that takes into account the differences between populism and antielitism or anti-intellectualism.

Scholars who suggest that 1970s neoconservatism did include populist elements have underscored two aspects of the movement's writings at the time. At times, scholars simply highlight the antielitist or anti-intellectualist aspect of neoconservatism—that is, new class thought—and suggest that the existence of this dimension as such justifies the populism label.[29] A different line of scholarly analysis draws attention to the fact that neoconservatives in the 1970s "added social scientific heft" to some popular views on social issues—for example, "tough" views on crime and critical views on forced busing as a method of desegregation—and points out that neoconservatives thus "elaborated on the crude conservative populism of George Wallace's presidential campaigns."[30] Still, these aspects of neoconservative writing (taken individually or together) do not necessarily suffice as a justification for labeling 1970s neoconservatism as "populist."

As political theorist Jan-Werner Müller notes in his perceptive book *What Is Populism?*, "It is a necessary but not a sufficient condition to be critical of elites in order to qualify as a populist." (Almost everyone criticizes the elites, he aptly notes.) In addition to being antielitist, Müller writes, populists always claim that they are the true representatives of an ideal people that is "presumed to be morally pure and unerring in its will."[31] While Müller's study focuses on populist politicians, we are here more interested in populist *language* or *logic*—which, as Michael Kazin notes, is sometimes made use of by political actors and thinkers who cannot easily be categorized as *populists*.[32] Nonetheless, Kazin's and Müller's studies (and many others) agree that populism, as a form of persuasion, depends on a very distinct idea of "the people"—namely, that one part of the sum total of actual citizens (the "common," or "real" people) is a noble assemblage and an unerring source of wisdom.[33] If populism is understood in this way—as a form of persuasion that constructs an opposition between the elites and the common people and presents the people as the unerring source of truth—then the mere observation of the use of new class rhetoric *as such* is not sufficient as a rationale for the populism label.

What about the remark that neoconservatives in the 1970s added social scientific weight to popular views on crime and busing? As such, this is an accurate observation, and it is certainly true that the neoconservatives' distrust of social engineering did encourage them to contrast some supposedly overly ambitious and naive plans of the American elites (such as those about forced busing as a desegregation method) with the "average American's" commonsensical desire for moderation.[34] Still, there simply is too much (counter) evidence suggesting that key neoconservative theorists in the 1970s neither portrayed the common people as an unerring moral or political guide nor attempted to depict themselves as the true representatives of the people. Indeed, Kristol and other neoconservative writers put much time and effort into exploring the *deficiencies* of the "moral character" of the American people at the time. Particularly in the early and mid-1970s, Kristol tended to attribute moral characteristics to *improved* individuals or social classes, as opposed to *all* (common) people as *natural* selves. The concept of (good) moral character was typically used to highlight this distinction between individuals or social classes with a history of moral improvement and those with no such history.

The new moral philosophical, or civic republican, forms of neoconservative thought that developed a few years after the inauguration of the *Public Interest* developed, then, to a significant degree as general reflections on the somewhat defective moral character of ordinary Americans. The importance of a strong moral character and the distinctions between improved and natural selves were most thoroughly articulated by Kristol in his explicitly pro-"republican" writings.

The essay "Republican Virtue versus Servile Institutions," in which Kristol defended "the original republican idea of self-government," is one such text. The republican idea, as Kristol put it, presupposed that "the self which is supposed to govern is necessarily conceived of as being a better self than the self which naturally exists, and the purpose of the republic, in all its aspects, is inherently a self-improving one." The "later democratic idea of self-government" was more problematic, Kristol maintained, since it was "based on the premise that one's natural self is the best of all possible selves, and that it is the institutions of society which are inevitably corrupting of natural goodness." For Kristol, the sorry consequence of the latter ("democratic") idea was that it led to concerns about whether institutions such as Congress, churches, and schools were "'responsive' to the people as they are" and to the assumption that "any discordance between the two constitutes strong evidence that the institution needs to be changed." As Kristol saw it, "The only authentic criterion for judging any economic or political system, or any set of social institutions, is this: what kind of people [in a moral sense] emerge from them?"[35]

In the late 1960s and early 1970s, Kristol clearly held that the American system, because it had discarded the republican ideals of self-improvement and sacrifice for the common good, had not been able to breed citizens with strong moral character. For example, in "Urban Civilization and Its Discontents," he argued that the American people were "more and more behaving like a collection of mobs."[36] It was the "democratic idea" (as opposed to the "republican" one) that reigned supreme in modern America, Kristol insisted, and therefore one had to be prepared for the possibility that "as we remake . . . our traditional institutions to suit us, we may simply be debasing these institutions so that they will more snugly fit our diminished persons."[37]

Kristol well knew that because of comments like these, he would be criticized for showing "a remarkable lack of faith in the American common people." His anticipatory response was that he included himself "among those common people." He continued by saying, "Knowing myself as I do, I would say that anyone who constructed a political system based on unlimited faith in my good character was someone with a fondness for high-risk enterprises." He thus concluded, "I do indeed have faith in the common people, only I don't have very much faith in them."[38]

This sort of mistrust of the disorderly "common people" and a concern for an improved moral character characterized not only Kristol's writings but those of other neoconservatives as well at the time. Bell, for example, argued strongly against Jacksonian celebration of the common man in the early 1970s—the problem with Jacksonianism, as Bell put it, was that "thought was replaced by sentiment and feeling, and each man's sentiments were held to be as good as any others."[39] Further illustrations of this neoconservative mistrust of the people can be found in Samuel P. Huntington's distressed *Public Interest* article discussing a "democratic surge" in the 1960s. For Huntington, writing in 1975, the recent "upsurge of democratic fervor" in America involved "challenges to the authority of established political, social, and economic institutions" to such an extent that the country was in danger of becoming ungovernable. Thus he argued that in order to save democracy, "what is needed . . . is a greater degree of moderation in democracy."[40]

Journalist Peter Steinfels, who wrote the first book-length study of neoconservatism in 1979, in fact argues that neoconservatives were essentially *afraid* of the common people and contemptuous of populism in the 1970s, despite their occasional ingratiating comments about the people's commonsense moderation and attachment to traditional mores. It was because of this "fear," Steinfels argues, that neoconservatives at the time distanced themselves from the notion of democracy as active participation and equality, which was advocated by the New Left.[41]

Steinfels also makes the case that the 1970s neoconservatives, despite their criticism of America's new liberal elites in the government, academia, and the media, should not be understood as presenting an antielitist position. Rather, as he sees it, the neoconservatives acted in the 1970s as a kind of counterelite. That is, neoconservative intellectuals, while they portrayed as elitist those *other* American elites besides themselves—namely, those all too optimistic "reform professionals" who still had faith in social engineering—they nevertheless advocated a role for a new, different kind of elite that would, in Moynihan's words, "keep the other elites of the country from tearing the country apart."[42] Moynihan—a social scientist, a regular contributor to the *Public Interest*, and a politician in the Democratic Party (New York senator from 1977 to 2001)—introduced such an idea in the late 1960s and early 1970s in such books as *Maximum Feasible Misunderstanding: Community Action in the War on Poverty* (1969), where he argued that the new elites should use social science not to elaborate social policy but to measure its results.[43]

Moynihan's ideas about the new elites serving as some kind of moderate referees or rule-makers and Kristol's disparaging comments about the misbehaving "common people" suggest then that the key *Public Interest* intellectuals for much of the early 1970s drew the line between the mentally and morally improved and the unimproved between conservative or moderate intellectuals like themselves and the great majority. Despite the intensifying anti-intellectual tendency (i.e., the opposition to liberal intellectual elites) and the occasional references to the average American's common-sense moderation, neoconservative moral and political language was still antipopulist rather than populist at the time. The remaining parts of this chapter will show how and why the emerging neoconservative enthusiasm for "the Anglo-Scottish Enlightenment" after the mid-1970s ultimately helped subvert this balance.

The Economic Crisis of the 1970s and the Neoconservative Discovery of Adam Smith

The growing neoconservative enthusiasm for the Scottish Enlightenment and the entering of the morally virtuous neoconservative "common man" into political discourse did not mean that the demanding civic republican idea of moral character lost its status in the neoconservative camp. Many neoconservative thinkers, to be sure, remained anxious about the "demoralization" of their home country until the century's end, never ceased blaming "the sixties" (the New Left) for the moral downturn, and kept reminding their audience that government should not create a class of demoralized, dependent citizens. Yet these continuities, as important as they are, should not obscure the fact that Kristol and others increasingly suggested throughout the 1980s and 1990s that moral wisdom came from the moral sense of ordinary Americans, instead of claiming that this moral sense is defective and needs to be cultivated. Moreover, increasingly, the neoconservatives explicitly claimed to be speaking *for* the people as they promoted their cause in domestic affairs.

The Scottish Enlightenment, as noted earlier, had experienced a sort of a renaissance in the American academy in the 1970s due to new historical interpretations of the American Revolution. In the case of the neoconservatives, though, it was the economic crisis of the mid-1970s that first caused them to turn to Smith and the moral sentimentalist school around him. In terms of pure economics, the crisis that afflicted the United States between 1973 and 1975 was about inflation—higher prices, especially for energy—which, exceptionally and unexpectedly, coincided with a recession (or, more appropriately, a period of anemic economic growth and high unemployment accompanied by rising prices or inflation, a phenomenon that came to be known as stagflation).[44] Yet importantly, the economic crisis was also a crisis of economic theory, or even of American social thought more generally. As Daniel Rodgers notes in *Age of Fracture*, the moment was made particularly bleak not so much by the economic crisis itself but by the complementary crisis of understanding: no one understood at the time why the reigning economic (Keynesian) paradigm "had failed to explain or to make sense of the unexpected." Such a moment, "a crisis in ideas and intellectual authority," was obviously likely to generate in due time some new forms of economic and social thought.[45] For the neoconservatives, as for many others, this crisis in ideas and intellectual authority was an opportunity to take hold of some of that authority.

Kristol and other neoconservatives decided during the economic recession that it was impossible to leave economics out of the neoconservative analysis of American society.[46] It is, in fact, commonplace to think of the evolution of neoconservative thought in the 1970s as a transition from an analysis of the Great Society and the New Left to a study of capitalism. The key neoconservative works typically cited as proof of this development are Bell's *The Cultural Contradictions of Capitalism* (1976), Kristol's *Two Cheers for Capitalism* (1978), and Michael Novak's *The Spirit of Democratic Capitalism* (1982).[47]

The common feature of these works, typically considered as the neoconservative approach to capitalism, is a conditional defense of capitalism: capitalism is a better economic system than any of its alternatives, but its success is simultaneously its (moral) dilemma, since capitalism itself (or the affluence it breeds) tends to destroy the moral capital—the ethic of hard work, frugality, and self-control—that was created by the Western religious and moral culture that preceded it. Political scientist Jean-François Drolet argues in *American Neoconservatism: The Politics and Culture of a Reactionary Idealism* (2013) that the moral deficiency that neoconservatives perceived in the capitalist system—that capitalism does not properly sustain the "republican conscience" of citizens—deeply worried them, and therefore they wanted *the state* to take responsibility for the moral cultivation of the civic mind.[48] Importantly, what has not been recognized by Drolet and others who make a similar argument is that the new focus on the logic of capitalism in the 1970s and early 1980s not only made many neoconservative thinkers anxious about the declining moral capital in the West but also gave birth to a new, more confident, Adam Smith–inspired moral and civic language that portrayed the "ordinary people" as a stable source of moral values and social order.

Kristol and Gertrude Himmelfarb were the two neoconservative writers who at the time explored the Scottish ideas on the moral sense and moral sentiments and who laid the foundation for the more explicitly populist neoconservative texts of the later culture wars era. The first one to do so was Kristol, soon to be followed by his wife, Himmelfarb. At the time of the mid-1970s crisis, Kristol saw it as important to study a thinker whom he considered the greatest theorist of capitalism, Smith. Kristol thought it was necessary at this moment of bleak economic visions to see what one might learn from the "founding text of modern capitalism," Smith's *Wealth of Nations*.[49] Himmelfarb, for her part, began at the time a nearly twenty-year research project on the Victorian ideas of poverty and compassion, in which Smith's political economy and moral philosophy were important starting points. Crucially, as the married couple familiarized themselves with Smith's capitalism, they came to realize that his economics was inseparable from eighteenth-century Scottish moral sentimentalist philosophy.

To properly understand how Kristol and Himmelfarb—and later Wilson and even later still Francis Fukuyama—*reshaped* the Scottish moralists' ideas about a natural moral sense and moral sentiments into a neoconservative sensibility, we need to have a general conception of what the original eighteenth-century moral sentimentalists said about the moral sense and moral sentiments and for what purposes.

The Morality of Ordinary People in Scottish Philosophy

The Scottish Enlightenment was an extremely wide-ranging intellectual flowering, but here I will restrict the discussion to eighteenth-century Scottish moral philosophers, particularly to the ones that the neoconservatives regarded as their intellectual companions: Hutcheson, Hume, and Smith.[50] Together with Reid, these three moral philosophers composed the forefront of eighteenth-century Scottish philosophy. With the exception of Reid, they were all moral sentimentalists (as opposed to moral rationalists), but they still argued among themselves and, as one would expect, modern-day scholars are continually reinterpreting their distinctive contributions and intentions. What is clear is that the moral sentimentalists shared the general view that morality originated not from reason alone but at least partly from sentiments.[51] One helpful way to see the Scottish sentimentalists' general contribution is to look at them, like philosopher Michael Gill does, as thinkers who contributed to "a Copernican Revolution in moral philosophy, a shift from thinking of morality as a standard against which human nature as a whole can be measured to thinking of morality as itself a part of human nature."[52]

The exceptional flowering of moral philosophy in eighteenth-century Scotland was, in this sense, part of a larger emergence of naturalistic, secular ethics in Britain in the seventeenth and eighteenth centuries. Ethical thought at the time first disengaged itself from Christianity, then from theistic ideas altogether (Hume was a skeptic, and Smith abandoned Christianity but remained a theist).[53] According to Gill, the primary force behind these crucial intellectual developments was the British thinkers' concern with answering a question that Gill terms the "Human Nature Question"—that is, "Is it natural for us to do the right thing, or must we resist something in our nature in order to do what is right?"[54]

In eighteenth-century Scotland, the moral sentimentalists were among the best-known contributors to this discussion; they argued against not only moral rationalists but also Calvinists (original sin) and Hobbesians (egoism) that all humans—not only sophisticated individuals—were capable of distinguishing between right and wrong because of a certain kind of natural "moral sense" or, alternatively, "moral sentiments."[55] Hume's contribution to the debate was particularly important in the sense that he ultimately undermined the question about humanity's goodness or badness and therefore helped the progress of a "science" of morality and human nature. In a word, the key philosophical advancement brought about by the Scottish moral sentimentalists was the growing use of empirical observation in the study of morality and human nature.[56]

While Hutcheson, Hume, and Smith thus shared the view that morality rested on feeling and that all humans were capable of making moral judgments, they nevertheless disagreed between themselves on the nature and existence of a specific "moral sense." Hutcheson, who is often referred to as the father of the Scottish Enlightenment, was the only one of these three key philosophers to consistently suggest that humans possess a distinct moral sense by which we can distinguish virtue and vice in ourselves and others.[57] That is, Hutcheson's "moral sense" was a special faculty that "senses" moral properties just as the eye senses visual properties.

To understand Hutcheson's moral sense theory, it is imperative to understand that for him, human nature was inherently virtuous in the sense that benevolence, a disposition to wish happiness for others for their own sake rather than for our own sake, was part of the original constitution of human nature. Hutcheson's "moral sense" was, then, the capacity to approve or disapprove of a motive, or, as philosopher and historian D. D. Raphael explains, "a disinterested feeling of approval naturally evoked when we come across the disinterested motive of benevolence, and a similar feeling of disapproval for motives with a tendency opposed to that of benevolence." Consequently, in Hutcheson's system, virtue was benevolence approved.[58]

In contrast to Hutcheson, Hume is typically not seen as a moral sense theorist in a strict sense. He used Hutcheson's term only in the title of the section on morals in his *A Treatise of Human Nature* ("Moral Distinctions Deriv'd from a Moral Sense"), writing instead of "feeling" or, more often, "sentiment."[59] Famously, Hume used the concept of "sympathy" to psychologically explain the human capacity to feel approval and disapproval (i.e., what Hutcheson had called the moral sense). In Hume's system, sympathy (in most cases) meant not the same as compassion or pity or any other feeling but rather the sharing of feelings of those influenced by an action.[60] The feelings of approval and disapproval, in turn, are (in Raphael's words) "feelings of pleasure or displeasure of a particular kind, and they arise from *sympathy* with the pleasure or pain of the person or persons affected by the action judged." For example, benevolence pleases the observer "because he sympathizes with the pleasure that benevolent action brings to the benefited." Importantly, however, Hume did not restrict virtue to benevolence, as did Hutcheson.[61] In *Enquiry concerning the Principles of Morals*, Hume wrote that virtue is "*whatever mental action or quality [that] gives to a spectator the pleasing sentiment of approbation*; and vice the contrary" (emphasis in original).[62] In other words, whereas Hutcheson had argued that the moral sense evaluates benevolent and non-benevolent motives and evokes a feeling of approval or disapproval, Hume claimed that moral judgment was directed at the character, or toward a character trait, of the agent being judged.[63]

The third prominent Scottish thinker to develop a sentimentalist theory of ethics was Smith. One of the basic presuppositions of Smith's thought was that Hume had convincingly demonstrated that moral distinctions arise from feeling. Therefore, Smith took sentiment as the basic element of his key moral philosophical work, *The Theory of Moral Sentiments*, in which he attempted to delineate the principles that people follow when they judge other people's and their own conduct and character.[64] The most important component and main legacy of Smith's book is the concept of the "impartial spectator," which Smith used to develop an original theory of *conscience* ("the man within the breast").[65] According to Smith's hypothesis, conscience (the approval or disapproval of oneself) was a product of both social opinion and one's own imagination. We judge others as spectators, and we see other spectators judging us. In Smith's own words, "We begin, upon this account, to examine our own passions and conduct, and to consider how these must appear to them. . . . We suppose ourselves as the spectators of our own behaviour, and endeavour to imagine what effect it would, in this light, produce upon us. This is the only looking-glass by which we can, in some measure, with the eyes of other people, scrutinize the propriety of our own conduct."[66]

This means that in Smith's system, we eventually begin to assess our own behavior by imagining whether an impartial spectator would approve it or not. Especially in the later editions of *Theory of Moral Sentiments*, Smith highlighted the effect of imagination, as opposed to social opinion, on one's judgments concerning oneself, pointing out in the sixth edition that it is vanity to be flattered by social praise and to ignore the more valid judgment of conscience. Smith therefore made the distinctions between love of praise and love of praiseworthiness and between dread of blame and dread of blameworthiness.[67]

As noted earlier, Reid, along with the sentimentalists, has to be counted among the leading moral philosophers of the Scottish Enlightenment. Reid's famous common-sense philosophy is the best-known example of how eighteenth-century Scottish thinkers aimed to defend the everyday logic of the average person.[68] Crucially, though, when it comes to the role of feeling in making a moral judgment—a question that captivated the neoconservatives—Reid's position was "plainly at odds with moral sentimentalism," as philosopher and historian Alexander Broadie notes. That is, Reid—in contrast to Hutcheson, Hume, and Smith—argued that "feeling wells up because of the antecedent [moral] judgment; it is not that the judgment is formed in the light of the feeling."[69]

In the United States between the mid-eighteenth and mid-nineteenth centuries, as noted earlier, Reid's common-sense moralism, along with the moral theories of other Scottish thinkers such as Hutcheson and Adam Ferguson, provided the language with which universities could teach the cultivation of character and a good republic without divisive theological and denominational claims. Reid's common-sense philosophy was in fact most popular among the leaders of American intellectual life in the eighteenth and nineteenth centuries.[70] For us, the case of Reid is very interesting precisely because the largely secular neoconservatives generally *neglected* the famed common-sense philosopher who had earlier received so much support in the United States (even though they repeatedly invoked the term *common sense*). As will be shown in the remaining parts of this chapter, for the neoconservatives, it was crucial that their favorite Scottish thinkers had positioned "moral senti-ment" or the "moral sense" at the center of their philosophical systems. This has not been properly understood by earlier students of the neoconserva-tive movement who point out that it was the "modesty and humanity of the Anglo-Scottish tradition" (as opposed to the more utopian or hubristic French Enlightenment) that inspired the neoconservatives.[71]

This short overview should make clear that there is no such thing as a unified "Anglo-Scottish Enlightenment ethics"—the moral sense theory of Hutcheson, the moral sentiments philosophy of Hume and Smith, and the common-sense philosophy of Reid were never meant to be compatible with one another. It might be better to think of competing Scottish schools of thought emerging from Glasgow (Hutcheson being a central figure), Ed-inburgh (Hume), and Aberdeen (Reid). (Smith was a student of Hutcheson at the University of Glasgow and later taught there for more than a decade, yet his ideas on moral sentiments were much inspired by Hume, a critic of Hutcheson's.) These three schools of thought were both divided within them-selves and pitted against each other. While the moral sentiments school of Hume and Smith is related to a variety of later forms of subjectivism and empirical-psychology-informed ethical naturalism, Hutcheson's moral sense school is closer to intuitionism and nonnaturalistic forms of moral objectiv-ism. Reid and the common-sense school draw on Hutcheson's ethics, yet they also incorporate elements of the rationalism of such Enlightenment philoso-phers as Samuel Clarke and Richard Price.[72]

Crucially for our purposes, the three eighteenth-century Scottish schools of thought differ from each other when it comes to their populist potential. While there is some populist potential in the idea of a universal moral sense or widespread common sense, the moral sentiments have more elitist impli-cations. Indeed, the leading philosophers of the moral sentiments school—Hume and Smith—while agreeing with other Scottish moralists that all hu-man beings were capable of making moral judgments, were highly suspicious of uncultured moral sentiments and emphasized the importance of sentimen-tal education. That is, far from celebrating the unrefined moral sentiments of the common man, Hume and Smith argued that moral sentiments were *not* reliable in the absence of proper education. Hume, for example, held that sentiments could be genuinely moral yet biased (e.g., in favor of our friends and those whose characters are most like our own). Thus he took a lot of ef-fort to explain the "correction" and "progress" of sentiments—that is, how our undeveloped, narrow sense of sympathy could be broadened and our partial moral sentiments made impartial.[73] Smith, in turn, argued that "untaught and undisciplined feelings" needed persistent tutoring—that "constant practice" was needed to learn to view oneself from the impartial spectator's perspective and to feel what is appropriate to feel.[74] Because of this emphasis on sentimental education, it is highly problematic to rationalize one's populist celebration of the instinctively moral and pure everyman with the help of Hume's and Smith's moral sentimentalism. As we will see, the neoconservatives often played down the idea of sentimental education and the fact that moral sentiments, as Hume and Smith saw them, could be biased or corrupted.

Irving Kristol on Shared Moral Sentiments and the Bourgeois Way of Life

Kristol laid out his initial thoughts on Smith's philosophy in a 1976 essay entitled "Adam Smith and the Spirit of Capitalism." His key idea was, in short, that all those economically distressed and intellectually confused Americans who were recurrently asking if capitalism "works" or not should turn to Smith to regain their confidence in the bourgeois way of life and to discover the answer to the crucially important and more elementary question about "what kind of society capitalism is supposed to create." At this moment of uncertainty and austerity, Smith could provide Americans with inspirational insight, Kristol thought, since Smith had skillfully expressed an "optimistic" idea that capitalism leaves everyone free, not "to become prosperous as he saw fit" (as American libertarians would have it), but to "better his condition." Studying Smith could thus help Americans once again see that in the (Smithian) capitalist system, "the individual . . . was freed *from* various traditional tyrannies, large and petty, and was free *to* participate in a bourgeois way of life whose ethos and institutions were taken for granted." For Kristol, it was thus very important that Smith had "defined freedom in a way that retained a firm connection with an idea of virtue to which the free individual submitted." It was, then, this kind of larger vision of capitalism and the bourgeois way of life as a moral lifestyle that Kristol wished to see reconsidered and modified in the crisis-ridden United States of the mid-1970s.[75]

Now, importantly for our concerns, Kristol suggested that this optimistic Smithian idea of capitalism ultimately rested on moral sentimentalist assumptions about human nature. Kristol's point was that Smith, when presenting his argument that capitalism "leaves everyone free" to take part in the moral-economic bourgeois way of life, had assumed that all individuals necessarily—simply because they were human beings—shared the same moral and intellectual capabilities that were required for such a morally understood bourgeois life. This "Smithian" assumption about "an inclination toward virtue" within human beings, Kristol pointed out, was in fact shared by many other moral philosophers of "the Anglo-Scottish Enlightenment," writers such as Shaftesbury, Hutcheson, and Hume whose work on the moral sense and moral sentiments predated Smith's texts by several decades.[76]

As regards the evolution of neoconservative thought, the most important aspect of Kristol's 1976 text is, then, that here *the* key neoconservative theorist emphasized that a sound and inspirational social and moral vision could flow from an egalitarian assumption about *everybody's* ultimately moral nature—a viewpoint that significantly differed from Kristol's earlier "republican" philosophy that not only highlighted the distinction between morally improved individuals and the disorderly masses but also explained moral characteristics as something opposed to our "natural selves." (As we will later see, Kristol did not play down the selfish aspects of human nature in Smith's philosophy, but he emphasized that Smith had found both moral and selfish dimensions in human nature.)

Kristol's aim in his 1976 article was not to defend Smith's moral sentimentalist view of human nature as compatible with modern psychology or social science—to the contrary, he reckoned that the Scottish philosophical psychology of "benevolent affections" had "little academic standing today, at a time when psychology strives to be as 'scientific' as possible." Instead, Kristol aimed to understand how Smith, as an eighteenth-century Scottish thinker, had ended up with such an optimistic vision of capitalism and the bourgeois way of life.

Despite Kristol's historical and somewhat reserved approach to eighteenth-century moral sentimentalist philosophy, it is important to understand how he portrayed this view of human moral psychology in his pioneering 1976 article, since these or similar ideas about human moral nature later came to inform neoconservative cultural warfare. To be exact, in 1976, Kristol was mostly talking about *Smith's* sentimentalist ideas: while he noted that Smith wrote in "the line of thought traced by Locke, Shaftesbury, and (to a lesser degree) Hume," he concentrated more on Smith's sentimentalism, since he thought it was Smith who, in his *Theory of Moral Sentiments*, "provided that theory of human nature [i.e. moral sentimentalism] with its most extensive and persuasive rationale."[77]

Three observations need to be made concerning Kristol's interpretation of Smith's moral sentimentalism. First, Kristol, as one would expect, discussed Smith's *Moral Sentiments* as a work of descriptive psychology and made the general point that Smith had argued in favor of common human moral abilities and emotions. In this sense, he interpreted Smith's sentimentalist ideas by and large as they are dealt with by contemporary Smith scholars. Kristol drew attention to Smith's key concepts, such as "sympathy" and the "impartial spectator," and noted how Smith had analyzed both the impact of the community on the development of moral ideas and the birth of conscience. As Kristol put it, Smith had strived to explain how the expressed opinions of the community and the "approbativeness" of certain behaviors were important influences on people. In addition, Smith had argued that "all human ambition and striving operates under a kind of 'inner check' as well. This takes the form of an ideal 'impartial spectator' who resides within each of us, and who internalizes the community's approbation and disapprobation."[78]

Second, Kristol interpreted Smith's *Moral Sentiments not only* as a work of descriptive psychology. That is, he argued that Smith's goal had been "the creation of a more humane and elevated bourgeois community"—namely, that Smith had aimed to discover common sensations and sentiments that "could serve as the foundation for a more 'realistic' definition of the good life and a more 'realistic' foundation for a good society."[79] This kind of assumption about the normative aspects of Smith's project is shared by only some modern Smith scholars.[80]

Third, Kristol's reading of the so-called Adam Smith Problem was somewhat different from that of many Smith scholars and slightly confusing (the question is about whether Smith contradicted himself in *Moral Sentiments* and *Wealth of Nations* by highlighting in each of them two very different elemental characteristics of human nature, sympathy and selfishness). Modern Smith scholars almost unanimously argue that there is no fundamental contradiction between the two books, and they point out that Smith's works, like the selfish and moral aspects of human nature, complement each other.[81] Kristol, however, saw the inconsistency as real and important: while *Moral Sentiments* was "cheerful and benign," "even in some ways an inspirational book," *Wealth of Nations* was "more objective in its rhetorical mode and is not infrequently dour and acerbic—almost Veblenesque—in its judgments on all classes of humanity." Moreover, Kristol emphasized that there was "an obvious intellectual difference between the two works, a difference in their conception of human nature and of the principle that shapes human behavior." Yet Kristol also made the case in the same essay that in *Wealth of Nations*, Smith had *not* forgotten the ideas about the moral nature of human beings presented earlier in *Moral Sentiments*. Indeed, Smith had supposed in his work on the "natural system of liberty," to use Kristol's words, that "man's 'natural' instincts and man's reason, if given their freedom, will in the end lead to decent rather than to vicious behavior. In this sense, *The Wealth of Nations* is decidedly an 'optimistic' book. . . . Man could not learn it [decent behavior] if his nature were such as to make such learning impossible."[82] Kristol's point appears to be that in *Moral Sentiments*, Smith emphasized moral characteristics as part of the original constitution of human nature, while in *Wealth of Nations*, he stressed that everyone can *learn* moral behavior because of how human nature operates. Yet in fact, moral and sentimental education is an important theme in *Moral Sentiments* too—not only in *Wealth of Nations*.

Eventually, Kristol came to rework these Scottish sentimentalist ideas—or his reading of them—and to incorporate them into his campaign against America's liberal cultural elites. One such text was his essay "The Adversary Culture of Intellectuals," a widely noticed 1979 article in which the neoconservative leader explored America's intellectual and educational culture (he, in other words, presented a neoconservative reading of Trilling's concept of the "adversary culture"). In the article, a frustrated Kristol made the point that his own (Western) civilization was perhaps the first civilization in all of recorded history "whose culture was at odds with the values and ideals of that civilization itself." Kristol was also upset because it was *taken for granted* in his home country that the contemporary intellectual and educational culture "is unfriendly (at the least) to the commercial civilization, the bourgeois civilization, within which most of us live and work."[83] The article's purpose was to explain this situation—that is, to offer a historical account of the rise of the adversary culture in the West, beginning from the rise of Romanticism in the late eighteenth century. What is most interesting for our purposes is how Kristol reworked and used for political ends Smith's ideas on the moral nature of human beings as he stood up for the "prosaic" bourgeois society whose values and ideals were constantly under attack by the adversary culture.

Kristol's aim, in the most general sense, was to defend bourgeois society as a society that was "popular among the common people" and, moreover, as a society that was "interested in making the best of this world, not in any kind of transfiguration, whether through tragedy or piety." He insisted that the bourgeois world view placed "the needs and desires of ordinary men and women at its center" and that, accordingly, bourgeois society was "organized for the convenience and comfort of common men and common women, not for the production of heroic, memorable figures." According to Kristol, such a world view and a social system that, admittedly, had given up on the very highest moral and intellectual ideals relied on a modest but at the same time realistic "'democratic' assumption about the equal potential of human nature," by which he meant that it was supposed that everyone was both self-interested and, to some extent, a sympathetic, social, and moral being. Kristol's point was that a bourgeois society that was "interested in making the best of this world, not in any transfiguration," did wisely to rely on such a level-headed, but not dismissive, democratic assumption about humanity's moral abilities. True, bourgeois society had given up on the very highest ideals, and it was pretty much inevitable that this would result in the formation of an irritated intellectual class. Nevertheless, it was only realistic to suppose that "only a few are capable of pursuing excellence" and, moreover, that "everyone is capable of recognizing and pursuing his own self-interest."[84]

Had Kristol left it at that—self-interest as such—one could conclude that Kristol's case for bourgeois society relied on a rather cynical argument about human nature and motivation, perhaps under the influence of Smith's *Wealth of Nations*. Yet Kristol's subsequent comment on the assumptions about human nature underlying bourgeois society makes it clear that his case rested not only on Smith's 1776 work on economics but also on the "cheerful and benign," "even in some ways an inspirational book," *Moral Sentiments* from 1759. That is to say, Kristol elaborated on the bourgeois world view by pointing out that such a world view *also* supposed that "the average individual's conception of his own self-interest will be sufficiently 'enlightened'—that is, sufficiently far-sighted and prudent—to permit other human passions (the desire for community, the sense of human sympathy, the moral conscience, etc.) to find expression, albeit always in a voluntarist form."[85] Needless to say, this kind of "democratic assumption about the equal potential of human nature" that took into account both the "self-interested" and moral or "sympathetic" qualities of human nature was familiar to Kristol from Smith's moral philosophy that the Scottish author had outlined in his two key works. For Kristol at least, this multifaceted Smithian view of human nature was not only realistic but also humane—in short, it was a view of human nature that he readily accepted as the foundation for his moral philosophy of bourgeois society.

Importantly, Kristol's particular interpretation of Smith's moral philosophy was not intrinsic to Smith's thought. It is true that in *Moral Sentiments*, Smith grounded morality in common dispositions of human nature—sympathetic imagination, the desire for approbation, and the internalization of the views of an impartial spectator as conscience—which perhaps can be seen as "democratic" or "egalitarian." However, Smith's classic text actually confirms a *hierarchical* vision of society by stressing the relatively greater sympathy that flows from below to above and encourages a system of deference. As Smith himself put it, "This disposition to admire, and almost to worship, the rich and the powerful, and to despise, or, at least, to neglect persons of poor and mean condition, though necessary both to establish and to maintain the distinction of ranks and the order of society, is, at the same time, the great and most universal cause of the corruption of our moral sentiments."[86] Smith continued by noting, somewhat sullenly, that "the great mob of mankind are the admirers and worshippers, and, what may seem more extraordinary, most frequently the disinterested admirers and worshippers, of wealth and great-ness."[87] So while Smith's view of human nature might be democratic in con-ception, his views of society and politics were not—in fact, the democratic moral sentiments, when "corrupted," end up confirming and stabilizing a hi-erarchical system.

Kristol's "Adversary Culture of Intellectuals" was then an important mile-stone in the evolution of neoconservative thought in the sense that in it, the godfather of neoconservatism refashioned the moral philosophy of Smith and other Scottish thinkers into a "democratic" neoconservative sensibility—namely, a response to the elitist adversary culture of liberal intellectuals. By reading Smith's *Moral Sentiments* together with *Wealth of Nations*, Kristol had settled upon a supposedly humane concept of the moral nature of human be-ings that he then presented as a minimum standard for a common moral cul-ture in post-1960s America. His serious engagement with the Anglo-Scottish Enlightenment had encouraged him to consider, and advocate in public, the idea that ordinary people *as natural selves* were decent and virtuous (indus-trious, morally conscious, "sympathetic") people, always willing to "better their condition" while taking into account their fellow citizens and that a (relatively) positive view of bourgeois capitalist society in fact rested on such an idea.

Significantly, by articulating a moral vision of capitalism that placed virtu-ous ordinary citizens at its center, Kristol also helped bridge the gap between neoconservatism—that primarily focused on moral and cultural issues—and "neoliberal" and "libertarian" free market advocacy. Although Kristol, in "Adam Smith and the Spirit of Capitalism" and elsewhere, attacked the vulgar economic reductionism of modern "libertarians"—and pointed out that "the 'economic man' of modern economics is not quite the same creature as the [socially, politically and morally understood] 'bourgeois man' of *The Theory of Moral Sentiments* or even *The Wealth of Nations*"—his Smith-informed vi-sion of capitalism and the bourgeois way of life offered free market advocates useful moral arguments in favor of capitalism at a time of a serious economic crisis.[88] One might even say, as historian Gary Gerstle does, that neoconserva-tives provided the post-1970s "neoliberal order" with a moral perspective. Yet while Gerstle identifies this neoconservative moral perspective with primar-ily Himmelfarb's "neo-Victorian" advocacy of self-discipline and self-control, perhaps even more relevant for the "neoliberal order" was Kristol's Smith-inspired moral vision of capitalism that was based on the idea of an indus-trious, morally conscious, "sympathetic" everyman, always willing to "better his condition."[89] Indeed, it is significant that in the mid-1970s, at the dawn of the neoliberal order (which presumably replaced the midcentury's "New Deal order"), the neoconservatives refocused on Enlightenment thought, Smith, and other eighteenth-century Scottish moral philosophers.

Kristol's late 1970s texts on Smith's moral philosophy, bourgeois capitalism, and the adversary culture of intellectuals were then early examples of Kristol's own efforts to redefine neoconservatism by attuning it with a "Scottish" view of human nature and the moral life—or to put it differently, to rework the Scottish tradition into a political instrument in the culture wars against elitist liberal intellectuals. More attempts to reconstruct the moral philosophical foundation of neoconservative thought were to follow in the early 1980s, and like Kristol's 1970s work on Smith, they make evident that neoconservative cultural battles against the liberal elites were at the time closely tied to questions about capitalism.

The Sentimentalist Enlightenment:
A Neoconservative Interpretation

The first one to follow Kristol into the world of the Anglo-Scottish Enlightenment was Himmelfarb. She, like Kristol, came to argue that Smith's vision of capitalism—or in Smith's words, "the natural system of liberty"—ultimately relied on a "democratic" view of human nature that reflected the more widespread moral sentimentalist ideas of the Scottish Enlightenment. She discussed the Scottish ideas in her historical works, in which she, the academic historian, not only reaffirmed Kristol's historical arguments about Smith as an eighteenth-century moral sentimentalist but further elaborated on the alleged critical differences between the sentimentalist Scottish Enlightenment and the rationalist French Enlightenment. Importantly, despite Himmelfarb's academic credentials, the version of the Scottish Enlightenment put forward by the neoconservative historian in her comparison with the French Enlightenment was not an entirely accurate reflection of a real historical difference between the French and Scottish traditions but rather served the needs of neoconservatives in their culture wars conflict with liberal intellectuals. Nevertheless, Himmelfarb very much substantiated the neoconservative reading of the Scottish philosophers as champions of the common people and the idea that a high respect for shared (moral) sentiments—rather than reason—is key for democratic thought.

Himmelfarb's neoconservative reinvention of Smith and the Scottish Enlightenment can be found in two massive books, together totaling about one thousand pages, which dealt with the idea of poverty in eighteenth- and nineteenth-century England. The books grew out of two articles written in the early 1970s, which is to say that she spent some twenty years on a project that resulted in *The Idea of Poverty: England in the Early Industrial Age* (1984) and *Poverty and Compassion: The Moral Imagination of the Late Victorians* (1991).[90] In these two works, Himmelfarb introduced Smith as a moral philosopher whose ideas about ordinary people and the poor strongly contrasted with Malthus's bleak views and served as one starting point for Victorian ideas on and attitudes toward poverty as a social problem (rather than as a natural condition). It is a strong indication of Himmelfarb's and her husband's coordinated intellectual endeavors that she, like Kristol—who took a sabbatical from New York University in 1976–77 to study economics and Smith's capitalism—devoted the academic year of 1976–77 to conduct research for a project that studied Smith's philosophy.[91]

Although Himmelfarb discussed Smith's thought both in *Idea of Poverty* and in *Poverty and Compassion*, it is her first book on English poverty (from 1984) that includes an entire chapter on Smith titled "Adam Smith: Political Economy as Moral Philosophy." In the chapter, Himmelfarb portrayed Smith's two key works very much like Kristol did in "Adam Smith and the Spirit of Capitalism," in that she described them as inseparable "parts of [Smith's] grand 'design.' " Like her husband, she gave emphasis to *Moral Sentiments* in particular, arguing that despite Smith's late twentieth-century reputation as the writer of *Wealth of Nations*, Smith should be seen primarily as a moral philosopher who had written two major works, not one.[92]

Himmelfarb's discussion of Smith from 1984 is to be seen as a companion to Kristol's 1976 and 1979 essays on Smith and America's "adversary culture," which, as noted, are neoconservative milestones because they turned the supposedly "democratic" Scottish moral philosophy into an intellectual weapon used in a political battle against contemporary liberal elites and their antibourgeois elitism. Indeed, Himmelfarb's chapter on Smith is no less seminal a neoconservative text, since she—the eminent historian—now explicitly introduced Smith's emotivism as the key that the great Scottish thinker had used to access the moral minds of ordinary people, and she contrasted Smithian ideas with French rationalist elitism. To repeat an earlier point, the use of language that distinguishes between the people and the elites and portrays the people as an unerring source of truth is by definition a populist use of language. Himmelfarb's book was an academic study on the idea of poverty, and accordingly, she introduced the essential concepts while discussing Smith's ideas about "the poor." She noted that the "people" and the "poor" played important roles in Smith's theory in *Wealth of Nations* and that Smith's concept of the nation (in the title *Wealth of Nations*) "referred not to the nation in the mercantilist sense—the nation-state whose wealth was a measure of the power it could exercise vis-à-vis other states—but to the people comprising the nation. And 'people' not in the political sense of those having a voice and active part in the political process, but in the social and economic sense, those working and living in society, of whom the largest part were the 'lower ranks' or 'poor.' "[93]

Now, what makes Himmelfarb's treatment of Smith a key moment in the evolution of neoconservative thought is that she more or less openly celebrated Smith for his sympathetic approach to "the people" by contrasting Smith's view with the "not a conspicuously democratic doctrine" of the philosophes of the French Enlightenment. Moreover, anticipating Wilson's and Fukuyama's culture wars tracts of the 1990s, Himmelfarb stressed that the democratic quality of Smith's philosophy and the larger Scottish Enlightenment derived from the Scottish philosophers' great respect for emotion, whereas the French Enlightenment had become an elitist endeavor because of its rationalist tendencies— that is, the French highlighted the learning, reason, and visionary capacities of the few.[94]

Importantly, Himmelfarb was here playing down the fact that both the Scottish *and* the French Enlightenments could be seen as propagating a democratic vision of human nature—consider, for example, the French 1789 Declaration of the Rights of Man and of the Citizen proclaiming that "men are born and remain free and equal in rights. Social distinctions may be founded only upon the general good."[95] Moreover, each of these enlightenments could be used to confirm a relatively egalitarian model, or a more hierarchical one—consider Smith's claim that the "disposition to admire . . . the rich and the powerful, and to despise, or, at least, to neglect persons of poor and mean condition" was "necessary both to establish and to maintain the distinction of ranks and the order of society."[96] In other words, there is nothing inherent in the argument for an order based on rationality rather than an order based on sentiment that would cause one to come to a conclusion that favored elite rule.

The point is, then, that Himmelfarb not only incorporated into her historical works her husband's dualistic and ideological reading of the evolution of Western political thought as a competition between the "modest" and politically moderate Anglo-Scottish Enlightenment and the "utopian" French Enlightenment; she further elaborated on it by highlighting the contrast between the two Enlightenments as an opposition between a sentimentalist and democratic Scottish Enlightenment and a rationalist and elitist French Enlightenment. In the latter, "reason was paramount," whereas "to Smith (and the Scottish Enlightenment in general), it was not reason that defined human nature so much as interests, passions, sentiments, sympathies."[97] As a professional historian, Himmelfarb naturally brought academic credibility to this neoconservative reading of the Scottish and French Enlightenments.

Yet Himmelfarb clearly exaggerated the contrast between a rationalist and elitist French Enlightenment with a sentimentalist and democratic British Enlightenment. There were plenty of rationalists in both England and Scotland—writers such as Ralph Cudworth and Samuel Clarke—and there were French and other continental sentimentalists, including Johann Gottfried von Herder and Montesquieu.[98]

Earlier I noted that both Hume's and Smith's sentimentalist ethics have certain elitist implications in the sense that the two writers were suspicious of unrefined moral sentiments and emphasized the importance of sentimental education. Himmelfarb, however, downplayed this aspect of Smith's moral sentimentalism and emphasized that it was the sentimentalist view of human nature that largely explained Smith's favorable view of "the poor" and more generally, "the people." She referred to this sentimentalist view as an "optimistic view of human nature." It was an optimistic view not only because the sentiments, sympathies, and interests were shared by all people but because they were shared "not in some remote future but in the present." In the coming years, Wilson and Fukuyama, as neoconservative social scientists, would emphasize that these shared sentiments were part of biological human nature. Himmelfarb however pointed out that "on the nature-nurture issue, as we now know it, Smith was unequivocally on the nurture side."[99]

On the first glance, Himmelfarb's comment about "nurture" may look like an important difference between her and the two neoconservative social scientists—namely, that Himmelfarb was here emphasizing sentimental education instead of inherent moral sentiments. Yet the three writers' views were actually largely compatible, since Himmelfarb was here drawing attention to Smith's emphasis on nurture when it comes to individual variations in intelligence.[100] With respect to people's moral and emotional characteristics, she portrayed Smith as a theorist who underlined our inherent shared nature. Himmelfarb's key point about Smith's moral theory concerned the "virtues inherent in human nature"—namely, that Smith had presumed that the poor "have the same virtues and passions as everyone else." Like Kristol some years earlier, Himmelfarb argued that it was precisely because of these shared virtues and passions that everyone, the poor included, in Smith's system, "were capable of working within the 'system of natural liberty' and profiting from it." In contrast to the French idea that the most highly talented and rational leaders were to "do for society what the people could not do for themselves," the Scottish thinkers believed that the people were "capable and desirous of bettering themselves, capable and desirous of exercising the virtues inherent in human nature, capable and desirous of the liberty that was their right as responsible individuals."[101]

While Himmelfarb, in *Idea of Poverty*, did not claim Smith's ideas as her own, there is no doubt that she sympathized with Smith's defense of capitalism and his supposedly "democratic" views on the moral nature of human beings and ordinary people. Considering that Himmelfarb's husband at the time was reconsidering his civic ideas along the lines of Smith's moral philosophy, we might conclude that by the early 1980s, the rather nervous "republican" insistence on moral *improvement* was no longer the only philosophically grounded neoconservative message for, or argument about, "the people." A revised, more confident neoconservative moral-political language grounded on the notions of the "moral sense," "moral sentiments," "a democratic view of human nature," and "shared virtues" was evidently in the making. Indeed, by the turn of the 1980s, Kristol had already begun to use these ideas to contest the antibourgeois elitism of liberal intellectuals in his article "The Adversary Culture of Intellectuals."

Speaking for Average White Americans: Neoconservatives and the Republican Party

Kristol and Himmelfarb's reinvention of Scottish moral philosophy established, then, the building blocks for the populist logic that in the 1980s and 1990s came to inform the neoconservative response to America's cultural liberalization, fracture, and the allegedly un-American "adversary culture of intellectuals." However, the neoconservatives' populist turn in the early 1980s was a response to both new intellectual influences and political trends. While the neoconservatives at first studied Smith and other Scottish thinkers to find a cure for the crisis of confidence that resulted from the economic slump of the mid-1970s, they held on to and reworked Scottish "democratic" ideas about human moral nature because of some of the same political trends and cultural developments that in the 1970s and 1980s provoked the larger conservative movement, including the Republican Party, to flirt with populist rhetoric. Particularly important in this sense was the series of liberal Supreme Court rulings (mostly in the 1970s)—sometimes called the "rights revolution"—that provoked a disapproving reaction from large sections of the population (working- and middle-class whites, in particular) and that, in turn, inspired the rebirth of the Republican Party as a representative of the average white American. While the rights revolution of the 1960s and 1970s thus shaped the language of both the Republican Party and neoconservative intellectuals, the new neoconservative language of the moral sense and moral sentiments differed in important respects from the Republican notions of both the "silent majority" and even "common sense" as they were used by Nixon and Reagan, respectively.

The rights revolution, of course, refers to the great expansion of civil rights and civil liberties in the United States in the 1960s and 1970s via a series of Supreme Court decisions. While the more famous landmark pieces of civil rights legislation enacted by Congress in 1964 and 1965—the Civil Rights Act and the Voting Rights Act—were largely supported in the country, the Supreme Court made at around the same time several important decisions that were much more contested.[102] Among them were *Engel v. Vitale* (1962) and *Abington School District v. Schempp* (1963), which banned school prayer and mandatory Bible reading in public schools; *Griggs v. Duke Power Co.* (1971), which made affirmative action a standard policy in the nation's workplaces; *Regents of the University of California v. Bakke* (1978), which allowed race to be one of the factors considered in choosing a diverse student body in university admission decisions; *Swann v. Charlotte-Mecklenburg Board of Education* (1971), which allowed federal courts to mandate busing black students to white schools, and vice versa, in order to desegregate schools; and *Roe v. Wade* (1973), which legalized the majority of abortions during the first two trimesters of pregnancy.[103]

That a large part of the American public resisted many of these rulings by the liberal courts of the 1960s and 1970s became evident when pollsters began to study the issues. In Gallup polls taken since the 1960s, the rulings against school prayer and reading the Bible in school consistently ranked as the most unpopular. The polls, for their part, enabled critics to label the rulings as "undemocratic." Religious conservatives in particular saw the secularization of schools as elitist and unfair, since 96 percent of Americans believed in God according to some Gallup polls.[104] Analogously, in the early 1970s, the majority of white Americans (around 85 percent) opposed forced busing of schoolchildren as a solution to America's racial problems and saw affirmative action as un-American.[105] A large number of Americans were thus genuinely dissatisfied with the court rulings, which brought very real changes to both their own lives and the American way of life more generally.[106]

The liberal Supreme Court rulings, part of the country's general post-1960s cultural liberalization, and the negative reaction to them by a large part of the population—especially by working- and middle-class whites—naturally created opportunities for political conservatives to take advantage of the situation; the liberalization of the country, after all, very much seemed like a transformation forced "from above." And political conservatives did indeed take the opportunity. Republican activists and politicians practically reinvented themselves at the turn of the 1970s as the voice of average white Americans.[107]

Richard Nixon's "silent majority" was the key concept that informed the early Republican embrace of populist language. The exact phrase was first introduced by the president in one of his public speeches in 1969, although a similar theme had already been developed during the 1968 Nixon campaign. The importance of the concept lies in the fact that it critically shaped the national self-image. That is, it helped implant the idea during Nixon's time in power (1969–74) that there are two kinds of Americans. On the one side was the "silent majority," those from the "middle class, middle American, suburban, exurban, and rural coalition" who, as historian Rick Perlstein notes, "call themselves, now, 'Values voters,' 'people of faith,' 'patriots,' or even, simply, 'Republicans'—and who feel themselves condescended to by snobby opinion-making elites, and who rage about un-Americans, anti-Christians, amoralists, *aliens*. On the other side are the 'liberals,' the 'cosmopolitans,' the 'intellectuals,' the 'professionals,'—'Democrats.'"[108] Crucially, then, during Nixon's time as a candidate and later as president, thinkers in the Republican Party realized that defense of middle-class *values*—diligence, moral piety, and self-governing communities—could help them gather votes from a diverse collection of citizens who resented powerful liberals, left-wing movements, and the counterculture. Never before had a leading conservative attached his cause to an explicitly "populist" identity.[109]

When it comes to the neoconservatives and Nixon's silent majority theme, two observations need to be made. First, one must note that the Republican Party began to court the silent majority already in the late 1960s and early 1970s when the neoconservatives were still rather *suspect* of populism, "democracies" (as against "republics"), and the reliability of the common man. The neoconservatives thus did not use Nixon's populist silent majority theme in the early 1970s, even if they took shared stances on many domestic policy issues (such as crime and busing).[110] On the other hand, the key idea included in Nixon's populist language—that there are two kinds of Americans, the moral middle class and snobby, amoral elites—soon became a staple of neoconservative discourse, albeit Kristol and others expressed the idea in a somewhat different form, focusing on popular moral sentiments as opposed to elite rationalism. Therefore, one should not rule out the possibility that Nixon and his aides had some (indirect) impact on the development of neoconservative thought.

During Nixon's time in power, and until the late 1970s, most neoconservatives were Democratic voters (Kristol and Himmelfarb were two exceptions:

they switched to the Republican Party already in 1972).[111] However, by the turn of the 1980s, neoconservative thinkers were moving one by one behind Ronald Reagan.[112] Importantly, Reagan, like Nixon, was fond of phrases familiar from populist rhetoric, and this time, the Republican Party's populist message was communicated by a leader whom many neoconservative thinkers recognized as their own.

A characteristic feature of Reagan's populist language was that he adopted the centuries-old concept of common sense to articulate the party's new proximity to, and understanding of, the common people. While Nixon's concept—the silent majority—had divided Americans into two opposite groups, Reagan used the concept of common sense to express a preference for the everyday logic of common people as opposed to the out-of-touch elite approaches. Rosenfeld points to Reagan as a particularly influential transformative figure in the political history of the common-sense idea, in that he helped make common sense one of the lead themes of *conservative* populism in the late twentieth century.[113] In 1976, right after serving eight years as the governor of California and several years before he took office as the president of the United States, Reagan argued that "what we did in California can be done in Washington if government will have faith in the people and let them bring their common sense to bear on the problems bureaucracy hasn't solved. I believe in the people."[114] During his time in the White House, Reagan kept up the theme, so much so that in his farewell address in 1989 he described the so-called Reagan Revolution as "the great rediscovery, a rediscovery of our values and our common sense."[115] In line with typical populist rhetoric, Reagan told Americans he was one of the people.[116]

This begs an important question: Was there a link between Reagan's common-sense discourse and the emerging neoconservative language of moral sentiments and the moral sense? To be sure, Reagan's aims differed from those of the neoconservative intellectuals. The Republican Party recreated itself as the voice of average white Americans in order to gain votes. The neoconservatives in turn took it as their task to counter the impact of the adversary culture of intellectuals and to help rebuild a foundation for a common moral culture. Moreover, unlike Reagan, the neoconservatives drew from Scottish moral sentimentalism, not Paine's common-sense thought. As Rosenfeld points out, Reagan "frequently mined the pages of [Paine's] original 1776 *Common Sense* for pithy, patriotic quotes about the necessity of limited government or the spirit of revolution" and thus ironically helped the eighteenth-century political radical and nonbeliever become the hero of late twentieth-century conservative populists and a symbol of "power to the fed-up people as opposed to the powers that be."[117]

As a justification for populism, the concept of the moral sense bears a resemblance to common sense. Yet whereas the concept of common sense lauds people's *experiences* with the "real world" (as opposed to the alienated elite's high-flown rationality), the language of the moral sense highlights the ordinary citizen's *emotions* rather than reason and innate factors along with experiences. The neoconservatives did appeal to "common sense" along with the "moral sense" and "moral sentiments," but they did so in a loose way and without reference to previous common-sense theorists; that is to say, when they aimed to offer a more penetrating analysis of ordinary people's mental and moral capacities, they invoked (Hutcheson's) "moral sense" or (Smith's) "moral sentiments" instead of (Paine's) "common sense." Despite these differences in aims and moral vocabularies, the neoconservatives in all likelihood advanced the cause of the Republican Party by reinventing Scottish moral philosophy to encourage the exclusion of the liberal elites so that Republicans—the conservative party—began to look like the party of "true," "ethical" Americans.

While the neoconservative discourse on everyman's moral sense or moral sentiments was from the beginning a more intellectually ambitious attempt to discuss ordinary people's mental capacities than Reagan's conversationalist populist slogans, "populism" in itself was not a label that the neoconservatives were particularly troubled by any longer in the early 1980s. This holds true with Kristol at least. He discussed populism in a positive light on several occasions in the early and mid-1980s.

One such text is Kristol's introduction to his essay collection *Reflections of a Neoconservative* from 1983—a text in which Kristol (re)considered the nature of neoconservatism and the relationship between neoconservatism and traditional conservatism. Anyone reading the text cannot miss the fact that at the time, the question of populism, and especially neoconservatism's position on it, was foremost in Kristol's mind. Indeed, Kristol made the case that one might best understand the differences and similarities between neoconservatism and conservatism proper by comparing and contrasting their respective attitudes toward "the people." As the leading neoconservative theorist now saw it, neoconservatism was a version of "conservatism" in the sense that it insisted on "standards of excellence and virtue." "Neoconservatism," he continued, "is anything but populist in that respect, and indeed would seem to be what we have come to call 'elitist.'"[118] Yet Kristol quickly retreated from this idea of neoconservatism as elitist by adding that neoconservatism was a *new* conservatism precisely because it—unlike traditional conservatism—understood that such an insistence on moral standards was instinctive to "the people." Or, as he put it, "The 'neo' in neoconservatism is its insistence that the American people have always had an instinctive deference toward such standards [of excellence and virtue], and that the American democracy has never been egalitarian in this sense. Economic and cultural egalitarianism—as distinct from the social and legal egalitarianism essential to a viable democracy—has been a passion of the intellectual class, never of the people. This is another way of saying that the American people remain profoundly bourgeois, in their populism as in so many other respects."[119] Although Kristol did not here directly refer to Smith or to any other Scottish sentimentalist thinker, he invoked an idea that was familiar to him from his own, and his wife's, studies on the Scottish Enlightenment—that is, the idea that all people, not only sophisticated individuals, were instinctively capable of making distinctions between virtue and vice, good and bad, merit and demerit. Hence it is not unreasonable to suppose that Kristol's (self-)understanding of neoconservatism was in the early 1980s essentially informed by his reading of Scottish moralists, in particular when one keeps in mind that Kristol had possessed a strikingly *low* opinion of the American people's mental and moral capacities just before he began to study Smith's philosophy in the mid-1970s.

One must also note that in the previous quote, Kristol referred to the idea of a shared instinctive sense of moral standards as an antidote to the contemporary intellectual elite's economic and cultural egalitarianism. That is to say, whereas in 1983 Kristol no longer viewed the common people as untrustworthy or morally deficient and adhered to the idea that most people did possess an equal moral consciousness and virtuous potential, he also realized that this idea of a commonly shared moral consciousness could function as a rhetorical means to renegotiate the line between the decent and deserving individuals and others. In other words, by referring to the sentiment-based natural standards of virtue of "the people," he and the neoconservatives could now argue—as if they were speaking *for* the people—against any policies or moral failings that supposedly did not meet the instinctive moral standards of the people. This populist logic was to play a crucial role in the neoconservative culture wars in the 1980s and 1990s.

Kristol's 1985 essay, tellingly entitled "The New Populism: Not to Worry," provides some early evidence of this new neoconservative logic. It also shows that common sense, rather than the moral sense or moral sentiments, was sometimes the selected word of the neoconservatives when the occasion did not call for a more thorough analysis of the people's mental capacities. In the article, Kristol made it clear that neoconservatives should not feel embarrassed if they were associated with the populist forces that were rising in the United States in the 1980s. He took note of the fact that populist rhetoric had recently become increasingly common among the nation's political leaders, but he argued that there was no need to worry—indeed, Kristol made the point that the ordinary citizen's commonsensical attitudes toward "issues of education and crime clearly illustrate why this new populism exists and flourishes." The American people were commonsensical, for example, in not caring about the fuss that educationists, courts, and legislators had made over school prayer. "American parents," very sensibly, only wanted schools to make their children "literate, to instill good study habits, to acquaint them with the importance of discipline." Similarly, the American people were sensible in wanting the criminal justice system, as its first priority, to punish the guilty—"*not* [like the unwise elites] to ensure that no innocent person is ever unfairly convicted."[120]

Considering that in 1974 Kristol himself had put forward a philosophically grounded argument *against* the American "democratic" idea that institutions should be "responsive to people as they are" (and not as they could be), we might conclude that in just over ten years, between 1974 and 1985, the godfather of neoconservatism had fundamentally renegotiated the role of "the people" in neoconservative political rhetoric. In the mid-1980s, he clearly was much more willing than before to argue that American institutions *should* be "responsive to people as they are"—in other words, that the institutions should reflect the instinctive moral standards, or the moral sense, of "ordinary people." Thus finally, in the early Reagan years, the neoconservative figure of the moral everyman had fully entered the political arena.

James Q. Wilson and the Rehabilitation of Emotions

Ultimately, it was James Q. Wilson who became the most detailed neoconservative interpreter of Scottish moralism. From his neoconservative friends—Irving Kristol and Himmelfarb—Wilson adopted the dichotomy between the sentimentalist Scottish Enlightenment and the rationalist French Enlightenment and, while invoking the moral vocabularies of Francis Hutcheson and Adam Smith, reshaped the Scottish thinkers' ideas on the moral sense and moral sentiments into a neoconservative sensibility. While Wilson as a social scientist clearly admired especially Smith's and David Hume's philosophical works as such, as a culture warrior, he applied their concepts and perspective to public issues that would have been alien to them. Neither Smith nor Hume ever used their ideas on moral sentiments to launch an attack on contemporary cultural "elites," but Wilson did, and therefore it is clear that Wilson's borrowing from the Scottish philosophers was a reinvention of their thought in populist terms. Moreover, Wilson brought together various strands of mostly Scottish ethics— especially the moral sense school of Shaftesbury and Hutcheson and the moral sentiments school of Hume and Smith—that were never meant to be compatible with one another. For these reasons, Wilson, like Kristol and Himmelfarb, was a shaper of the Scottish intellectual tradition rather than being shaped by it.

Wilson added force to a neoconservative reading of the sentimentalist tradition in two ways. On the one hand, he made a general effort to show that something that could be called a natural moral sense *did* exist and that the moral sense of the so-called average American was a viable alternative to the American intellectual elite's morally silent, scientific way of knowing. On the other hand, Wilson invoked the moral sense and moral sentiments to defend conservative positions in specific cultural conflicts, such as those over crime and punishment, abortion, and gay marriage.

This chapter explores Wilson's self-imposed task to raise the status of moral emotions in the United States during the culture wars era. To paraphrase Kristol's 1983 assertion that "it is the self-imposed assignment of neoconservatism to explain to the American people why they are right, and to the intellectuals why they are wrong," Wilson took it as his task in the late 1980s and 1990s to explain to the American people why their moral sentiments on contemporary moral issues were justified and right and to the intellectuals why their rationalism and moral relativism were wrong.[1] In this sense, Wilson, like Kristol, acted like a true representative of the unerring "ordinary people," in genuine populist fashion. Thus whereas in the mid-1960s the mission of the *Public Interest* intellectuals had been to offer relevant social scientific data to the nation's liberal, technocratic decision-makers, twenty-five years later, Scottish philosophy and modern social science were used by Wilson, the distinguished social scientist, to defend popular moral emotions as a viable alternative to any morally silent, data-based, or "scientific" way of knowing.

That it was Wilson who, of all the neoconservative social scientists, first took it as his task to explain "scientifically" to the American people why their moral sentiments were justified is hardly surprising given the fact that Wilson was among Kristol's and Himmelfarb's closest friends and, in Kristol's words, the "leader" of the social scientists within the neoconservative camp.[2] Wilson had been particularly close to Kristol ever since the first days of the *Public Interest* in the mid-1960s (Wilson contributed to the second issue), and he remained so until Kristol's passing in 2009. In his later years, Kristol—who as the editor of the *Public Interest* and the public face of neoconservatism was naturally concerned for neoconservatism's public standing—was deeply grateful to Wilson for "providing neo-conservatism with academic social science credentials"—in other words, for being "the leader of that group [of scholars committed to making the *Public Interest* work]."[3]

Considering Wilson's long academic career and his reputation among colleagues, Kristol's remark about him being the leader of the neoconservative social scientists does not seem exaggerated. Between the late 1950s and his death in 2012, Wilson had a remarkably successful career in political science and as a theorist of criminal policy at some of the country's best universities, first at the University of Chicago (PhD in political science, 1959), then at Harvard (1961–87) and the University of California, Los Angeles (1987–97). An Oxford bibliography notes that Wilson is "by many accounts, the most influential criminal justice scholar of the twentieth century" due to his role as perhaps the most important intellectual architect of the punitive turn in American criminal policy in the 1970s.[4] Related to this, Wilson is remembered as the codeveloper (together with George Kelling) of the "broken windows" theory of crime that inspired New York City's controversial "quality of life," "zero tolerance," and "stop-question-and-frisk" policing methods in the 1990s.[5] Besides these well-known accomplishments as a theorist of criminal policy, Wilson also had a career as a student of government, and in 1991–92, he served as president of the American Political Science Association. Finally, in 2003, he was granted the highest civilian award in the United States, the Presidential Medal of Honor, by President George W. Bush, who stated that Wilson was arguably "the most influential political scientist in America since the White House was home to Professor Woodrow Wilson."[6] On the basis of the vast number of obituaries written for him, Wilson had a reputation among his colleagues as a fact-driven, humble and polite, yet intellectually tough scholar—fellow scholars and thinkers such as Michael Sandel, George F. Will, and Charles Murray praised him for being "a model of the modest scholar" (Sandel), "the most accomplished social scientist of the last half-century" (Will), and "my hero" (Murray).[7]

Emotions as a Way of Knowing

It is somewhat ironic that Wilson, despite his reputation as a data-driven social scientist, was himself deeply, and increasingly, unsatisfied with modern social science as a means of producing (purely descriptive) knowledge. Indeed, from the mid-1980s onward, Wilson became more and more critical of the "moral silence" of contemporary social science and political philosophy.[8] He claimed that there was an increasing "public demand" for "more ethics" in the United States by "children, government officials, and business leaders," and thus he blamed American social scientists and philosophers, both privately and publicly, for their incapacity to respond to this demand.[9] In a 1988 commencement address given at the University of Redlands, he made the general observation that "it is as if it were a mark of sophistication for us to shun the language of morality in discussing the problems of mankind."[10]

Two years later, in a grant application to the liberally oriented Sloan Foundation, he lamented that "Western philosophy and social science have called into question the idea that people can make moral statements that are true, useful, or generally applicable." "Much of modern social science," Wilson continued, "has been devoted to showing that there are in fact no universal moral standards. At best, morality is a set of learned cultural 'norms' that may prevail in many societies but certainly do not prevail in all places. At worst, morality is a code word for the inculcated oppression of a ruling class (Marxism) or the learned repression of people with unresolved sexual anxieties

(Freudianism)."[11] Wilson made a similar point in an unpublished (and un-dated) outline entitled "The Moral Sense," claiming in it that "almost every tendency in modern thought has in common a rejection of the possibility of defending moral judgments." He referred to Marxism, logical positivism, "narrow utilitarianism," and cultural relativism and noted that all four "have in common a belief that reason equals science (even the pretend science of Marxism). The scientific method is the only form of knowing, and it cannot know, in the sense of defend, morality."[12]

Wilson's most forceful criticisms of the "morally silent" social sciences date from the late 1980s and early 1990s, a period that was arguably the most heated moment of the American culture wars, beginning with the publication of Allan Bloom's 1987 bestseller *The Closing of the American Mind*. Bloom fa-mously claimed that the American liberal "virtue" of "openness" was in fact a closedness to the truth, since it relied on a dogmatic relativism—that is, on a view that all value judgments are equally true (or false). As Bloom put it, this was understood in the United States not so much as a "theoretical insight but [as] a moral postulate," one that thus stood as the only moral claim that was not relative.[13] In the extremely heated intellectual atmosphere of the late 1980s and early 1990s, Wilson, as a conservative thinker, was thus hardly alone in pressing charges against unprincipled liberal scholarship or liberalism more generally.

What was more original in Wilson's writing in that period was his idea that the *intuitively moral* perspective of the average citizen could be seen—and defended—as a viable alternative to the moral silence of social science and other scientific ways of knowing. As Wilson put it in a letter to Arthur Singer of the Sloan Foundation, he could "think of few subjects [other than morality] on which expert and popular opinion are more at odds. While phi-losophers confidently assert that 'ought' statements cannot be logically de-rived from 'is' statements, the average person goes about his or her life con-fident that there are certain fundamental moral rules the truth of which is self-evident." The average person, Wilson clarified, had no doubt that "killing innocent children is wrong," that "no man should be a judge in his own case," or that infanticide and incest are wrong.[14] For this reason, Wilson had come to the conclusion—this is how he put it in an unpublished outline—that

there are other ways of knowing [than the scientific method that could not defend morality], one of which is an intuitive or directly felt sense of the stan-dards one ought to apply, at least when one thinks disinterestedly about a choice. We do not intuitively know moral rules or principles but we do have a moral sense that shapes these principles, and this sense is universal: it occurs

in all cultures and at all times, and can be found among all but the most bi-
zarre ind[ividuals]. I draw from Aristotle, Hume, Adam Smith + Cha[rles]
Darwin [Wilson has added Darwin later with a pen].[15]

This idea about the average person's moral perception of the world as an alternative to the moral silence of social science inspired Wilson to launch a
new research project on morality in the late 1980s, after having published a
series of widely noticed and influential criminological studies (most recently,
Crime and Human Nature in 1985 with the Harvard psychologist Richard
Herrnstein). He described his new idea to Singer in early 1990: "Whenever on
a matter of great importance and everyday personal experience public opinion differs from elite opinion, it is my bias to think that the people may know
something that the experts do not and my inclination [is] to look for ways
in which the popular view might be better understood. This entire venture
that I propose to Sloan might be simply stated as an effort to give intellectual
substance to common understandings about right conduct."[16] Wilson's aim,
then, was nothing less than to defend popular sentiment as a viable alternative to elite rationalism when it came to managing public issues in contemporary America. Or, as Wilson himself put it elsewhere (in private), he set for
himself an "intellectual task" "to *rehabilitate* the scientific, evolutionary, [and]
philos[ophical] status of *emotions*" (emphasis in original).[17]

Wilson's private writings thus reveal quite well how he—the alleged leader
of the neoconservative social scientists—positioned himself and his new research project on morality in relation to social science: on the one hand, he
launched his new project to defend the intuitively moral perspective of the
ordinary citizen *against* the unprincipled contemporary social science; on the
other hand, he, *as a social scientist*, attempted to understand—drawing on
Aristotle, Hume, Smith, and Darwin—the emotions that more or less shaped
the average citizen's moral responses to the conduct and character of other
people.

Wilson's unpublished papers also make visible the links and differences
between his post-1985 project on everyday morality and Kristol's and Himmelfarb's earlier writings on eighteenth-century Scottish moralism and "the
new populism." As we saw earlier, Himmelfarb had suggested in 1984, in *The
Idea of Poverty*, that the democratic nature of the Scottish Enlightenment (as
opposed to the elitist French Enlightenment) was the result of the Scottish
thinkers' great respect for emotion (not opposed to but together with reason).
A year later, Kristol suggested in "The New Populism: Not to Worry" that the
nonexpert sentiments of ordinary Americans relating to such questions as the
education and justice systems showed not only that the people were capable

of making sensible decisions on such issues but that the opinions of ordinary Americans were *more* sensible than those of the educated (liberal) elite. Now after the mid-1980s—in the evermore polarized national atmosphere of the culture wars—it was left to Wilson, one of Himmelfarb's and Kristol's closest friends, to provide academic social science credentials for the idea that the average Joes of America were in fact capable of making important judgments in order to participate meaningfully in public life—perhaps even being the most reliable source of moral truth. That Wilson's new research project was in many respects an extension of Kristol's and Himmelfarb's earlier commentary on Smith and other Scottish thinkers became evident at least when Wilson in 1993 published his major "moral philosophical" work *The Moral Sense*. In it, Wilson fully embraced Kristol's concept of "the Anglo-Scottish Enlightenment." That is to say, he not only adopted Kristol's otherwise seldom used term but also paid respect to the "commonsensical views" of the eighteenth-century British philosophers, which he contrasted, just like Kristol and Himmelfarb did, with the "more strident and extreme claims of some of their French counterparts."[18] Eventually, the study and interpretation of Scottish ideas on human moral nature, and the effort to understand and explain their significance in the contemporary culture wars environment, occupied Wilson from the late 1980s to the early 2000s.[19]

How Ordinary People Think

As noted earlier, Wilson recorded in his private writings that he "drew from" Hume and Smith to reach his aim of defending the intuitive sense of standards of the average citizens. But how exactly did Wilson draw from the Scottish thinkers—or more precisely, reshape their ideas—as he attempted to create an alternative way of knowing to that of purely descriptive modern social science?

To properly understand Wilson's reading of the Scottish philosophers, one must be familiar with the two roles Wilson had in American intellectual life in the late twentieth century—namely, his roles as both a social scientist and a culture warrior. As a social scientist, Wilson often seems to have been studying Scottish ideas from a purely scientific perspective. On the other hand, as a culture warrior, he took elements of the Scottish tradition as a resource that could be reinvented to serve present political needs in the culture wars environment.

For Wilson the social scientist, Hume and Smith were key precursors to the modern science of human behavior, who, however—unlike modern social scientists—had understood that science and morality were not opposites.

He construed that for the Scottish thinkers, a better understanding of human nature had been a prerequisite for saying something meaningful about the good life. Scottish moral philosophy was perhaps not the last word on human nature and morality, but it provided a foundation upon which to develop an enhanced understanding of moral development in children and moral judgment in general. Wilson thought that the Scottish philosophers had built an excellent foundation for such an effort, since they had understood that humans were above all social beings and because they had realized that morality was based not on reason, dogmas, books, or a study of doctrines but on the repertoire of (moral) emotions that all healthy human beings shared.

It seems that Wilson became more and more respectful of the Scottish moral philosophers as he studied their ideas in the late 1980s and early 1990s. Throughout his published works from the 1990s—such as *The Moral Sense* and *Moral Intuitions*, as well as in his correspondences, grant applications, outlines, and lecture notes—Wilson described his sympathy toward the Scottish thinkers and assessed the merits of their moral philosophy. Smith was perhaps the dearest to his heart, so much so that he wrote in a 1994 letter to Richard Herrnstein that he "couldn't resist the chance to have a title [for his 1993 book *The Moral Sense*] the initials of which would match *The Theory of Moral Sentiments*. It is as close as I will ever get to Adam Smith."[20] Wilson admired both of Smith's key works, seeing Smith as "the preeminent economist of all time" and "the preeminent moral philosopher of his time."[21] He had just as high a regard for Hume, whom he once described as an "old friend" and "a philosopher from whom I have learned a great deal and whose writing I enormously admire."[22] It was thus only natural that Wilson portrayed his major work on morality, *The Moral Sense*, as "a continuation of work begun by certain eighteenth-century English and Scottish thinkers, notably Joseph Butler, Francis Hutcheson, David Hume, and Adam Smith."[23]

Perhaps surprisingly, Wilson typically introduced Hume to his readers and listeners by noting that the renowned Scot was the major philosopher from whom American academic experts, at some point in their studies, learned the fundamentals of their nihilist attitudes. As Wilson put it in *The Moral Sense*, "legions" of philosophy students in American universities had learned from Hume's *Treatise of Human Nature* that one cannot infer an "ought" from an "is"—that is, that one cannot infer values from facts. To do so was simply logically untenable. From Hume, Wilson wrote, the American intellectual elite had "acquired reasoned doubts about the possibility of saying anything meaningful about the good life."[24]

Wilson argued that this was a seriously flawed understanding of Hume. Having himself conducted a more systematic reading of Hume for his 1993 book, he had concluded that "the rest of Hume's book [*Treatise of Human Nature*, after the is-ought passage] is a discussion of morality in which he uses language that seems to contradict his own admonition [against inferring an ought from an is]." For Hume, Wilson pointed out, "benevolence—that is, being 'humane, merciful, grateful, friendly, generous'—'universally express[es] the highest merit.'" "These sentiments are 'natural,'" Wilson continued quoting Hume, "and even though they are fainter than self-love, 'it is impossible for such a creature as man to be totally indifferent to the well or ill-being of his fellow-creatures, and not readily, of himself, to pronounce, where nothing gives him any particular bias, that what promotes their happiness is good, what tends to their misery is evil.' Moral sentiments are 'so rooted in our constitution and temper, that without confounding the human mind by disease or madness, 'tis impossible to extirpate and destroy them.'"[25]

These aspects of Hume's philosophy are debated by modern Hume scholars. What is relevant for us is that Wilson—the cultural critic—highlighted the moral sentimentalist aspects of Hume's philosophy in a way that suited his attempt to rehabilitate the status of (moral) emotions in contemporary America. He portrayed Hume as a thinker who had argued that healthy human beings "naturally"—due to their ability to "sympathize" with the feelings of others—judge as "good" those benevolent actions that promote the well-being of their fellow creatures and as "bad" those actions that promote their suffering. Wilson greatly appreciated Hume's idea that "humane, merciful, grateful, friendly, generous" acts—that is, benevolence—would always receive moral approbation from people. For Wilson, this meant that Hume had understood that there was a psychological, if not logical, bridge between is and ought, and therefore Wilson held it "clear that Hume's famous separation of 'is' from 'ought' was meant as a challenge only to those systems of moral thought that attempted to rely purely on reason to prove a moral obligation, and only to 'vulgar systems' at that. Morality, he said, rests on sentiment."[26] The famous Scottish thinker, Wilson wrote elsewhere, had "simply said you had to work carefully from an is-statement to an ought-statement." Hume's understanding of the is-ought issue was therefore a far cry from the ideas of those like English philosopher A. J. Ayer, who later argued that "ought" statements are meaningless.[27]

As Wilson's reference to Ayer suggests, he was deeply frustrated by developments in Western moral philosophy after Hume's era, particularly the reception of Hume himself. Wilson lamented that "only the 'is' versus 'ought' statement by Hume survives among many educated people" despite the fact that Hume's "view about the nature of moral intuitions was much more complicated than a simple and sharp distinction between what is and what ought to be."[28] Wilson understood this misunderstanding of Hume by Western thinkers to have deeply disturbing consequences. In the 1990s, he repeatedly made the argument that this misinterpretation of Hume had importantly contributed to the abandonment of the old Western idea that there were "self-evident moral truths" that, "before about 1800, almost every philosopher in the Western world believed." This "great transformation"—that is, a transition to the world "since about 1800" in which "very few philosophers have held the view that moral truths are self-evident"—Wilson sometimes described as a turn toward "positivism," "relativism," and "cynicism."[29] He defined "positivism" as the idea that "moral discussions are meaningless"; "relativism" as the notion that "my morality is as good as yours, and every culture is equally good"; and "cynicism" as the belief that "moral statements are covers for self-interest."[30]

For Wilson as a cultural critic, the heart of the matter was not that some early modern philosopher—however important—had been misunderstood by later scholars but that a combination of cynicism, relativism, and positivism, which supposedly had come to dominate Western moral discourse by the second half of the twentieth century, was "the cause of several disturbing attitudes" relating to extremely important social issues such as school, children, drugs, families, welfare, gangs, the law, and international affairs.[31] To respond to such supposed destructive tendencies in Western elite thought, Wilson repeatedly stressed in his speeches and published works that resorting to cynicism, relativism, and positivism was "not how ordinary people think." He admitted that ordinary people might be cynics, especially about politicians, but he added that they were cynics "only up to a point," since they considered unfairness in politics as disgusting even if it had no direct harmful effects on them. Moreover, ordinary people were not positivists, since they did not hesitate to state, for example, that "playing with babies is better than torturing them." Finally, the common people were "not relativists: [for them] cultures are bad if they encourage murder, good if they try to prevent it." Wilson's conclusion was that "the people are right, though they are often confused by their inability to argue with others."[32]

Regarding Hume, Wilson's aim was thus to contest the "conventional" understanding of the Scottish thinker as someone whose work could be used to justify positivism, relativism, and cynicism. Correspondingly, and just as importantly, Wilson wished to rationalize and justify ordinary people's everyday habit of making meaningful judgments about right and wrong—for example, relating to murder and the treatment of children—as being congruent with Hume's "true" philosophy, which aimed to explain just such everyday moral judgments with reference to natural "moral sentiments" and the concept of sympathy. All this is to say that Wilson took from Hume—whose moral philosophy has been described by some scholars as "common sense moralism"[33] but who clearly was not a "populist"—his perspective and concepts and reinterpreted them in a culture wars context that, needless to say, would have been alien to Hume. For Wilson, Hume's ideas were primarily an instrument in a political battle against America's liberal intellectual and cultural elites—a battle whose terms were set by the emergence of post-1960s liberalism and an intensifying multiculturalist and relativist ethos.

The Man within the Average Joe's Breast

Wilson's neoconservative reinvention of Hume's concepts and perspective thus had its roots in Wilson's genuine respect for Hume as a theorist of human nature. This holds true with Smith too: Wilson's decision to entitle his 1993 book *The Moral Sense* so it would have the same initials as Smith's *Theory of Moral Sentiments* speaks volumes of Wilson's high opinion of Smith as a student of human nature.[34] The importance of this naming decision is underlined by the fact that *The Moral Sense* was not just another one of the twenty-nine books that Wilson wrote or edited in his career but the one that he was most proud of.[35] Still, Wilson, in *The Moral Sense* and elsewhere, was not merely echoing Smith's moral philosophy; instead, he translated the famous thinker's ideas into an argument that served his goal of rehabilitating popular emotions against elite perspectives.

Generally speaking, Wilson's interpretation of Smith was similar to his reading of Hume: Smith had given a very convincing explanation of the tendency of the ordinary person to make meaningful moral judgments that are ultimately based on emotions. However, while Wilson in the case of Hume concentrated on the misreading of Hume by Western scholars and the unfortunate consequences of this error (while offering a rather rough sketch of Hume's "true" moral sentimentalist philosophy), in the case of Smith, he used more time and ink to examine the actual content of the Scottish thinker's sentimentalist philosophy. Wilson's most penetrating analysis of Smith can be found in *The Moral Sense*, in which Wilson discussed every one of the key concepts of Smith's *Theory of Moral Sentiments*—that is, "sympathy," "imagination," "the impartial spectator," praise and praiseworthiness, and "the man within the breast." In using Smith's concepts in the context of his own theory of "the moral sense," Wilson ignored the fact that the Scottish philosopher had himself concluded that his theory of the moral sentiments was incompatible with Hutcheson's theory of a moral sense properly speaking.[36] Such inconsistencies between the various Scottish moral philosophies were of no interest to Wilson, however, for his focus was on the opposition between eighteenth-century sentimentalism and modern relativism.

Sympathy is, as we saw earlier, *the* key concept of Smith's *Moral Sentiments*. It is no wonder then that Wilson was particularly "impressed" by Smith's "pre-scientific" analysis of sympathy, which, as Wilson noted, had recently been substantiated by modern studies on the subject.[37] By *sympathy*, Wilson meant, like Smith, "the human capacity for being affected by the feelings and experiences of others." This mental capacity was a crucial factor in human social life, having immense consequences, since it often "restrains us from acting cruelly" and sometimes also "leads us to act altruistically." "And even when it does not inspire benevolent actions," Wilson continued, "sympathy is an important source of the moral standards by which we judge both others and ourselves. Sympathy, in other words, is both a motive and a norm."[38]

Although Wilson drew heavily from Smith to outline his conception of sympathy, the previous idea that sympathy is both "a motive and a norm" differs somewhat from the Smithian concept. Smith scholars, as we have seen, are generally in agreement that in Smith's ethics, sympathy does not play a prominent role as a motive for action but instead is a key element of moral judgment.[39] Despite this small difference in emphasis, Wilson surely was mainly interested in sympathy as a "standard"—that is, how the concept could be used, and had been used by Smith, to explain the natural human tendency to make moral judgments. After all, Wilson originally set out to write what became *The Moral Sense* in order to explain and to justify ordinary Americans' tendency to rely on emotion when they *pass judgment* on contemporary social issues. It is this intention that in the end makes a critical difference: while Smith's primary aim in *Theory of Moral Sentiments* was to explain in scientific or philosophical terms how emotion enters into the making of moral judgments, Wilson, as a culture warrior, underscored in *The Moral Sense* the contrast between "the moral sense of the average person" and "the moral relativism of many intellectuals."[40]

The second chapter of *The Moral Sense* titled "Sympathy" illustrates quite well how Wilson reinvented Smith's ideas on moral judgment. Wilson's starting point here was the idea (a Smithian idea in itself) about the fundamental sociability of humans—namely, that "we have a natural desire to be admired by others; to be admired by them, we must please them. Since our happiness depends somewhat on the goodwill of our fellows, we naturally seek to understand what may please or offend them." Wilson next moved on to explain the human capacity to change places imaginatively with other individuals, which is a prerequisite for Smithian sympathy or fellow feeling:

"To do this [i.e. to understand what may please or offend others] we seek to enter into the minds and feelings of others, and we are aware that others try to grasp our own thoughts and feelings. We cannot, of course, know what others feel, and so we must imagine it."[41] Finally, Wilson explained, in Smithian terms, how one forms a moral judgment on the basis of his or her capacity to change places in fancy with others and sympathize with them: "But we do not simply share the feelings we imagine others to have; we also judge them. More particularly, we judge whether the actions and feelings of another person are proportionate. . . . We approve of the conduct and character of another person if, when we imagine ourselves in his position, our feelings correspond to those that we think motivate him. . . . Sympathy—our sense of another's feelings and of their appropriateness given the circumstances—is the basis of our judgment. More bluntly, to sympathize *is* to judge."[42] Wilson's notion of sympathy as such is quite similar to that of Smith. Yet Wilson, in a book that found much fault with relativist liberal elites, seems to have been particularly keen on highlighting sympathy as a *natural* human characteristic—one of the "moral senses," a concept that Smith did not use—along with the role it plays in the human tendency to judge. By starting his book with a full chapter on the natural human predisposition to sympathize—which, "more bluntly, is to judge"—Wilson could call into question the liberal elites' seeming tendency to *avoid* meaningful moral judgments. The eminent neoconservative social scientist thus interpreted Smith's concepts and perspective in a framework that was very different from that of Smith: the famous Scottish thinker did not use his scheme of the sympathetic imagination, the desire for approbation, and the internalization of the views of an impartial spectator as moral conscience to attack contemporary "intellectuals" in populist terms.

The final Smithian idea that Wilson reinvented in *The Moral Sense* was "the man within the breast"—that is, Smith's notion of conscience. As noted earlier, the one truly original contribution of Smith's *Theory of Moral Sentiments* was to develop the concept of the "impartial spectator" as a theory of conscience. Wilson, for his part, reworked in *The Moral Sense* this Smithian notion of "the man within the breast" to make the case that "a conscience-driven moral sense is natural to man."[43] To repeat the important point, Smith did not accept Hutcheson's idea of a separate "moral sense" and wrote of "moral sentiments" in more sociological terms. Once again, then, the particular interpretations of Smith's moral sentimentalism made by Wilson were not those intrinsic to Smith's moral philosophy. What is true, though, is that the general description of the development of conscience formulated by Wilson was close to Smith's argument:

As we grow from childhood to adulthood, we increasingly judge ourselves as we judge others. We do so at first because we imagine what others must think of our motives when they see us acting in a certain way. Since we want to be admired, we want to conform, within reason, to the expectations of others. But at some point a remarkable transformation occurs in how we judge ourselves. We desire not only to be praised, but to be praiseworthy. As Adam Smith put it, "man naturally desires, not only to be loved, but to be lovely." . . . [That is,] finally we judge ourselves as an impartial, disinterested third party might. The importance of this last step can hardly be exaggerated, because the "man within the breast," unlike some other person, *knows* our real motives. We can fool our friends, but not ourselves.[44]

The practical result stemming from the acquiring of a strong conscience was, according to Wilson, that "in our calmer moments . . . we reflect bitterly on how wrong it was—and not merely how inconvenient—to have allowed our actions to be governed by the wrong motives." "Even in our daily lives," Wilson continued, "there will be innumerable cases of our obeying rules, resisting temptations, and doing the honorable thing for no other reason than that we instinctively act that way and reflexively feel guilty when we don't."[45]

For anyone familiar with Wilson's long career as a student of crime and criminals, it may be surprising that he, in *The Moral Sense*, presented such a sanguine image of the moral nature of human beings. To be sure, as an experienced theorist of criminal policy, Wilson was more than well aware that not all people had a strong conscience—of which his remarks on "psychopaths" are a reminder.[46] *The Moral Sense* actually does have a very significant exclusionary dimension to it that will be examined in chapter 4 as part of an analysis of how the neoconservatives turned the language of the Scottish moralists into a political instrument in the culture wars debate over the criminal black "underclass." Before that, I will turn to another key battleground of the culture wars—namely, the conflict over the American family—to find out if and how the neoconservatives employed the language of Scottish moral sentimentalism to respond to the increasing diversity of opinion about family issues in late twentieth-century America. From the more philosophical aspects of Wilson's *The Moral Sense*, we now move on to some of the most heated political battlegrounds of the 1980s and 1990s.[47]

Family Values as Moral Intuitions:
Neoconservatives and the War over the Family

At the heart of the culture wars were the spirited battles over the family, sexuality, and gender issues. This conflict between liberal and conservative Americans over "family values" and the "decline" of the traditional two-parent family with a working father and a stay-at-home mother who are biologically related to their children is often portrayed in both scholarly and journalistic literature as a battle between secular liberals and religious conservatives.[1] The question of family values was, however, equally important for the largely secular neoconservative intellectuals. Ever since the late 1960s, intellectuals around the *Public Interest* and its neoconservative ally *Commentary* (such as Daniel Patrick Moynihan, Midge Decter, Irving Kristol, and James Q. Wilson) wrote extensively on such issues as the traditional nuclear family as the foundation of society, the social pathologies related to the African American family structure, and the paradoxes of feminism.[2]

At first, in the mid to late 1960s, the *Public Interest* group developed, via Moynihan's lead, a distinct voice with regard to the troubles of black families.[3] By the early 1980s, however, deviations from the nuclear family ideal that had been associated with black families—having children out of wedlock and single parenthood—had become more common also in white America, with the result that the neoconservatives, like many other American scholars and intellectuals, came to see family decline as a general American (and even global) challenge. In responding to such challenges and perceived threats—including the relaxing cultural attitudes toward different types of families and the feminist celebration of more fluid conceptions of gender and sexuality—the neoconservatives came to play a crucial part in the post-1960s debates on the American family, a conflict that, according to historians such as Robert O. Self, helped realign the entire political culture in the United States.[4] As Self convincingly argues in his *All in the Family: The Realignment of American Democracy*, the emergence of "family revival" as a conservative and Republican concern in the 1970s and 1980s greatly helped conservatives gain political power in the last decades of the century.[5]

Some aspects of neoconservative thought on the family have been comprehensively discussed in the existing literature. Historians have covered quite well the controversy generated by Moynihan's 1965 report *The Negro Family: The Case for National Action* throughout the late 1960s and early 1970s.[6] Similarly, literature on neoconservatism includes some helpful analyses on neoconservative criticism of academic feminists and other new class thinkers who challenged the midcentury bourgeois family norms in the post-1960s decades.[7] Yet scholars have largely ignored the fact that key neoconservative theorists such as Irving Kristol, James Q. Wilson, and Gertrude Himmelfarb responded to the collapse of "traditional" family norms by following Kristol's 1983 neoconservative and populist scheme of explaining to "the people" why they were right. This chapter shows how two of these writers, Kristol and Wilson, responded to the liberalization of family norms in the 1980s and 1990s by reintroducing and reshaping the moral language of the Scottish Enlightenment—the moral sense, moral sentiments, and common sense—to set consensual parameters for debate on family values. That is, the focus is on how Kristol and Wilson reworked these Scottish concepts to give new validity to the supposedly conservative family values of ordinary Americans and also to delegitimize and marginalize the liberal views of many experts, intellectuals, and journalists—those whose takes on issues such as child-raising, schooling, abortion, and same-sex marriage allegedly did *not* represent people's shared moral sense, moral sentiments, or common sense.

At times, the neoconservatives simply used the *vocabulary* of eighteenth-century Scottish moral philosophers to delegitimize liberal positions in the context of key culture war debates—for example, when Wilson criticized the landmark *Roe v. Wade* abortion decision for being at odds with the "moral sentiments" of ordinary Americans and when Kristol called for "common sense" in the debate over sex education. At other times, the neoconservatives instead borrowed from Adam Smith and other Scottish philosophers more specific ideas that they then refashioned into a neoconservative political argument. Wilson, in particular, when making a case for the traditional two-parent family, was eager to cite Smith's views on moral education within the family as well as Smith's account of how people formed judgments concerning the propriety of conduct and the underlying sentiments within the family.

Kristol and Wilson were the writers primarily responsible for the introduction of the neoconservative moral everyman to the family values debate. By appealing to the moral sentiments and common sense of the imagined ordinary Americans, these two writers defined the boundaries of an acceptable—not only "moral" but also "democratic" and "American"—discourse on family matters. In so doing, they deviated from the ideas of Moynihan on recent American nonjudgmentality presented in his oft-cited 1993 essay "Defining Deviancy Down."[8] It is a commonly held view in scholarly literature that Moynihan's text best captures the neoconservative view of America's moral landscape in the 1990s. In the article, Moynihan famously claimed that "deviant" behavior, such as having children out of wedlock, had increased in the post-1960s decades so much so that Americans no longer recognized deviancy as such—in other words, that Americans had "defined deviancy down." While Moynihan's essay in the *American Scholar* was favorably cited in the 1990s by political leaders ranging from President Bill Clinton to the mayor of New York, Rudolph Giuliani, and by several neoconservatives, some of the most renowned neoconservative cultural critics—such as Kristol, Wilson, Himmelfarb, and Francis Fukuyama—actually turned away from Moynihan's comments on contemporary Americans' *inability* to distinguish between right and wrong when it came to family issues.[9] Indeed, Wilson, Kristol, and Himmelfarb made in the 1980s and 1990s considerable efforts to show that ordinary Americans *were* perfectly capable of differentiating morally between alternative families and traditional families, bad parenting and good parenting, and sex education and character cultivation in schools—certainly more capable than many members of the liberal intelligentsia in the ivory tower.

The conflict over the family was, along with the (in many ways related) debates over the rise of a criminal black underclass and criminal justice (see chapters 4 and 5), the primary culture wars debate in which the neoconservatives claimed to speak in the name of "the people." This is hardly surprising, given the distinctively down-to-earth theme of the family wars and because this cultural conflict clearly had great relevance for conservatives, for whom the ongoing transformations of family life appeared as a breakdown of the American family. From a foreign politics perspective, the early 1990s, when the family values debate reached a high point, could have been a time of celebration for American conservatives—Soviet communism had finally been defeated—but as historian of neoconservatism Murray Friedman notes, such a Cold War victory did not mean much to neoconservatives if at the same time culture at home (family norms in particular) "continued to spin out of control."[10] The neoconservative reinvention of Scottish moral philosophy was in part an effort to respond to this concern.

The story of how *Public Interest* intellectuals first became defenders of the traditional family begins, however, long before key neoconservative theorists such as Kristol and Wilson embraced their paradoxical roles as educated experts in common sense and popular moral sentiments. In the mid to late 1960s, in the movement's formative years, writers around the *Public Interest* stood up for the traditional two-parent family as the preferred form of family arrangement not only in response to the rise of the women's liberation movement but also because of the accumulation of social scientific data on the impact of family background on educational achievement as well as the idea that family instability was a cause of social pathologies among African Americans.

The Emergence of Family Values as a Neoconservative Theme

Some of the early neoconservative discussions on the family that emerged in the late 1960s and 1970s specifically targeted the women's liberation movement. Journalist and author Midge Decter was particularly keen among the neoconservatives on disparaging feminists in her early 1970s books *The Liberated Woman and Other Americans* (1971) and *The New Chastity and Other Arguments against Women's Liberation* (1972).[11] For Decter, as a conservative thinker, the problem was not that women felt liberated at a time when the radical feminists of the women's liberation movement—together with the liberal reformists in organizations such as the National Organization for Women (NOW; founded in 1966)—questioned old social attitudes toward women. Nor did she dislike feminists because of their achievements at the legislative level that affected women's lives at home, in the workplace, and in the educational system.[12] Rather, she attacked the women's movement because the women who wanted freedom from male oppression, to her, did not seem to be prepared to accept responsibility for the decisions that their new freedom imposed on them.

For Decter, it was obvious that women were not victims, and for them to claim so was "merely an expression of their terror in the face of the harshnesses and burdens of a new and as yet not fully claimed freedom." For example, women's liberation's discussion of work was "a response not to the experience of exclusion but to the discovery that the pursuit of career is but another form—in some ways more gratifying, in many ways far more bruising—of adult anguish." Women were *already* free to take a job or not to take one, Decter emphasized, but they could not stop being women, and thus she fiercely opposed what she referred to as the women's liberation's "demand no longer to be mothers." In opposition to radical feminists, Decter thus positioned herself as a defender of more traditional notions of the family and motherhood or, as she put it, "what life itself imposes on mortal beings."[13]

Another more influential and better-known line of early neoconservative thought on family and gender issues drew from two mid-1960s government reports that seemed to indicate that traditional middle-class family life had a positive effect on an individual's life changes. The first author from the *Public Interest* group to engage seriously with such issues was, as noted, Moynihan, who in the mid-1960s called attention to the situation of African American families. The key political events of the moment offered much reason for hopefulness to both blacks and white liberals, for the Civil Rights Act of 1964 and the Voting Rights Act of 1965 ended Jim Crow segregation and granted formal equality to African Americans. Yet Moynihan held that the United States was at the time "approaching a new crisis in race relations," since African Americans demanded economic equality that went "beyond civil rights." Moynihan was at the time a member of President Lyndon B. Johnson's administration, expressing these concerns in the now-famous government report entitled *The Negro Family: The Case for National Action.* This report became a starting point for much of the neoconservative discussion over the family in the post-1960s decades, and ultimately, it became one of the most important political documents of the era.[14]

In the report, which soon came to be known simply as the Moynihan Report, Moynihan argued that even with equal civil rights, the "crumbling" family structure of lower-class blacks would greatly hinder their efforts to escape poverty. Moynihan alluded to the "matriarchal pattern of so many Negro families" that was reflected in the relative abundance of female-led single-parent households and the high numbers of out-of-wedlock births. Such a family structure was, according to Moynihan, "at the center of the tangle of pathology," which included juvenile delinquency, drug abuse, and poor educational achievement: "So long as this situation persists," Moynihan wrote, "the cycle of poverty and disadvantage will continue to repeat itself." Since poor blacks were entangled in such a pattern of pathological behavior, Moynihan reasoned, it would require a lot of government aid to ensure upward social mobility for them (antidiscrimination legislation would not meet the case alone). Although Moynihan's ideas were at first warmly received inside the Johnson administration, the report provoked heavy protests among black and liberal intellectuals after this internal government memorandum had been leaked. Most famously, Moynihan was accused of "blaming the victim."[15]

Despite some weaknesses in the Moynihan Report—such as that it left open the question of whether (black) family instability should be seen as a cause or consequence of inequality—the report was critically important for the emerging neoconservative movement in the sense that it provided the

movement's key theorists with clues about the significance of traditional family life and steered the discussion on such issues for many years to come.[16] But
it was not the only government report that had this effect. In summer 1966,
while the debate over *The Negro Family* was still in its initial stages, the US
government made available the *Equality of Educational Opportunity Report*,
the end result of a massive study conducted by sociologist James S. Coleman
and his research team. The report, commonly known as the Coleman Report,
was commissioned by Congress as part of the Civil Rights Act of 1964, and the
aim was to conduct a study on the absence of equal educational opportunities
for minority children throughout the Unites States (four thousand schools
and six hundred thousand students were studied).[17] While the intention was
to document educational disparities between whites and African Americans
and while Coleman initially expected to find a gross inequality of educational
resources between black and white schools, his conclusions surprised nearly
everyone and defied conventional wisdom. Coleman's startling conclusion
was that the money spent by the federal government on education did not significantly impact the success of children in schools. Family background and
the social environment at schools—other students and teachers—seemed to
be more important.[18]

Such conclusions, which underlined the importance of cultural values at
home, supported the arguments of the Moynihan Report, and Moynihan and
many other *Public Interest* intellectuals—such as Kristol, Wilson, and Daniel
Bell—did their share to keep discussion on the Coleman Report alive in the
following years. Bell, for example, argued in a 1972 essay that the Coleman
Report was a serious setback for those 1960s liberals who aimed to broaden
equality of opportunity through the schools: "What Coleman was saying,"
Bell explained to his readers, "was that the public schools—or the process
of education itself—were not the social equalizers American society imagined them to be. Children achieved more or less in relation to family background and social class, and these were the variables that would have to be
changed [in order to attain equality]."[19] Thus together with *The Negro Family*,
the Coleman Report made the neoconservatives both more sensitive to and
appreciative of the cultural values instilled in the home and more skeptical of
the ability of the welfare state to alleviate all social problems. Taken together,
these two reports set the tone for much of the neoconservative discussion on
families for the next several decades.

Although the early neoconservative discourse on families was often more
about tentative observations and assumptions than about elaborate arguments on the superiority of the traditional family, the movement's work contributed to the emergence of "family revival" as a conservative concern in

the aftermath of the liberation movements of the 1960s and early 1970s. Yet despite all the fuss that arose around the family and feminism in the 1970s, Moynihan and his neoconservative friends turned their attention in other directions in the latter half of the decade. Most importantly, Moynihan himself, who had been more seriously involved in the debates over the family than any other writer from the *Public Interest* group, was hurt by the accusations of "blaming the victim," and he soon found himself serving as the American ambassador to India in 1973–75 and then as the US ambassador to the United Nations in 1975–76 before serving for a long time as a New York senator (1977–2001). The staunch antifeminist Decter, for her part, channeled much of her energies after 1972 into the Coalition for a Democratic Majority, which was founded that year to counterbalance the George McGovern wing of the Democratic Party—in other words, to revive the principles of containing communism and accepting America's international responsibilities.[20]

Despite the subsidence of the neoconservative discourse on families in the latter half of the 1970s, the broader American debate on the issue between conservative and liberal Americans was about to accelerate at the time.[21] This was quite predictable due to the contemporary challenges to and ongoing decline of the male breadwinner family model and the rapid alteration of women's and men's lives in the country. These changes were due not only to the legislative victories of 1970s feminism but also to deindustrialization, the development of the service economy, and partly as a corollary of these changes, the economic independence of women. Because of the economic transformations, women's increasing participation in the workforce, and the legal victories of feminism, women's lives had changed considerably in a short period of time by the late 1970s: people married later, sexual codes had loosened, and the numbers of divorces had increased massively—in 1979, the divorce rate was two and a half times that of the mid-1950s.[22]

The New Era of Sentiment in American Politics: Irving Kristol's Family Wars

After some relatively quiet years in the mid to late 1970s, family issues returned to the neoconservative agenda in the early 1980s. This was due to two interrelated developments: first, a general alertness in the country toward a "crisis" of the American family and second, a revival of interest in the Moynihan Report by the media.[23] Moynihan's major concern in the mid-1960s had been the rising number of single-parent families among blacks, but in the 1970s and 1980s, the number of such households grew steadily among *all* Americans. In 1970, single-parent families with children represented 13 percent of all family

groups but grew to 22 percent by 1980 and to 26 percent by 1984.[24] The rising
numbers did not go unnoticed in the press, as Moynihan himself noted in the
fall of 1980. At the time, he wrote to Wilson and other friends that the subject
of the Moynihan Report "[all] of a sudden emerges from the past." However,
he thought there was little he could "do in this subject any longer, but one
could wish that someone else would take up the matter."[25]

Moynihan's growing excitement about the media's reawakening to the issue was soon taken up by his neoconservative friends, such as Nathan Glazer,
who began to ponder how they could "deal with this delicate matter at *The
Public Interest*."[26] That it was now the American family *in general* that needed
special attention was noticed by, among others, Coleman, author of the Coleman Report, who wrote to Moynihan in 1984 that "what began in the 60s as
a problem of disorganization of the black family comes . . . to be in the 80s
a problem of disorganization of the American family as a whole, with the
whites trying hard to catch up with the blacks."[27] (In reality, the *gap* between
blacks and whites was not diminishing; in 1984, black single-parent families
with children made up 59 percent of all black family groups, compared with
nearly 20 percent among whites.)[28]

When the neoconservatives in the early 1980s began to reconsider the
troubles of American families, the country's political scene had experienced a
thorough makeover that equaled the transformation of family life. The White
House was now occupied by Ronald Reagan, who had achieved an electoral
victory by promising to cut taxes and defend traditional (family) values. Reagan's campaign had profited from the support of the Christian Right, which
had burst onto the scene in the late 1970s.[29] The Christian Right had its roots
in 1920s Protestant fundamentalism, but at the turn of the 1980s, it was becoming a considerable force in politics at the same time that it was beginning
to express greater interest in the upsetting trends of American family life. At
the same time, academics, such as William Julius Wilson and Charles Murray,
began to greatly impact the public view of the troubles of American families.
Both writers drew attention to the types of troubles of black families that
Moynihan had focused on in 1965. Wilson, a liberal African American sociologist, encouraged liberal social scientists to take the various troubles of the
urban black poor seriously, drawing attention to the fact that black family dis-
solution, as portrayed by Moynihan in 1965, had by the mid-1980s "reached
catastrophic proportions," which was the reason "welfare dependency among
poor blacks ha[d] mushroomed" and why "economic hardship ha[d] become
almost synonymous with black female-headed households."[30]

Both the actual transformations in family life—above all, the rising illegitimacy and divorce rates—and the influential conservative arguments on

family decline ensured that family issues became *the* center of the culture wars in the 1980s and thereafter. However, while out-of-wedlock births, divorce, abortion, and many other bones of contention separated conservative commentators from liberals, the overall endeavor to further the cause of families expanded during the 1980s into an entire family revival movement that crossed all conventional political boundaries. By 1987, Democratic Party analysts suggested, as reported by the *New York Times*, that "by focusing public attention on children's issues . . . the party could rekindle support for government programs and end the seeming Republican monopoly on the phrase 'family values.'"[31] Another *New York Times* article from 1987 reported that "with one eye on the shifting demographic data and another on the 1988 Presidential election, many liberal groups are trying to wrest the 'pro-family' label from its conservative proprietors." Thus the left and right were now fighting "for custody of [the] 'family' issue."[32] One sign of the changed atmosphere was that Moynihan was now portrayed in the media as a visionary who had foreseen the collapse of the black family.[33] If Moynihan had been extremely sorry for the liberal and leftist response to *The Negro Family* in the mid-1960s, now, twenty years later, he could celebrate with his publisher the "most exceptional response" and the "nicest reviews and commentary" of his report's twentieth-anniversary lectures (published as *Family and Nation* in 1986).[34]

Provoked by both the perceived decline of the American family and the heated exchange of words between conservatives and liberals, key neoconservative theorists joined the debate over the family in the early 1980s. Two of these writers, Irving Kristol and James Q. Wilson, redirected neoconservative discourse on the family by consistently approaching the issue following Kristol's 1983 program of explaining "to the American people why they are right, and to the intellectuals why they are wrong."[35] At a time when the midcentury's imagined consensus on the traditional two-parent family and parenting was being seriously challenged and when Republicans and Democrats were struggling over custody of the family issue, Kristol and Wilson introduced to the family debate the neoconservative common man with an instinctive sense of right and wrong.

Kristol opened the discussion on everyman's morality in his 1984 *Wall Street Journal* essay titled "Whatever Happened to Common Sense?" According to the neoconservative godfather, issues related to families and children, especially child-rearing and schooling, were prime examples of everyday issues in which the average American's moral intuitions ought not to be questioned. Kristol was therefore upset to see that recently, so many educated Americans seemed to have come to a different conclusion. In his rather pessimistic essay, Kristol lamented the growing notion in the country that an ordinary citizen would need expert guidance in order to raise a family. Kristol responded to such suggestions by highlighting child-rearing as a truly "prosaic human experience" that only recently had become "mysterious" in the US. He emphasized that all Americans were capable of making simple moral distinctions that were needed in child-rearing, and he attributed such moral judgments to "common sense." "Children need love, children need discipline," Kristol wrote, "and there is no expert who can provide the precise mixture appropriate to a particular child of particular parents in a particular family. We all know, without ever having read a book, the difference between caring parents and uncaring parents. We even know, by virtue of our common sense, the difference between sensible parents and silly parents."[36]

Kristol continued with the theme by modifying his language somewhat, suggesting next that these moral distinctions between caring and uncaring parents arise from "intuition" rather than "common sense" (the latter is typically understood to be a result of everyday experience, while the former refers to instinctive feeling). He insisted that such "gross [moral] discriminations are intuitively available to us all, and [that] they are quite sufficient for purposes of child-rearing."[37] It is noteworthy that Kristol, an admirer of Smith, did not here cite Smith, who had argued in *The Theory of Moral Sentiments* that it was a generally shared human trait to feel hatred and even horror when one faced "a parent without parental tenderness."[38] (Wilson did not miss the opportunity to cite this Smithian idea when discussing similar issues, as we will later see.) But Kristol's anti-intellectual rhetoric was potent nonetheless. He used the idea of commonly shared moral intuitions to portray the liberal ideas of many family experts as both eccentric and amoral, pitting ordinary parents—the intuitive educators—against "ethicists" who supposedly taught morals to children but could only "teach them about moral beliefs in general, but not the difference between right and wrong." The intuitive understanding of the ordinary parent, which Kristol called "the 'populist-conservatism' among ordinary Americans," was instead "marked by an outraged assertion of the validity of received wisdom as against abstract, academic 'innovative' theorizing." He contended, cheekily, that "if the average parent needs expert guidance in order to rear the average child—well, that is a pretty accurate sign that the culture as a whole has lost its moorings."[39] Kristol's point was that American culture needed to retain its links to the shared moral intuitions of ordinary Americans in order to stay firmly anchored.

A year after the essay on common sense, moral intuitions, and child-rearing was published, Kristol again invoked the common-sense idea to delegitimize the ideas of professional educationists and to push for a moral consensus in children's issues, this time in relation to America's school system, in his 1985 piece "The New Populism: Not to Worry." "The American people," Kristol declared, posing as an expert in popular opinions and common sense, "have always had perfectly reasonable expectations about our educational system." In Kristol's telling, typical American parents simply wanted schools "to improve their children—to make them literate, to instill good study habits, to acquaint them with the importance of discipline, self-discipline, and deference toward authority." This "modest cast of mind" of the American people stood in stark contrast to the "trendy fantasies" of professional educationists and decision-makers who had recently made a fuss about such issues as school prayer and sex education. Kristol posed as someone who could effortlessly gain access to the minds of the American people, and he claimed—without citing any polls—that "most parents," unlike professional educationists and decision-makers, did "not really care whether their children pray in school."[40] (In fact, according to polls, about 60 percent of Americans still disapproved of the Supreme Court's school prayer ban of 1962 in the mid-1980s and continued to do so until the 2010s.)[41]

Kristol tried to delegitimize the views of experts by telling his readers where common sense was *absent*: "If our educationists, our courts and our legislators had not been bereft of all common sense about education, if they had not succumbed to trendy fantasies, there would be very little fuss about the matter." As the neoconservative author saw it, it was only after the introduction of sex education into the curriculum—which, according to Kristol, seemed to encourage, or at least not discourage, teenage promiscuity—that school prayer had begun to seem like an antidote to the corruption of the American educational ethos. The antidote that Kristol himself recommended was to go back to the basics of instilling good study habits and discipline—an idea that he branded as common sense. In his telling, it was the "un-wisdom of our elites" that accounted "for the populist rebellion against our current educational practices—a rebellion whose demands are basically common-sensical, not at all extreme."[42]

For Kristol, who had been known as a critic of populism in the 1960s and early 1970s, it seemed to be imperative to rationalize in historical terms his new willingness to rely on popular intuitions in educational practices and other public matters in the 1980s. Kristol made at the time serious efforts to explain to his readers how late twentieth-century Americans had ended up in a situation in which it was perfectly reasonable—more reasonable than before— for decision-makers to rely on nonexpert sentiments as a guide to public affairs. Historical arguments and narratives were, of course, nothing new when it came to Kristol's political writing. We have already seen in chapter 1 how Kristol, in his dour and demanding early 1970s "republican" writings, formulated a powerful historical narrative about a turn from early America's firm republican mind-set to the later years ruled by a decadent democratic spirit—a narrative that was meant to rationalize his strict demands for a return to civic and bourgeois virtue. A few years later, in 1976, Kristol portrayed the evolution of Western political thought as a rivalry between the hubristic French Enlightenment and the modest and civilized Anglo-Scottish Enlightenment, indicating that modern Americans needed to reject the traces of French big government collectivism and fortify the links with the eighteenth-century British tradition of humane individualism in order to find new confidence in the capitalist system at the time of the mid-1970s economic slump. In the mid-1980s, when the culture war was intensifying and Ronald Reagan had been in the White House for a couple of years, Kristol seems to have felt that the occasion demanded a new historical narrative to justify the increasingly frequent use of anti-intellectual and populist language by himself and other neoconservatives.

What Kristol did at the time was construct a historical argument that matched with Reagan's claim that his presidential policies embodied the common sense of the people. That is, Kristol formulated a historical narrative in which the leftist political activism of the 1960s youth was portrayed as nothing but daydreaming and the conservative backlash of working- and middle-class whites that followed it in the 1980s as common sense. In other words, Kristol not only argued that "the American people" had "edged rightward" during the Reagan era, but he also made the case that this apparent conservative turn by the people was a natural turn of events after the decadent 1960s. In Kristol's narrative, "ordinary Americans" had been sensible enough to keep abreast of the times and to move on from the ideological (leftist) illusions of the previous decades. Kristol made this argument in a 1986 *Wall Street Journal* column "American Universities in Exile," in which he contrasted the average American's commonsensical right turn with the allegedly abnormal, stagnant state of American universities, in which a similar turn was *not* observable. The major American universities, Kristol wrote, since they had not been impacted in any way by the Reagan presidency (if anything, they had moved "rapidly and massively to the left"), were living in a "time warp." Universities thus had "militantly divorced themselves from the sentiments and opinions of the overwhelming majority of the people." Whereas the common people's conservative turn epitomized sound "sentiments" or "common sense" for Kristol, major American universities were dominated by "a whole spectrum of radical modes of thinking" that were all "constructed on premises that range from the relativist to the nihilist, and all imply that traditional values (moral, aesthetic, political) along with traditional institutions are artifacts that are arbitrarily imposed on the people by a ruling elite."[43]

At least by the early 1990s, Kristol had become fully aware of the political value of such common-sense populism. Although his own populist vocabulary was secular, it was the Christian Right that helped him realize the full political potential of such language. At the time, Kristol seemed to be impressed by how America's Christian Right was transforming the country's political landscape by listening to and utilizing the moral intuitions of the working and middle classes. At the height of the nationwide debates over out-of-wedlock childbirths, divorce, and single mothers, Kristol reflected on the Christian Right's recent political rhetoric in various *Wall Street Journal* op-ed pieces. He argued that by using language that appealed to public sentiments regarding the family, parenting, and education, the Christian Right had in fact initiated a "counter-reformation," or even a "new era," in American politics.[44] Most importantly, the Christian Right had expanded the conservative agenda beyond its traditional economic focus by "putting a new conservative emphasis on family and education."[45] By focusing on these topics, which grabbed the attention of and were graspable to the great majority of Americans, the Christian Right had once again enabled conservatism to become a populist movement. Indeed, the Christian Right and the entire social-cultural conservative movement, whose "popular base is the working class, the lower-middle class, and the self-employed middle class," was potentially more popular than the economic right that spoke "to this disposed class in a language that does not appeal to human sensibilities."[46]

Although Kristol was clearly impressed with the Christian Right's ability to touch a popular nerve, his own language of "sentiments," "intuitions," and "common sense" was notably different from the religious populism of the Christian Right—which always rested on the idea of "God's people."[47] That Kristol used a secular vocabulary to discuss the moral mind-set of the American people reflected the more general neoconservative secularism. Kristol's personal outlook on religion was notoriously ambivalent, but he always underscored its social effects (its contribution to moral order in the liberal-capitalist system) while occasionally discussing the cleansing of the individual soul.[48] Tellingly, the neoconservative writer once explained his spirituality to a reporter by noting that he had always been a "believer" but that he should not be asked what he believed in: "That gets too complicated. The word 'God' confuses everything."[49]

Crucially, then, Kristol had an important double role in the rise of conservative populism in late twentieth-century United States. Most importantly, he used the common-sense idea to encourage the exclusion of liberal experts, intellectuals, and journalists, those who supposedly did not epitomize common sense but rather nonsense or amoralism. Insofar as he simultaneously inspired doubts about inherent biases among all establishment sources of information or expertise, his writings can be seen as counterproductive, contributing to the development of a posttruth phenomenon (or moment), which ultimately undermines efforts to find common ground—which was Kristol's ultimate goal—since it leaves individuals and groups alone to settle their disputes.[50]

Equally important was Kristol's rationalization of recent religious populism. In the early and mid-1990s, he used the case of the Christian Right to encourage the Republican Party to appeal to popular sentiments in order to gain votes. The Christian Right, Kristol suggested, had shown by its successful appeals to public "sentiments" how the political right in general could triumph at the ballot box. Taking public sentiments and interests seriously, Kristol remarked, had enabled the religious and cultural right "to enlist the active support of some tens of millions of ordinary Americans who are profoundly concerned about the very shape and substance of American civilization, in all its dimensions." He did take note of contemporary criticism of such populism—namely, that the idea of "bringing into the political arena masses of 'simple-minded' people" and "even allow[ing] salient issues to emerge from sentiments" had been criticized by Europeans and the American liberal media as "democratic excess." Kristol nonetheless dismissed such notions, arguing that "a democratic populism" of the kind demonstrated by America's Religious Right could actually be "a corrective to those defects of democratic politics arising from our secular democratic elites."[51]

Thus although Kristol did label the Religious Right's political language, which prioritized public sentiments, as "populist social conservatism," he clearly meant not to condemn it—to the contrary, he rationalized such populism by introducing it as true democracy. What Kristol ignored was the possibility that his own version of common-sense populism or the populism of the Religious Right would *undermine* the core of democracy—namely, the idea of fallible and contestable judgments by shifting majorities. As Sophia Rosenfeld suggests, this is what common-sense populism typically does in democratic societies where the "faith in information provided by key institutions including government agencies, the academy, and a free press should temper the impulse to trust exclusively one's own experiential sense of the world" (in contrast to totalitarian societies where common sense is "the only potential source of truth that remains").[52]

The Moral Sense as a Policy Compass: James Q. Wilson on Abortion and Gay Marriage

Wilson soon joined Kristol in making the argument that the moral sentiments of ordinary Americans ought to be taken seriously in the political arena. Wilson was active on several fronts of what he called "the family-values debate," including the clashes over abortion and same-sex marriage, in which he, among the neoconservative intellectuals, most consistently followed Kristol's 1983 program of explaining to the American people why they were right. That is to say, in Wilson's hands, the vocabulary of "common sense," and especially of the "moral sense" and "moral sentiments," became a means to delegitimize and marginalize the liberal elites' positions on family issues and to define the boundaries of acceptable discourse in the contemporary family wars.

In writing about moral sentiments and family issues, Wilson also took the neoconservatives once again somewhat closer to Smith and his fellow eighteenth-century moral sentimentalist philosophers. Kristol, as we saw, ultimately settled for a rather ambiguous concept of popular moral sentiments—that is, morally relevant gut feelings or intuitions of "the people"—and he no longer, in the 1980s and 1990s, delved into the Scottish thinkers' more serious analyses of the specific nature of commonly shared moral sentiments or the moral sense. Wilson instead kept bowing to the Scottish sentimentalist philosophers throughout the 1990s, as if they were the primary inspiration for his works on the moral sense of the average American.

Before exploring Wilson's takes on abortion and gay marriage, let us look at his understanding of the nature of the general culture war itself. Significantly, Wilson's portrayal of the culture war departed from that of many later analysts and instead echoed the presuppositions of Kristol's populist neoconservative guideline from 1983. While historians and social scientists typically define the culture war as a conflict between two elite blocs, Wilson portrayed it as an intellectual battle between the elites and the ordinary people—a battle in which the neoconservatives took the side of the people. Along these lines, he insisted that it was the cultural war between ordinary people and the elites that was "far more consequential than any of the other cleavages that divide us."[53] The paradox here is, of course, that neoconservative intellectuals, such as Wilson, were very much part of the intellectual elite. However, Wilson and his fellow neoconservative writers portrayed themselves as some kind of educated experts in public morality and common sense in the style of the mid-eighteenth-century Aberdonian Common Sense School.

Where Wilson's understanding of the culture war coincides with that of later historians is that both highlight the struggle over the family as the most important dimension of the more general cultural conflict. According to Wilson, the family values debate, as a major culture wars conflict, had emerged because the "family life that most Americans want is regarded by the eminences of the media and the academy as a cartoon life, fit only for ridicule and rejection."[54] Wilson's most essential premise in the family values debate was, then, that the views of ordinary Americans differed from those of the liberal elites in the sense that average Americans had genuine affection for the family. In his most grandiloquent mood, Wilson would even declare in 1995 that "there is no more radical a cultural division in all of history than that between the attachment ordinary people have for the family and the hostility intellectuals display toward it."[55] This theme showed up in a major part of Wilson's writings in the 1990s, including *The Moral Sense*, in which he declared that the key issues in the present "cultural war" were "divorce, illegitimacy, crime, and entertainment."[56]

Another essential discrepancy between the people and the liberal elites, aside from having an affection for the family, was, in Wilson's telling, that ordinary citizens—unlike the elites—regarded most of the transformations in American family life over the past few decades (such as the mounting divorce rate and the growing number of nonmarital children) as a negative development. Similarly, Wilson's "ordinary citizens" (or "the people" or "most Americans") supposedly saw that most of the country's social problems—such as the deficiencies in communal life, crime, drugs, teenage pregnancies, and welfare dependency—ultimately resulted from what could only be referred to as the decline of the American family. As Wilson put it in a 1994 column in the *Wall Street Journal*, "What these problems have in common in the eyes of most Americans is that they result from the weakening of the family."[57] He also stressed that the American people did not "need studies to tell them that these outcomes [the dramatic increase in divorce, single-parent families, and illegitimate children that had taken place over the last 30 years] are generally bad, because they have had these outcomes happen to them or to people they know."[58] Thus Wilson, like Kristol, at times referred also to ordinary people's *experience* with real life—and not only to an innate moral sense—to vindicate middle American views.

Lastly, Wilson took the side of the people against the out-of-touch liberal elites when he suggested that the average American intuitively understood the basic function of the family. He praised the ordinary citizen for recognizing that "the family is the place in which the most basic values are instilled in children." While this view was, according to Wilson, not disputed among the public, no such consensus was found among intellectual and policy elites. Thus he noted in "The Family-Values Debate," published in *Commentary* in 1993, that the "beliefs about families that most people regard as virtually self-evident are hotly disputed among people whose job it is to study or support families." Wilson criticized scholars for being unable to figure out decisively whether the conventional two-parent family was as critically important for the healthy development of children as was once thought. He argued that the American people instead well understood that teenage single mothers, for example, were not as capable of instilling basic values in their children as were traditional two-parent families and that due to this incapacity, the children of teenage moms had less self-control.[59]

Following the populist logic that Kristol had defined in the early 1980s as neoconservative, Wilson wanted to explain to the people why they were right. While admitting that some key scholarly disputes on family issues were currently unsettled, he nevertheless was eager to show that popular views had recently gained support from social scientific research. Teenage motherhood, for instance, was just such an issue, and so was divorce. While not denying that divorce was sometimes "right and necessary," Wilson made the case that "in general divorce makes people worse off: the woman becomes poorer and the children more distressed. . . . If scholars say that the evidence is not conclusive, so much the worse for scholars. But now, I believe, scholars are starting to find hard facts to support popular impressions."[60]

Related to the larger theme of family values, there were two specific policy debates in which Wilson delved into the moral mind-set of ordinary Americans particularly methodically—that is, those on abortion and gay marriage. In the context of these two debates, he used the language of the Scottish moralists and explicitly urged American decision-makers to formulate family policy in a way that took into account the "moral sentiments" of the people— namely, the commonly shared moral emotions that (he claimed) profoundly shaped the public's approach to such issues. In fact, at first in 1994, Wilson considered the possibility of applying the moral sentimentalist concepts to policy questions on a broad scale in an extensive policy-oriented sequel to the more philosophical *The Moral Sense* that would have dealt with questions ranging from abortion to pornography and drugs.[61] Yet in the end, he gave up this idea and applied the Scottish moral vocabulary to select policy issues only (in journal articles and in one short book), some of which concerned the family (chapter 5 of this book explores Wilson's takes on crime and the criminal justice system).

The first of these family-related policy issues was abortion. In an article published in *Commentary* in 1994, Wilson criticized the current American abortion law, particularly the critical *Roe v. Wade* decision (1973), which legalized abortion and, as Wilson put it, did not protect life in moral terms. The problem with the current American ruling (according to which a woman had an unqualified right to terminate her pregnancy at will during the first trimester) was that many women did not "always clearly see, and thus fully sense, what is at stake" in the abortion decision, at least not in a moral sense— that they did not see the moral dimension of the issue resulted in turn from the fact that they had not personally experienced the moral sentiments that were related to the issue.[62]

In order to make American women more conscious of the moral side of the question, Wilson suggested that every woman considering an abortion had to be brought "under moral pressure" by showing them "exact color photographs of the human embryo" at various stages of embryonic development. While speculating that each woman would react to such pictures in her own way (to some extent), Wilson nevertheless believed that the natural human moral sentiments thus awakened could provide "a useful guide to our actions" in the context of the abortion decision. While many women would, after seeing the pictures, still undoubtedly choose abortion, at least they would have personally seen—and felt—what was at stake in terms of human life in the decision during each phase of pregnancy. Moreover, Wilson thought it was possible to identify the "rough stage" in embryonic development when "our moral sentiments" would "begin to be most powerfully engaged," insofar as the person in question was "made unmistakably aware of" the state of the embryo. Wilson's idea was that people would "treat as human that which appears to be human [and that they would] treat as quasi-human that which appears quasi-human." According to this logic, Wilson then speculated that "most people" would identify "a baby" probably around seven to nine weeks after fertilization, when the embryo had acquired humanlike features (legs, arms, eyes, eyelids), and that they would then make their more attentive moral decisions based on these observations and on the moral sentiments that had been awaked by the pictures.[63]

The abortion issue illustrates quite well that Wilson, while using the same moral vocabulary as Smith had done—that is, "moral sentiments"—applied it in an entirely different manner in a radically different political context than the Scottish philosopher had done. What Wilson did here in political terms was use the language of the Scottish moralists to delegitimize contemporary American abortion policy. While the previous procedure suggested by Wilson was clearly desirable for American conservatives in the sense that it would highlight the moral dimension of abortion, it could not easily be achieved, nor did Wilson think so. To the contrary, he noted that it would require nothing less than "that this nation [w]ould start afresh" and abandon the current abortion policy. Such drastic changes were in any case necessary, Wilson argued, since the currently effective rules "were at odds with public opinion." These rules had been made by the courts instead of legislatures, and the issue, as it was defined by the courts, was delineated in terms of individual rights instead of moral responsibility.[64]

For Wilson, abortion was above all a question of the intrinsic value of life and the (parents') moral responsibility toward it, and he, posing as an expert in the moral sentiments of the common people, claimed that most Americans would agree with this assessment.[65] Yet his article was criticized by both liberals and conservatives, and soon, Wilson admitted himself in a letter to Michael Joyce of the conservative Bradley Foundation that his article "satisfied almost no one" and that he was "not yet certain it really satisfied me." He intended to tackle the issue again in his planned policy-oriented sequel to *The Moral Sense*, but as noted, this project was never finished.[66]

Another hot-button issue in which Wilson appealed to human moral sentiments to delegitimize liberal positions and to set limits for debate was gay marriage. Just a few months before President Clinton's Defense of Marriage Act (1996) defined marriage for federal purposes as a union of one man and one woman, Wilson argued in "Against Homosexual Marriage" that America's challenge was to "find a way of formulating a policy with respect to homosexual unions that is not the result of a reflexive act of judicial rights conferring, but is instead a considered expression of the moral convictions of a people."[67] Although Wilson did not explicitly invoke natural "moral sentiments" in this particular article, his references to "mankind" and to culturally widespread moral distinctions between homosexual and heterosexual marriages had the same effect, which is to say that in "Against Homosexual Marriage," Wilson once again appealed to the idea of a universal instinct for right and wrong as a bulwark against liberal standpoints and the unwanted diversity of opinion in family matters.[68] That Wilson did approach gay marriage from a (reworked) "Scottish" viewpoint is confirmed by Wilson's 1994 letter to the Bradley Foundation, in which Wilson outlined a plan for his unrealized sequel to *The Moral Sense*. As noted earlier, in the new book, Wilson intended to apply his Scottish-inspired moral sentimentalist philosophy to various policy questions, including "homosexual unions (or 'marriages')."[69]

The key premise of Wilson's article on same-sex marriage was that the natural moral sentiments shared by the human species included retributive moral emotions that disapproved of homosexual sex and unions and approved of heterosexual sex and marriage. In the article, Wilson claimed, among other things, that for "the average citizen," it was typical to intuit that "homosexual uses of the reproductive organs violate the condition that sex serve solely as the basis of heterosexual marriage." From such premises, Wilson claimed that "thinking of laws about marriage as documents that confer or withhold rights" was not typical to "mankind," while it perhaps was to American lawyers—thus marginalizing lawyers' views by leaving them outside the range of certain allegedly universal moral sentiments. Societies differed "scarcely at all," Wilson pointed out, "over the distinctions between heterosexual and homosexual couples" so that heterosexual couples were "overwhelmingly preferred" over homosexual couples. Such distinctions were made not entirely out of misinformation or irrational prejudice, Wilson asserted, but instead they "involve the nature of marriage and thus the very meaning—even more, the very possibility—of society."[70]

While Wilson's argument against gay marriage *did* reflect popular attitudes in the United States in the mid-1990s, there is some historical irony in the fact that he bolstered his case by referring to the American citizenry's steady antigay attitudes just a few years before public attitudes began to change considerably.[71] Just fifteen years after Wilson wrote his *Commentary* article, it would have made no sense to argue against gay marriage, hoping that the policy would be "a considered expression of the moral convictions of a people."[72] Support for same-sex marriage has grown steadily in the United States since 2004, when the majority of Americans still opposed it (60 percent opposed, 31 percent favored), such that by 2019, 61 percent of Americans supported it while only 31 percent opposed.[73]

It needs to be stressed then that although Wilson in *The Moral Sense* and elsewhere presented his own work on the average American's moral sense as a continuation of the work of eighteenth-century Scottish thinkers, he, as much as Kristol, reinvented Scottish philosophy in populist terms—namely, he shaped it to fit the contemporary political climate and the neoconservative agenda in the ongoing culture wars. Even if Wilson borrowed a vocabulary (and some ideas) from the Scottish thinkers and stated in public that Smith and Hume were his intellectual heroes (see chapter 2), he still invoked the Scottish moral concepts in the contemporary American political context to articulate a neoconservative moral sensibility.

Part of this reinvention process was that he interpreted the Scottish philosophers' concepts in light of modern science. Modern sociobiology and the so-called self-control theory of crime were particularly important influences on Wilson as he reinterpreted the Scottish thinkers. He touched on this question in a 1994 letter to Richard Herrnstein, renowned Harvard psychologist, noting that if he "hadn't worked on [their 1985 book *Crime and Human Nature*] with you, it never would have occurred to me to write *The Moral Sense*, or if it would have occurred to me I wouldn't have known how to begin."[74] By this, Wilson meant that the collaboration with Herrnstein had taught him to look at "people" like a modern biologically oriented psychologist, sociobiologist, or evolutionary psychologist would do: as naturally evolved biological beings whose minds were formed in the evolutionary process by the interactive forces of nature and nurture. Moreover, the teamwork with Herrnstein had helped Wilson understand the (slight) differences in the genetic constitutions of individuals.[75]

Wilson's sociobiological approach to the moral sense had important repercussions for his understanding of religion's role in society. That is, it made him much more consistent than Kristol was on the issue of religion. While Kristol at times seemed unable to decide whether to highlight ordinary people's inherent moral intuitions or religious education as the primary foundation of family values and moral order, Wilson was unwavering in arguing that the natural moral sense was the key foundation of society's moral order. For him, religion was a social force that could *strengthen* the natural moral sense. This is not to say that Wilson did not see the importance of religion: as he put it, religion offered "a transforming experience to people who have resisted these moral intuitions and so have descended into pathology."[76] But the foundation of morality was the moral sense—namely, as Wilson put it in *The Moral Sense*, "a sense that is formed out of the interaction of [people's] innate dispositions with their earliest familial experiences."[77]

Later in the book, Wilson discussed the "moral senses" in the plural—referring to the different aspects of the moral sense—that is, sympathy, duty, fairness, and self-control—and argued that these senses "are to some important degree innate, and they appear spontaneously amid the routine intimacies of family life."[78] Wilson's concept was therefore largely faithful to a modern understanding of nature-nurture interaction. Yet to the extent that Wilson highlighted the *innate* nature of the moral sense—a fact that is underlined by his use of the Hutchesonian concept of "the moral sense"—his sentimentalist vocabulary differed somewhat from the theory of "moral sentiments" of Smith, Wilson's greatest Scottish hero. As explained in chapter 1, Smith had been a critic of Hutchesonian moral sense theory, arguing that no such (innate) "sense" existed and that moral judgments did not emerge from human constitution or emotions in any direct way.[79] Wilson was not entirely consistent on these issues, though, at least not in the sense that Francis Hutcheson and Smith were. To the contrary, Wilson used the concept of moral sentiments as often as he used the moral sense, using both terms to refer to the natural human capacity (or tendency) to make moral judgments. Furthermore, by the moral senses, as noted earlier, he was referring to the various aspects of the moral sense (duty, sympathy, fairness, and self-control).

While Wilson was unwavering in highlighting the importance of the moral sense as the primary source of moral order, he was, then, more ambiguous in describing the *nature* of the moral sense, particularly when it came to the question of innateness. This ambiguity actually gave him an important rhetorical advantage in the culture wars milieu in the sense that he could use the moral sense idea in multiple ways to defend conservative positions in the family wars. On the one hand, he could—in the context of certain specific policy debates such as those involving gay marriage and abortion—underscore the universal nature of certain moral preferences that arose from natural, universally shared (moral) emotions, suggesting that "ordinary Americans" necessarily judged these issues in a characteristically conservative fashion. One the other hand, he could stress the interaction of nature and nurture in the development of the moral sense to make the case that morality was best cultivated in conditions that were not too far from the bourgeois family ideal. In both cases, his arguments functioned as a defense of the traditional family consisting of a married heterosexual couple and children.

A Neoconservative Philosophy of Moral Education

Earlier I noted that Wilson, in writing about shared moral sentiments and conservative family values, kept bowing to the eighteenth-century Scottish moralists as if they were his key inspiration. This holds true especially on the question of moral development within a family environment. Indeed, Wilson adopted many of Smith's views on moral education within a family environment or, more precisely, refashioned Smith's philosophy into a neoconservative political argument for the traditional two-parent family. While citing many of Smith's ideas on moral education, Wilson reworked them to form a neoconservative argument for the traditional family as the site where an individual's "law-abidingness" develops and which, therefore, was the seedbed of social order. At a time when the traditional two-parent family with a breadwinner father, a stay-at-home mother, and biologically related children as a collective American ideal was being seriously challenged by feminists and other left-liberals—and when Americans' attitudes toward divorce, cohabitation, and nonmarital children were relaxing considerably—Wilson aimed to reassert the status of traditional family life by making the case for the two-parent family as the seedbed of an individual's moral sense, understood as law-abidingness.[80] Similarly, he expressed concern for the numerous "at-risk" children who did not experience the benefits of a conventional middle-class family environment and, assumedly, suffered the consequences in later life. Unlike the many conservative writers who in late twentieth-century America lamented that feminism and left-liberalism more generally threatened *religious* (typically Christian) family values and the social order that supposedly was dependent on them, Wilson argued in secular terms that it was the child's natural moral sense—and thus his or her future law-abidingness—that was at risk in modern America.

Having studied Scottish moral philosophy for *The Moral Sense*, Wilson well knew that Smith, Hutcheson, and Hume had written on family issues, including moral education in the family, affection between family members, and the development of moral sentiments. These and other eighteenth-century Scottish authors had explored the role of the family as an explanation of human morality and sociality. Hume, for example, attributed the origin of society to the "natural appetite betwixt the sexes" and parents' natural affection for their children.[81]

Yet Wilson, in writing about the family and moral education, drew especially from Smith. While Smith did not provide a systematic analysis of the ways in which the moral mind develops in early life, he argued in *Theory of Moral Sentiments* and *Lectures on Jurisprudence* in general terms that the love and care provided by parents help children learn "self-command" and view themselves from the "impartial spectator's" standpoint and thus act virtuously. For Smith, the necessary condition for the development of the moral self was a child's natural sociability and the mirroring process of sympathy, or more accurately, a child's innate desire to be sympathized with.[82] In order to satisfy the expectations of their parents—the first "spectators" in their life—children learned to tone down their passions and to restrain their will. In Smith's system of moral education, the role of the parents was thus critical in the sense that they, in philosopher Charles Griswold's words, show "by example, as well as precept, that self-command makes one not only lovable but able to love; thanks to sympathy, the process by which one comes to have perspective and proper concern for one's self is inseparable from that by which one has the same for others."[83]

This is not to say that family life was, for Smith, the only social environment in which the moral self developed. In *Moral Sentiments*, Smith drew attention to the deficiencies in parental education, noting that parents as "partial protectors" were not ideal as teachers of self-command, which was learned effectively later in school or elsewhere when children encountered people with no such "indulgent partiality."[84] The general emphasis in *Moral Sentiments* was, however, on the importance of early family life in moral education, and Smith stated clearly in the book that in order to educate children "to be dutiful to their parents, to be kind and affectionate to their brothers and sisters," one should "educate them in your own house."[85] In *Lectures on Jurisprudence*, Smith noted optimistically that even the children of "most profligate and wicked parents" learned to tone down their passions and restrain their will because of their desire to be sympathized with by others.[86] In the same spirit, Smith was quite critical of contemporary public education and universities, arguing that the "education of boys at distant great schools, of young men at distant colleges, of young ladies in distant nunneries and boarding-schools, seems, in the higher ranks of life, to have hurt most essentially the domestic morals, and consequently the domestic happiness, both of France and England. . . . Domestic education is the institution of nature; public education, the contrivance of man. It is surely unnecessary to say, which is likely to be the wisest."[87]

In Smith's system, proper parental care and moral education were dependent on the natural affection between family members. What was necessary for both family stability and proper childcare was not only parental affection but also a constant passion between the sexes.[88] According to Smith, it was necessary that this passion, which helped keep the parents together, was a permanent force. After all, newborn children are in need of parental care for a long period of time, considerably longer than any other species. As Smith put it in *Lectures on Jurisprudence*, the care of children required "that union of the parents should be of a very long continuance." He took it for granted that "the affection of the sexes is therefore constant and does not cease on any particular occasion; and as the children, at least some of them, require the attendance of the parents pretty far in their life, this affection and love betwixt them which is the foundation of their union generally continues the greatest part of their lives."[89]

Smith's main goal in *Moral Sentiments* was not to discuss moral education but to delineate the principles that people follow when they *judge* other people's and their own sentiments, conduct, and character. What most interests us here is Smith's account of how people formed judgments concerning the propriety of conduct and the underlying sentiments within the family. Smith proceeded from the notion that typically "the objects of [one's] warmest affections" were, after himself, "the members of his own family, those who usually live in the same house with him, his parents, his children, his brothers and sisters." According to Smith, these people were "naturally and usually the persons upon whose happiness or misery his conduct must have the greatest influence. He is more habituated to sympathize with them."[90] (For Smith, "affection" was "in reality nothing but habitual sympathy.")[91] Then consistent with the main goal of his book, Smith went on to claim that people not only ordinarily found that "a suitable degree of affection" did take place among family and friends but "naturally expect[ed] that it should" and felt "horror" if it did not:

Relations being usually placed in situations which naturally create this habitual sympathy, it is expected that a suitable degree of affection should take
place among them. . . . The general rule is established, that persons related
to one another in a certain degree, ought always to be affected towards one
another in a certain manner, and that there is always the highest impropriety,
and sometimes even a sort of impiety, in their being affected in a different
manner. A parent without parental tenderness, a child devoid of all filial reverence, appear monsters, the objects, not of hatred only, but of horror.[92]

For Wilson, whose aim in the culture wars environment was to build a case for a
reinforced family culture in the United States, Smith's ideas on moral education
in the family, affection between family members, and judgments concerning
the propriety of sentiments and actions within the family offered much potentially useful intellectual weaponry against what he referred to as the "countless"
modern critics of marriage and the nuclear family.[93] Although Smith was rarely
Wilson's only source of inspiration in issues related to parenting and moral development, the neoconservative author was eager to cite Smith's views on the
family and moral development that corresponded with his own.

The most important of such corresponding issues was the general idea
that moral sentiments develop at an early age in the context of ordinary family life. Wilson drew attention to the parallels between his views and Smith's
own in his 2002 book *The Marriage Problem: How Our Culture Has Weakened Families*. In the book, he noted approvingly that Smith, and Hume too,
had supported the idea that morality was best cultivated at home, and he
cited Smith's idea that "domestic education" is "the institution of nature," unlike public education.[94] Wilson's most thorough discussion of the issue can
be found in *The Moral Sense*—the book that he introduced as "a continuation of work begun by" eighteenth-century Scottish writers such as Hume
and Smith.[95] While Smith's ideas on the family were among the sources that
inspired the book's arguments on moral development, Wilson relied more
heavily on recent findings by child psychologists who, as Wilson explained to
the Sloan Foundation's Arthur Singer in 1990, increasingly saw the child "as an
organism predisposed by its constitution to value—and initiate—sociability
and to convert learned behaviors into moral standards."[96] Broadly speaking,
Wilson's argument on the development of the moral sense reaffirmed that of
Smith (on moral sentiments) in that both writers stressed that the development of the moral mind was not entirely spontaneous but necessitated a caring family environment in an individual's early years.[97]

Despite the overlaps in Smith's and Wilson's arguments on moral education within the family—and Wilson's allusions to the Scottish thinker as his

inspiration—the neoconservative scholar did much to rework Smith's ideas with the help of modern social and natural science, which, in turn, enabled him to make the political argument for the traditional two-parent family as the seedbed of not only the moral sense but also law-abidingness and social order. Scientifically, Wilson's argument as to the development of a "natural" and "universal" moral sense within a family setting was contingent on his ability to show that there were "fundamental social bonds," in particular "the practice of child nurturance," that could be thought of as human universals.[98] Here, Wilson could not rely solely on Smith, who, as explained earlier, took it for granted that both mother and father would indeed be there for their children continually because of the constant affection between the sexes. In his 2002 book *Marriage Problem*, Wilson openly admitted that the Scottish philosophers' ideas needed to be revised, since both Hume and Smith "took for granted the conventional marriage, a man and a woman solemnly united for the purpose of raising children." Hume and Smith, Wilson wrote, "did not think much about" the possibility that "one could in principle devise alternatives to [the traditional family]. A child might be raised by an unwed parent, or a marriage designed to bring children into being might be terminated when they went off to become apprentices, or a man and a woman might live together without anything like a marriage agreement." Moreover, Smith never confronted "the question of the promiscuous male."[99]

To rework the Scottish thinkers' ideas on the family and to make a convincing, scientifically valid argument for the family as the seedbed of a child's moral sense and social order, Wilson turned to sociobiological research. Such contemporary sociobiological writers as Robert Trivers, William Hamilton, Donald Symons, and Lionel Tiger had recently written on family-related human emotional patterns, yet Wilson seemed to be most impressed by the pioneering "sociobiological" work of Edward Westermarck—a Finnish anthropologist and philosopher. Westermarck's work on the family, familial emotions, and morality dating from the late nineteenth and early twentieth centuries was experiencing a renaissance in the last decades of the twentieth century (among both liberal and conservative scholars and writers) in the wake of the rise of sociobiology and evolutionary psychology.[100] As a keen follower of both the Scottish sentimentalist tradition and Charles Darwin, Westermarck had written several landmark studies on the family and morality that treated such familial emotions as maternal and paternal sentiments as products of human evolution.[101] For Wilson, Westermarck's scholarly work was, then, useful in the sense that it gave him an evolutionary explanation (and anthropological evidence) for the naturalness and universality of the familial emotions that Smith had taken for granted. This in turn enabled Wilson to present an argument on the "universal" and "natural" moral sense that developed from early on in a family environment.

In scientific terms, then, Wilson's argument about the development of the moral sense within a family environment was a revised version of Smith's philosophy of moral education. As a neoconservative author on crime, however, Wilson redefined the concept of moral sense in a way that underscored its significance as the psychological source of social order in the United States, where the increase in crime since the 1960s was considered by the public as a major source of concern (see chapter 5). That is, Wilson maintained that the moral sense that developed early in life in a normal family environment ought to be seen as the psychological basis of an individual's law-abidingness.

More specifically, as a theorist of criminal policy, Wilson interpreted Smith's philosophy of moral education and later scientific findings on the development of the moral sense in light of criminologist Travis Hirschi's influential self-control theory of crime, in particular the idea that criminality could not be properly understood unless one first understood why most people did *not* break the law. Already before he adopted the moral sentimentalist vocabulary of the Scottish philosophers at the turn of the 1990s, Wilson had come to think that respect for the law, or the psychological traits that predicted such behavior, developed at an early age in family surroundings as the child interacted with his or her parents.[102] In his 1985 book *Crime and Human Nature* and in articles such as "Raising Kids" (1983), Wilson argued, following Hirschi's theory, that juvenile delinquents and criminals often came from broken families that had been unable to instill self-control and strong moral character in their children. In "Raising Kids," for example, Wilson cited studies showing that "large family size, parental criminality, low family income, and poor child-rearing practices" were among the most important factors that predicted "which boys would become delinquent."[103]

A few years later, at the turn of the 1990s, Wilson then borrowed the concept of the moral sense from the Scottish thinkers and used it as an explanation for most people's law-abidingness. In *The Moral Sense*, he noted that "we already know that criminality is importantly influenced by biological factors, including sex; it stands to reason that noncriminality should be influenced by such factors as well. To believe otherwise is to believe that law-abidingness is wholly learned, while criminality is a quasi-biological interruption of that acquired disposition. That is, to say the least, rather implausible."[104] In Wilson's Scottish-inspired, yet heavily revised moral theory, the notion of "the moral sense" thus referred to an individual's moral capacities, which formed out of the interaction between biological factors and social and cultural experiences and which contributed to one's law-abiding tendencies.

The political argument that Wilson made on the basis of these social scientific premises was that America's political and intellectual elites ought to do all they could to strengthen the traditional two-parent family that was indispensable for the normal development of the moral sense—that is, law-abidingness—in children. In Wilson's estimate, "the prevalence of divorce and illegitimacy" were obvious signs of a decline in the family institution in the United States, one that could have detrimental effects on the development of the moral sense in children, thus leading to social problems such as the increase in crime. In such conditions it was imperative, Wilson implied, to consciously cultivate the natural but vulnerable family bonds. Only thus would it be possible to shield and develop the natural moral sense, "our persistent but fragile disposition to make moral judgments."[105] In suggesting that American moral and social order rested on a "fragile" moral sense of ordinary people, Wilson fused Scottish moral philosophy with a conservative understanding of civilization as delicate, easily disrupted, and in need of constant protection. Here, again, he was thus a shaper of the Scottish tradition rather than being shaped by it.

Wilson's willingness to stand firm in defense of the traditional family was, for sure, based on a genuine concern about the risks that supposedly followed from a child's inability to experience the benefits of a middle-class family ethos. After finishing *The Moral Sense*, Wilson looked for solutions to the problem of "at-risk children"—children who came from broken families and who did not learn the moral habits that were necessary to succeed in life. Wilson suggested that boarding schools and orphanages were plausible solutions. Citing new historical studies, he argued that orphanages in the late nineteenth and early twentieth centuries had been "decent places run by caring professionals who maintained close ties to the community."[106] Most importantly, in modern orphanages, a child's moral mind could be cultivated by creating an environment that, insofar as possible, resembled the type of ordinary middle-class life in which self-control and related values were highly regarded. Another conceivable solution for at-risk youth was to relocate them and their parents "to neighborhoods with intact social structures and an ethos of family values."[107]

Having closely witnessed the controversy over the Moynihan Report for several decades, Wilson understood that to speak in moral terms about good middle-class family structures and corrupt ones would "annoy some readers" who would see it as a way of "stigmatizing" people. Still, Wilson saw nothing wrong with this kind of moral approach to families, and he insisted that "wrong behavior—neglectful, immature, or incompetent parenting; the production of out-of-wedlock babies—*ought* to be stigmatized."[108] In this case, as in many others, Wilson cited Smith's *Moral Sentiments* as an authoritative account on the issue. That is, in *Marriage Problem*, Wilson alluded to Smith's work on moral judgments concerning family life to endorse the idea that it was only natural to stigmatize bad parents. He pointed out that Smith "surely spoke for almost everyone when he said that a 'parent without parental tenderness, a child devoid of filial reverence, appear monsters.' Then as now, everyone is appalled at the sight of parents who care nothing for their children or of children who despise their parents."[109]

In a sense, Wilson was here elaborating on Kristol's more rudimentary ideas about ordinary Americans' moral evaluations concerning family life from the 1980s; as we have seen, Kristol had responded to the rising authority of family "experts" in American life by making the case that ordinary Americans were instinctively capable of making moral distinctions between good parents and bad parents. Above all, with the help of Smith's ideas on moral education and moral judgments concerning good and bad parenting, Wilson was trying to impose a moral consensus on the importance of traditional family life. Wilson used Smith as a source of authority who could help promote the view that the United States needed to bring into being a culture that supported traditional two-parent family life and therefore, social order. Yet crucially, in using Smith to make the argument that conventional family life was necessary for the raising of a law-abiding citizenry, Wilson had to rework Smith's ideas with the help of modern sociobiology and criminology and to apply them to a late twentieth-century American context that—with widespread cohabitation, single parenthood, and the modern welfare system (among other things)—was unimaginable to Smith himself.

The Battle over Nonjudgmentalism and the New Definitions of Deviancy

Despite Daniel Patrick Moynihan's consistent rejection of neoconservatism as a label (and identification with FDR liberalism), his much-discussed 1993 article "Defining Deviancy Down" is often taken as a text that captures the neoconservative position on America's moral and cultural condition in the early 1990s.[110] Such an interpretation is problematic not only due to Moynihan's dissociation from the movement but because his position is not exactly representative of the movement's thought on Americans' moral perceptions of the world.

Moynihan was prompted to write about the American moral landscape after being puzzled about "why there has in fact been so little response" to the serious troubles of American families in the past decades.[111] In the summer of 1992, he had begun "to see the outline of an argument." "The values issue that has come to consume American politics," Moynihan asserted in a letter to Harvard economist Richard T. Gill, "is an argument on redefining deviancy."[112] Moynihan had come up with a theory, following sociologists Émile Durkheim and Kai T. Erikson, according to which "too much deviancy becomes intolerable and gets defined away."[113]

Soon, Moynihan published his theory in the *American Scholar* in an article that immediately grabbed the attention of not only scholars and journalists but also the nation's leading politicians, including President Bill Clinton and New York Mayor Giuliani. Moynihan thus wrote to his friend James Q. Wilson about the "strange and odd turn of events" that his text had turned out to be one of the "principal texts for the new Republican administration of City Hall in New York."[114]

In "Defining Deviancy Down," Moynihan's key argument was that in recent years, deviant behavior had increased so much in the country that Americans were no longer able to recognize it as such. Consequently, Americans now defined as more or less normal many behaviors that had been defined as deviant previously, and they seemed to tolerate all kinds of dysfunctional behavior. In particular, attitudes toward alternative family structures and violent crime, as well as the deinstitutionalization of mental health patients, had become too relaxed, Moynihan claimed. Despite the fact that "of children born in the years 1967–69, some 22.1 percent were dependent on welfare . . . before reaching age 18" (15.7 percent of white children, 72.3 percent of black children), there was "little evidence that these facts are regarded as a calamity in municipal government. To the contrary, there is general acceptance of the situation as normal. Political candidates raise the subject, often to the point of dwelling on it. But while there is a good deal of demand for symbolic change, there is none of the marshaling of resources that is associated with significant social action. Nor is there any lack of evidence that there is a serious social problem here."[115]

In one sense, Moynihan's much-discussed article indeed is illustrative of how many *Public Interest* intellectuals, and many others in the country, felt about America's moral condition in the early and mid-1990s; the idea of "decline" was in the air, so to speak.[116] Yet "Defining Deviancy Down" does not illustrate equally well how many neoconservatives spoke about ordinary Americans and their moral mind-set. Moynihan himself spoke of Americans at a general level, arguing consistently that "we" (Americans) do not recognize many forms of deviancy anymore.[117] However, as we have seen, key neoconservative theorists, such as Irving Kristol and James Q. Wilson, were much more careful to differentiate between the moral world view of ordinary people and that of the political and intellectual elites. Indeed, Moynihan's argument about Americans was a far cry from that of Wilson, who in *The Moral Sense* and in his articles on gay marriage and abortion argued that the American people, unlike the country's intellectual elite, habitually used moral concepts to differentiate between right and wrong. In *The Moral Sense*, after all, "the pivotal problem" was "the moral sense of the average person versus the moral relativism of many intellectuals."[118]

A particularly illuminating perspective into the neoconservative discourse on everyday Americans' moral standards in the 1990s is offered by the debate sparked by sociologist Alan Wolfe's 1998 book, with the lengthy title *One Nation, after All: What Middle-Class Americans Really Think about God, Country, Family, Racism, Welfare, Immigration, Homosexuality, Work, the Right, the Left, and Each Other.* The neoconservative response to the book, which was overall negative, is, together with Kristol's and Wilson's writings on common sense and moral sentiments, another indication that Moynihan's "Defining Deviancy Down" is unrepresentative of the neoconservative outlook on America's moral landscape and their approach to the culture wars in the 1990s. Wolfe's book inspired several key neoconservative theorists, notably Himmelfarb, Fukuyama, and Wilson, to reflect on everyman's morality in the late 1990s, since Wolfe concluded that "nonjudgmentality" was a major principle uniting the contemporary American middle class—a conclusion that bears a resemblance to Moynihan's thesis about the recent normalization of deviant behavior.

Wolfe's book was based on interviews with two hundred middle-class Americans from eight suburbs around the country. A key finding was, in Wolfe's words, that the current "culture war" was being fought "*primarily by intellectuals, not by most Americans themselves*" (emphasis in original). The leading liberal sociologist wrote, "To exclude, to condemn, is to judge, and middle-class Americans are reluctant to pass judgment on how other people act and think." Wolfe even declared provocatively that "middle-class Americans have added an Eleventh Commandment, best formulated by [one of his respondents] Dolores Wales of Sand Springs, Oklahoma: 'Thou shalt not judge.'"[119]

The family values issue, Wolfe suggested, reflected this general middle-class "nonjudgmentalism." The largest cluster of attitudes he and his group of researchers had found on the question of the proper family form fell into the "ambivalent" category (as opposed to "traditional," "postmodern," and "realist"). Such results indicated, for Wolfe, that "the culture war lies within: middle-class Americans believe in both the traditional and the modern version of the family simultaneously. Longing for a world that no longer exists but having no intention of giving up the one that does, they are torn between nostalgia and necessity. . . . What the sociologists Peter and Brigitte Berger called 'the war over the family' [in their 1983 book with that title] may not be a war at all, but an inevitable, and perhaps even healthy, conflict between two different sets of needs, both of which have compelling reasons to exist."[120]

Wolfe's argument about middle-class nonjudgmentalism thus called into question Wilson's claim in *The Moral Sense* that ordinary Americans "talk constantly [in moral terms] about being or not being decent, nice, or dependable; about having or not having a good character; about friendship, loyalty, and moderation or fickleness, insincerity, and addiction."[121] Thus it is no wonder that in the neoconservative camp, Wolfe's conclusions about the American middle-class value system aroused much interest. The response was mostly critical, although the merits of his study were also highlighted by some.

One particularly trenchant critic was Himmelfarb, who challenged Wolfe's conclusions in the very title of her book *One Nation, Two Cultures*, which was published a year after Wolfe's book came out. Himmelfarb blamed Wolfe for "obscuring the reality" of America's two cultures, which "emerges in one poll after another about one important issue after another." The neoconservative historian stressed that there *was* a true culture war going on in the country between the "dominant culture" found in the media, universities, and entertainment industry (that, ironically, had its roots in the counterculture) and the "dissident culture" that supported traditional values.[122] Even if Moynihan's distressed 1993 article had managed to encapsulate "the social and cultural situation of our time," "ordinary people," for Himmelfarb, were still more prone to perceive the world in moral terms than were the out-of-touch elites, even if such ordinary people had not been able to resist countercultural ideas completely. Thus in contrast to Wolfe's "nonjudgmentality" thesis, Himmelfarb argued that among "the public at large," "morality" and "virtue" "testify to something real and commendable."[123]

Himmelfarb saw much evidence of this popular understanding of morality in late 1990s America. Above all, she saw more and more signs of a conservative moral response to the "defining deviancy down" phenomenon Moynihan had described in 1993. One could perceive this conservative response in the issue of family values: students were "becoming less permissive in their sexual attitudes," so that in 1998, only 40 percent of college freshmen approved of casual sex, whereas 51 percent did in 1990. Correspondingly, a decreasing proportion of college freshmen thought that abortion should be legal (from 62 percent in 1990 to 50 percent in 1998). Teenagers, too, were "becoming somewhat disenchanted with their sexual liberation"—more than

half of girls had told pollsters that sex before marriage is wrong, Himmelfarb noted—and older people were "also reconsidering the permissiveness of
their own youth," so that among adults in their forties, attitudes toward premarital sex and divorce had tightened from what they had been twenty-five
years previously (when they had been in their twenties). Himmelfarb thus
concluded against Moynihan's 1993 thesis that it was "not only conservatives
(religious and secular) who now deplore the breakdown of the family, liberals
do as well, responding to the irrefutable evidence of the consequences of that
breakdown."[124]

Fukuyama also spoke his mind regarding Wolfe's findings on several occasions in the late 1990s and early 2000s. His understanding of the issue differed
somewhat from that of Himmelfarb. While Himmelfarb criticized Wolfe for
obscuring the reality of America's two cultures, Fukuyama was more sup-
portive of Wolfe's observations about middle-class Americans' generally tolerant inclinations. The Monica Lewinsky impeachment scandal, according to
Fukuyama, bolstered Wolfe's findings. A "substantial number of Americans,"
Fukuyama pointed out in a 2000 article in the *Wall Street Journal*, had dis-
liked Republican moralism even more intensely than President Clinton's behavior. While Fukuyama highlighted the importance of recent social changes
relating to sex and the social role of women as the "single source that virtually all of the 'culture wars' stem" from and while he argued that Americans
were "extremely opinionated about sex, family, homosexuality, feminism, and
judgmentalism in general," he reckoned that in the end, Americans were not
consistent (i.e., persistently conservative or liberal) in their approach to family values. Drawing on Wolfe, he noted that Americans seemed to be intensely
worried about "moral decline" but "just as steadfastly opposed to people who
were 'judgmental.'" Thus Fukuyama concluded that Americans were "genuinely divided on these issues."[125]

What Fukuyama here meant by division was very different from Wilson's
and Himmelfarb's ideas on America's "two cultures" but similar to Wolfe's
conclusions: whereas the two first-generation neoconservatives spoke of the
rift between the dominant liberal elites and the beleaguered defenders of traditional values, Fukuyama understood the situation as more complicated in
the sense that individual Americans often seemed unable to decide what to
think on moral questions. This was the case in the questions of homosexuality and gay marriage, for example. Unlike Wilson, who a few years earlier had
argued that ordinary Americans intuitively opposed gay marriage, Fukuyama
pointed out that Americans, despite the fact that they had strong doubts about
these matters, did not want to discriminate against gays. He concluded that
"ironically, the greatest moral passion of contemporary Americans turns out

to be hostility to 'moralism' in areas related to sex and family life."[126] Or, as he put it in his 1999 book *The Great Disruption*, "contemporary Americans . . . seek contradictory [moral] goals."[127] (Here, Fukuyama's view fits closely with that of sociologist Irene Taviss Thomson, who argues in *Culture Wars and Enduring American Dilemmas* that Americans typically defend morality but oppose moralism and "tribalism.")[128]

Ironically, Fukuyama's own accounts of the value system of everyday Americans were not entirely consistent either. In discussing Wolfe's work, he clearly indicated that he agreed with the author about the generally tolerant attitudes of average middle-class Americans. Yet in many books and articles that he authored in the late 1990s and early 2000s, Fukuyama described humans, and by the same token ordinary Americans, as natural rule-makers and suggested that the present dominance of liberal nonjudgmentalism on such issues as the family was only a *temporary* phenomenon. That is, while Fukuyama agreed with Wolfe that contemporary middle-class Americans avoided passing judgment on other people's behavior and searched for contradictory ethical goals, he nevertheless argued—like Himmelfarb did at around the same time—that more conservative family values were making a comeback in the United States after thirty years of family disruption. Divorce rates, for example, had gone down and illegitimacy rates had leveled off, if not declined, which provided "evidence that more conservative social norms have made a comeback."[129] Another sign of this kind of "renorming" was that the idea of male responsibility was making a comeback, as such recent phenomena as the 1995 Million Man March to Washington (in which African American men demonstrated their joint willingness to fight against the social ills in black communities) and Promise Keepers (a new organization of evangelical Christian men who promised to cherish their families) indicated. Moreover, in the late 1990s, a popular radio show advised its listeners "to stop indulging themselves and accept responsibility for spouses and children." Fukuyama contrasted these trends and events with the ethos of the 1960s and 1970s, when liberationist therapists "advised people to 'get in touch with their feelings' and discard social constraints that would stand in the way of 'personal growth.'"[130]

A conservative approach to family values was, for Fukuyama, in some ways a more *natural* approach than an unreserved openness toward alternative families. This is why it was to be expected that the conservative trend toward "more restrictive norms" would continue—human beings were biologically driven to establish moral values. As will be shown in more detail in chapter 6, Fukuyama's understanding of human moral nature and the "spontaneous" generation of values owed much to the moral sense theory of both the eighteenth-century Scottish thinkers and Wilson. Here, it suffices to note that with his moral sentimentalist, naturalist perspective on conservative family values, Fukuyama was in the end quite close to Wilson's and Kristol's positions on everyman's morality.

Wolfe's claims about middle-class nonjudgmentality in *One Nation, after All*, and later in *Moral Freedom: The Search for Virtue in a World of Choice* (2001), provoked a reaction from Wilson too. As one would expect from the author of *The Moral Sense*, Wilson found Wolfe's arguments about middle American nonjudgmentality not entirely plausible. He criticized the methods that Wolfe had used to find out about middle-class morality as severely limited in the sense that they were of no help in discovering how people in fact acted and felt about issues in their *daily life* (as opposed to what they *reported* about their value system). Wilson had no trouble believing that many of Wolfe's interview subjects had told him they were unwilling to judge other people's moral choices or lifestyles. But when Wolfe had presented them with a real murder case in Texas where the accused (Karla Faye Tucker) claimed she had become a born-again Christian in the fifteen years since her crime, Americans had been much less forgiving than Wolfe had expected. For Wilson, Wolfe's mistake was to explain the case as an "exception" to their nonjudgmentalism. "What really happened," Wilson suspected, "is that a concrete case rather than a moral abstraction was presented to Mr. Wolfe's interview subjects, and they responded concretely. Suppose he had asked them in detail about an unmarried teenage girl having a baby and living off welfare, one's spouse being sexually unfaithful or Timothy McVeigh blowing up an office building in Oklahoma. I suspect we would have had some sharp moral judgments made with little equivocation." Wilson concluded by invoking the vocabulary of the Scottish moralists: "I am as puzzled as Mr. Wolfe by the moral sentiments of Americans, but I doubt they can be fully understood with interviews about abstractions." When "a real, concrete case of a particular human being behaving in an unmistakable manner intrudes," Wilson insisted, "suddenly the moral ambiguity of Americans disappears."[131]

It is clear then that Wilson held tightly to the view that ordinary Americans were consistent in their (conservative) moral judgments rather than "nonjudgmental." And therefore, scholars such as James T. Patterson who see Wilson as one of those "nostalgic" conservatives who claimed in the 1990s and early 2000s that Americans had "defined deviancy down" are only partly correct. It is true, as Patterson notes, that Wilson argued, in his 2002 book *Marriage Problem*, that the celebration of personal freedom and individual self-expression had weakened the social stigma that had been attached to unwed pregnancies, drug use, and male idleness.[132] What Patterson does not take note of, though, is that Wilson emphasized in the same book that Americans still *were* "judgmental" when "what is being judged is something we care about." To clarify this point, the neoconservative scholar referred to polls showing that "half of us approve of *other* people's daughters having children out of wedlock, but hardly any of us approve of that for *our* daughters."[133] Thus in *Marriage Problem*, Wilson once again denied Wolfe's thesis about middle American nonjudgmentality.

Wilson's responses to Wolfe in *Marriage Problem* and elsewhere illustrate quite well how the neoconservatives often fought the culture wars: to respond to feminists and other thinkers and experts who in the last decades of the twentieth century challenged the traditional two-parent family, they invoked the figure of a morally alert man in the street who still knew the difference between right and wrong. This holds true especially with Kristol, Wilson, and Himmelfarb, three key neoconservative theorists who tried to *build up* a moral consensus on family values by insisting that a consensus (or near consensus) *already* existed among ordinary Americans. At times, the key neoconservative culture warriors simply lamented America's post-1960s moral decline or the defining deviancy down phenomenon, although typically they, in one way or another, followed Kristol's program of explaining to the people why they were right and to the intellectuals why they were wrong. Often, they used the eighteenth-century Scottish philosophers' concepts of the moral sense, moral sentiments, and common sense to do so. Such rhetoric had a powerful appeal in a country with a deep passion for democracy, but the moral sentiments of Americans were always more varied than the neoconservatives suggested and in many respects always historically changing, often moving in a more liberal direction. One may conclude, then, that in the hands of the neoconservatives, the eighteenth-century Scottish moral vocabulary became a political tool intended to delegitimize and marginalize the increasingly widespread liberal views of many family experts, intellectuals, and journalists. In a word, by appealing to the "moral sense," or to some of its variants, they tried to impose, informally, a moral consensus on the question of family values.

Moral Sentiments of the Black Underclass:
Race in the Neoconservative Moral Imagination

In the early 1980s, at about the same time that the neoconservatives recon-
ceptualized family decline as a general American dilemma instead of just a
black one, they and many other Americans perceived in urban black America
another, even more disturbing, manifestation of cultural decline. That was
the rise of an "underclass"—that is, an increase in the numbers of inner-city
blacks who were, in James Q. Wilson's words, "permanently poor" and "habitually criminal."[1] In different contexts, the flexible term could refer to welfare
dependents, school dropouts, teenage mothers, the homeless, beggars and
panhandlers, drug and alcohol addicts, street criminals, or gang members.[2]

The debate over the black underclass emerged in the 1980s and 1990s as
one of the key domestic policy debates that aggravated the divide between
liberal and conservative Americans. Liberals emphasized structural forces,
location, resources, and discrimination as roots of African American poverty and depicted (black) offenders as disadvantaged or poorly socialized.
Conservatives instead stressed the need for bourgeois values, such as self-
initiative among urban black poor; highlighted welfare dependency as an
expanding *moral* problem; and advocated stricter punishments for urban
America's "predatory" career criminals. While it was occasionally noted at
the time that many ethnic groups were found among the underclass, it was
typically perceived to be a black phenomenon.

This chapter explores the debate over the urban underclass as another key
battleground of the culture wars of the 1980s and 1990s, one in which neoconservative writers—in this case, Wilson and Gertrude Himmelfarb—consistently appealed to the supposedly conservative moral sentiments of ordinary Americans to provide consensual parameters for debate and to influence
decision-makers and public policy. Wilson wrote regularly about the criminal

behavior of urban black youngsters, policing, and the criminal justice system, while Himmelfarb concentrated on the questions of poverty, the welfare state, and private charity. Both Wilson and Himmelfarb reinvented the vocabulary of the Scottish moralists—the moral sense, moral sentiments, and common sense—in the context of the underclass debate, like Irving Kristol and Wilson did within the framework of the family wars by turning it into a conservative political instrument.[3]

Himmelfarb, and especially Wilson, while suggesting solutions to urban problems, such as crime and welfare dependency, claimed to be speaking for (and about) "ordinary Americans," implicitly or explicitly referring to work-ing- and middle-class citizens, mainly whites, some of whose moral sensi-bilities were grounded in racism of various forms and degrees. Such popular attitudes have been explored by scholars such as Martin Gilens, who shows in *Why Americans Hate Welfare: Race, Media, and the Politics of Antipoverty Policy* (1999) that "Americans oppose welfare, that they hold cynical views of welfare recipients, and that their thinking about poverty and welfare is per-meated by their beliefs about blacks."[4] Was neoconservatism, or the strand of neoconservative thought that claimed to speak for ordinary Americans, then a form of white backlash—and if so, how and to what degree?

Currently, in the existing scholarship, there is no consensus on neocon-servative thought on race. One group of scholars makes a clear distinction between racist ideologues and the neoconservatives who, as urban New York intellectuals, gave voice to a "color-blind" world view. These scholars cor-rectly note that neoconservative intellectuals defended a merit-based social system and opposed quotas and affirmative action while frowning on provin-cial bigotry.[5]

Many other scholars instead suggest that neoconservative thought did include racist elements, and nearly always they highlight crime and welfare dependency as the issues through which the neoconservatives viewed Afri-can Americans. Perhaps most notably, political scientist Jean-François Drolet argues in *American Neoconservatism: The Politics and Culture of a Reaction-ary Idealism* that the "neoconservative political community presupposes con-flict. It comes into being and acquires its normative content by facing and overcoming the undesirable other." As Drolet sees it, the black underclass, including criminals and welfare cheats, was the key enemy of the neocon-servatives in the culture wars. Drolet even claims, following critical theorist Thomas McCarthy, that the neoconservative discourse on the "socially dys-functional behaviour" of the underclass "operates according to the same logic as the biological racial theories of society and development discredited in the second half of the twentieth century," at least "to the extent that" it "relies on psychological and cultural patterns to explain social structures and pro-cesses."[6] Drolet is by no means the only writer to suggest that neoconser-vative thought included racist elements. To take another example, historian Elizabeth Hinton argues in her well-received 2016 book on the post-1960s War on Crime that Wilson, like his fellow *Public Interest* intellectuals Edward Banfield and Daniel Patrick Moynihan, saw "crime and violence as somehow innate among African Americans."[7]

This chapter reconsiders neoconservative thought on race from a new perspective. It takes an in-depth look at how Wilson's and Himmelfarb's dis-course on human moral nature—the "moral sense"—relates to their concep-tions of the black underclass. To whom, in fact, did they refer when they spoke of ordinary people's natural moral sense, which in their telling was needed to counterbalance the moral relativism or amoral rationalism of out-of-touch liberal elites? Did Wilson or Himmelfarb argue that the black underclass pos-sessed a moral sense? If so, then what does that tell us about neoconservative racial attitudes?

What this focus on Wilson's and Himmelfarb's Scottish-inspired language of the moral sense reveals is that the neoconservatives relied on the logic of color blindness in a way that distinguished them from scientific racists. As we will see, throughout the 1990s, Himmelfarb consistently invoked the Scottish moral ideas to rationalize welfare state contraction by emphasizing that the moral sense—understood as a willingness and a capacity for self-improvement—ought to be understood as an attribute of the poor and rich alike and suggested that the proponents of a generous welfare state did *not* appreciate the moral sense of the disadvantaged. That is, even when the focus of her analysis was the underclass—permanently poor blacks and a smaller number of poor whites—it was the presumably white liberal intellectuals who were the subject of her criticism. Wilson, in turn, tried to persuade his read-ers of the value of the "ordinary citizen's" moral perspective as a cure for the troubles of the black underclass. In other words, he saw a greater contrast be-tween the moral capacities of the underclass and those of "ordinary citizens" than Himmelfarb did—especially when it came to "self-control." Yet he, like Himmelfarb, blamed America's mostly white elite culture for the sorry condi-tion of the black underclass.

This chapter argues then that for neoconservative culture warriors, the black underclass was not so much their required enemy but an unprotected, poorly socialized victim of a larger American cultural malaise initiated by the cultural left; therefore, it was the liberal cultural and political elite who was the primary foe in the neoconservative culture wars, and it was the liberal elites whose views and policies on poverty reduction, crime, and punishment

Wilson and Himmelfarb strived to discredit in the 1990s by invoking the natural moral sense of ordinary citizens. In the context of a national debate over the underclass in which Afrocentrists and cosmopolitan intellectuals of the left challenged right-wing ideas on black "culture of poverty," genetic differences, and race and IQ, the Scottish notions of the universal moral sense and moral sentiments offered the neoconservatives a seemingly sophisticated vocabulary with which to distinguish between the supposedly amoral and eccentric liberal perspectives and the ethical, democratic, and "American" approaches to certain social problems often related to the urban black underclass—namely, poverty and crime.[8] While the neoconservatives' moral sentimentalist language that highlighted the shared moral capacities of "ordinary people" seemingly embraced democratic ideals, it simultaneously fell short as a language of national solidarity, for it encouraged the exclusion of academic and other elites and—especially in the case of Wilson—the underclass from the idealized group of morally pure "ordinary citizens."

To understand the neoconservative preoccupation with the underclass, I will begin this chapter by looking at how the national debate over the topic emerged in the 1970s and 1980s and how the neoconservative outlook on the issue took shape. I will then analyze how and why both Himmelfarb and Wilson came to invoke—and reshape—eighteenth-century ideas on the moral sense and moral sentiments in the context of the underclass debate and how these two key neoconservative cultural warriors viewed the role of the intellectual elites in the emergence of America's urban crisis.

The Discovery of the Underclass: Urban Decay as a Question of Character

The background to the national and neoconservative debate over the urban underclass can be traced to the "rediscovery" of American poverty in the early 1960s. Since poverty, in fact, was nothing new in America, it is, as James T. Patterson notes, "much easier to observe that poverty became a subject of debate than to explain why." Rather than to any clear increase in the number of poor Americans, the nation's "discovery" of destitution is commonly traced to journalistic depictions of mass deprivation that became frequent after 1962.[9] The most important of these texts was the activist Michael Harrington's passionate book *The Other America* (1962), which contested the complacent midcentury assumptions about American affluence and exposed the deprivation of forty to fifty million Americans. These "new poor" included, according to Harrington, different people ranging from "old people suddenly confronted with the torments of loneliness and poverty" to "minorities facing a wall of prejudice."[10]

The path from these journalistic accounts to social policy was opened when President John F. Kennedy read Harrington's book and set his staff to study the question. After inheriting this staff work, it was President Lyndon Johnson who then launched a full War on Poverty in 1964. The aim of Johnson's program was to prevent poverty by a legislative agenda relating to education, job training, and improvement of housing, but at least in the short run, it reduced deprivation only marginally. As Patterson remarks, by the time the War on Poverty lost its political appeal (after the 1960s), "its limitations had intensified the country's doubts about the ability of experts to diagnose, much less cure, the ills of the poor."[11] Crucially, after the mid-1960s, the issue of poverty became increasingly mixed with questions of inner-city violence, crime, and race. As one historian notes, after the Watts riots in Los Angeles in 1965, "the hottest and fiercest political issue of the day" was "the problem of poor, angry black people in the inner cities."[12]

The debate on the urban "underclass" picked up steam in the late 1970s and 1980s. The term was first used already in the 1960s by liberals and social workers, who used it to refer to families that were the most disadvantaged and uneducated among the poor—families that were especially hard for welfare case workers to reach.[13] Over time, the term began to take a conservative coloring, however. This occurred in the late 1970s and 1980s at a time when American cities, in Daniel Rodgers's words, became flooded with "homeless men and women, pushed out of mental institutions and cheap rental housing" and as "crack cocaine ratcheted up the drug economy's levels of trade and violence."[14] In conservative use, the reference was not only to individuals at the bottom of society who were *unable* to hold a permanent job but also to those who were *unwilling*. Rodgers aptly describes how the image of the poor congealed in the 1980s "into the new verbal clichés: Black, urban, crime-wracked, hypersegregated, welfare-dependent, isolated from and indifferent to mainstream American values: the underclass label described a people who were, by definition, aliens in their own land." Thus by the 1980s, the idea of an underclass had greatly assisted in creating a growing consensus that poverty had become a more enduring problem, with lots of people stuck in a reality of low income and mobility.[15]

To be sure, there has never been a consensus over the exact meaning of the underclass concept, even among liberal or conservative writers. Such widely noticed works by liberal writers as sociologist William Julius Wilson's *The Declining Significance of Race* (1978) and *The Truly Disadvantaged* (1987),

journalist Ken Auletta's *The Underclass* (1982), and sociologist Orlando Patterson's *The Ordeal of Integration* (1997) defined the concept in rather different terms (Auletta, in a 1999 edition of the book, positions himself as neither
liberal nor conservative).[16] In Auletta's book, which did much to inspire a dialogue on the issue in the early 1980s, the underclass concept referred to those
who were affected by one or more socioeconomic problems, such as enduring poverty, criminal records, or drug addiction. This was a broad definition:
there were nine million of these people, 70 percent nonwhite, representing
one-fourth of the black population.[17]

Wilson, in *Declining Significance of Race* in 1978, similarly wrote about a
"huge black underclass," "close to a third of the black population," while
stressing economic factors: blue-collar jobs were leaving the inner cities, and
access to the new higher-paying jobs in the rapidly growing corporate and
government sectors was based on educational criteria, which widened the
gap between the well-educated black middle class and the unskilled inner-
city black poor. Thus Wilson, an African American himself, argued that race
was losing its significance as a determinate of blacks' chances in life, and class
was growing in importance.[18] Wilson's critics felt that his focus on economic
factors left too little room for important cultural explanations. Patterson was
perhaps the most prominent of such writers. In his major works, many of
them dating from the 1990s, underclass referred not to all poor people but
to a "small hard core of dangerous people with multiple problems." In Patterson's estimate, there were about nine hundred thousand of such people in
1997, no more than 10 percent of the black poor. According to Patterson, the
number of such people had not grown in previous decades, but the underclass had "certainly become more deadly, taking its toll on the more vulnerable inner-city Afro-American communities."[19]

Social scientist William Kelso discusses in *Poverty and the Underclass:
Changing Perceptions of the Poor in America* (1994) both the conservative and
the liberal side of the underclass debate of the 1970s and 1980s. Kelso notes
that it was only at the time of economic decline in the 1970s, when family
earnings ceased growing, that conservatives actively began to look for real
alternatives for liberal ways of managing the poverty problem. Conservatives
criticized liberals for becoming too concerned to shelter the poor from the
demands of society and, as Kelso puts it, "hoped to create a new 'opportunity society' that relied on market incentives and cultural values to promote
upward mobility." Kelso makes a useful distinction between "market conservatives" and "civic conservatives." Among the diverse group of conservative
thinkers, "market conservatives" relied on economic incentives to reduce
the number of poor Americans. "Civic conservatives" in turn held that such

efforts would not work out unless the poor first absorbed vital cultural values, such as self-reliance. The aim of civic conservatism was, then, to battle urban decay by making deliberate efforts to promote among the poor the virtues of a shared middle-class culture.[20]

In discussing the civic conservative side of the conservative poverty debate, Kelso singles out political scientist Lawrence M. Mead—who is known for his argument for a program of workfare to replace older forms of welfare—as "the most prominent civic conservative."[21] Yet he also cites two books by James Q. Wilson, written in the 1980s and early 1990s, that discussed the question of "moral character": *Crime and Human Nature* (1985), cowritten with Richard Herrnstein, and the essay collection *On Character* (1991).[22] Importantly, these texts by Wilson differ significantly from those written in the early days of the neoconservative movement in the late 1960s and early 1970s, when Wilson and others in the movement had been known for their remarkably *skeptical* attitudes toward the predicament of the urban lower class rather than for any suggestions as to the solution of its problems. Although several reference points (such as welfare dependency and crime) of the early neoconservative discourse did persist until the 1980s, many neoconservative thinkers learned, after their more cynical early years, to view the same problems from a more solution-oriented perspective.

To get a grasp of this shift in attitudes from the very low expectations of early neoconservatism toward the increasing, yet still guarded, optimism of the 1980s underclass discourse, one needs to be aware of two features of the early neoconservative discourse on inner-city decay. First, a key neoconservative idea was that the main causes of the underclass problem were not to be found in any economic and structural factors but largely in the poor people's own resilient "culture of poverty" that was distinct from the American mainstream and very difficult to change. Among the pioneers of this discourse was Edward Banfield, the supervisor of Wilson's dissertation (1959) at the University of Chicago, who moved to Harvard in 1959, with Wilson soon following him (in 1961).[23] Banfield made a reputation as a maverick sociologist in 1970 with his controversial book *The Unheavenly City*, which argued that poor people in America's inner cities would never be able to compete successfully in the job market due to their distinct value system. Unlike the members of the upper, middle, and working classes, "the lower-class individual" could not, according to Banfield, "discipline himself to sacrifice a present for a future satisfaction." Banfield also held that neither of the two "mammoth government programs" presently underway to aid the cities (i.e., the improvement of transportation and housing) were "intended to deal with the serious problems"—namely, the "existence of huge enclaves of people (many, but not all of them, Negro) of low skill, low income, and low status."[24] On the whole, these programs—which had forced "hundreds of thousands" of low-income people out of low-cost housing and which would likely reduce the number of jobs in inner cities—would probably only aggravate urban problems.[25] At the time, Wilson sympathized with his former teacher's view on the importance of class ethos, arguing that "social class . . . is a much better predictor of behavior than race."[26]

If it was typical of the early neoconservatives to associate the urban, mainly black lower class with a self-destructive social ethos (a lack of future-orientedness), then it was even more characteristic of them to link black family structure with social failure. As noted in chapter 3, it was another good friend of Wilson, Pat Moynihan, who was the key figure in taking the neoconservatives—including Wilson—to this direction with his 1965 argument that the black family structure would greatly hinder African American efforts to escape poverty.[27]

At the time of the Moynihan Report, and especially by the time Banfield published *Unheavenly City* in 1970, Wilson was, as much as his neoconservative friends, mugged by the dim reality of America's inner cities (to paraphrase Kristol's famous description of neoconservatives as liberals mugged by reality). Although Wilson had begun his academic career as a political scientist already in the late 1950s, it was only now in the mid to late 1960s, in the midst of worsening urban violence, that he found his specialty in crime.[28] At a time when America's cities generally seemed "dirty, dangerous, and locked in a cycle of continuing decline," Wilson wanted to focus his energies on "predatory" street crime, which at the time ranked number one when average citizens were asked about the biggest problem facing the city.[29]

As a result of this refocusing of research agenda, between 1965 and 1975, Wilson went on to challenge the orthodox conception of postwar liberal criminology (more tax money spent on the problems of unemployment and poverty would solve the problem of rising crime rates) and argued that raising punitive costs through long-term prison sentences was the only measure that would indisputably reduce crime.[30] A striking feature of Wilson's thought on crime—and of his attack on liberal criminology—was his view that current knowledge was simply not enough to justify any view of the "root causes" of crime. The "tangle of pathologies" (Moynihan's term) observed in inner cities was very intricate, and it would take time for criminologists to make sense of the roots of the crime problem. It is here that we meet the true sources of Wilson's low expectations at the early stages of his career. The attempt to reduce crime by attacking its root causes was "futile," as Wilson later aptly described his own earlier outlook, since "we did not know what these root causes were, and the most likely candidates for such causes, human character and the intimate social settings in which it was formed, were beyond the reach of public policy in a free society."[31] Because of the prevalence of such attitudes toward governmental efforts to cope with crime in the 1970s, criminologist Franklin Zimring refers to this period as the "nothing works era" in American crime response.[32] Tellingly, in 1971, Wilson wrote to Kristol that "the state of our knowledge about what can and cannot be done [about crime] has substantially improved [since 1966], especially with reference to what cannot be done."[33]

The "tangle of pathologies" in America's inner cities was a major concern just as much for Himmelfarb. However, as a historian, her role as a social commentator was very different from Wilson's—and it began at a later stage of her career. Until the mid-1990s, Himmelfarb was better known as a historian of Victorian England, albeit as a conservative one rather than as a social analyst. Her more detailed analyses of contemporary American urban problems emerged in the 1990s in books such as *On Looking into the Abyss: Untimely Thoughts on Culture and Society* (1994), *The De-moralization of Society: From Victorian Virtues to Modern Values* (1995), and *One Nation, Two Cultures* (1999). Some of these works from the mid to late 1990s will be explored later, but here it needs to be pointed out that Himmelfarb had already made her diagnosis for late twentieth-century urban America earlier—as evidenced by her two-volume study on poverty in Victorian England, written mainly in the 1980s.[34] In the latter volume, Himmelfarb argued that with the emergence of the underclass problem, America had confronted "a culture of poverty" similar to "the 'Mayhewian' poor a century and a half ago." According to her, the "symptoms" were "a growing rate of illegitimacy and single-parent families, a 'social pathology' of crime, violence, and drugs, and a dependency on welfare that cannot be entirely attributed to unemployment and low wages." In fact, such a troubled underclass had recently emerged not only in America but in England as well. But only in America "this class ha[d] attained the status of a major social problem."[35]

Against the background of early neoconservatism's skepticism—visible especially in Banfield's and Wilson's works—one can appreciate the "solution-orientedness" that the new "civic conservative" perspectives of the 1980s articulated (although neoconservatives were continually aware of the gravity of existing urban problems). In Wilson's case, this change of perspective meant a reconsideration of his political thought on at least two different fronts.

First, unlike in the 1970s—when he took it for granted that the "character" of American citizens was "beyond the reach of public policy in a free society"—Wilson was now, by the mid-1980s, more willing to acknowledge and even emphasize that the federal government had, and should take, a role in the moral cultivation of American citizens. He admitted that the American republic had been founded on a different understanding of politics but added that whatever the proper role of government was in eighteenth-century America, in the contemporary United States, the government necessarily took part in character formation. The most widely noticed article by Wilson along these lines was "The Rediscovery of Character: Private Virtue and Public Policy" from 1985, which pointed out that "if we wish [the federal government] to address the problems of family disruption, welfare dependency, crime in the streets, educational inadequacy, or even public finance properly understood, then government, by the mere fact that it defines these states of affairs as problems, acknowledges that human character is, in some degree, defective and that it intends to alter it."[36] After all, it was "in almost every area of important public concern [that] we are seeking to induce persons to act virtuously, whether as schoolchildren, applicants for public assistance, would-be lawbreakers, or voters and public officials. Not only is such conduct desirable in its own right, it appears now to be necessary if large improvements are to be made in those matters we consider problems: schooling, welfare, crime, and public finance."[37] On a more practical level, Wilson linked the opportunities for cultivating character to such issues as "invigorating the work requirement associated with welfare," "preparing children for school and equipping parents to cope with unruly offspring" in order to reduce crime, and "a desirable school ethos" with "an emphasis on academic achievement, the regular assignment of homework, the consistent and fair use of rewards (especially praise) to enforce generally agreed-upon standards of conduct, and energetic teacher involvement in directing classroom work."[38]

In part, Wilson's new emphasis on the importance of (governmental) efforts at improving moral character was meant as an answer to the general tendency in both conservative and general American policy analysis to concentrate all attention on "incentives." He held that the country had come face-to-face over the past two decades "with problems that do not seem to respond, or respond enough, to changes in incentives. They do not respond, it seems, because the people whose behavior we wish to change do not have the right 'tastes' or discount the future too heavily. To put it plainly, they lack character." Therefore, the need was, above all, "to explore, carefully and experimentally, ways of strengthening the formation of character among the very young."[39] In 1991, Wilson made this new perspective the focus of his book *On Character*, a collection of previously published and revised essays.

The other important reconsideration by Wilson (besides the government's role in character cultivation) concerned the underclass. Previously, Wilson had sympathized with Banfield's view that the underclass problem was largely caused by the lower classes' own inborn culture of poverty, which left the urban poor with very little chances for upward social mobility. Now Wilson was coming closer to an interpretation of the underclass as a victim of a more general moral and cultural debasement in America and a lack of advice on how to regulate behavior.

Wilson's emphasis thus shifted from the lower classes to America's intellectual and political elites who had lost both their confidence in traditional middle-class values, such as self-control, and their willingness to promote those values among the citizenry. The deeper historical background was, according to Wilson, that between 1860 and 1960, "elite opinion underwent a change, from advocating self-control to endorsing self-expression."[40] Such an ideological change among the elites had had important implications for nearly all Americans, for the reason that the elite's "public philosophy alters how they define the proper policy for others."[41] The implications were different, however, for different people. For most people, such a cultural change toward the ideal of self-expression had meant "extraordinary social benefits" without significant harms, such as increased illegal activity—namely, because "their parents and peers have intuitively rewarded decency and punished selfishness and because these people have entered markets and neighborhoods that reinforced the lessons of their early training." Unfortunately, the change in elite ideology was a disaster for "some people [who] lack either the earlier training or the later environment, and so become especially vulnerable in the self-indulgent tone of modern elite culture. Black Americans have been especially vulnerable in this regard."[42] The upside of this interpretation was that the underclass, after all, might not be permanently trapped by the destructive qualities of its own culture. But to bring about changes in the habits of the black urban poor, American elites needed to restore their own motivation to stand up for and knowingly promote the unfashionable "middle-class values."

In Himmelfarb's works from the same period (the late 1980s and the turn of the 1990s), one can perceive similar, cautious contentment: Americans seemed to have found a proper course of action as regards the urban underclass. In her 1991 book *Poverty and Compassion*, Himmelfarb noted with pleasure that her compatriots, after "making the most arduous attempt [in the name of the welfare state] to ... divorce poverty from any moral assumptions and conditions," were ultimately "learning how inseparable the moral and material dimensions of that problem are."[43] To back up this idea of looking at the poverty problem in moral terms, Himmelfarb drew attention to late Victorian England as a model society that had actually succeeded in alleviating poverty while perceiving the question in moral terms. The key to the late Victorians' success had been an ethic founded on a specific idea of "compassion"—that is, compassion not in a "sentimental" but in an "unsentimental mode." "In its sentimental mode," Himmelfarb argued, implicitly referring to liberal enthusiasts of the welfare state, "compassion is an exercise in moral indignation, in feeling good rather than doing good." But in its unsentimental late Victorian mode, "compassion seeks above all to *do* good, and this requires a stern sense of proportion, of reason and self-control."[44]

The key to the late Victorian ethic thus was in the realization that it was in the best interest of the poor that compassion was sometimes "curbed" and benevolent impulses "restrained" so that not every one of the poor was aided and that those cases could be sorted out in which charity could be used "to create the power of self-help," leading, eventually, to self-support.[45] Such an ethos had been the foundation of countless philanthropic and legislative initiatives relating to housing, schooling, and work, and they had been particularly beneficial to the laboring poor. Because of these successful efforts, Americans had "much to learn from the late Victorians."[46] That Himmelfarb indeed meant her historical work to contribute to the current American public debate is confirmed by her 1991 letter to Wilson, in which she stated that she had "tried to make some of the same points [that Wilson makes in *On Character*]—about character, virtue, the idea of respectability—but so obliquely, with reference to another country and another century, that I am not at all sure that the larger principles emerge."[47]

By the turn of the 1990s, both Wilson and Himmelfarb thus felt that they had found some means to alleviate the social ills in America's inner cities. Wilson was more inclined to emphasize the role of the political elites: their need to regain their confidence in "middle-class values" (particularly self-control) and to use public policies to mold the character of citizens—especially that of the underclass. Himmelfarb also emphasized the moral dimensions of the problem, but she was more prone to stress the importance of private poor relief as an instrument through which to instill the virtue of self-reliance.

Why, then, did Wilson and Himmelfarb, in the early and mid-1990s, turn away from these original "civic conservative" viewpoints on "character" cultivation and embrace a new perspective that centered on the Scottish moralists' idea of the natural "moral sense"? The reason is, I believe, that by doing so, they could synthesize their older moralist agenda—moral arguments about poverty, the underclass, and crime—with the neoconservatives' new populist logic. As we have seen, both Wilson and Himmelfarb were, in the 1980s, adopting elements of Kristol's 1983 neoconservative program of explaining to the people why they were right and to the intellectuals why they were wrong. In the 1990s, Wilson and Himmelfarb came to apply a parallel logic to contemporary debates over American inner cities and the black underclass, yet again speaking for the Americanized figure of the common man with a moral sense.

The Wise and Virtuous Everyman and Other
Americans in James Q. Wilson's *The Moral Sense*

Wilson's most important work on the natural moral sense—*The Moral Sense* from 1993—was, on the surface, a descriptive analysis of human moral psychology. This work provides us an opportunity to shed light on neoconservative thought on race, for we may examine how his ostensibly color-blind discussions on the moral sense of ordinary people linked to, or contrasted with, his conceptions of the poor criminal black underclass inhabiting the inner cities. The book, in fact, is a prime example of how Wilson used the concept of the moral sense to distinguish between the supposedly amoral and eccentric liberal perspectives and the ethical, democratic, and "American" approaches to certain social problems often related to the urban black underclass—namely, poverty and crime.

Wilson himself introduced *The Moral Sense* as basically a social scientific work intended to provide further evidence for the eighteenth-century Scottish and English claims about the existence of the natural moral sense. Importantly, though, Wilson stated another aim in the first pages of the book: By showing that such a moral sense did exist, he wanted "to help people recover the confidence with which they once spoke about virtue and morality."[48] That is, while he introduced his book on the moral sense as an attempt to demonstrate its actual existence, he justified his literary effort by referring to the rising tide of cultural and moral relativism. Very much like the eighteenth-century common-sense moralists from Aberdeen that we met in chapter 1, Wilson was here working to erect an intellectual bulwark against moral relativism or uncertainty.

Wilson used a large part of the book's introductory chapter to build an argument against such relativist thinkers as Richard Rorty and A. J. Ayer. To oppose further diffusion of relativism in America, it was crucial, Wilson maintained, to be able to demonstrate that something like a natural moral sense indeed existed; in his words, that "mankind has a moral nature to which we commonly and inevitably appeal when trying to defend our moral arguments."[49] "The moral 'sense,'" he wrote, "exists in two meanings of the word: First, virtually everyone, beginning at a very young age, makes moral judgments that, though they may vary greatly in complexity, sophistication, and wisdom, distinguish between actions on the grounds that some are right and others wrong, and virtually everyone recognizes that for these distinctions to be persuasive to others they must be, or at least appear to be, disinterested. Second, virtually everyone, beginning at a very young age, acquires a set of social habits that we ordinarily find pleasing in others and satisfying when we practice them ourselves."[50]

In *The Moral Sense*, Wilson introduced "four examples" or "dimensions" of the moral sense, referring to them also as "moral senses." They were (1) sympathy—that is, "our sense of another's feelings and of their appropriateness given the circumstances";[51] (2) fairness, in its three forms as equity, reciprocity, and impartiality;[52] (3) self-control—namely, an ability to take a longer view of one's interests and to forgo immediate pleasure;[53] and (4) duty—that is, "the disposition to honor obligations even without hope of reward or fear of punishment."[54]

For a correct understanding of Wilson's idea of the moral sense, in philosophical terms, it is important to bear in mind Wilson's aforementioned notion that "the moral sense exists in two meanings of the word." That is, Wilson claimed not only that it was a universal commonplace to acquire "social habits" relating to sympathy, fairness, self-control, and duty; he also claimed that it was a universal commonplace to believe that one *ought to* sympathize with others, be fair in dealings with others, control one's impulses, and honor obligations. Wilson thus underlined that even if he was "interested in why people act as they do," he was "more interested in why people *judge* actions as they do." The moral senses, according to him, were "the basis for much of that judging," and therefore it was those that he wanted to "dissect."[55] Moreover, Wilson wanted to "stress that these are four aspects of the moral *sense*, not four moral rules or laws." His book was "not an effort to state or justify moral rules." Indeed, Wilson denied that he wrote *The Moral Sense* in order to "discover facts that will prove values" or "to make a case for or against some currently disputed moral question."[56] As noted in chapter 3, his plan was to write a different kind of book on "those policy questions that engage our moral sentiments" after the publication of *The Moral Sense*.[57]

The moral relativism of intellectuals was, then, an explicit theme in *The Moral Sense*, which in itself makes the book a contribution to the culture wars of the 1990s. The book is an important document of the neoconservative culture wars not only because of this anti-intellectual dimension but also because of the implicit role of the urban black underclass in it. That is, in the book, Wilson embraced the social role of an expert in public morality while using the moral sense idea to establish common guidelines for debate about the urban black underclass, a debate in which, he hoped, "bourgeois" virtues, such as self-control, would not be despised as outdated and reactionary means to repress the lower orders. To justify an interpretation of Wilson's 1993 book as a normative response to late twentieth-century American inner-city decay, it must be shown first that in Wilson's understanding, there still were, at the time, pressing urban problems to solve. Second, it must be shown that normative elements were at least *blended into The Moral Sense*—in other words, that his methods were an amalgamation of descriptive and normative elements. As we will see, such a reading of *The Moral Sense* indeed is possible.[58]

Today we know that in 1992–93, when *The Moral Sense* was about to go to press, many of the most pressing inner-city problems, in particular different forms of crime in both urban and rural areas, had just begun to moderate—albeit this change of direction was barely observable at the time. The general picture of crime in the United States in the second half of the twentieth century is that the half century divides, as Franklin Zimring puts it, "into two trendless periods—one prior to 1964 and another between 1974 and 1993—and two clear trends: one a decade after 1964, when the homicide rate more than doubled, and the period after 1991, when it dropped consistently."[59] The 1990s is known among criminologists for its great crime decline, which was "the longest and deepest decline in crime by far in the United States since World War II."[60] For most "index crimes"—homicide, rape, robbery, aggravated assault, burglary, auto theft, larceny—the decline in the nine years after 1991 was between 35 and 40 percent (only in larceny and aggravated assault the reduction was significantly smaller), with the year 1992 being "the first year that homicide rates were lower than the previous annual total."[61] However, it was only in 1996 and 1997 that mounting evidence began to indicate a non-standard decline in crime rates. Indeed, for those who were thinking about (urban) crime rates in the first years of the crime decline of the 1990s, the experience of the previous decade was not very encouraging: even if crime had declined sharply also in the early 1980s for four years, it had increased very rapidly—by 1991—back to the highs of 1974 and 1980.[62]

Considering that in 1992–93 those who were considered experts in the field of crime did not yet know whether one was witnessing a nonstandard decline in urban crime rates or ordinary cyclical variation without any specific causes, it is not surprising that Wilson claimed in 1993 that there still were pressing inner-city problems to solve. In the opening chapter of *The Moral Sense*, he wrote about the global crime wave that had begun around 1960. The choice of words in phrases such as "rising crime rates worry Americans" indicates not only that he approached the question from the perspective of the ordinary citizen but also that he highlighted urban decay as an acute social problem. Unlike most liberal criminologists, Wilson underscored cultural change as one root of those social ills. He found it intriguing that crime had increased over the past couple of decades in the United States, as well as elsewhere in the world, even if it had been a time of economic growth. (In fact, as noted, the significant increase in crime rates in the United States had occurred in just about ten years between 1964 and 1974, after which it stayed on a high level.) The high crime rates during a time of economic growth encouraged Wilson to make the general argument that the world had experienced, over the course of the last hundred years, "a shift from an era in which crime chiefly responded to material circumstances to one in which it responds in large measure to cultural ones." More specifically, he pointed to the "collapse in the legitimacy of what once was respectfully called middle-class morality" as one of the many causes of that shift.[63] This is, of course, consistent with the interpretation of *The Moral Sense* as a normative response to the urban decay of the post-1960s decades.

While it is true that Wilson's aforementioned remark about a "crime wave" was a reference to the *global* crime wave and while it was only a short section in the book's introductory chapter, it is also the case that in the later chapters of the book—which discuss the various aspects of the natural moral sense (sympathy, self-control, duty, fairness, moral development, and the gender differences associated with moral valuation)—an attentive reader can discern a rather gloomy diagnosis of the American urban condition. Four representative examples from different parts of the book should be enough to prove the point: In a chapter on the gender aspects of the moral sense—in which Wilson discussed gender differences in temperament, socialization, reproductive success, and moral orientation—he remarked that "marauding male gangs have excited fear for as long as man has lived in cities" and that "American gangs" that "are found chiefly among the inner-city poor" are only the latest chapter in this story.[64] In a chapter on sympathy, Wilson discussed at length the weak status of altruism and cooperation in large cities, in which people were more likely to "reward individual achievement."[65] Sympathy was easily aroused "by the sight of one hungry child," but as easily, it disappeared "by the sight of thousands," and by the same logic, America's city dwellers had been willing to help homeless people in the streets when there had been only a few of them around, whereas today, "the sight of scores of importuning people causes some onlookers to feel anger rush in to replace a waning sympathy."[66] To continue with the American urban theme, in a chapter on family and moral development, Wilson argued that "teenage mothers in American cities . . . often do not make very good mothers."[67] And to take one more example from the concluding chapter, Wilson noted that he was writing "these lines not long after terrible riots [i.e. the 'Rodney King riots' of 1992] wracked the city that I love, Los Angeles."[68] Thus at the very least, one may conclude that Wilson had the problems of the American inner-city poor in his mind while he was writing *The Moral Sense*.

While the essential subject matter of "civic conservatism"—namely, the degradation of inner-city life in America—thus was very visible in *The Moral Sense*, there was also one obvious linguistic divergence from the older mainstream civic conservatism. That is, Wilson did not explicitly refer to the "underclass" in his 1993 book. Yet the black urban underclass was an *implicit* theme in *The Moral Sense*. The fact that Wilson defined both the underclass and the moral sense in relation to "self-control"—defined as a willingness to postpone gratification—indicates that he saw a connection between these two subjects. Equally importantly, when one compares Wilson's choice of words in his 1993 book and in his other writings that tackled the underclass problem explicitly, an almost inevitable conclusion is that Wilson makes an implicit point about the (largely) African American underclass in *The Moral Sense*. In order to see this, one needs to keep in mind that Wilson had, in the 1980s, shifted toward an interpretation of the black underclass as a victim of elite culture. That is, he had mused over the possibility to "interpret the underclass as simply that group in our society most vulnerable to false prophecies [of the elite]." The underclass was, according to this interpretation, "a 'dialect' of the elite culture that celebrates personal liberation, denounces conformity, values the avant-garde, and regards the core traditions of the republic as nothing more than a camouflage for repression and greed. Elite culture is a curse inflicted by the haves on the have-nots."[69] Second, one must be aware of Wilson's view that the underclass was a small fraction of the whole society, to the point that, although it was "perceived to be a black phenomenon," it accounted "for only a small fraction of the black community."[70] When these two views—not presented in *The Moral Sense* but in Wilson's other works— are acknowledged, one will be in a perfect position to see that Wilson had the urban black underclass in mind when he, in his 1993 book, referred to the "tiny fraction" of people that was most susceptible to fall into criminal habits under the influence of deleterious cultural change.[71]

To be entirely accurate, in *The Moral Sense*, Wilson implicitly suggested a twist on the interpretation of the underclass as a "dialect of the elite culture." That is, in the first chapter of the book, he argued that most people—but not quite everyone—possessed a kind of immunity to dubious elite thought systems that might encourage a life of crime: "To the extent that there is something in mankind that leads us to hold back from a life of crime, it must be something that, at least for most of us, is immune to the philosophical doubts, therapeutic nostrums, and ideological zealotry with which the modern age has been so thoroughly infected." Alongside this immunity-possessing mainstream, Wilson identified some "marginal persons at risk for crime," individuals who made up "a tiny fraction of all people." Due to prosperity and modern technology, this "small cohort of serious offenders" had acquired "the ability to commit crimes over a much wider territory, to reach more victims, and to take more lethal actions than once was the case," insomuch that there was "at least three times as much violent crime today as there was thirty years ago."[72] Bearing in mind that Wilson defined the mostly black underclass as the most crime-prone fraction of the nation ("the permanently poor" and "the habitually criminal"), the absence of the exact term (black) *underclass* from *The Moral Sense* begins to look like a minor semantic detail.[73] And due to this implicit presence of the African American underclass, it is justified to say that Wilson's 1993 book—and his neo-conservative version of moral sense theory in general—distinguished between *three* different social classes, not only the "relativist" elites and the working- and middle-class "ordinary people" but also the disoriented and dangerous black underclass.

In Wilson's *The Moral Sense*, there was, then, an acute awareness of a pressing social problem in America—the decay of inner cities—that largely resulted from the black urban underclass' embrace of a present-oriented and criminal lifestyle after having fallen victim to the moral relativism of the liberal elites. Did Wilson provide any solutions? He did, and he introduced them as flowing from what he called the "ordinary citizen's" instinctive moral sense capacity.

Here we confront head-to-head the question of the normative elements of *The Moral Sense*, as well as Wilson's method of populist persuasion and implicit white identity politics. Even if the core chapters of Wilson's book consist mainly of excursions into social science intended to illuminate "such topics as gender differences, family dynamics, the origins of our moral sentiments, and why the human animal is the way he/she is" (as Irving Kristol described the book's contents), both the opening and the concluding chapters are best understood as efforts to persuade the reader of the value of the "ordinary citizen's perspective" as a cure for those social ills that we just saw him diagnosing.[74] It is in these parts of the book that Wilson most candidly indicated that his text was intended as a response to (and remedy for) both the social problem of urban decay and the allegedly sorry condition of current moral philosophy that was for him an important source of such decay. Wilson's point seems to have been that "ordinary people's"—here referring to working- and middle-class citizens—perspective on moral issues was exactly what was needed to "bring our governing elites to their senses" (as Kristol would say) because this perspective was "balanced" among the four different moral senses.[75] Elite perspectives, to say nothing of the value system of the black underclass, were in this regard defective and, indeed, harmful.

Wilson implicitly introduced himself as a spokesperson for these "ordinary citizens," therefore becoming just the latest incarnation of the social type that was born in eighteenth-century Britain—the educated expert in popular moral sensibilities.

To understand Wilson's method of populist persuasion, one should take notice of both his relatively optimistic treatment of the supposed general ways of judging a fellow citizen's character in America in the concluding chapter and his gloomier anti-intellectual observations in the preface and first chapter. In the context of a discussion on the rise of moral relativism in American academia early in the book, Wilson lamented that the dubious moral theories put forward by America's intellectual elite had, despite the ordinary Americans' alleged "immunity" to the elite's "ideological zealotry," also made ordinary citizens confused about their own moral feelings. The citizen had "gone to great lengths to deny that he has a perspective to take," and he was "nervous or on guard when hearing someone speak of virtue or character." All in all, American "intellectual culture" had left ordinary men and women "alone to cope with" a frightening prospect—namely, "the possibility that by behaving as if no moral judgments were possible we may create a world that more and more resembles our diminished moral expectations." For this reason, Wilson wanted to help "rebuild" "the basis of moral judgments," which, according to him, required "us to take the perspective of the citizen."[76]

An elucidation of such a salutary citizen's perspective followed in the last chapter of *The Moral Sense*, which discussed the regular ways of judging a good character in America. Here the essential concept was the "balance" of the moral senses. Wilson saw it as encouraging that it was still common in the United States, in spite of the recent cultural changes, to judge fellow citizens' character according to *all four* moral senses—namely, sympathy, fairness, self-control, and duty. He acknowledged that some expressions that had been used in reference to a good (balanced) character had grown old-fashioned but added that there were still in use certain terms with which to denote persons with a good "balance sheet" of different virtues. The talk of "ladies" and "gentlemen" might have been a "vanishing" discourse among ordinary citizens, to say nothing of the liberal elite, but it was still common to think and speak of certain fellow citizens as "nice persons" or "good guys."[77]

Although Wilson was here discussing the supposed common American ways of judging a character, one may—considering his frustration with the confusion induced by relativist elite culture—take it for granted that he was explicating *his own* ideal of a virtuous character when he wrote about the "human balance sheet." In the beginning of his book, Wilson, as noted earlier, remarked that he "wrote the book to help people recover the confidence with which they once spoke about virtue and morality," but it seems that he also had a more specified "civic conservative" goal: by giving "self-control" and "duty" a place in the "human balance sheet," he specifically wanted to help people recover the confidence with which they once spoke of duty and, in particular, self-control.[78] Through this, he was setting parameters for debate about the "present-oriented" underclass. As Wilson was sketching a portrait of "a nice person" who had a good balance sheet of the different virtues, he remarked that such a person was "fair in dealings with others" and took "into account the feelings of others." However, Wilson promoted his key normative message when he described how such a "nice person" "has prudent self-control; that is, . . . the nice person [unlike the present-oriented member of the underclass] tries to take the long view when the more distant goal is clearly superior to the immediate one. . . . When this is difficult he looks for ways to force himself to do the right thing."[79]

Wilson's discussion on the citizen's perspective and of the four "moral senses" in which it was rooted in is best understood as a "naturalization" of the older mainstream civic conservative argument. In *The Moral Sense*, Wilson used the language of the eighteenth-century Scottish moralists to transform into ahistorical psychological categories (i.e., "moral senses") the "bourgeois" values of duty and self-control, which allegedly had fallen out of favor in American elite culture and which mainstream civic conservatism had claimed to be necessary to combat urban problems. That is to say, Wilson identified human moral nature with many of the values and norms that were commonly prized in midcentury white middle-class America (what Andrew Hartman refers to as the "normative America" of the 1950s), values that included personal responsibility (duty), delayed gratification (self-control), and individual merit.[80] In contrast to mainstream "civic conservatism," including Wilson's older works such as *On Character*, his main point no longer was that self-control was part of a bygone "bourgeois interior" or "middle-class" value system. Instead, he now argued that self-control was part of a nearly universal moral code that was based on biological factors. The all-important virtue of self-control appeared in a totally new light owing to the fact that it was presented as one of the four universally respected virtues or character traits alongside fairness, sympathy, and duty. Of course, the same goes also for the old, reviled Anglo-American ethos of self-control, which had been suppressed by an ethos of self-expression. Seen from this novel naturalistic and anthropological perspective, if there was something questionable in late twentieth-century American moral discourse, it was not the "old-fashioned" or "conservative" ethos that valued self-control over self-expression but the liberal elite's hostility toward such an ethos that was, after all, based on the evolved characteristics of the human mind.

To make such an argument concerning a moral code that was rooted in "natural" or "innate" moral senses but that had then (partly) collapsed, it was essential to emphasize that innateness did not signify any sort of old-fashioned biological determinism. Rather, the moral senses were more about an inherited *potential.* In fact, it was just the fact that Wilson defined the moral senses in the context of the modern idea of nature-nurture interaction that it became possible for him to link an "innatist" idea of the moral senses with the civic conservatives' earlier *cultural* argument about the recent loss of respect for self-control in America. As Wilson put it in *The Moral Sense* (rather vaguely), the "strength of the moral senses" were revealed only "when circumstances permit their fuller expression and wider effect."[81]

The key concept that tied together Wilson's biopsychological argument about the nature of the human psyche and the cultural critical argument of civic conservatism was, in fact, not "innate moral sense" but "fragile moral sense" (the word fragile appears four times in *The Moral Sense* in connection with "moral sense" or a corresponding concept).[82] When the moral sense had been described as fragile, indeed, as "a small candle flame . . . flickering and sputtering in the strong winds of power and passion, greed and ideology," Wilson could move rather smoothly between the two languages of moral innatism and cultural criticism.[83] He could make, for example, the ominous remark that the moral sense was "not always and in every aspect of life strong enough to withstand a pervasive and sustained attack."[84] Most importantly, by emphasizing the "fragility" of the natural moral sense, Wilson highlighted the dramatic situation—especially in the inner cities—of his home country.

What does all this then tell us about Wilson's, and neoconservative, racial thought? It suggests that the eminent neoconservative crime specialist did not see "crime and violence as somehow innate among African Americans," as Hinton claims in her book on the post-1960s War on Crime (which studies an earlier period, the 1960s and 1970s).[85] Rather, Wilson suggested in his 1990s works that the current condition of the black underclass was in large part a result of twentieth-century liberal elites' unwillingness to stress the importance of a life of virtue. *The Moral Sense*, the personal favorite of Wilson among his many books, offers strong evidence for the claim that the neoconservatives' major opponent in the culture wars was not the black underclass but the mostly white liberal intellectual and cultural elite that allegedly fostered nonjudgmentality and uncertainty. To be sure, in Wilson's works, the black underclass was not portrayed in a favorable light either: it was not an active player in any positive meaning but rather a victim of a relativist elite culture—a victim that behaved badly largely because it lacked a healthy family environment and a normally developed moral sense that made "ordinary Americans" immune to demoralizing relativist ideas. Still, Wilson's thought on the underclass does not include racist assumptions about black inferiority seen in early twentieth-century biological racism.

The hero of Wilson's *The Moral Sense* was the intuitively moral working- and middle-class "ordinary citizen." His method of persuasion was that of moral populism in the sense that moral wisdom, in his book, came from an ordinary citizen's instinctive capacity to perceive the world in moral terms, and the ordinary citizen was defined in opposition to intellectual elites. In fact, Wilson himself made it explicit after his book had come out that *The Moral Sense* dealt with the question, *In whom* should Americans trust when the nation wished to define what is right and what is wrong? He was forced to make this question explicit shortly after the publication of *The Moral Sense*, after one of the book's reviewers had (correctly) accused Wilson of "moral populism."[86] In his response, Wilson admitted that he actually *did* wish to make a case for the superiority of the ordinary citizen's moral sensibility over the views of the American elites. "I will plead guilty," Wilson wrote, "to being a bit of what [Elliot Turiel] calls a 'moral populist.' . . . In retrospect I suppose that I did overstate the difference in moral sensibility between intellectuals and what I persist in thinking of as real people. Had I two of the classic virtues—temperance and prudence—in greater supply, I would have tempered that language without entirely abandoning the point."[87]

Wilson's unpublished papers affirm that the populist spirit of *The Moral Sense* was not the result of oblivion or carelessness. As noted in chapter 2, he already wrote in 1990 to the Sloan Foundation's Arthur Singer that he wanted to write what became *The Moral Sense* "to give intellectual substance to common understandings about right conduct."[88] Wilson's book was, then, a populist work, and populism, as Jan-Werner Müller notes, is by definition an exclusionary form of identity politics in the sense that it dismisses parts of the citizenry "as immoral and not properly a part of the people at all."[89] One may or may not agree with Wilson that self-control is a virtue that ought to be encouraged among people residing in the inner cities, but by portraying middle Americans as the *only* "real people" (as he admitted to have done)— that is, by encouraging the exclusion of academic and other elites as well as the underclass from this idealized group—Wilson ignored the fact that (liberal) democracy requires the acceptance of pluralism and that we, as Müller puts it, "find fair terms of living together as free, equal, but also irreducibly diverse citizens."[90]

A Poor Man's Moral Sense and the Ethic of Self-Help

Earlier in this chapter, we saw that Himmelfarb affirmed in a 1991 letter to Wilson that she had "tried to make some of the same points [that Wilson made in *On Character*]—about character, virtue, the idea of respectability— but so obliquely, with reference to another country and another century [nineteenth-century Britain]" that she was "not at all sure that the larger principles emerge[d]."[91] In the 1990s and early 2000s, she turned her scholarly attention to the previous century—"the British Enlightenment"—yet these works seem to have been similarly intended as commentaries on America's present cultural condition and politics rather than solely as historical analyses of eighteenth-century thought. In articles such as "The Idea of Compassion: The British vs. the French Enlightenment" and the 2004 book *The Roads to Modernity: The British, French, and American Enlightenments*, the neoconservative historian discussed eighteenth-century British thinkers and social actors from Adam Smith to Methodist preacher John Wesley and argued that at the heart of the "social ethic" of the British Enlightenment had been a widely held belief in a natural "moral sense."[92]

Despite being, outwardly, historical studies of Enlightenment thought, many of Himmelfarb's texts on eighteenth-century moral sense philosophy were intended as contributions to contemporary debates over poverty and the welfare state. That is, she reintroduced the moral sense idea to her American readers to illustrate how they ought to view, in moral terms, the underprivileged citizens of their country—namely, the ordinary people, the potential receivers of welfare benefits—as people who were capable and willing to enhance their lot and to better themselves. If revived in late twentieth-century America, the British Enlightenment idea of the commonly shared moral sense, she suggested, would help resuscitate a social ethic based on the virtue of self-reliance after the allegedly failed post-1960s attempts to construct a generous welfare state.

Equally importantly, by implying that the proponents of a generous welfare state did *not* appreciate the moral sense of ordinary people, Himmelfarb painted a picture of liberal decision-makers and intellectuals as condescending elitists. Inasmuch as Himmelfarb reinvented British Enlightenment ideas to serve as instruments in a political battle whose terms were set by the emergence of post-1960s liberalism, she—the preeminent neoconservative historian—must be seen as a shaper of the Scottish tradition rather than as an objective chronicler of it. Put differently, Himmelfarb's 1990s and early 2000s writings on the British Enlightenment and the moral sense idea follow the logic of "civic conservatism" in the sense that they were meant to show

how contemporary Americans ought to battle poverty and how they could "rescue" the underclass from welfare dependency and related problems by bringing them within middle-class culture.

For Himmelfarb, the need for a reconsideration of America's system of poverty reduction and the revival of a social ethic based on the moral sense idea stemmed from two factors. First, as we saw earlier, she had argued in *Poverty and Compassion* in 1991 that the welfare-statist crusades, such as the War on Poverty, had been all but failures in both economic and moral terms. Himmelfarb drew attention to this theme, focusing on the urban underclass, throughout the 1990s. Drawing on journalist and historian Myron Magnet's widely noticed 1993 book *The Dream and the Nightmare: The Sixties' Legacy to the Underclass*, she claimed in her own similarly popular *De-moralization of Society* (1995) that the underclass was a legacy of the social and cultural revolutions of the 1960s: the welfare programs of the Great Society had provided "counterincentives to leaving poverty," and the cultural revolution had "disparaged the behavior and attitudes that traditionally made for economic improvement—'deferral of gratification, sobriety, thrift, dogged industry, and so on through the whole catalogue of antique-sounding bourgeois virtues.'" Like Wilson, Himmelfarb thus considered the underclass "not only the victim of its own culture, the 'culture of poverty,'" but "also the victim of the upper-class culture around it."[93]

While Himmelfarb considered the underclass to be mainly a black phenomenon, she stressed that the "two nations in America today," one of them suffering from a "pathology of poverty" and the other one not, were "distinguished neither by money nor by class. Nor are they two racially divided nations. . . . The distinctive features of our two nations are ethos and culture rather than class, race, or ethnicity."[94] Drawing on Wilson and others, she claimed that it had been "conclusively demonstrated" that the single-parent family was "the most important factor associated with the 'pathology of poverty'—welfare dependency, crime, drugs, illiteracy, homelessness." Thus she did not regard race as an all-important factor in the underclass phenomenon and noted in 1995 that a "white underclass with much the same pathology as the black" was currently developing. At the time, in the mid-1990s, the white underclass was, according to her, "smaller and less conspicuous than the black (partly because it is more dispersed) but rapidly increasing."[95] On the last point, she drew on Charles Murray's widely noticed 1993 *Wall Street Journal* article "The Coming White Underclass."[96]

Second, the need for the restoration of a social ethic based on the moral sense idea, for Himmelfarb, stemmed from current political and intellectual elite's condescending approach to the poor and their moral powers. In her

1991 book *Poverty and Compassion*, she had argued that in the nineteenth century, upper and middle-class confidence in ordinary people's moral potential had been the key to successful poverty relief. In Victorian England, she wrote, "the primary objective of any enterprise or reform was that it contribute to the moral improvement of the poor—at the very least, that it not have a deleterious moral effect." Himmelfarb underlined that such "compassionate" acts from the part of the Victorian upper and middle classes were made possible by an underlying confidence in the virtuous potential of ordinary people. The entire late Victorian ethic would have been unthinkable, she insisted, unless the virtues admired by the Victorians (respectability, responsibility, decency, industriousness, prudence, temperance) would not have been considered "common, everyday virtues, within the capacity of ordinary people."[97]

It was, then, the fall of this late Victorian social ethic that was behind Himmelfarb's urge to reintroduce in present-day America the moral sense philosophy of the Scottish philosophers. The first blow to the late Victorian social ethic had been given in the early twentieth century by Bloomsbury's modern artists and writers, such as Virginia Woolf, who had postulated a strict dichotomy between themselves and ordinary people, insisting on a complete freedom from any kind of moral obligations or duties. According to these influential cultural revolutionaries, Himmelfarb maintained, "Ordinary people were bound, as they had always been, by the habits and customs devised for 'timid natures who dare not allow their souls free play.'"[98] In *One Nation, Two Cultures* (1999), Himmelfarb showed how the final blow to the Victorian social ethic had been given by the counterculture of the 1960s that disseminated the ethic of self-expression to parts of the wider public.[99]

Himmelfarb's decision to write a series of works on the eighteenth-century moral sense idea in the 1990s and early 2000s was then at least partly motivated by a desire to show that it would probably pay off to reclaim the moral sense idea in contemporary America in order to revive the key intellectual element of the old successful individualistic social ethic of the eighteenth- and nineteenth-century British society. For her, a widely held belief in the natural moral sense of ordinary people was a prerequisite for an effective poverty alleviation based on private charity that was badly needed after the economically and morally failed attempts to reduce poverty via a generous welfare state. An alternative to the current American system of poverty relief was desperately needed, Himmelfarb insisted, for she still, even in the late 1990s—a time of declining welfare dependency and crime rates—considered poverty and related urban problems to be a serious social crisis. "The lowering or stabilization of some of the indices of social disarray," she asserted in 1999, "does not begin to bring us back to the status quo ante, before their precipitous rise in the 1960s and '70s."[100]

Himmelfarb's neoconservative reinvention of Scottish moral sense philosophy in the 1990s was encouraged by Wilson's *The Moral Sense*. When
Wilson published his 1993 book, Himmelfarb seized on the moral sense idea
almost immediately. In her 1995 book *De-moralization of Society*, she noted
how "James Q. Wilson suggests that hidden behind the present usage of 'values' is the idea of a 'moral sense,' so that 'values' has become a code word
for 'virtues.'"[101] A year later, she lectured on eighteenth-century moral sense
philosophy in Castel Gandolfo near Rome by the title "Armut und zweierlei
Aufklärung" (Poverty and the two kinds of enlightenments). In many public
lectures and texts, including *Roads to Modernity*, she kept up the theme, so
that between the mid-1990s and early 2000s, her work no longer revolved
around the late Victorian ethic and the idea of "compassion" but around the
British Enlightenment and *its* "social ethic." Making moral sense the philosophical hub of her work, her new thesis was, in short, that "'benevolence,'
'compassion,' 'sympathy,' 'fellow-feeling,' a 'natural affection for others'—
under one label or another, this moral sense (or sentiment, as Smith preferred) was the basis of the social ethic that informed British philosophical
and moral discourse for the whole of the eighteenth century."[102] She intended
to remind Americans "of those 'habits of the mind' and 'habits of the heart'
that produced a social ethic all too easily ignored in the light of the more
dramatic claims of the French Enlightenment." The British Enlightenment,
she suggested, was reformist rather than subversive, and its social ethic was
more humane than the French Enlightenment's.[103]

One of the striking aspects of Himmelfarb's neoconservative reading
of Scottish moral philosophy was the connection she made between the
eighteenth-century moral sentimentalism and populism. She underlined how
the ideas of common sense and the moral sense—the latter of which for her
included the "moral sentiments" school of Hume and Smith—made the British moral philosophers "respectful of the common man." Such eighteenth-
century ideas, for the neoconservative historian, "made for a social ethic that
was populist and, in a profound sense, egalitarian, for the moral sense and
common sense were the common denominators of rich and poor alike, the
believer and non-believer, the educated and uneducated, the enlightened and
unenlightened."[104] It is, however, hard to make a case that Smith's and Hume's
philosophy was "populist" in its orientation if one agrees with modern students of populism who define it as a form of persuasion that constructs an opposition between the elites and the common people and presents the people
as the unerring source of truth.[105] Since Smith and Hume never portrayed the
people as the infallible source of truth nor systematically attacked elitism—
and Smith even claimed that "the great mob of mankind are the admirers and

worshippers . . . of wealth and greatness"—one must conclude that Himmelfarb's account of the "two Enlightenments" exaggerated the difference between the sentimentalist and democratic Scottish and rationalist and elitist French traditions and, in so doing, served the needs of neoconservatives in the 1980s and 1990s.[106] Moreover, as noted earlier, there were many rationalists in both England and Scotland, and there were French and other continental sentimentalists.

Such inaccuracies notwithstanding, Himmelfarb used both her historical works and shorter political commentaries to promote the moral sense idea as an important perspective in current poverty reduction debates. In her historical studies, she claimed that the idea of the moral sense was all-important in eighteenth-century Britain because it had become a foundation for a morally egalitarian social ethic that underlined poor people's capacity for moral, spiritual, material, and social self-improvement.

It was Francis Hutcheson's influence on eighteenth-century Methodists, Himmelfarb explained, that best exemplified moral sense philosophy's potential as a foundation for an ethic that was "not only social and religious but also, in important respects, individualistic."[107] John Wesley, she remarked, had "admitted a philosophical affinity with Francis Hutcheson, whose religious views he deplored but whose idea of a moral sense he recognized as akin to his own idea of an 'internal sense,' or 'conscience,' that made men relish the happiness of others." The Methodist preachers' special merit was not their philosophical refinement but that they "were giving practical effect to that idea [of the moral sense] by spreading a religious gospel of good works, engaging in a variety of humanitarian causes, and welcoming the poor into their fold."[108] A crucial outcome of this social ethic was that the "poor themselves were caught up in the same ethos that motivated the reformers and philanthropists, an ethos that combined a communal spirit with that of self-help. The Friendly Societies—insurance clubs, essentially—founded by workers for their mutual aid, were voluntary and independent, self-governing and self-supporting."[109] Insofar as Himmelfarb, in her 2004 book *Roads to Modernity*, hoped to make a (normative) point about general principles along with the aim of illuminating past reality—as she had done in her earlier books according to her letter to Wilson—she was here using the eighteenth-century British thinkers to *promote* both the idea of the moral sense and the principle of self-help, portraying them as cornerstones of a social ethic that was humane, respectful of the poor, and in a positive sense "populist."

Himmelfarb invoked the moral sense idea to encourage an ethos of self-help also in her political commentary. A particularly good example is her analysis of George W. Bush's Republican ideology of "compassionate conservatism." In this commentary that dates from the Bush era and beyond, Himmelfarb argued that contemporary American conservatives who were reconsidering their social policy ideas would profit from taking instruction from the Scottish moral philosophers and social and religious activists. She advised the present-day conservatives to reconsider the Scottish ideas of "compassion," as well as "sympathy," "moral sense" and "moral sentiments," "social affections," and "social virtues"—ideas that, according to her, had given a unique character to the British Enlightenment.[110] During Bush's first term, she commended American political conservatives in the politically oriented epilogue to *Roads to Modernity*, for they seemed to be breaking loose from their earlier contempt for the idea of compassion, a term easily associated with the liberal, generous welfare state. The Republican Party's recent embrace of "compassionate conservativism" was a testament to this. The party's intention was not to expand government programs, Himmelfarb explained, but to "strengthen civil society and thus reduce the role of the state by channeling the sentiment of compassion into voluntary and communal endeavors." The ultimate purpose of such efforts, the neoconservative historian stressed, was "to enhance the moral sense of the giver and the receiver alike, to encourage the social affections of the one while respecting the moral dignity and integrity of the other."[111]

A couple of years after Bush's presidency ended, though, Himmelfarb grew dissatisfied with what had resulted from the policy of compassionate conservatism. She confessed in the neoconservative *Weekly Standard* that ultimately it had meant "yet another round of programs conceived and financed by the government and farmed out to 'faith-based' (a euphemism for 'religious') institutions."[112] The foremost neoconservative authority on intellectual history saw this failure as an opportunity to call attention, again, to the eighteenth-century Scottish moralists. A "new generation of conservatives," she suggested, "may well look to some old sages for inspiration—to Adam Smith most notably, not only for his economic principles but also for the moral vision that informed them." The merit in Smith's philosophy, for Himmelfarb, was that it "moralizes the economy even as it liberalizes and liberates it from the government and the state," at the same time as "the people are moralized." Himmelfarb suggested that Smith's philosophy moralizes and liberalizes the economy because it shows that poverty reduction could be, for the most part, left to compassionate individuals and "societies." It also moralizes the citizenry because "the working classes, including the very poor," were said to have a motive to help themselves. Thus what Himmelfarb wanted conservatives to do was "to recapture compassion from the liberals," since, "properly understood," compassion was "a preeminently conservative virtue."[113]

Do Himmelfarb's writings on the moral sense of ordinary people, includ-ing the "very poor," then, offer evidence for the claim—made by such scholars as Jean-François Drolet and Thomas McCarthy—that the neoconservative discourse on the "dysfunctional behaviors" of the underclass "operates ac-cording to the same logic as the biological racial theories of society and de-velopment discredited in the second half of the twentieth century"?[114] Do they offer evidence for Drolet's related argument that the black underclass was a vital enemy of the neoconservatives in the culture wars, an "undesirable other" that neoconservatism as a thought system necessarily needed?[115] Or do Himmelfarb's writings give evidence for the more moderate interpretation of neoconservative thought on race—namely, that the neoconservatives were cosmopolitan intellectuals who gave voice to a color-blind world view while ignoring the unique history of discrimination against blacks in America?[116]

Before drawing conclusions, one should first ask whether it is useful to speak in general terms of a "neoconservative" outlook on race. A comparison between Himmelfarb's and Wilson's respective takes on the moral qualities of ordinary citizens and the urban underclass reveals some significant differ-ences between the "racial" thought of even these two close friends and fel-low neoconservatives. Wilson, in *The Moral Sense*, drew attention to the *dif-ferences* between working- and middle-class "ordinary citizens"—who were typically raised in the stable and caring environment seen necessary to the development of the moral sense—and a relatively small number of habitual criminals in the inner cities (i.e., the black underclass). The latter group, Wil-son implied, lacked a normally developed moral sense that allegedly was im-mune to demoralizing, relativist elite ideas. Himmelfarb, for her part, spoke of the moral sense of ordinary people to highlight the considerable moral ca-pacities of even the most disadvantaged, including the very poor (receivers of welfare benefits), whether black or white. Himmelfarb's approach was color-blind also in the sense that she claimed that the dependent underclass was not solely a black phenomenon and in the sense that she viewed the underclass as a victim of the liberal cultural elite that was mainly white. With Himmelfarb, then, Drolet misrepresents the case when he argues that neoconservative dis-course on the "dysfunctional behaviors" of the underclass operated according to the "same logic" as the scientific racism of the early twentieth century.

Himmelfarb's moral language was thus color-blind, but it was hardly sym-pathetic of the many black or white poor people whose livelihoods were tem-porarily dependent on social welfare programs. Indeed, she invoked the moral sense idea to set consensual limits for debate about welfare dependency—that is, to rationalize welfare state contraction by emphasizing that the moral sense (understood as a willingness and a capacity for self-improvement) ought to

be understood as an attribute of the poor and rich alike and to criticize proponents of a generous welfare state for *not* appreciating the ordinary citizen's
moral sense. She was not entirely against safety nets, but the thrust of her
argument was to show that efforts to deal with poverty had been both more
successful and more honorable in the past when individuals who were helped
were also expected to show signs of moral virtue and self-help.

This kind of color-blind self-help approach to poverty reduction was a
logical follow-up to those neoconservative statements of the 1960s and 1970s,
according to which the many problems of black communities could best be
met by black private organizations. In other words, as Nathan Glazer wrote in
Beyond the Melting Pot, the key tasks of racial advancement were ones "that
conceivably no one but Negroes can do" (Moynihan, though, in the Moynihan
Report in 1965, did not promote Glazer's argument about the primary necessity of racial self-help but instead suggested that "the Negro family" needed
special attention from the government).[117] Somewhat ironically—but consistent with the general neoconservative meritocratic ethos—Himmelfarb, a
Jewish historian, in her 1990s and early 2000s writings on the moral sense
idea, played down the distinctive history of oppression of African Americans in the United States to make a right-wing argument for welfare state
contraction.

What Himmelfarb added to the neoconservative corpus of the 1990s and
early 2000s with her works on the British Enlightenment was, in effect, a philosophical and historical rationalization of a "conservative welfare state," one
that borrowed the vocabulary of eighteenth-century moral sentimentalist
philosophers rather than Smith's notion of an "invisible hand" in the *Wealth
of Nations*. A "conservative welfare state" was a term used by Kristol to describe a version of the welfare state in which the "general rule has to be: If it
is your own behavior that could land you on welfare, then you don't get it, or
you get very little of it."[118] Himmelfarb refashioned the Scottish philosophies
of the moral sense and moral sentiments to articulate an alternative to the
social democratic ethic of a generous welfare state and to delegitimize liberal
ideas about the welfare state as condescending and elitist, disrespectful of
ordinary people. The Scottish moralists, needless to say, wrote at a time when
nothing like a welfare state existed, and we will never know what they would
have thought about such a system of government entitlements and benefits.
Thus it is questionable, to say the least, to promote (welfare) state contraction
in the name of eighteenth-century Scottish authors. Many present-day advocates of unregulated free market economy, for sure, pretend that Smith attacked state power as such, but he never did—instead he criticized a state that
worked to further the interests of the great manufacturers and merchants at

the expense of consumers and workers, especially the poor. While Smith did oppose government's micromanaging of the economy, he also advocated a role for government in providing education and public works such as canals, roads, and postal services.[119] Once again, then, a neoconservative writer—in this case a renowned historian—using the vocabulary of the Scottish moralists, reinterpreted and actively shaped the Scottish ideas into a neoconservative moral sensibility.

Retributive Sentiments and Criminal Justice: James Q. Wilson on Crime and Punishment

After finishing *The Moral Sense*, James Q. Wilson continued to invoke the moral sense, moral sentiments, and common sense to buttress his politics, now in the context of the exceptionally animated crime control debates of the mid-1990s. This chapter examines Wilson's thinking on criminal justice. In doing so, it continues the theme of chapter 4—neoconservative thought on race—by exploring how Wilson, the foremost neoconservative author on crime, responded to such racially dividing events as the 1992 Los Angeles riots, Bill Clinton's Crime Bill of 1994, and the era's televised and sensationalized court cases such as the O. J. Simpson case, the Lorena Bobbitt case, and the Menendez brothers' case. What we will see is that Wilson's neoconservative reinvention of eighteenth-century Scottish moral philosophy was in part an effort to illustrate and give credibility to the tough-on-crime views of many late twentieth-century Americans and to marginalize liberal experts' seeming tendency to explain rather than to judge criminal behavior. Although Wilson made use of Adam Smith's moral vocabulary in the context of the 1990s crime debates, he distanced himself from Smith's actual ideas on punishment and an "impartial spectator's" possible sympathy for the offender.[1]

Wilson's work on crime and punishment from the 1990s is rarely explored in the literature on neoconservatism. His wide reputation as a theorist of criminal policy is largely based on *Thinking about Crime* from 1975 and "Broken Windows: The Police and Neighborhood Safety" from 1982. The latter text has been described as the "most influential media article on crime policy of its era," one that "provided the rationale for a new strategic emphasis on maintenance of order as a police objective."[2] Together, these works have brought Wilson a reputation as the most sophisticated intellectual architect of the punitive turn in American crime response in the 1970s and 1980s.[3]

It is much less well known how Wilson's ideas and rhetoric on crime and punishment evolved in the 1990s and how he used Scottish moral vocabulary at the time to legitimate a conservative tough-on-crime policy as both right and representative of the people. During this time, America's murder rate first reached its peak (in 1991) and then started to decline, and such sensational-ized court cases as the O. J. Simpson case and the Menendez brothers' case (in the mid-1990s) made Wilson and his compatriots rethink the dilemmas of the American legal system. The mid-1990s was, according to criminologist Franklin Zimring, "one of the angriest and most fearful periods in the mod-ern politics of criminal justice—an era of three 'strikes and you're out' laws and truth-in-sentencing crusades [to abolish or curb parole]. . . . The United States was well into the 1990s crime decline before anybody noticed."[4] Corre-spondingly, in the public eye, crime was the number one problem facing the nation in the mid-1990s.[5]

The Mid-1990s Tough-on-Crime Frenzy and Wilson's Penal Populism

Wilson discussed "ordinary people's" views on crime and the proper role of popular moral sentiments in the justice system repeatedly through the 1990s but tackled the question most comprehensively in his 1997 book *Moral Judg-ment: Does the Abuse Excuse Threaten Our Legal System?* Shorter essays and speeches such as "What to Do about Crime" (1994), "Reading Jurors' Minds" (1996), and *Moral Intuitions* (2000) examined such issues more cursorily. Some of these texts ought to be seen as expressions of penal populism. Ac-cording to criminologist John Pratt's useful definition, penal populism "speaks to the way in which criminals and prisoners are thought to have been favoured at the expense of crime victims in particular and the law-abiding public in general. It feeds on expressions of anger, disenchantment and dis-illusionment with the *criminal justice* establishment. It holds this responsi-ble for what seems to have been the insidious inversion of commonsensical priorities: protecting the well-being and security of law-abiding 'ordinary people', punishing those whose crimes jeopardize this. And as with populism itself, penal populism usually takes the form of 'feelings and intuitions.'"[6]

Wilson used penal populist language not only to convince other Ameri-cans to join his side on questions relating to the criminal justice system but also to define America's crime problem in the mid-1990s. As noted earlier, national statistics showed that levels of crime had begun to decline around the country in 1992–93 (following a sharp rise from the mid-1960s to mid-1970s and a subsequent plateau). The ultimate "fear" crime—homicide—began to drop around 1991.[7] Yet Wilson insisted in the mid-1990s that urban crime—and black crime in particular—was still a deeply troubling issue in the United States. In language typical of penal populism, he approached the question from the perspective of an imaginary, fearful, ordinary citizen.

In a 1994 *Commentary* essay "What to Do about Crime," for example, Wilson argued that the "public" was "quite correct" in its assessment "that today's crime problem is different from and more serious than that of earlier decades." The public was right, Wilson affirmed, to claim that the crime problem had been actually getting worse lately, since America's youth, and black youth especially, had gotten out of control in the late 1980s and early 1990s: these "youngsters" were "shooting at people at a far higher rate than at any time in recent history."[8] That is, Wilson rationalized the public unrest by noting that despite the leveling off or even dropping of the *adult* homicide rate between 1980 and 1990, youth homicide rates had "shot up" after 1985. Relying on a recent criminological study, he noted that between 1985 and 1992, "the homicide rate for young white males [aged fourteen to seventeen] went up by about 50 percent but for young black males it *tripled*."[9] What Wilson did not tell his readers was that *whenever* the public has been polled about changes in crime rates, most people have responded that they believe crime rates have been increasing rapidly. This is not to say that Americans were entirely wrong about crime rates in the 1990s: they were right in thinking that over a long-term period, about thirty years, the (general) crime rate had increased.[10]

Wilson's definition of America's current crime problem thus underlined the opposition between the violent black youngsters and the frightened ordinary Americans. Two days after the devastating 1992 Los Angeles riots—which erupted after four white policemen charged for beating an African American taxi driver, Rodney King, had been acquitted and during which sixty-three people lost their lives—Wilson drew attention to white fear of the black underclass. "So long as black men commit violent crimes at a rate that is six to eight times higher than the rate found among whites," he wrote, "that perception [of the underclass as a black phenomenon] will persist. And so long as that perception persists, fear will heighten our anxieties and erode our civility."[11] Consequently, two years after the Los Angeles riots, Wilson correctly pointed out that fear of crime had recently had a major impact on national politics. It was only during the 1992 presidential race, in contrast to the 1984 or even 1988 elections, that crime had challenged "the economy as a popular concern and today [in late 1994] it dominate[d] all other matters."[12] It tells a lot about the mood in the country at the time that during his 1992 campaign, presidential candidate Bill Clinton promised that he would not permit any Republican to be perceived as tougher in crime than he was.[13]

There is some historical irony here, since the most important crimes feared by the public—homicide, rape, robbery, and burglary—were declining at a faster rate than other crimes at the time, ultimately dropping 40 percent between 1990 and 2000.[14] Nevertheless, Wilson drew attention to "terrified" ordinary Americans—and spoke on their behalf—when in 1994 he considered why the crime issue now overshadowed all others: "The reason, I think, is that Americans believe something fundamental has changed in our patterns of crime. They are right. Though we were unhappy about having our property put at risk, we adapted with the aid of locks, alarms, and security guards. But we are terrified by the prospect of innocent people being gunned down at random, without warning and almost without motive, by youngsters who afterward show us the blank, unremorseful faces of seemingly feral, presocial beings."[15]

Some of Wilson's reflections on an appropriate crime response were similarly replete with references to ordinary Americans and penal populist language in the early and mid-1990s. For years, Wilson had placed his greatest (yet always moderate) hopes on deterrence, incapacitation, and community policing as the best immediate means to combat crime. Correspondingly, he did not put much faith in liberal remedies such as gun control or reducing violence on television. The reasons for Wilson's distrust of such remedies were largely in social scientific data (or in its absence), but from our point of view, it is most relevant that Wilson promoted his conservative views on crime control by suggesting that his position was in fact the public's position, which, unlike the expert views, was the correct one.[16] That is, Wilson, a crime expert himself, set the people's views against those of the experts and—distancing himself from *other* experts—took the role of an educated spokesman for the people. The "folk wisdom that swift and certain punishment is more effective than severe penalties," Wilson explained, was "almost surely correct."[17] More generally, Wilson sided with "the public" who, in his telling, wanted "more people sent away for longer sentences," in contrast to the "many (probably most) criminologists" who "think we use prison too much and at too great a cost and that this excessive use has had little beneficial effect on the crime rate."[18]

Presenting himself as an outsider in the study of crime (he was a political scientist by training), Wilson attacked the "expert view" that was expressed in "countless op-ed essays" and that complained about America becoming "the most punitive nation on earth." Such a view was seriously out of touch, according to Wilson, since it did not consider that the probability of being arrested for a given crime was lower in the mid-1990s than it had been two decades earlier. Moreover, Wilson claimed that the disoriented experts ignored that the average amount of time served in state prisons had been "declining more or less steadily since the 1940s." The costs of crime had thus declined, especially between 1960 and 1980. Around 1980, the costs had begun to inch up again, which was mainly the result "of an increase in the proportion of convicted persons who were given prison terms."[19]

In the mid-1990s, Wilson had good reasons to be quite satisfied with how his tough-on-crime approach was breaking through in the political arena. On the national level, the key event in American crime response at the time was President Clinton's $30 billion crime bill, formally titled the Violent Crime Control and Law Enforcement Act of 1994. In many ways, the law that the president signed in mid-September 1994 was a triumph of Wilsonian thought on crime, even if Wilson also criticized some parts of it. The crime bill provided money for one hundred thousand new policemen in communities around the country and for the construction of prisons. It also encouraged states to lengthen prison sentences, expanded the death penalty, and included a "three strikes and you're out" penalty for federal crimes (the three-strikes law imposes a protracted prison term on repeat offenders). It speaks volumes of 1990s thinking on crime and the general atmosphere in the country at the time that every Democratic senator except two voted in favor of Clinton's crime bill, which has been severely criticized later for destroying numerous American lives, especially among minorities.[20] The Justice Policy Institute has observed that Clinton's " 'tough-on-crime' policies resulted in the largest increases in federal and state prison inmates of any president in American history."[21]

Wilson naturally applauded the fact that US politicians were "energized" over crime in the mid-1990s.[22] Clinton's crime bill satisfied him only up to a point, however. In a *New York Times* interview just after the signing of the law, Wilson described the bill as "a Christmas tree designed by Salvador Dalí."[23] Elsewhere, he reiterated that the crime bill included many untested ideas— those relating to prevention programs, for example, and the deterring effect of "executions, as they work in this country (which is to say, after much delay and only on a few offenders)." Wilson was also critical of the so-called three-strikes laws, since "they suffer from an inherent contradiction. If they are carefully drawn so as to target only the most serious offenders, they will probably have a minimal impact on the crime rate; but if they are broadly drawn so as to make a big impact on the crime rate, they will catch many petty repeat offenders who few of us think really deserve life imprisonment." Wilson thus noted uncharacteristically that "the average person" exaggerated "the faults of the present system and the gains of some alternative (such as 'three strikes and you're out')."[24]

On the whole, then, Wilson had mixed feelings about America's current crime problem and crime response in the mid-1990s. On the one hand, the foremost neoconservative crime authority could note with pleasure that his ideas on community policing—that is, his "broken windows" theory—were just being implemented by some of the nation's top law enforcement officers and decision-makers. Most famously, New York mayor Rudolph Giuliani (in office 1994–2001) seized on the theory of broken windows during his first term as he aimed to restore order to his city.[25] NYPD commissioner Bill Bratton (in office 1994–96), too, was inspired by Wilson and George Kelling's 1982 *Atlantic* article (which greatly pleased Wilson, partly because Wilson was a "great admirer" of Bratton, as Daniel Patrick Moynihan told the police chief in private).[26] Evidently referring to Giuliani and Bratton's work in New York, as well as to the work of other police chiefs, Wilson could thus note with pleasure in late 1994 that it was "now widely accepted" that the police needed to be "proactive: to identify, with the aid of citizen groups, problems that can be solved so as to prevent criminality, and not only to respond to it."[27] Similarly, Clinton's 1994 crime bill, at least in some ways, reflected Wilson's views on deterrence and incapacitation. Moreover, crime rates in general were declining, which naturally pleased Wilson—even if he did not claim that the declining rates resulted from crime control measures alone (as he noted in 1994, there were 1.5 million fewer boys between the ages of fifteen and nineteen by 1990 than there had been in 1980, and these were the ages at which criminality peaks).[28] On the other hand, Wilson argued that underclass youngsters— mainly black—had become more lethal than ever and more dangerous for innocent passersby. A related concern was the crack epidemic that had erupted in the mid-1980s and resulted in higher punishments for crack cocaine offenses and a massive growth in America's prison population after 1986.[29] The drug problem was difficult to solve by sending people to prison, Wilson noted—a new dealer appeared in the street corner right after the previous one had been sent away—but while one waited for truly effective prevention or treatment programs, it was "necessary either to build much more prison space, find some other way of disciplining drug offenders, or both."[30]

Moral Sentiments and Criminal Justice

It was in this mid-1990s context of rising and more lethal youth violence and national panic over crime that Wilson wrote a series of analyses on the American criminal justice system and the proper role of shared moral sentiments in it. He, like many other Americans, was urged to review recent developments in and the performance of the American justice system due to the high-profile court cases of O. J. Simpson, Lorena Bobbitt, and Erik and Lyle Menendez—three cases of violent crime with decisions of not guilty or mild sentences.[31] O. J. Simpson, an African American football star, was arrested on charges of killing his ex-wife Nicole Brown Simpson and her friend Ronald Goldman, both white. The nationally televised trial lasted for nine months in 1995 and, as James T. Patterson notes, "millions of Americans fixated on the many sordid details of the murders."[32] Ultimately, in October 1995, Simpson was acquitted of first-degree murder charges, but the case, like the Rodney King case in 1991–92, showed how polarized along racial lines were the attitudes toward the criminal justice system—soon after Simpson was arrested, 63 percent of whites believed that his trial would be fair; 69 percent of blacks disagreed. Similarly, in a 1994 poll, 63 percent of whites believed Simpson was "probably" or "definitely" guilty; only 22 percent of blacks did so.[33]

In another mid-1990s case that received a huge amount of attention on television and in tabloids, Lorena Bobbitt had cut off her husband's penis while he was asleep.[34] During the trial, Mrs. Bobbitt testified that during the marriage, her husband had raped her and battered her on several occasions. The defense argued that Mrs. Bobbitt snapped psychologically after her husband raped her, producing an "irresistible impulse" to retaliate. Several expert witnesses, including psychologists and psychiatrists, concluded that she was a "battered woman" suffering from serious depression and possibly suffering from post-traumatic stress disorder. The jury found Mrs. Bobbitt not guilty of all criminal charges, deciding that she had been temporarily insane when she mutilated her husband.[35]

Wilson was particularly interested in the trial of Lyle and Erik Menendez, or "the Menendez brothers," which became a national sensation in 1993 when Court TV broadcasted the event for the nation. Ultimately, these two rich boys from Beverly Hills, sons of a Cuban-born father and a white American mother, were sentenced to life in prison for killing their parents for financial gain: the brothers spent over $500,000 within a few weeks after they slaughtered their parents, buying a Porsche, a Rolex, and a restaurant in Princeton.[36] In the first trial, however, two juries were divided between convicting them for murder or manslaughter. During the trial, the brothers claimed that childhood sexual and psychological abuse had driven them to kill their parents. The defense called a series of experts to witness, including psychologist Ann Tyler, who explained that intense, repeated abuse results in a condition called "learned helplessness"; therefore Erik Menendez, on the night of the murders, had been "in a box with no way to get out."[37]

In *Moral Judgment* and elsewhere, Wilson used the case to highlight the divergence of the views of "ordinary people" and lawyers, law professors, and other experts concerning the nature and goals of the justice system. Wilson noted how the audiences of his public lectures had wondered, "How could the Menendez brothers have gotten off? . . . The criminal justice system could not convict them [in the first trial] of what they surely deserved, first-degree murder. My audiences were profoundly upset about what they—and I—regarded as an indefensible outcome."[38] Obviously, Wilson's rhetoric here fed on the popular expressions of anger and disillusionment toward the criminal justice establishment.

The Menendez brothers' case, together with other recent cases including claims of abuse, encouraged Wilson to question the ability of the American justice system to foster law-abiding behavior among the citizenry. The case of the two brothers, Wilson bemoaned, was indicative of a deeply disturbing trend in the American law courts: crimes were being increasingly *explained* rather than judged. The American justice system, in other words, increasingly used medical and social scientific "expert" witnesses who aimed to explain criminal behavior by various syndromes, fears, intoxication, the people's past, and the like. This meant that the so-called experts had begun "expanding on what mental states may weaken self-control, enlarging on what constitutes self-defense, and exploring what might amount to a provocation," which, according to Wilson, was all destined to obscure the notion of personal responsibility for criminal acts. It was "a dubious proposition," Wilson argued, "that the greater the degree to which a crime was caused by something other than free choice, the lesser the penalty that should attach to it."[39] Indeed, for Wilson, it was "the central failing of American criminal law" that it blurred "the boundaries between imperfect science and commanding law, with the consequent admission into courts of questionable expert testimony." This created "a tension between judging and explaining a killing." Because psychiatric and social scientific expert witnesses did nothing but blur the idea of personal responsibility, Wilson wanted them banned from court altogether.[40]

To place these expert views on crime and punishment outside the boundaries of commonly shared moral life and to encourage the banning of expert witnesses from court Wilson appealed to the "moral sentiments" of ordinary people. That is, he once again invoked the moral vocabulary of Adam Smith only to reshape Smith's ideas—in this case, to advance a neoconservative moral agenda on punishment. This time, unlike in the case of family values, Wilson did not cite or appeal to Smith's more specific insights on the particular issue at hand—that is, crime and punishment. One might find this somewhat surprising, since crime and punishment were Wilson's main professional interests, and Smith—Wilson's intellectual hero—had discussed these issues in *The Theory of Moral Sentiments* and elsewhere. Yet it is conceivable that Wilson *intentionally* ignored Smith's theory of punishment in order to underline an entirely different aspect of the issue than Smith had done. That is to say, Wilson employed the Smithian notion of universal "moral sentiments" in his 1990s works on the criminal justice system not to refer to any of Smith's specific ideas on crime and punishment but to use the concept to illustrate and give credibility to the tough-on-crime views of late twentieth-century Americans and to marginalize the experts' recent explanatory approaches to crime. I will return to Smith's ideas in short.

Wilson's key work here is *Moral Judgment*, which is to be seen in light of both penal populism *and* "civic conservatism." That is, in *Moral Judgment*, Wilson used penal populist language to convince his readers that the criminal justice establishment ought to foster self-control in black communities and elsewhere where it was supposedly lacking. "A goal of the legal system," the neoconservative crime authority asserted, "is to foster self-control by stigmatizing and punishing its absence."[41] Much like in *The Moral Sense*, in *Moral Judgment*, the black urban underclass was an implicit theme rather than an explicit one—Wilson neither used the term nor especially highlighted the problems of urban blacks, such as gangs and teenage motherhood, even if he did bring up drugs, illegitimacy, and absent fathers as symptoms of America's current cultural malaise. In the wake of the Menendez brothers' case and other cases including claims of abuse, Wilson's aim was to encourage a moral consensus on the role of the American justice system—namely, that it ought to foster law-abidingness among "people most lacking in self-control."[42] Knowing that Wilson in the 1990s consistently described the mainly black and "habitually criminal" underclass as the most present-oriented fragment of the nation—that is, the segment most lacking in self-control—it is very likely that here, like when writing *The Moral Sense*, he had in mind the urban black underclass even if he did not explicitly state it.[43]

To rationalize the self-control-cultivating agenda for the justice system and to make a case against the left-liberal experts he disagreed with, Wilson used the Menendez brothers' case and the reactions of his audiences to highlight the disillusionment of "the public" with the criminal justice establishment. What he described as the bewilderment of ordinary citizens, this time in the face of the justice system's failure to convict the brothers for first-degree murder, reflected a larger critical issue—namely, personal responsibility. "Many Americans worry," he insisted, "that the moral order that once held the nation together has come unraveled. Despite freedom and prosperity—or worse, perhaps because of freedom and prosperity—a crucial part of the moral order, a sense of personal responsibility, has withered under the attack of personal self-indulgence." The problem of personal responsibility, Wilson stressed, was nowhere greater than in criminal law: "The public worries that criminals are too often excused rather than punished or, if they are punished, that the sentence is too short when imposed and even shorter in practice."[44]

In addition to this kind of conventional penal populist rhetoric, Wilson reinvented the Smithian language of moral sentiments to set boundaries for public debate, insisting that the law "ought to reflect the most widely shared moral sentiments of the people."[45] As we have seen, Wilson had already advocated a tough-on-crime position for decades by the 1990s and had underlined that he was only articulating the view held by ordinary Americans. However, not until the 1990s did he really try to validate his argument about the critical relevance of "ordinary people's" perceptions on crime and criminal justice (as opposed to expert views). In this context, by referring to the "moral sentiments" of ordinary people, Wilson seems to have aimed to *establish* a sufficient level of conformity as to the proper level of punishment and personal responsibility that, according to him, was threatened in the United States because of the increased use of social scientific expert witnesses in court. In other words, by implying that a consensus on crime and punishment already existed among the people, he tried to encourage such a consensus.

It is a well-established fact in criminology that the public in the United States and elsewhere is generally not well informed about the true nature and volume of crime in their society or about the effectiveness of punishment and deterrence. As criminologists Julian Roberts and Loretta Stalans note in their 1997 study on the public perception of crime in the United States, "the public systematically over-estimate critical statistics such as criminal recidivism rates and crime rates." Studies show that the public also underestimates the severity of the justice system.[46] Moreover, although members of the public typically consider the criminal justice system too lenient, they, as criminologists Francis Cullen, Bonnie Fisher, and Brandon Applegate note, "moderate their punitiveness when less stringent interventions have utility for victims, the community, and offenders." The public also believes that rehabilitation ought to be an important goal of the penal system.[47] The issue of public perception of crime is further complicated by the essential fact that the public are far from unanimous in their attitudes. For example, black and white Americans have different views about criminal justice policies, reflecting the fact that incarceration rates for black Americans are much higher—in the mid-1990s, they were approximately seven to eight times higher than for whites.[48] Blacks, on average, are less punitive than whites. Rural whites are the most punitive, while they are least likely to be victims of crime.[49]

As an experienced theorist of criminal policy, Wilson could not have been unaware of such facts concerning public image of and attitudes toward crime.

Indeed, he did take note of *some* of these criminological research results in *Moral Judgment* and elsewhere. In "Reading Jurors' Minds" in 1996, he noted that "paradoxically, the public itself is of two minds."[50] However, he did not mean that blacks and whites disagreed about the justice system but that there was a "tension between what people say in their capacity as citizens and what they do in their capacity as jurors." Studies of public opinion, he continued, "show that the average citizen wants the system to be tough on criminals by imposing harsher sentences. Studies of juries, by contrast, suggest that the average juror aims to do justice by understanding the defendant and by devising a verdict that will take into account his subjective state and the circumstances of his offense." Citizens, *as jurors*, in other words, were "interested in explanations."[51]

Despite his punitive and penal populist tendencies, Wilson did not simply suggest, in "Reading Jurors' Minds," that the legal system ought to respect the punitive attitude of "the people"; rather, he actually wanted the public "to be of two minds about certain things, and not the least of these is justice." That is, he insisted that the "explanation-hungry, story-seeking, context-searching temperament of a juror confronting a case must be held sharply in bounds by the skeptical, judgment-prone, verdict-seeking attitude of a nonjuror, an ordinary citizen, facing the same case." Moreover, the idea that citizens as jurors would bring their shared "moral sentiments" to influence decisions about the severity of punishment was complicated by historical record; Wilson suspected that, for example, in Mississippi in the 1920s, jurors relying on their sentiments had treated blacks and whites very differently. (Wilson did not here mention the unequal treatment of blacks by the justice system in the *contemporary* United States, although he did so later in other texts.) Objective written law was therefore for Wilson an absolutely necessary counterpart to moral sentiments.[52]

While Wilson acknowledged these complexities regarding public perception of crime in "Reading Jurors' Minds," in *Moral Judgment*, he played down the fact that the public typically overestimates crime rates and that different social groups have diverse views of criminal justice. In the book, he claimed loosely that the "popular belief" concerning the withering of personal responsibility was validated by the "high rates of crime, the prevalence of drug abuse, and the large number of fathers who desert children and women who bore them."[53] Besides claiming that the supposedly unanimous "public" was correct in its estimate of the seriousness of this cultural malaise, Wilson insisted on the moral point that the law indeed ought to reflect the moral judgments that all mentally fit people make in "our daily lives," in which "each one of us assigns to others blame and credit for many of their actions." Wilson continued, sarcastically, referring to the expert witnesses who tended to *explain* wrong-doings, "We do not [make moral judgments] because we are lousy social scientists or eager accomplices in myth maintenance. We [make them] because we really believe that people can morally be held responsible for all but a relatively small number of actions that are truly involuntary or the product of manifest duress."[54] Moreover, Wilson once again used the language of common sense to delegitimize the expert views as nonsensical. As he put it, it was simply a "commonsense view" to think, as ordinary citizens allegedly did, that people were responsible for their actions "unless those actions are caused by a pure reflex or a delusional state utterly beyond rational control."[55]

Wilson's overall idea seems to have been, then, that criminal justice ought to *reflect* the retributive moral sentiments of ordinary citizens in order that it could appropriately *cultivate* the moral sentiments, or self-control, of crime-prone citizens. Although admitting that "we all on occasion lack self-control," Wilson argued, consistent with the principles of "civic conservatism," that the law's "prohibitions are addressed to people most lacking in self-control."[56] For him, it was "the task of the law to raise, not lower, the ante in these circumstances. . . . It is the task of the law not only to remind us of what is wrong—almost all lawbreakers know they acted wrongly—but also to remind us that we must work hard to conform to the law."[57] It is here—in Wilson's willingness to ensure that the law maintains its function in cultivating self-control, especially of the people most lacking it—that we encounter the key philosophical differences between Wilson's and Smith's theories of punishment and the most likely reason Wilson did not here follow Smith's line of thought as he did in some other topics (such as sympathy and conscience; see chapter 2)—even if he used Smith's language of moral sentiments.

The key idea of Smith's theory of punishment is that people make judgments concerning a proper level of punishment by looking at a wrongdoing from the perspective of the impartial spectator. What is essential for Smith is the impartial spectator's sympathy for both the victim and the offender. As the Scottish philosopher put it in *Theory of Moral Sentiments*, someone appears to deserve punishment if he is "the natural object of a resentment which the breast of every reasonable man is ready to adopt and sympathize with."[58] In *Lectures on Jurisprudence*, Smith further claimed that "in all cases the measure of the punishment to be inflicted on the delinquent is the concurrence of the impartial spectator with the resentment [felt by] the injured." Smith clarified this by noting that "if the injury is so great as that the spectator can go along with the injured person in revenging himself by the death of the offender, this is the proper punishment."[59] As philosopher Richard Stalley notes, implicit in Smith's theory was the idea that "impartial spectators will

148 CHAPTER FIVE

go along with a punishment only when it is inflicted for an act which was done with the intention of doing harm (or at least with some awareness that it might cause harm) and from a motive of which impartial spectators cannot approve."[60] Smith wrote in *Moral Sentiments*, "Before we can adopt the resentment of the sufferer, we must disapprove of the motives of the agent, and feel that our heart renounces all sympathy with the affections which influenced his conduct. If there appears to have been no impropriety in these, how fatal soever the tendency of the action which proceeds from them to those against whom it is directed, it does not seem to deserve any punishment, or to be the proper object of any resentment."[61] Thus in Smith's system, the impartial spectators will judge punishment to be misplaced when they sympathize completely with the perpetrator's motives. However, as Stalley points out, Smith's account does not tell us clearly what happens in cases when spectators object to an act yet have *some* sympathy with the motives of the offender.[62]

As a determined advocate of a punitive and morally cultivating criminal justice system, Wilson evidently wished to avoid this kind of confusion that resulted from the idea that the severity of punishment ought to be decided on the basis of an impartial spectator's sympathy for the offender. Instead of following Smith's line of thought here, Wilson insisted that the law ought to "rein in our natural tendencies toward sympathy or vindictiveness." Indeed, he applauded the fact that the law did *not* show "much empathy for the defendant." For individual human beings, it was natural to have a different amount of understanding, or sympathy, for various kinds of perpetrators, for example, battered wives, war veterans, or people representing one's own ethnic group. Individual citizens, when acting as members of a jury or as judges, "often" did show empathy, Wilson noted, "and so verdicts and penalties are adjusted to take into account human frailties and particular circumstances." As Wilson saw it, this was as it should be but only "up to a point." "A law that permits compassion," he pointed out, "also permits revenge." In the past, some judges and juries had shown "boundless understanding to whites who lynched blacks while denying any trace of sympathy to blacks who killed whites." This had been a "tragic mistake," and to prevent such things from happening again, it was "important that we let neither science nor compassion decide legal precepts."[63]

Wilson's *Moral Judgment* bears the marks of penal populism not only because he reinvented the notions of moral sentiments and common sense to delegitimize the explaining mentality of "experts" but also because of his historical argument concerning ordinary citizens' allegedly *diminished* chances of influencing the criminal justice system. As Sophia Rosenfeld remarks, it is a well-known argument in the history of populism and common-sense rhetoric "that 'the people' have in recent times been denied a power that they once freely and rightfully possessed."[64] Wilson made such an argument when he claimed that it was the rationalist liberal elite, the judges and social science experts, who, because of their willingness to explain rather than judge criminal acts, were responsible for the present relatively unhealthy condition of the criminal justice system. The neoconservative crime expert asserted that things had been better in the 1970s and 1980s when "American public opinion redirected American penal policy, leading to a sharp increase in the chances that a convicted offender would go to prison."[65] Now in the mid-1990s, in the aftermath of the cases of the Menendez brothers and Lorena Bobbitt, Wilson's *Moral Judgment* implied, it was time to give power back to the people.

Neoconservative Moral Sentimentalism, Color Blindness, and Mass Incarceration

What can we learn, then, about neoconservative thought on race from Wilson's and Gertrude Himmelfarb's writings on the black underclass, urban social dysfunction, and the natural moral sense of so-called ordinary Americans? Did Wilson, along with his fellow *Public Interest* intellectuals Daniel Patrick Moynihan and Edward Banfield, see "crime and violence as somehow innate among African Americans," as Elizabeth Hinton claims?[66] Or did Wilson's and Himmelfarb's writing exemplify the general neoconservative colorblind world view that fits their status as cosmopolitan intellectuals, as others suggest?[67]

In the post–civil rights era, most Americans, especially whites, have seen color blindness as an antidote to America's long-standing problem of racial discrimination and tension.[68] Yet many writers and academics, perhaps most notably civil rights lawyer Michelle Alexander, claim that color blindness is in fact a problem itself and certainly not the best solution to America's race question.[69] Alexander argues in her widely read 2010 book *The New Jim Crow: Mass Incarceration in the Age of Colorblindness* that during the "era of colorblindness" in the years after the civil rights movement of the 1960s, Americans developed a "racially sanitized rhetoric of 'cracking down on crime'" and, with or without malign intent, began to use the "criminal justice system to label people of color 'criminals' and then engage in all the practices we supposedly left behind [with the Jim Crow]."[70] A use of racial code speak— not only the "criminal" label but also "undeserving" poor, "welfare queens," "crack whores," and so on—enabled politicians such as Nixon and Reagan to exploit, in the War on Crime, white working-class resentment against ethnic minorities who had suddenly entered the job market on equal terms after the enactment of the 1960s civil rights legislation. The evolution of America's carceral state (or "the new Jim Crow," as Alexander calls it), especially after Reagan launched the War on Drugs in 1982, ultimately led to a situation where African Americans labeled "criminals" were discriminated against like blacks had been in the Jim Crow era.[71] It became perfectly legal to prevent "felons" from voting, deny them food stamps and other public benefits, and limit their right to public education, for example. Thus Alexander claims that "we have not ended racial caste in America; we have merely redesigned it." For her, the only way to overcome the current system of racial caste is a commitment to "compassionate race consciousness."[72]

Does the history of neoconservative moral sentimentalism, then, lend support to the claim that color blindness, instead of providing the solution, is in fact part of the problem of lingering racial inequality in America? The case of Himmelfarb suggests that it does but not exactly in the way Alexander suggests. Unlike Alexander's subjects who used the racial code speak of "criminals" and "crack whores" as a justification for discrimination, Himmelfarb refashioned the language of the Scottish moralists—most often, the notion of the moral sense—to legitimize private charity and a "conservative welfare state" as a color-blind approach to poverty reduction. She emphasized that the moral sense and the related psychological disposition, a "willingness to better oneself," ought to be understood as attributes of the rich and poor alike, including the (black) underclass, in order to rationalize welfare state contraction and private charity as a key poverty reduction mechanism, as well as to deny the necessity of special treatment of minority groups by the government. The eminent neoconservative historian thus played down the history of oppression of an important ethnic minority—African Americans—in the United States to make a right-wing argument about social policy.

While Himmelfarb did not publicly express a particularly strong historical understanding of the status of African Americans in the United States—or "compassion" in the liberal or "color-conscious" sense that Alexander uses the word—an analysis of her case does not lend support to the argument that the neoconservative discourse on the dysfunctional behaviors of the underclass operated according to the same logic as the scientific racism of the early twentieth century. Himmelfarb did not see the disoriented underclass *solely* as a nonwhite phenomenon, and she argued that the underclass, with its many social problems, was, to a significant extent, a victim of white upperclass culture.

What about Wilson, then? There is no question that his reflections on the criminal justice system also aimed at the ideal of color blindness. Wilson condemned what he claimed to be the recent tendency in the justice system to recompense past injustices by showing understanding to offenders representing minorities or women. He drew attention to the recently grown "desire to recognize within the criminal justice system the existence of social inequality and to use trials (or pleas) as a way of reducing that inequality—or at least what are taken to be its effects." While there was a "long list of factors, both hereditary and environmental, that increase the likelihood of criminal behavior," the "growing tendency of judges" was, Wilson claimed, "to validate those factors that embody the claims of the putatively disadvantaged defendant. We wish to help veterans suffering from posttraumatic stress disorder or wives systematically abused by their husbands, but we are much less moved by the claims of men suffering from high levels of testosterone, low levels of manganese, minor physical anomalies, inadequate schooling, or low verbal intelligence."[73] Moreover, Wilson strongly criticized the suggestion put forward by critical race theorists—who did not believe that the profoundly racist American society could apply neutral laws in judging the behavior of nonwhites—that trials should "involve more 'storytelling,' by which they mean giving free rein to the expression of racially formed accounts of group experiences and group suffering."[74] As to African Americans, Wilson acknowledged that they had "suffered countless indignities." There were, according to him, "many ways by which some recompense can be offered." When it came to the justice system, though, the crucial means to offer recompense was, for Wilson, to treat black people the *same* way everyone else was treated—that is, "a promise of fair treatment based on individual accountability." The law simply could not offer more, since that would mean "the end of the law."[75]

Despite—or in some cases because of—Wilson's adherence to color-blind ideals, many of his critics have stressed his questionable contribution to and responsibility for the late twentieth- and early twenty-first-century mass incarceration that destroyed lives, especially in black communities. Many critics have noted that Wilson strongly and influentially advocated the stop-and-frisk policing procedure that was, in their view, race-driven profiling instead of crime-driven profiling.[76] Furthermore, criminologist Mark Kleiman argues that since Wilson treated punishment as a morally neutral or justified tool, he could not properly see that he was endorsing (unnecessary) cruelty.[77]

Even if one would generally agree with these claims, it would be fair to point out that Wilson did argue, at least by the late 1990s, that the use of prisons had gone too far and that African Americans had suffered too much from it. As he put it in 1998, the "defenders of the deterrent and incapacitative effects of punishment . . . now concede that the financial and human costs of this strategy are, indeed, very large. We have more than a million inmates in state and federal prisons (plus many in jails)." This, Wilson acknowledged, had "affected racial groups very differently. An Afro-American male born today will, if present imprisonment and crime rates continue, have more than a one in four chance of being in state or federal prison before he dies." Thus he concluded that it was "hard to be sanguine about a policy that produces so profound a racial divide in our society." But despite these concessions, Wilson held on to the view "that higher levels of punishment have in fact lowered crime rates in the United States."[78]

It is important, then, to differentiate between Wilson's color-blind ideals and racist ideologies or explicit white nationalism and to note that his later writings show signs of hesitation, if not regret, as to the much-increased use of prison and its effects on African Americans. Still, it is equally important to recognize that Wilson effectively highlighted the supposedly profound behavioral differences between the urban black poor and "ordinary Americans" in many of his writings on crime from the 1990s. As one of the country's leading authorities on crime, Wilson helped reinforce an image of African Americans as members of an alien subculture that had failed to cultivate the "moral sense" of its youth—thus explaining why black underclass youngsters had become such a dangerous force in the country, generating fear among fellow citizens. Indeed, the way Wilson defined the American crime problem overly emphasized the role of the black underclass. In reality, crime is committed by a wide range of offenders in the United States, so much so that in the late 1990s, state information systems stored criminal record information on fifty million people, a fact that is known by few members of the public.[79]

Wilson downplayed such facts and highlighted the outcast nature of the black underclass by placing it in opposition to the imagined, morally pure "ordinary citizen" whose alleged fears of black violence and neighborhoods he exploited to promote his personal, or neoconservative, views on punishment. Partly as a result of the era's many sensationalized media accounts of career criminals and "superpredators"—including many neoconservative texts—the public in the United States tended to overestimate especially violent offender recidivism.[80]

That Wilson invoked the Scottish notions of the natural moral sense and moral sentiments while discussing the ordinary citizen's tough views on crime and moral preference for individuals with self-control, as well as the criminal underclass's *lack* of self-control, speaks of his willingness to indicate that it was not a sign of racism or a reactionary ideological position to criticize black criminals of a weak character. His choice of words was intended to show that it was, instead, a universal commonplace to judge *anyone* based on their conduct and character—for example, their lack of self-control.

Seen from a critical point of view, however, Wilson's language of the moral sense must be understood in relation to power. For Wilson and many other first-generation neoconservatives, the (a)moral world view of the urban underclass signified a dangerous threat to an imagined, or hoped-for, moral consensus that was a necessary condition for safe American communities. Wilson's claims about the "moral sense" or "moral sentiments," like most claims about "common sense" within the last two hundred years, were polemical claims whose aim was to discredit competing perspectives—in this case, the "relativist" ideas of the liberal elites and the "present-oriented" moral system of the urban underclass. When associated with the notion of "ordinary people," Wilson's idea of a shared moral sense created new forms of exclusion more than national solidarity because it existed, like "common sense" as shown by Rosenfeld, "in contrast to other views perceived as superstitious, marginal, or deluded, on the one hand, or overly abstract, specialized, or dogmatic, on the other."[81] The notion of the moral sense, to borrow the words of Rosenfeld (who here follows Pierre Bourdieu's understanding of common sense), "turned into an unspectacular instrument of domination that works constantly and silently not only to keep individuals in line but also to exclude outlying voices as either criminal or crazy and to limit the parameters of public debate."[82] Furthermore, Wilson's and Himmelfarb's claims about a shared moral sense, moral sentiments, and common sense often created new intellectual conflicts—rather than national consensus—since many liberal writers, unsurprisingly, refused to accept at face value Wilson's understanding of the evolutionary roots of the moral sense or the neoconservatives' exclusive right to define common sense.

Were Wilson's and Himmelfarb's neoconservative reinventions of Scottish moral philosophy, then, a form of white backlash? Not primarily. Instead, they appealed to the moral sense or moral sentiments of ordinary people above all to offer an antidote to late twentieth-century relativism, expert nonjudgmentality, and liberal policymaking. According to the neoconservatives, the liberal elites, experts, and policymakers had undermined important moral codes relating to personal responsibility and delayed gratification, and by so doing, they had shattered the social order by way of negatively impacting the poorly socialized and therefore vulnerable lower classes in disorderly neighborhoods and families. Despite the aggression and violence that the criminal underclass directed against its victims, the present-oriented underclass was, for both Wilson and Himmelfarb, itself a victim of the more general cultural malaise that originated from the mostly white liberal elites. The neoconservative concepts of the moral sense and moral sentiments were thus primarily counterweights to harmful elite ideas and policies—that is, moral relativism and a generous welfare state. To respond to such perceived problems, the neoconservatives articulated an idealized notion of an ordinary American who was tough on crime and strongly in favor of personal responsibility. In a country in which democratic faith is, in historian Mark Hulliung's words, "omnipotent" and efforts to operate outside it are futile, such an image of ordinary people was extremely useful as a political instrument.[83] Overall, by refashioning the Scottish philosophies of the moral sense and moral sentiments in the framework of the underclass and crime debates, Wilson and Himmelfarb not only vindicated politically conservative ways to deal with poverty and crime as "ethical," supposedly "democratic," and "American" but also delegitimized and marginalized liberal conceptions of, and solutions to, inner-city unrest.

Elite Multiculturalism and the Spontaneous Morality of Everyday People: Francis Fukuyama's Culture Wars

In this book, I have argued that at the heart of neoconservative culture wars discourse was a populist logic and an epistemology that claimed that moral truth came from the average American's instinctive capacity to perceive the world in moral terms. This neoconservative logic, I have argued, was informed by the Scottish Enlightenment philosophies of the "moral sense," "moral sentiments," and "common sense." Yet as noted in the introduction, some scholars make the claim that neoconservatism as a movement was characterized by an elitist "Straussian" world view that distinguished between the superior few and the inferior majority whose impulses needed to be restrained by a conventional morality.

Especially following the US invasion of Iraq in 2003, many scholars and journalists argued that neoconservative foreign policy hawks—both intellectuals such as William Kristol (the son of Irving Kristol and Gertrude Himmelfarb) and politicians such as Paul Wolfowitz—were vitally influenced by the philosophy of Leo Strauss. Strauss's philosophy, according to these scholars and journalists, tutored the neoconservatives in the importance of the intellectual elites and their need to tell "noble lies" to the masses that supposedly were unable to handle hard truths about the world, such as the nonexistence of God or natural support for justice. According to this account, then, Strauss taught the neoconservatives that lies about God, justice, and the good were necessary to keep the masses under control.[1]

While this reading of Strauss has been disputed by scholars and while "Straussianism" was not the dominant discourse in either neoconservative foreign policy or neoconservative cultural warfare, there is no doubt that certain writers within or near the neoconservative circle—including cultural analysts such as Francis Fukuyama and his teacher Allan Bloom—made use of the ideas of continental European thinkers such as Nietzsche and Strauss.[2] For these neoconservative followers of Strauss, as well as for many other so-called Straussians, the famed philosopher taught above all a high reverence for ancient political thought that aimed at grand and inspiring high virtues, as well as the more or less pessimistic idea that modernity entailed the "lowering of sights."

In this final chapter, I will dig deep into the logic of these two poles of neoconservative culture wars thought—namely, *Public Interest*–style moral sentimentalism and Straussian cultural pessimism. I will do this by analyzing how and why Fukuyama—a leading second-generation neoconservative theorist and the world-renowned author of the post–Cold War bestseller *The End of History and the Last Man*—replaced many of his earlier Straussian notions with the vocabulary of the eighteenth-century Scottish moralists in his mid to late 1990s works.[3] Because of this rather swift transition from Straussianism to a Scottish-informed moral sentimentalism, Fukuyama's 1990s work provides us the best opportunity to compare and contrast these two divergent neoconservative ways of thought.

The first three sections of this chapter explore how Fukuyama first employed the ideas of Strauss, Nietzsche, and other continental philosophers to analyze the American mind—that is, the ordinary liberal democratic citizen—and how he then moved from these more pessimistic and elitist Straussian-inspired notions to a moral optimism based on eighteenth-century Scottish (and later) ideas on moral sentiments in the mid to late 1990s. An analysis of Fukuyama's intellectual journey makes strikingly clear the inconsistency between Straussianism and *Public Interest*–style Scottish-informed moral sentimentalism as viewpoints on America's cultural condition in the late twentieth century. The earlier Fukuyama, in the early 1990s, followed Strauss in articulating the idea that the typical liberal democratic citizen was best described as Nietzsche's "last man" who had lost his spiritedness and was unwilling to make any moral judgments. The later Fukuyama, in turn, followed the first-generation neoconservatives in invoking the language of the Scottish moralists to articulate an optimistic vision of American bourgeois capitalist society that was based on high confidence in the moral capacities of the American common man.[4]

Fukuyama's intellectual journey also reveals why Strauss's pessimistic philosophy of the "last man" lost much of its appeal as an analytical perspective on the liberal democratic mind in the latter half of the 1990s. Indeed, much of Fukuyama's writing on the culture wars dates from the late 1990s, which was an era of optimism at least for those cultural analysts who were at the time paying attention to (improving) statistics on family life, civic participation, and crime. For Fukuyama, these statistics, as well as his newly begun study of evolutionary psychology and works such as Adam Smith's *The Theory of Moral Sentiments* and James Q. Wilson's *The Moral Sense*, opened a new perspective into the moral mind of everyday Americans and stimulated his shift away from Straussian cultural pessimism.

After discussing how Fukuyama backed off from pessimistic Straussianism, I will analyze Fukuyama's late 1990s moral sentimentalism as a response to the question of how to "re-moralize" America. I will argue that his late 1990s oeuvre—including *The Great Disruption: Human Nature and the Reconstitution of Social Order* (1999)—is to be seen as a guardedly optimistic response to a perceived post-1960s crisis of values that combined elements of *Public Interest*–style moral sentimentalism with Friedrich von Hayek's economics of "spontaneous order" and evolutionary biology to produce an updated neoconservative argument for both bourgeois values and limited government. That is, by introducing the natural moral instincts and sentiments of ordinary people as the biological origins of the human capacity for "spontaneous order," Fukuyama made a case against distorted elite multiculturalism and overly rationalist and potentially counterproductive government efforts to rebuild and reshape social order in America.

Moreover, I will argue that Fukuyama, in using Adam Smith's ethics to construct a morally reassuring view of the American people and bourgeois capitalist society, helped reinforce the moral foundations of the post-1970s "neoliberal order" that otherwise lacked a proper moral perspective. Here Fukuyama was following in the footsteps of Irving Kristol, who already in the 1970s turned to Smith's moral philosophy to articulate a moral vision of capitalism that placed virtuous ordinary citizens at its center. I will also draw attention to the differences between neoconservatism and neoliberalism as moral systems. Significantly, both neoconservative intellectuals such as Kristol and Fukuyama *and* neoliberal thinkers such as Hayek, Milton Friedman, and Ronald Coase claimed Smith's legacy, yet only the neoliberals tended to avoid Smith's conception of the moral individual while selectively using Smith's authority to advance unambiguous ideas of the self-interested man in the marketplace. The differences in the reception of Smith, I suggest, reveal essential aspects of the nature of these two conflicting yet intertwined ideologies of the late twentieth century—namely, neoconservatism and neoliberalism.

Straussian Cultural Pessimists and the Failures of Liberalism

Fukuyama's worldwide reputation is, as noted, due to his international bestseller *End of History* (1992), which extended the arguments first published in a 1989 article in the *National Interest*, a bimonthly magazine that was founded in 1985 by Irving Kristol.[5] The mixed response to the book and the article from contemporary and later readers reveals that Fukuyama's key message was not easily grasped. One of the most disputed questions pertaining to *End of History* has been whether the book should be seen as a celebration of liberal democracy's triumph over its twentieth-century competitors or rather as a gloomy jeremiad on liberal democracy's lack of "the 'striving spirit' that gives humanity its sense of direction."[6] The very title of Fukuyama's book was ambiguous: "end of history" signaled an optimistic outlook in the line of Hegel and Marx, while "the last man" referred to Nietzsche's pessimistic caveats.[7]

Today, serious commentators seem to agree that the widespread first reaction to Fukuyama's book as a triumphalistic work was at least to some extent a misconception: Fukuyama never predicted the end of all conflict, and although he held that liberal democracy had prevailed over its competitors in the sense that no other ideology had durable and universal appeal, the "deeper and more profound question" (as Fukuyama himself put it) in the book was a normative one; that is, whether liberal democracy was *good* or not.[8] In the end, much of the academic analysis on Fukuyama's book asked not whether the author was being triumphalistic or pessimistic but what in fact had made him so gloomy and which thinkers in the European tradition of "Kulturpessimismus"— Nietzsche, Strauss, Alexandre Kojève, or someone else—had most inspired his bleak visions on liberal democracy's moral dimensions.[9]

To properly understand Fukuyama's fascination with the tradition of European cultural pessimism, a more general understanding of the American cultural atmosphere in the early 1990s is necessary. In this study, I have approached the larger debates over America's alleged moral corrosion from the perspective of the culture wars, looking at the debates as conservative America's attempt to come to terms with the cultural liberalization and fracture of the post-1960s decades. Yet although it is typical to associate concerns about "demoralization" with conservative thinkers, moral regeneration was demanded in the 1980s and 1990s not only by the American right but also by many center-left writers who reacted with alarm to certain contemporary trends such as citizens' prolonged dependency on welfare, electoral passivity, unrestricted individualism, and family disruption.[10]

Much of this nationwide debate over America's supposedly growing individualism or demoralization revolved around the notion of "community" and what became known as "communitarianism" (of the political right, left, and center). As political scientist Robert Booth Fowler noted in 1999, "community" or "increased community" was proclaimed by American intellectuals in the 1990s "as the answer to almost everything," including crime, unwanted pregnancy, divorce, corruption, citizen apathy, greed, and the environmental crisis. "The pervasiveness of the call for community (or more or strengthened community) is," Fowler wrote, "an explicit declaration that something has gone wrong in much of the political and social culture of the United States. Almost always the culprit is identified as liberalism or too much liberalism."[11] In these debates over demoralization and excessive individualism, the notion of "virtue" had a rather similar healing function, even as it meant, of course, different things to different people.[12]

Fowler is hardly alone in identifying liberalism as the main culprit in much of the debate over America's cultural dilemmas in the 1990s. It was noted by many cultural analysts in the late 1990s that liberalism was "under siege."[13] The cure for liberalism's failures might be identified as community or virtue, but the fact remained that both Democrats and Republicans shunned "liberal" ideas in the 1990s.[14] As intellectual historian James Kloppenberg noted in 1998, "Republican Party loyalists accuse liberals of being overly interested in using government to achieve equality and insufficiently sensitive to individual property rights. Academic radicals accuse liberals of being insufficiently sensitive to egalitarian aspirations and overly interested in protecting individual property rights. Conservative critics charge liberals with glorifying diversity by celebrating toleration; critics in the academy fault liberals for trivializing difference by pretending to tolerate forms of cultural diversity that they secretly wish to silence."[15] To this diverse collection of critics, one must add one more group of intellectuals that had received a lot of attention in the United States since the late 1980s: the "Straussian" conservatives who drew from the tradition of European Kulturpessimismus and in whose ranks Fukuyama belonged to at the turn of the 1990s.

The key figure behind Straussianism is, as noted, German-born political philosopher Leo Strauss (1899–1973), who is famous for his contention that the modern world had confronted a serious intellectual crisis. Significantly, Fukuyama was taught by Strauss's most widely known and most controversial student, Allan Bloom, at Cornell University in the 1970s.[16] While all Straussians take as a key starting point Strauss's influential arguments on the differences between modern and ancient political thought, Bloom is known as a particularly extremist voice within the intellectual "movement," in the sense that he was deeply pessimistic about American culture as an outcome of modernity. The fact that Straussianism moved from the margins to the center of the American cultural debate in the late 1980s is in fact very much attributable to Bloom's 1987 bestseller *The Closing of the American Mind*, which is today considered by some historians as the single most important text of the American culture wars.[17]

In his blockbuster book, Bloom claimed that the American "virtue" of "openness" was in fact a closedness to the truth, since it relied on a dogmatic relativism—which, in turn, was a threat to a free society, since it undermined the intellectual and moral commitments upon which free societies had to rely.[18] Bloom also famously held that value relativism—or "Nietzscheanization"— had turned university students into incurious conformists and impoverished the American "soul."[19] Intellectual historian Jennifer Ratner-Rosenhagen, who has studied the American reception of Nietzsche, summarizes Bloom's position by noting that for Bloom, the "problem with the democratic mind of the late twentieth century . . . was not that it was closed, but that it was too radically open, too indiscriminate to understand Nietzsche's subtle moral criticism and his warnings about nihilism."[20]

From Strauss and the Straussians, Fukuyama adopted not only their general reverence for ancient thought but two specific key concepts in *End of History*—namely, the Nietzschean concept of the "last man," as well as the Platonic notion of "thymos" (spiritedness). Strauss had used these concepts in the context of his general argument that the modern world had confronted a serious intellectual crisis—he called it "the crisis of the West" and "the crisis of our time." In Strauss's estimate, modernity entailed a "lowering of sights," or a moral diminution of humanity (brought about by Machiavelli and Hobbes), in the sense that human beings in modernity aimed not at human excellence or holiness but "comfortable preservation" or "self-expression."[21] As political philosophers Catherine and Michael Zuckert explain, it was, in Strauss's understanding, due to the "aim of actualization" that "the modern moral and political orientation makes peace with the passions and becomes reconciled to man-as-he-is, not [like the ancients] aiming at man-as-he-could-be. . . . In reconciling with the passions, modernity aims at what is in reach of all (or almost all) and therefore democratizes the moral scene. . . . This democratization occurs in terms of the lowest common denominator, and thus we find a steady depreciation of high and rare moral qualities like courage and nobility."[22]

Nietzsche's notion of the last man came into play in Strauss's analysis in the sense that he, as the Zuckerts aptly explain, "frequently cited Nietzsche's concern that modernity produces 'the last man,' human beings with nothing to strive for beyond a house in the suburbs with a patio and a gas-fired barbeque grill, a decent job, and the ability to get their children into good schools." The last men, as Nietzsche and Strauss and later also Fukuyama saw them, are human beings who pursue merely trivial pleasure and whose lives fixate on modest delights, entertainment, and conformism.[23]

The second key concept, besides the last man, that both Strauss and Fukuyama used to describe modernity's impact on individuals is Plato's notion of thymos. Both Strauss and Fukuyama used thymos to clarify what they meant by the last man: for them, the last man was the character who represented the decline of thymos, or spiritedness, in modernity.[24] Strauss often voiced his misgivings about modernity and liberalism in his correspondence with Russian-born French philosopher Alexandre Kojève, which was the central inspiration for Fukuyama's *End of History*. Fukuyama held that the Strauss-Kojève debate was the "most serious" discussion of the "crisis of modernity," or the normative grounding of modern liberal democracy.[25] In this debate, Kojève argued in historical terms that human beings would achieve satisfaction of their deepest needs by way of equal and universal recognition (for being human beings capable of moral choice) in what he called the "universal and homogeneous state" that could be understood, and was understood by Fukuyama, as liberal democracy.[26] Strauss meanwhile, in the words of philosopher Robert P. Pippin, advocated "a kind of Platonic perfectionism and seem[ed] committed to the problematic claim that the true perfection of a human being transcends the human as such."[27]

The Liberal Democratic Citizen and the Lost Thymos

Fukuyama's understanding of the last man as the character who represented the eclipse of thymos thus laid the foundation for his critical analysis of average Americans and liberal democratic culture. Indeed, despite disagreements among scholars regarding the level of gloom in *End of History*, it is not controversial that in the book, Fukuyama adopted Nietzsche's analysis of the last man to describe "the typical citizen of a liberal democracy." For our purposes, it is particularly important to focus on Fukuyama's concept of thymos, for the neoconservative author used it to denote not only spiritedness but that part of the human soul, or human nature, that places *value* on things. In *Great Disruption*—and in his other contributions to the culture wars from the late 1990s and early 2000s—he used the Scottish idea of the "moral sense" to refer to essentially the same thing, although with very different implications.

To comprehend Fukuyama's philosophy of thymos, it is essential to understand that he associated Plato's thymos with Hegel's idea of "desire for recognition." While Fukuyama noted that both of "these terms refer to that part of man which feels the need to place *value* on things," he saw, after all, a small difference between the two concepts.[28] As the neoconservative scholar explained, "*Thymos* and the 'desire for recognition' differ somewhat insofar as the former refers to a part of the soul that invests objects with value, whereas the latter is an activity of *thymos* that demands that another consciousness share the same valuation."[29]

There are four aspects to Fukuyama's philosophy of thymos that are crucial for understanding his thinking on human moral nature and the typical liberal democratic citizen in the early 1990s, some of which express his pessimistic mood at the time and form a basis for his cultural criticism. To begin with, Fukuyama's "thymos" (unlike his later moral sense idea) draws attention to the egotistic side of human nature in the sense that he not only argued that thymos was a part of the human soul that "invests objects with value" but claimed that it principally evaluated the *self* and that it was inclined to overvalue itself. People "evaluate and assign worth to *themselves* in the first instance," he wrote, "[although] they are also capable of assigning worth to *other* people."[30] Thymos, or the desire for recognition was, for Fukuyama, "*a desire for a desire*, that is, a desire that [any] person who evaluated us too low should change his opinion and recognize us according to our own estimate of our worth." Thymos was therefore "something like an innate human sense of justice: people believe that they have a certain worth, and when other people act as though they are worth less—when they do not *recognize* their worth at its correct value—then they become angry." Therefore, thymos was the source of such emotions as not only indignation but also shame ("when other people see that we are not living up to our sense of self-esteem") and pride ("when we are evaluated justly").[31] Still, there was an obvious downside: "Since the thymotic self usually begins by evaluating itself, the likelihood is that it will *overvalue* itself," and therefore thymos was "closely related to selfishness."[32]

Second, and more directly pertaining to his cultural pessimism, Fukuyama made the case that there were two different manifestations of thymos—megalothymia and isothymia—and that megalothymia had been defeated in the modern world. This idea was crucial for Fukuyama's famous analysis of the "end of history" (a concept that had been used by Hegel and Kojève), and he emphasized it to highlight liberal democracy's discontents. Indeed, Fukuyama's main thesis rested on the idea that history could be understood with reference to the two different manifestations of thymos. History began with the coexistence of these two manifestations "around which the historical transition to modernity can be understood." "Megalothymia" was "the desire to be recognized as superior to other people," and it was a desire that animated the few, the great men. Its opposite, "isothymia," was "the desire to be recognized as the equal of other people," which was the thymos of the mainstream, the ordinary, the mediocre.[33] For Fukuyama, history was a conflict between these two desires, and his thesis was that this conflict was coming to its end with the rise of liberal democracy, since megalothymia had been largely defeated in a society where the "predominant ethos is one of equality."[34] On this basis, Fukuyama argued that the typical citizen of a liberal democracy—a human being lacking megalothymia, the psychological force that drives people to aim for greatness—could be identified with Nietzsche's "last man."[35]

Third, and most important for our concerns, Fukuyama described liberal democratic citizens' moral mind-set by claiming in more general terms that thymos had been "tamed" in the modern world. By this, Fukuyama meant not only that some aristocratic megalothymia had been tamed but that citizens of liberal democracies had generally become unwilling to make moral judgments. Megalothymia, first of all, had been tamed by the founders of modern liberalism such as Hobbes and Locke. The aristocracy with its code of honor had been "the social embodiment of megalothymia," and thus in one sense, the decline of thymos was associated with "the denigration of aristocratic pride."[36] But while Fukuyama often set the focus on megalothymia, he also held that the taming of thymos in the modern world signified a more general transformation as to the human tendency to place value on things. As Fukuyama put it in a chapter named "Men without Chests," it "becomes particularly difficult for people in democratic societies to take questions with real moral content seriously in public life. Morality involves a distinction between better and worse, good and bad, which seems to violate the democratic principle of tolerance. It is for this reason that the last man becomes concerned above all for his own personal health and safety, because it is uncontroversial." In a manner much reminiscent of Strauss's and Bloom's analyses, Fukuyama thus declared that typical American citizens no longer were (capable of) aiming for (moral) excellence. Instead, for "Americans, the health of their bodies—what they eat and drink, the exercise they get, the shape they are in—has become a far greater obsession than the moral questions that tormented their forebears."[37]

The fourth and last distinguishing feature of Fukuyama's philosophy of thymos (that is illustrative of his current thinking on human nature and liberal democratic citizens) was the view that the central moral distinction people made between different individuals was between those with megalothymia (like the old aristocracy) who were brave enough to risk death "in a battle for pure prestige" and those without megalothymia who were not similarly courageous.[38] The justification Fukuyama gave for this rather astonishing claim was that the human capacity (or freedom) to willingly risk one's own life for pure prestige was the key characteristic that distinguished human beings from animals. Consequently, Fukuyama made the case that people in general had more respect for those who displayed this truly *human* characteristic in real life (an idea drawn from Kojève). Later, in his moral sense philosophy, Fukuyama drastically revised these ideas concerning the human tendency to make moral judgments. A fundamental difference was that his

moral sense philosophy was to draw from recent biological research to highlight the evolutionary roots of human moral emotions, while his philosophy
of thymos instead postulated a strict dichotomy between morality and nature,
relying on the Hegelian-Kojèvean idea that "[man's] very humanity consists
in his ability to overcome or negate . . . animal nature."[39] As we will later see,
Fukuyama's revised, Scottish-cum-evolutionary psychological conception of
moral judgments made him much less inclined to long for the lost virtues
related to battling and death.[40]

Losing the Language of Straussian Pessimism:
Fukuyama's Moral Sense Idea

In the early 1990s, at the end of the Cold War, Fukuyama's philosophical analysis of humanity's ideological evolution had thus led him to upsetting ideas
about the typical democratic citizen as the Nietzschean "last man." This was
a sad picture of the average citizens of his home country, but it was not his
final attempt to evaluate the American mind. In the mid-1990s, Fukuyama
rethought his *Menschenbild* after having read James Q. Wilson's *The Moral
Sense*—a work in which Wilson introduced to his readers an Americanized
figure of the common man with an intuitive moral sense. Needless to say, in
Wilson's work, Fukuyama encountered a much more positive and dynamic
conception of ordinary Americans as makers of moral judgments and guardians of virtue than he had himself introduced at the turn of the 1990s.

Fukuyama's response to Wilson's ideas on ordinary citizens as virtuous
guardians of civilization was very positive, even enthusiastic. This is startling
considering his earlier claims on the typical nonjudgmental liberal democratic citizen. Why was Fukuyama from the start willing to side with Wilson's
portrayal of the average American? To comprehend his response to Wilson's
book, one must take note of his evolving moral-political agenda in the culture
wars context, as well as the country's shifting social indicators as to crime,
family life, trust, and civic participation around the mid-1990s. Moreover, to
comprehend Fukuyama's turn of mind, one must be aware of his understanding of contemporary developments in the rapidly rising field of evolutionary
psychology.

Fukuyama already greeted *The Moral Sense* with positive interest in his
first comments on the book in 1995.[41] After that, he repeatedly cited Wilson's
volume approvingly or invoked the "moral sense" in his late 1990s and early
2000s works, first in *Trust: The Social Virtues and the Creation of Prosperity*
(1995) and then in *The End of Order* (1997), *Great Disruption* (1999), and *Our
Posthuman Future: Consequences of the Biotechnology Revolution* (2002).[42] Fu-

kuyama's early remarks on Wilson in *Trust* were nonetheless short. He noted how Wilson's studies had shown that people—although "fundamentally selfish"—"also have a moral side in which they feel obligations to others, a side that is frequently at cross-purposes with their selfish instincts."[43] In *Trust*, Fukuyama actually highlighted cultural differences between the various "languages of good and evil" around the globe rather than the shared features of human moral nature, arguing that a culture's ability to create and sustain a shared moral language was a key factor contributing to the local creation of prosperity, since it helped people trust each other and thus made business easier. He also discussed "culture" for the most part as an autonomous system without allusions to human moral psychology. The earlier references to thymos as a psychological seat of values were no longer there, and the moral sense idea was not yet really put to use.

It was not until 1997 when Fukuyama began to formulate a distinctive reading of moral sense philosophy. He first used the actual concept of the "moral sense" in a 1997 article on the "revolution" in biology in the late twentieth century. His conception of "culture" was now significantly different from what it had been just two years earlier in *Trust*. Now Fukuyama argued that "what a culture can do is to build on this 'moral sense,' as James Q. Wilson has called it, in order to reinforce altruistic tendencies and to control other biological drives toward aggression and violence."[44]

Coming to 1999, Fukuyama had acquired a wide reading of Wilson on both morality and crime.[45] What is more, Wilson was among the colleagues who commented on Fukuyama's book in progress *Great Disruption*, which made extensive use of moral sentimentalist ideas (most often "moral emotions" or "moral instincts").[46] In this book and elsewhere, at about the same time, Fukuyama invoked the moral sense with reference to various themes such as America's necessary "re-moralization," social capital, biotechnology, and Smith's theory of moral sentiments.[47] In his 1999 article "How to Re-moralize America," which covered many of the same themes as *Great Disruption*, Fukuyama argued that commentators on America's supposed moral decline were easily led astray unless they took note of the natural moral sense. This was the case with religious conservatives who "underestimate the innate ability of human beings to evolve reasonable moral rules for themselves." But one had to be careful, Fukuyama cautioned, not to misunderstand what he, Wilson, and others meant by the "innate" psychological mechanisms sustaining human social life: "When we say that human beings are social creatures by nature, we mean not that they are cooperative angels with unlimited resources for altruism but that they have built-in capabilities for perceiving the moral qualities of their fellow humans. What James Q. Wilson calls the 'moral sense' is put there by nature, and will operate in the absence of either a law-giver or a prophet."[48]

What, then, explains the fact that Fukuyama, who in 1992 put forward a "Straussian" cultural pessimist argument about ordinary liberal democratic citizens as "last men," responded so approvingly to Wilson's 1993 book and its fairly confident view of ordinary Americans as morally pure guardians of virtue?

Most importantly, Fukuyama was forced to reassess the average American as a moral agent because of the positive turn in several key social indicators in the mid-1990s, at the same time as Fukuyama explored Wilson's book. New statistics relating to crime and family life that came available around the time that Wilson's *The Moral Sense* (1993) was published indicated that "moral" behavior was making a comeback in the United States after thirty years of in-creasing "indecency." This "moral turn" did not go unnoticed by Fukuyama. He discussed related statistics extensively in his books from the late 1990s, such as *End of Order* and *Great Disruption*. For example, in *Great Disruption*, Fukuyama noted that "culturally, the period of ever-expanding individualism is coming to an end, and that at least some of the norms swept away during the Great Disruption are being restored."[49] Crime and divorce rates had actu-ally begun to decline and civic participation to increase within the last few years, and for Fukuyama, these and other numbers provided "evidence that more conservative social norms have made a comeback."[50] Such social indi-cators thus enabled Fukuyama to see ordinary Americans in a more positive light as dynamic creators of value rather than as nonjudgmental "last men."

Fukuyama was, of course, not the only political thinker who had to mod-ify his moral language around the mid-1990s due to the improving trends in crime, family life, and civic engagement. This challenge faced all those conser-vatives whose public roles had been based on the idea that the United States was about to fall apart because of chronic moral corruption. This held true with politicians too. As British political writer Edward Ashbee noted in 2000, "the front-runners in the Republican presidential race" had become "increas-ingly less willing or able to evoke images constructed around threats to the fabric of American society." Instead of such dark visions, conservative poli-ticians had come to emphasize "the language of 'compassion' and 'tolerance' with increasing vigour."[51] Conservative politicians and writers who had been relying on social statistics to make a case about America's "moral decline" were now basically forced to adjust their message in order to be taken seriously.

Another important feature of the contemporary intellectual environment that helps explain Fukuyama's change of mind on everyday people is the devel-opment of evolutionary psychological study of human sociability and moral emotions in the last decades of the twentieth century. Notoriously, in the aftermath of World War II, many popularizers of evolutionary research, such as Konrad Lorenz and Robert Ardrey, had emphasized the animal roots of human aggression and warfare.[52] However, ever since the 1970s, more and more evolutionists, among them William Hamilton, Robert Trivers, and Edward O. Wilson, were highlighting the importance of sociability in human evolutionary history.[53] Fukuyama's understanding of the field was still marginal in 1993, when Wilson published *The Moral Sense*. Yet by 1997, Fukuyama had begun a serious study of leading evolutionists such as Hamilton, Trivers, Lionel Tiger, and Robin Fox. Fox, for one, was at the time very appreciative of Wilson's *The Moral Sense*, referring to it in a 1997 book as "a momentous contribution." Fox agreed with Wilson that "we have a moral sense" "for the same reasons Darwin gave"—namely, that natural selection "would have favored the development of what we call morality in any organisms that developed the levels of intelligence, consciousness, foresight, and sociality that humans did."[54] During the next couple of years, Fox and other evolutionists had a major impact on Fukuyama's thought as they coworked with the neoconservative scholar on two seminar series on new developments in science that Fukuyama chaired and commented on Fukuyama's book in the making, *Great Disruption*.[55]

In the latter half of the 1990s, Fukuyama was therefore becoming well informed about the overlaps between eighteenth-century Scottish moral sentimentalism and the cutting-edge study of biologically evolved moral emotions. Compared with many other time-honored notions about the human "soul," such as the Platonic "thymos," the ideas of a natural moral sense and moral sentiments were at the time becoming more attractive due to the scientific credibility that accompanied the rise of evolutionary psychology.[56]

Finally, Fukuyama's view of ordinary liberal democratic citizens, after *End of History*, was shaped by the expansion of the American debate on "civil society" and its ability to produce what had come to be called "social capital." It was political scientist Robert Putnam who most famously argued, in 1995, that social capital—people's ability to trust and their willingness to participate—had declined in the United States since the 1950s.[57] This decline of social capital was a serious challenge, Putnam claimed, since social capital was vital for a well-functioning democracy. Putnam's argument received enormous attention around the mid-1990s and made many social analysts concerned about American civil society and democracy. Yet some scholars almost immediately drew attention to various shortcomings in Putnam's data and argued that associational life (the main factor measured in the study) actually had not decreased in America—it was only that its forms had changed.[58] Fukuyama quickly joined Putnam's critics.

Fukuyama in fact first echoed Putnam's ideas in his *Trust* in 1995 but became more critical of his thesis after the mid-1990s.[59] While admitting that both public and private *trust* (trust in institutions and other people) had eroded in America over time, Fukuyama could not accept Putnam's thesis at face value, since participation in community affairs and volunteer work seemed to have increased over the same period. True, some kinds of organizations like labor unions had seen declines, yet "others like professional associations have seen increases."[60] After the mid-1990s, Fukuyama thus had many reasons to be critical of his earlier deeply pessimistic view of typical liberal democratic citizens as self-absorbed "last men" who care about little else than the health of their bodies. Statistics that pointed to American civil society's lasting ability to sustain and create social capital was one more factor that gave credibility to the Scottish ideas about natural human sociability and the ordinary citizen as a possessor of the natural "moral sense."

Fukuyama thus came to modify his previously pessimistic moral language along the lines of Wilson's *The Moral Sense*. The replacement of a continental European cultural pessimist vocabulary with a Scottish one meant that now Fukuyama sounded much more confident when it came to the moral capacities of ordinary Americans. But how exactly did his position on human moral nature change? First, Fukuyama rethought what it is that ordinary people actually value. In *End of History*, he had followed Kojève's philosophical anthropology in suggesting that it is typical for human beings to make a general moral distinction between people on the basis of their ends beings either materialistic or nonmaterialistic and that nonmaterialistic ends are considered "noble" or "admirable." In Fukuyama's assessment at the time, what truly set human beings apart from nature, or materialistic ends, was the quest for pure prestige and in particular the willingness to "risk one's life in a battle for pure prestige."[61]

Political theorist Shadia Drury, who has studied Fukuyama's *End of History*, makes an important observation when she notes that Fukuyama, although he was preoccupied with recognition, had not properly considered what it is that people admire. Fukuyama's claim that people admire strength and courage is as such undoubtedly true, and a willingness to risk one's life is a manifestation of courage. Drury points out, though, that strength is not admired for its own sake and neither is strength that is improperly used. Rather, it is strength that is used for good objectives, and not for pursuing self-interested "prestige," that is generally admired.[62] Drury perceptively notes that Fukuyama's narrow understanding of moral distinctions led him to an odd interpretation of the famous "dream speech" by Martin Luther King Jr. In his speech, King had hoped that his children and grandchildren will be judged by the content of their characters rather than the color of their skin. Drury is amazed to see that Fukuyama thinks King "is pleading for equal and mutual recognition *independent* of merit. . . . It does not occur to Fukuyama that there can be distinctions among people on the basis of their character. The only distinction he recognizes is between those who flirt with death and those who opt for slavery."[63] Drury's harsh conclusion is that "for all its contempt for America, [Fukuyama's] Kojèvean sensibility panders to the most vulgar aspects of her culture—her violent and anarchic qualities, and above all, her Rambo conception of valor."[64]

With the help of Wilson's *The Moral Sense*, Smith's *Theory of Moral Sentiments*, and recent evolutionary studies of moral emotions, Fukuyama learned his lesson, however. It was precisely the human tendency to make moral distinctions between people on the basis of their character that Fukuyama took note of after the mid-1990s when he examined the writings of Wilson, Smith, and the evolutionists. As noted earlier, Fukuyama, when he invoked Wilson's moral sense concept, wanted his readers to see that "we mean not that [people] are cooperative angels with unlimited resources for altruism but that they have built-in capabilities for perceiving the moral qualities of their fellow humans."[65] Here, Fukuyama referred to the key idea of Wilson's *The Moral Sense* that ordinary people naturally place high value on character traits such as self-control, fairness, capacity for sympathy, and respect for duty. Fukuyama's affirmative response to Wilson's moral sense idea clearly indicates that by the late 1990s, he no longer thought that a human being best achieves recognition by risking his life in a violent struggle for sheer prestige.

After *End of History*, Fukuyama revisited not only his conception of what people actually value but also the question of whether the valuing part of human nature indeed was "in decline" in America at the "end of history" and whether ordinary citizens in modern liberal democratic societies really were largely nonjudgmental.[66] That is, it appears that Wilson's moral sense idea— not by itself but in conjunction with both the new encouraging trends in crime and family life and Fukuyama's newly acquired knowledge of the evolutionary study of moral emotions—persuaded the author of *End of History* to rethink the persistence of human moral nature; he came to see that the psychological seat of values, understood as a built-in capacity "for perceiving the moral qualities of their fellow humans," was more deeply ingrained in human nature than he had suggested. Wilson, after all, had claimed that the moral sense was a product of human evolution and that it was firmly rooted in human nature, so that its spontaneous development in children could only be harmed by exceptional conditions (like those in the poor inner cities). Fukuyama had taken note of Wilson's arguments already in 1995 when he noted in *Trust* that Wilson had "documented at length that this moral side has a natural basis that is evident even in infants and young children who have not yet been 'socialized.'"[67] Fukuyama's approach was close to Wilson's at least by 1999 when he remarked that "what James Q. Wilson calls the 'moral sense' is put there by nature, and will operate in the absence of either a lawgiver or a prophet."[68]

Lastly, Fukuyama simply left out of his late 1990s works the idea that the psychological seat of values would principally evaluate the *self* and that it would therefore be related to selfishness. To repeat once more, Fukuyama's new understanding of the moral sense was such that human beings "have built-in capabilities for perceiving the moral qualities *of their fellow humans*" (emphasis added).[69]

By the late 1990s, then, Fukuyama could no longer stick to his earlier disturbing conception of the typical liberal democratic citizen. Contrary to what he had claimed (rather vaguely) in *End of History* in 1992, thymos, or the moral sense—whatever one should call the valuing part of human nature— simply could not be extinguished even if "liberal" culture did not support it in any significant way. The judging part of human nature seemed to be constantly active, making evaluations about people doing—or not doing—small good deeds in their community life, such as acts of sympathy and fairness. By the late 1990s, the violent battles for pure prestige no longer seemed so relevant for the world-renowned neoconservative author of *End of History*.

Fukuyama's Culture Wars: Elite Multiculturalism versus Popular Moral Sentiments

Despite Fukuyama's worldwide fame, the major scholarly works on neoconservative thought devote very little (if any) time to discuss Fukuyama's response to the culture wars. This is unfortunate, since *End of History* was hardly all that Fukuyama had to say about the moral culture in the United States in the 1990s. His later writings on such issues are an important testament to how the neoconservatives saw the post–Cold War situation, as well as how they reinvented eighteenth-century ideas of the moral sense and moral sentiments to wage cultural warfare. While there is reason to believe that Fukuyama genuinely changed his position on ordinary Americans as moral agents in the mid-1990s, it did not take long until he also used these reworked ideas about the morality of the common man to contest the ideas and politics of America's liberal intellectual elites and social reformers, as the first-generation neoconservatives had done.

That the culture war was high on Fukuyama's agenda in the 1990s becomes clear from his immediate reaction to Patrick Buchanan's famous culture wars speech at the Republican convention in August 1992. As Fukuyama put it in a 1993 *Commentary* essay, Buchanan was "right that a cultural war is upon us, and that this fight will be a central American preoccupation now that the cold war is over."[70] While Fukuyama agreed with Buchanan that "Anglo-American cultural values" were under threat in 1990s America, he disagreed with the Republican politician's nativist, paleoconservative view that third world immigration was a threat to such values. According to the neoconservative scholar, "the real sources of cultural breakdown" were not in some foreign cultures that newcomers brought to the United States but in broad socioeconomic factors such as capitalism, technological change, and economic factors at the workplace and in urban life. At least an equally important role was played by America's own "elite culture" that was not fully committed to "Enlightenment notions of the universality of human equality and freedom" but instead celebrated multiculturalism.[71] Fukuyama thus denounced Buchanan's conservative nativism and insisted, consistent with the more general neoconservative stance, that the "real fight, the central fight should not be over keeping newcomers out [but over] the question of assimilation itself: whether we believe that there is enough to our Western, rational, egalitarian, democratic civilization to force those coming to the country to absorb its language and rules, or whether we carry respect for other cultures to the point that Americans no longer have a common voice with which to speak to one another."[72]

In Fukuyama's culture war, then, like in Kristol's, Wilson's, and Gertrude Himmelfarb's, the "enemy" was America's "elite culture," and a key task was to oppose a supposedly perverse multiculturalism that "legitimates and even promotes continuing cultural differentness."[73] Besides the general celebration of "diversity," a more specific defect in America's elite culture was feminist mockery of "family values." The defense of the traditional two-parent family had been a neoconservative theme for decades by the 1990s, as we saw in chapter 3, but family values emerged at the center of public debate in the 1992 presidential campaign and in the related controversy over the sitcom Murphy Brown, which according to conservative critics, glamorized single motherhood.[74] Like Kristol, Wilson, and Himmelfarb, Fukuyama had relatively little understanding for cultural elites' "ideological assault on traditional family values—the sexual revolution; feminism and the delegitimation of the male-dominated household; the celebration of alternative lifestyles; attempts ruthlessly to secularize all aspects of American public life; the acceptance of no-fault divorce and the consequent rise of single-parent households."[75] Because of the multiculturalist and uncompromising feminist tendencies in America's own elite culture, the country's problem was "not the foreign culture that immigrants bring with them from the third world, but the contemporary elite culture of Americans. . . . In the upcoming block-by-block cultural war," Fukuyama asserted, "the enemy will not speak Spanish or have a brown skin. In [the cartoon character] Pogo's words, 'He is us.' "[76]

While Fukuyama thus defined America's elite culture, with its celebration of multiculturalism and feminism, as an "enemy" right after Buchanan's 1992 culture wars speech, much of his writing on culture wars issues dates from the latter half of the 1990s. As noted earlier, this was a period in which Fukuyama, like many of his fellow conservative Americans, felt encouraged by the recent comeback of "conservative" family norms, declining crime rates, and increasing associational life—social indicators that previously had made conservatives mourn over America's moral decline. Fukuyama did not think that the culture war was over by the decade's last years, however. To the contrary, in 1999, he still argued that "discussion, argument, even 'culture wars' " were required to turn down the misleading ideas about sex and family life that had been put forward during the post-1960s "great disruption"—ideas such as that "growing up in a single-parent family was no worse than growing up in an intact one" and that "children were better off if the parents divorced."[77] Indeed, he viewed the positive late 1990s social trends as only a *tentative* conservative turn. Thus in 1999, he cautioned his readers that it was "far too early to assert that these problems [of crime, divorce, illegitimacy, low levels of trust, and individualism] are now behind us."[78]

It was in this late 1990s context of an enduring culture war that Fukuyama harnessed the language of the Scottish moralists. At the time, Fukuyama put his mind into the question of "How to Re-moralize America"—the title of his 1999 essay and a key question in his 1999 book *Great Disruption*. Fukuyama's response to this question followed a similar logic as that of the first-generation neoconservatives in the sense that he, too, embraced the vocabulary of the moral sense and moral sentiments to make the point that anyone in America who wished to remoralize the country ought to place his or her faith in ordinary citizens instead of cultural or political elites. That is, Fukuyama—unlike the Religious Right that saw a religious revival (e.g., school prayer and Bible reading in schools) as the only proper means to remoralize America—used the secular language of the Scottish moralists to rationalize the idea that re-moralization ought to come "from below." Fukuyama agreed with religious conservatives that a remoralization process was necessary in the United States in the 1990s after several decades of moral decline. Yet he argued that "it is not clear . . . that the re-moralization of society need rely on the hierarchical authority of revealed religion. Against Nietzsche's view that moral behavior inevitably rests on dogmatic belief, we might counterpose Adam Smith, the Enlightenment philosopher with perhaps the most realistic and highly developed theory of moral action. . . . Smith argued that human beings are social and moral creatures by nature, capable of being led to moral behavior both by their natural passions and by their reason."[79] Thus consistent with Wilson's neoconservative reinvention of Scottish moral philosophy, Fukuyama argued that "religion is frequently not so much the product of dogmatic belief as it is a provider of a convenient language that allows communities to express moral beliefs that they would hold on entirely secular grounds."[80]

The Moral Sense and Spontaneous Order:
Neoconservative Moralism Meets the Neoliberal Order

In suggesting that culture wars era Americans had much to learn from Smith as the author of *Theory of Moral Sentiments*, Fukuyama was following in the footsteps of not only Wilson but also Kristol and Himmelfarb. Ever since the late 1970s, the neoconservatives had been arguing that contemporary Americans should study Smith and other eighteenth-century Scottish moral philosophers to see why ordinary people—not the intellectual elites—were the proper mainstay of social and moral order in the United States. Yet Fukuyama's line of reasoning on this issue differed somewhat from that of the older generation of neoconservatives. While Kristol's and Wilson's writings on the moral sense, moral sentiments, and common sense represented first-generation neoconservative moral populism that pitted the inherently moral and unerring ordinary people against the out-of-touch (antibourgeois) New Left intellectuals, Fukuyama's moral sentimentalism was an explicit response to a perceived post-1960s crisis of values that combined elements of *Public Interest*–style common-sense moralism with Hayek's economics of "spontaneous order" and evolutionary biology to produce an updated argument for bourgeois values and limited government. That is, Fukuyama introduced the natural moral sentiments and instincts of ordinary people as the biological origins of the human capacity for "spontaneous order" and, in so doing, made a case against multiculturalism and excessively rationalist government efforts to restore and reshape social order in America.

Fukuyama's reading of Smith's moral philosophy thus represents a new chapter in the neoconservative reception of the Scottish Enlightenment in two senses: not only did Fukuyama belong to a younger generation of neoconservative theorists, but he was also the first to merge the long-standing neoconservative anti-New Left spirit with the libertarian belief in the self-balancing and natural evolution of social order (which Hayek famously called "spontaneous order"). Indeed, in *Great Disruption*, Fukuyama made use of the Scottish concepts of the "moral sense" and "moral sentiments" (he used the latter concept when referring to Smith's book), as well as "moral instincts," "emotions," and "preexisting cognitive structures" to refer to the evolved psychological traits that could be counted on to act as persistent sources of a self-balancing moral order in human society.[81] While Fukuyama recommended some government action to reconstruct social order—relating, for example, to education and community policing—and explicitly distanced himself from "libertarians," the thrust of his argument was on the repertoire of natural moral instincts and sentiments as a foundation for a self-regulating community.[82] As Fukuyama put it in the first chapter of his book, one could expect the remaking of social order "to happen for a simple reason: human beings are *by nature* social creatures, whose most basic drives and instincts lead them to create moral rules that bind themselves together into communities. They are also by nature rational, and their rationality allows them to create ways of cooperating with one another spontaneously."[83]

Fukuyama's fervor for the idea of a self-balancing order derived in large part from recent research in biology and economics—including celebrated works such as Richard Dawkins's *The Blind Watchmaker: Why the Evidence of Evolution Reveals a Universe without Design* (1986) and Hayek's *The Fatal Conceit: The Errors of Socialism* (1988)—that had shown how order could emerge in a spontaneous fashion. The "systematic study of how order, and thus social capital, can emerge in a spontaneous and decentralized fashion" was, according to Fukuyama, "one of the most important intellectual developments of the late twentieth century."[84] As Fukuyama made clear, the biological theories that explained the role of natural moral instincts and emotions in the generation of spontaneous order were not entirely new, however. Already a hundred years before Dawkins, the Darwinian anthropologist Edward Westermarck—who was heavily influenced by both Smith's *Moral Sentiments* and Darwin's theory of the moral sense—had put forward a theory of the incest taboo that was, according to Fukuyama, "one of the best illustrations of how natural instincts can shape social norms in a rather direct way." Indeed, the incest taboo was "a good illustration" of norms that evolve "arationally" and "spontaneously"—in other words, without hierarchical organizations such as the state.[85]

If Fukuyama, in the aftermath of the period of the "great disruption" in moral values (mid-1960s to early 1990s), was enthusiastic about the natural human capacity for spontaneous order (and the scientific evidence for it), he was much less so about human rationality as expressed by government action. Government action was potentially harmful, he argued, in the sense that counterproductive actions might destroy social capital rather than help produce it and therefore make the country less hospitable to democracy and a healthy capitalist economy. In *Trust*, in 1995, Fukuyama already made the case that social capital "can be dissipated by the actions of governments much more readily than those governments can build it up again."[86] In the past, Fukuyama argued, many governments all over the world had by their counterproductive actions undermined "spontaneous sociability," which he saw as a key source of prosperity. This had also occurred in the United States, where "the weakening authority of civil associations has been connected with the rise of a strong state, through both the courts and the executive." The American welfare state had, for instance, encouraged "the breakdown of families" by subsidizing single motherhood. "Less obvious" was "how government policy can restore family structure once it has been broken."[87] The state had also encouraged a distorted multiculturalism and diversity in the school system. Therefore, Fukuyama noted that "one area in which the state needs to do less harm is in the question of assimilation of new Americans."[88] More generally, he concluded that "a first order of business might be to say that government policy should seek to do no harm, and in particular should not seek to undermine existing communal institutions in the pursuit of abstract diversity or openness."[89]

As a moderate critic of big government rationalism, Fukuyama thus invoked the moral sense, moral instincts, and related ideas to explain the human capacity to create order spontaneously. However, as a neoconservative culture warrior, Fukuyama had more specific claims to make about certain conservative values that according to him were necessary to "re-moralize" America. He underlined the importance of, and need for, such norms that best helped generate social capital—since that, in turn, helped sustain a healthy democratic political system and a flourishing capitalist economy. Societies "constantly need new rules," he argued, "to permit new forms of cooperative endeavor and to enable us to feel connected with one another in communities."[90]

Despite such references to the need of new rules in information age America, several themes in Fukuyama's late 1990s works suggest that for him, "re-moralization" meant a partial revival of what Andrew Hartman calls "normative America" of the postwar years—namely, the "cluster of powerful conservative norms [that] set the parameters of American culture" between 1945 and President Kennedy's assassination in 1963, including personal responsibility and delayed gratification as well as strict gender roles and stringent sexual expectations.[91] Indeed, Fukuyama naturalized some of the key norms of midcentury white middle-class culture by identifying virtues such as the meeting of obligations, honesty, and reciprocity—what he associated with Max Weber's "Puritan values" and what also overlap, to a significant degree, with "normative America's" high regard for deferred gratification, personal responsibility, and individual merit—with the biologically evolved moral sense of everyday people.[92] This was an effective means to defend these "Puritan" values, for once the aspects of the natural moral sense had been defined, all deviations from them seemed both unnatural and immoral. Toward the end of *Great Disruption*, he argued that ordinary citizens were "spontaneous" creators of just his own desired Puritan values. If left alone, he claimed, ordinary people "will, without much prompting, create order spontaneously simply by pursuing their daily individual ends and interacting with other people. . . . Honesty, trustworthiness, the keeping of commitments, and reciprocity in various forms will be practiced by many people much of the time and valued, at least in principle, by nearly everyone."[93] That ordinary people in fact did so was due to "the human emotional system [that] is equipped with [moral] feelings like anger, pride, shame, and guilt" that "come into play in response to people who either are honest and cooperate, or who cheat and break the rules."[94]

This was an interpretation of the natural "moral sense"—a term that he used once in *Great Disruption* and more systematically in his 2002 book on the consequences of the biotechnology revolution—that drew heavily from modern evolutionary psychology.[95] In stark contrast to religious conservatives of the era who associated their deepest moral commitments with God and rooted for a religious revival, but much like Wilson a few years earlier, Fukuyama argued that the moral sense—namely, the "special [moral] emotions or instincts"—had evolved by natural selection to "ensure that we . . . reward the angels and go out of our way to punish the devils."[96]

The use of the "moral sense," "moral instincts," and related ideas to naturalize the "Puritan values" was not Fukuyama's only means to wage cultural warfare in the late 1990s. He also directly confronted what he saw as unhealthy post-1960s relaxation of cultural attitudes toward the family and encouraged Americans to wage a culture war against such an ethos. While Fukuyama repeatedly denied that he advocated "anything like a return to Victorian values," he did encourage his fellow Americans to contest post-1960s conceptions of family life.[97] The post-1960s family norms, he argued, had "ended up hurting the interests of children: men abandoned families, women conceived children out of wedlock, and couples divorced for what were often superficial and self-indulgent reasons." In other words, during the post-1960s "great disruption," American culture had "produced many cognitive constructs that obscured from people the consequences of their personal behavior on people close to them."[98] Therefore, Fukuyama encouraged Americans to argue—to wage cultural warfare—against the post-1960s ideas that allegedly hurt the interests of children: "If it can be demonstrated to [parents] that their behavior

is seriously injuring the life chances of their offspring, they are likely to be-
have rationally and to want to alter that behavior in ways that help their children." In particular, Fukuyama stressed the importance of "male responsibility" and pondered whether women would eventually be persuaded to choose
to stay at home while their children are young.[99]

The promotion of "male responsibility" and the suggestion that small
children were perhaps best helped when mothers stayed at home, no doubt,
evoke images of "normative America" of the 1950s. Similarly, Fukuyama's criticism of contemporary American cultural ideals strengthens the impression
that he downplayed his sympathy for pre-1960s white middle-class cultural
standards, or at least for the self-confidence with which many middle-class
whites spoke of their value system in the postwar years. Fukuyama had res-
ervations about what he portrayed as the contemporary American "hierar-
chy of moral virtues" in which "tolerance ranks high and moralism—the attempt to judge people by one's own moral or cultural rules—ranks as the vice
among vices." Similarly, the contemporary American society was perhaps too
dedicated to "constant upending of norms and rules in the name of increasing individual freedom of choice." Such a condition was not for the benefit of
any society, Fukuyama cautioned, since in the end, such a society "will find
itself increasingly disorganized, atomized, isolated, and incapable of carrying
out common goals and tasks." He wanted his readers to recognize that a society's moral code might not be beneficial to it for the simple reason that "the
values may be the wrong ones."[100] Thus even if Fukuyama sympathized with
some aspects of the biological and economic spontaneous order literature,
he clearly wanted to dissociate himself from libertarian individualism that
(over)emphasized individual freedom of choice.

Fukuyama's response to the question of "How to re-moralize America?"
was, then, somewhat ambiguous. One the one hand, he reinvented the time-
honored ideas of the moral sense and moral sentiments in terms of biological
and economic literature on spontaneous order to explain how and why social
order would reconstitute itself if "the government get[s] out of the way of individuals and communities that want to create social order for themselves."[101]
On the other hand, he seems to have felt that ordinary Americans ought to be
encouraged by intellectual authorities such as himself to wage cultural warfare for proper family values. Moreover, to distance himself from libertarians,
he suggested that traditional hierarchies such as the state and church did also
have a role to play in the reconstitution of values.[102] Despite such ambiguity,
Fukuyama's primary point seemed to be that it was important to focus on and
learn from the spontaneous order literature. As he put it, what Americans
had lost in the postindustrial, post-1960s era was not universalistic principles

of individual rights and citizenship but "the ordinary morality"—namely, the habits of reciprocity, honesty, and trust—"that they were initially able to create for themselves." Thus in this situation, instead of relying on hierarchical authority in the form of religious and political authority to create social order, Americans should "presume that people will continue to use their innate capabilities and reason to evolve rules that serve their long-term interests and needs."[103]

While Fukuyama, in *Great Disruption*, embraced one of the key concepts of Hayekian free market advocates—spontaneous order—that was never popular with leading first-generation neoconservative theorists such as Kristol or Wilson, his late 1990s work on America's social and moral order is best seen as part of the neoconservative tradition rather than (what is sometimes called) "neoliberal" free market advocacy. Since neoliberal thought began, as historian Daniel Stedman Jones notes, "with a reductive reading of Adam Smith's premise of man as a rational, self-interested actor," Fukuyama' reinvention of Smith's thought is in fact a good example of how his thinking resembled that of Kristol and Wilson rather than "neoliberal" economists such as Hayek, Friedman, or Coase.[104] (Kristol and Fukuyama referred to this group of free market advocates as "libertarians"; in calling them "neoliberals," I am following the terminology of Stedman Jones and many other historians).[105]

In his late 1990s work, Fukuyama was following in the footsteps of older neoconservatives, such as Kristol, in the sense that both, as students of Smith's moral philosophy, took as their starting points optimistic ideas about human moral nature and proceeded from there to present relatively confident and morally encouraging ideas about ordinary Americans and the American bourgeois capitalist society. As we saw in chapter 1, Kristol, during the bleak days of the economic crisis of the 1970s, wanted to present an optimistic view of bourgeois capitalist society by drawing attention to the Smithian idea that ordinary people *as natural selves* were decent and virtuous—industrious, morally conscious, "sympathetic"—people, always willing to "better their condition" while taking into account their fellow citizens. Fukuyama, in turn, in the aftermath of the period of the "great disruption" in moral values, invoked Smith's *Moral Sentiments* and later works on moral instincts to remind big government rationalists and religious thinkers that ordinary citizens were moral beings by nature and capable of creating norms without hierarchical organizations such as the state.

While neoliberals such as Friedman, Hayek, and Coase, too, revered Smith as an inspiration, they tended to *avoid* Smith's conception of the moral individual while selectively using Smith's authority (i.e., *The Wealth of Nations*) to advance unambiguous ideas of the self-interested man in the marketplace, the invisible hand and the spontaneous power of the markets, and the virtues of limited government as opposed to government intrusion in the market-place.[106] As we have seen, Smith was much more ambivalent about such ideas, advocating a role for government in providing education and public works—such as canals, roads, and postal services—and warning of the "corruption of our moral sentiments" that followed from the disposition to admire the rich and to despise and neglect the poor. Yet Friedman, writing in 1976, claimed unambiguously that Smith "was attacking an entrenched system of govern-mental planning, control, and intervention," which in turn made Smith "a radical and revolutionary in his time—just as those of us who today preach laissez-faire are in our time."[107] What was important to neoliberal writers like Friedman was, then—as Stedman Jones puts it—"a virulent faith in the indi-vidual and his economic behavior under market conditions rather than any conception of cultivated behavior, manners, or Smithian moral sympathy."[108]

To say that the neoconservative interpretation of Smith differed from that of the neoliberal economists is not to say that the neoconservatives, as admirers of eighteenth-century Scottish moral philosophy, never sounded like allies—even if restrained allies—of less hesitating free market advocates. In showing how to use Smith's ethics to construct a (morally) encourag-ing view of American liberal-capitalist society, the neoconservatives can be seen as serving the cause of neoliberals. One might even say, as I noted in chapter 1, following Gary Gerstle's slightly different claim about neoconser-vative "neo-Victorianism," that the neoconservatives—with their Scottish Enlightenment–inspired ethics—endowed the post-1970s "neoliberal order" with a moral perspective.

Still, in the end, it is important to bear in mind that as moral thinkers, neoconservative theorists such as Kristol and Fukuyama clearly differed from libertarian and neoliberal free market advocates. Unlike Friedman and his coideologues, the neoconservatives never wholeheartedly celebrated the ac-tions of the rational, self-interested actor in the competitive marketplace as expressions of human freedom.[109] Instead, Kristol and later Fukuyama directly attacked the economic reductionism of modern "libertarianism" and empha-sized the need to engage in a cultural war against America's liberal intellectuals who had done much to disrupt the country's pre-sixties bourgeois moral order and social stability. It was precisely because of the neoconservatives' eagerness to throw themselves into the middle of a cultural war that they ended up de-veloping a distinctive, refined moral perspective. While this neoconservative moral perspective that associated virtues such as self-control, personal respon-sibility, and self-betterment with the moral sense of ordinary people, in a way, morally sanctioned the free market ideology of the post-1970s neoliberal order, it also conflicted with it, for the market—the leitmotif of neoliberalism—was indifferent to people's moral characters, hardly favored thrift and self-control, and encouraged a pluralism of identities and lifestyles.[110]

Coming to the late 1990s, Fukuyama had thus embraced many of the key ideas that characterized the *Public Interest* group's cultural warfare. In 1992, as a follower of Nietzsche and Strauss, Fukuyama had portrayed the ordinary liberal democratic citizen as the nonjudgmental "last man," but a few years later, he—like Kristol, Himmelfarb, and Wilson—described ordinary Americans as the guardians of civilization and pointed to America's post-1960s elite culture as a force that had helped damage valuable aspects of the bourgeois moral culture that had dominated postwar America.

Similarly, for Fukuyama, as for other neoconservative moral thinkers, an appeal to the "moral sense" was, very much like an appeal to "common sense" had been for British writers after the repeal of preventive censorship in the eighteenth century, a means of marking the limits of tolerable discourse and behavior. An inability to pay heed to ordinary Americans and their moral sense was, according to Fukuyama, Wilson, and others, behind America's post-1960s cultural decline and many (if not most) recent political mistakes. Indeed, when the neoconservatives drew attention to the moral system of average Americans as the place where the moral sense or common sense was present, they also indicated where it was absent: in the multiculturalist ethos of America's cultural elite and in overly rationalist enterprises of government bureaucrats. To remoralize America, one needed to get rid of the distorted multiculturalism and overly confident, excessive rationalism of the liberal elites and to get back in touch with the instinctive morality of everyday people.

Each one of these neoconservative writers—Kristol, Himmelfarb, Wilson, and Fukuyama—with their respective formulations of the "moral sense," "moral sentiments," and "common sense," in one way or another, rationalized white middle-class cultural standards of the 1950s—namely, self-control, deferred gratification, personal responsibility, dutifulness, and the traditional two-parent family model. Among historians, there is ongoing debate as to what extent such bourgeois norms actually dominated American culture in the 1940s and 1950s—and to what extent they were questioned at the time by an emergent mass culture of self-expression, sexual freedom, and rejection of paternal authority.[111] While few historians today argue that there was a full national consensus in the 1940s and 1950s, neoconservative culture wars rhetoric that pitted the antibourgeois post-1960s liberal intellectuals against the inherently moral ordinary people at least implied that there actually was a normative consensus based on ("commonsensical") bourgeois morality before the infamous sixties. In this book, I have suggested (in line with previous scholarship) that the culture war of the 1980s and 1990s was a result of very real and massive cultural contradictions of the 1960s—namely, that the 1960s universalized cultural fracture. Yet at the same time, it is important to bear in mind that many of the modernist ideas and social movements that contributed to cultural fracture in late twentieth-century America (and which the neoconservatives attacked) were already present in some form in the easily caricatured 1950s America.

The Scottish-inspired moral sentimentalist ideas of Kristol, Wilson, Himmelfarb, and Fukuyama were thus in important respects similar, but they were far from identical. A key difference between Fukuyama and the three first-generation neoconservatives is that Fukuyama's works are not easily—and should not be—categorized as populist. Earlier we have seen that Kristol's and Wilson's rhetoric in the culture wars was populist in the sense that these two writers constructed an opposition between the elites and the conservative-minded common people, presented the people as the unerring source of truth, and posed as educated experts in common sense or popular moral sentiments. Himmelfarb contributed to this discourse by helping establish a noble genealogy for neoconservative common-sense populism—that is, she connected neoconservatism with the (in her words) "populist" social ethic of the Scottish Enlightenment and placed it in opposition with the elitist rationalism of the French Enlightenment. Furthermore, Wilson used Scottish ideas such as the moral sense and moral sentiments to portray middle Americans as the *only* "real people" and thus encouraged the exclusion of academic and other liberal elites, as well as the black underclass, from this idealized group. This kind of rejection of moral or cultural pluralism in the name of a supposedly concerted "people" is, as noted earlier, a key feature of populism. Fukuyama, even if he, too, invoked the shared moral sense and related ideas to sanction his preferred (pre-1960s) moral values, did not paint a picture of the "real people" as morally pure or unerring but instead at times pointed out that, as we saw underlined in chapter 3, ordinary Americans "seek contradictory [moral] goals."[112] Moreover, Fukuyama did not divide the society into opposing camps of the black underclass and ordinary Americans. While Fukuyama did juxtapose ordinary citizens—who, according to him, were natural creators of moral values—with rationalist political elites in his late 1990s works, these texts were directed against the *over*confident, excessive rationalism of big government liberals, not so much against "elites," "experts," or "intellectuals" as such, as many of Kristol's and Wilson's texts were. These questions relating to the exclusive and inclusive dimensions of the neoconservative version of common-sense moralism will be elaborated on in the epilogue.

Conservative Intellectuals and the Boundaries of the People

Following the US presidential election of 2016, journalists and scholars repeatedly observed that many major conservative intellectuals from George Will to David Frum and David Brooks vehemently opposed Donald Trump. Trump's electoral victory and politics, it was said, shocked the intellectual right that had long defended the principles of free markets, limited government, and moral character. In the same spirit, prominent historians have suggested that studying the conservative intellectual movement—the "polite" wing of the post–World War II American right—is not particularly helpful in order to make sense of the rise of Trump's populist politics.[1]

The story of the neoconservative culture wars proves otherwise. Indeed, the history of neoconservatism's alliance with "ordinary" Americans and engagement with Scottish moral sentimentalist philosophy in the 1980s and 1990s is an important testament to the fact that the rise of Trump as a political actor was a consequence rather than the cause. Insofar as Trump's use of language represents conservative culture warfare in the late 2010s and early 2020s—a strong case can be made that @realDonaldTrump was the nation's premier conservative culture warrior in the years that saw the rise of #MeToo and Black Lives Matter—it resembles that of Irving Kristol and his coideologues who in the 1980s and 1990s wanted to explain to "the people" why they were right and to "the intellectuals" why they were wrong. Thus in order to understand the Trump phenomenon, students of US politics should pay more—not less—attention to the languages of right-wing public intellectuals such as the neoconservatives.

During the last two decades of the twentieth century, neoconservative intellectuals such as Kristol and James Q. Wilson followed a populist logic that, as Jan-Werner Müller points out, dismisses parts of the citizenry "as immoral and not properly a part of the people at all."[2] To borrow the words of political scientist Yascha Mounk, populists are thus "demarcating the boundaries of the *demos*."[3] In the neoconservative culture wars, the *in*-group consisted of working- and middle-class whites; namely, segments of the population that assumedly shared the neoconservatives' views on the need for traditional family values, severe punishments for criminals, and the bourgeois values of hard work, delayed gratification, personal responsibility, and individual merit.

In being a means to demarcate the boundaries of the ("real") people, the neoconservative language of "the moral sense," "moral sentiments," and "common sense," then, only seemed to be a unifying language. Despite this aspect of hypocrisy, one may ask whether the neoconservative intellectuals' systematic efforts to speak in the name of commonsensical "ordinary Americans" included, after all, some helpful building blocks for a truly unifying vision, one that transcends identity attachments and provides something in the way of a shared glue of "we-ness" in a fractured America. This theme is extremely relevant not only for the political right but also for the left, for, as intellectual historian David Hollinger writes, "A stronger national solidarity enhances the possibility of social and economic justice within the United States. This is a simple point, but an extremely important one. Any society that cannot see its diverse members as somehow 'in it together' is going to have trouble distributing its resources with even a modicum of equity."[4] Could nonconservatives, then, learn something from neoconservative culture wars thought that highlighted the moral intuitions and capacities shared by all or most Americans? Is there perhaps a way for left-liberals to capture some aspects of neoconservative thought for their project of social democracy?

To be sure, one can point to some elements in the moral language of the neoconservatives that might provide clues for those in search for a unifying vision. After all, the neoconservatives invoked everyman's moral sense, moral sentiments, and common sense precisely to respond to cultural fracture and the supposedly ill-conceived celebration of diversity by post-1960s liberals and praised the eighteenth-century Scottish moralists for their "democratic," morally "egalitarian" ideas. In the context of the culture wars of the 1980s and 1990s, in an environment in which feminists, Afrocentrists, and multiculturalists often seemed to settle for their own truths or celebrate relativism, this neoconservative language stood out as a seemingly universalist, color-blind alternative. Indeed, as articulate opponents of feminism, Afrocentrism, and multiculturalism, the neoconservatives anticipated post-2016 criticism of identity politics that, according to critics, erects "separate spheres for each cultural and ethnic group" and in doing so "embrace[s] principles that would ultimately destroy the very possibility of a truly open and multiethnic democracy."[5]

Moreover, those writers who yearn for national solidarity and criticize both right-wing populism a la Trump and leftist identity politics would probably agree with the neoconservatives of the 1980s and 1990s that a fractured America needs a renewed faith in moral principles such as fairness, self-control, duty, and sympathy—virtues and character traits that Wilson celebrated in *The Moral Sense*. Authors who search for a unifying moral and political vision would probably add that these virtues are desirable especially in the social media, which, as a platform for hate speech and fake news, divides the world into various groups of like-minded people and is itself one of the key factors behind the rise of populism (along with economic stagnation and rapid social changes).[6]

Because of Wilson's and his neoconservative friends' consistent emphasis on the need for "self-control" and other social virtues—and their praise for the common man's capacity for moral judgment in such issues—there are good grounds for asking whether they would have been horrified by everything that President Trump as a character represents. Indeed, while I have here emphasized the similarities between the neoconservatives' populist efforts to speak for the moral everyman and Trumpian pleas for the forgotten men and women of America, one should also keep in mind that Wilson, Kristol, and Gertrude Himmelfarb spent much of their careers writing and talking about the importance of "moral character"—indeed, "the moral sense," in their use, referred to a psychological seat for making moral judgments on people's character and behavior. Based on their praise for the common man's moral sense and criticism of elite "nonjudgmentalism," it seems quite evident that they would have strictly condemned Trump's impetuous behavior and coarse language—for example, his sexist comments on grabbing women by their genitals and racist comments on Mexican immigrants as rapists.

Himmelfarb, in fact, criticized the increasingly rude language used by some factions of the American right years before Trump's emergence as a political figure. She made it clear in 2006 that American conservatives should not respond to the country's emerging "PC culture" by going to the other extreme, to a *South Park*-style, vulgar and raunchy language. To her, the new breed of conservatives who rejected "the image of conservatives as uptight squares" by "boasting that they could drink, cuss, smoke . . . , tell dirty jokes, and be as raunchy as the best of them" were no conservatives at all. "South Park conservatism," to her, was "an oxymoron, being not only antiliberal but anticonservative as well."[7] It is very likely that Himmelfarb, in her last years, saw the Trump phenomenon in such terms as the latest and most powerful manifestation of an extremely undesirable vulgar trend in the American right (Himmelfarb passed away in December 2019 at the age of ninety-seven). Himmelfarb's strong repudiation of the emerging bad-mannered conservatism of the 2000s makes one wonder whether some of the older neoconservatives' moral ideas—or the Enlightenment theories that inspired them—could provide us with resources to counter the unwelcome rude tendencies in "Trumpian" right-wing populist discourse.

I have already noted that those seeking a cure for the "contempt machines of social media" may find some encouragement in the neoconservatives' Scottish-inspired works such as Wilson's *The Moral Sense* that was an explicit effort to "help people recover the confidence with which they once spoke about virtue and morality."[8] Yet as a cure for contempt, Wilson's work is flawed because of its confrontational anti-intellectual aspects. At a time when many observers complain that public discourse suffers from an overflow of raw emotion and the ridicule of those holding a different opinion, it might be best to consult the work of the original eighteenth-century moral sentimentalists—David Hume and Adam Smith. The neoconservatives, in their populist celebration of everyman's moral sentiments, largely ignored Hume's and Smith's ideas on sentimental education, which seem particularly relevant as guidelines for those seeking to combat the spreading of anger and contempt. Hume in particular, as we have seen, was highly suspicious of uncultured moral sentiments that favored our friends and those whose characters are most like our own. Thus he tried to explain how our undeveloped, narrow sense of sympathy could be broadened and our partial moral sentiments made impartial.[9] Smith, meanwhile, argued that our "untaught and undisciplined feelings" required continuous tutoring and worried about the "corruption" of moral sentiments. He also described how an impartial spectator as a voice of conscience developed through "constant practice" and acknowledged that learning facts about human moral sentiments could help us correct and refine those very sentiments (even if he held that the work of moral philosophers was basically descriptive).[10] That's why a better understanding of the Enlightenment moral theories that stimulated the neoconservatives may prove useful for those seeking ways to cultivate understanding across difference and a more constructive competition of ideas.

Political theorist Michael Frazer, in his *The Enlightenment of Sympathy: Justice and the Moral Sentiments in the Eighteenth Century and Today* (2010), builds on Hume's, Smith's, and Johann Gottfried von Herder's ideas on sentimental education and argues that "a sentimentalist theory of civic education" has much to offer to those who wish to build bridges over barriers of difference. As he puts it, the sentimentalist perspective underlines that one's "reflective capacities can only be developed through the education of the whole person— emotion and imagination included." It all begins at a young age, within the family, where children first develop their capacity to sympathize with the feelings of others. Most importantly, sentimentalists "offer a distinctive defense of the liberal arts by focusing on their power to lead students through the progress of sentiments, which they see as central to proper moral and political reflection." To give students "powers necessary to understand even those most different from themselves," liberal arts education must involve cultivating students' imaginative and emotional as well as rational capacities. "A sentimentalist educator," Frazer writes, "is thus neither a neutral provider of mere information nor an ideological indoctrinator, but rather a catalyst for the reflective and autonomous progress of sentiments necessary for mature moral judgment."[11]

While Hume's and Smith's sentimentalist theories may thus provide some building blocks for a renewed civic education necessary for building solidarity and understanding across difference, the neoconservatives' reworked language of moral sentiments and the moral sense was, more than anything, a conservative political instrument in the culture wars environment, not a helpful means to unify a fractured nation. A discourse centered on human moral nature—as opposed to an ethnos-centered discourse—does have the potential to increase solidarity by enlarging awareness of shared emotions and experiences.[12] Nonetheless, systematic efforts to define the nature of the moral sense are probably not particularly useful for political actors who see common culture as a necessary starting point for solidarity that is needed to build social democracy. In *Common Sense: A Political History*, Sophia Rosenfeld shows that historically, claims about common sense have typically provoked new schisms rather than convergence, since they are—"regardless of [common sense's] advocates' fervent claims of universality and moderation"—"almost always polemical: statements about consensus and certainty used to particular, partisan, and destabilizing effect."[13] The history of neoconservatism provides evidence that the same holds true with the language(s) of the moral sense and moral sentiments when such language is invoked by agents operating in the political arena. That the moral sentimentalist language of Kristol, Wilson, Himmelfarb, and Francis Fukuyama was not particularly useful as a means to bring together a fractured nation is hardly surprising given the depth of the chasm that "the sixties" created between the country's conservative and liberal elites and that the neoconservatives appealed to the moral sense and related concepts to champion many all-too-evidently conservative—and often Republican—political goals—namely, welfare state contraction, the traditional two-parent family, and stricter punishment for criminals.

Despite such shortcomings, one can take the history of the "neoconservative common man" as a reminder of the importance of being attentive to nontechnocratic voices in addition to experts—a plurality of voices is, after all, necessary for a well-functioning democracy. The neoconservative culture warriors, as we have seen, staged their battle against moral relativism, non-judgmentalism, and multiculturalism as a battle against "intellectuals" or "experts." Yet one can surely fight relativism and promote a unifying moral vision without pronouncing an all-out war on every authoritative source of information and expertise. Neoconservative culture warriors of the 1980s and 1990s consciously decided to use anti-intellectualist, even populist, language as a means of persuasion to convince other Americans to join their side and to endorse their views on particular issues, to the extent that it was sometimes regretted. "In retrospect," Wilson wrote in response to a reviewer of *The Moral Sense* in 1994, "I suppose that I did overstate the difference in moral sensibility between intellectuals and what I persist in thinking of as real people. Had I two of the classic virtues—temperance and prudence—in greater supply, I would have tempered that language without entirely abandoning the point."[14] Tellingly, despite such regret, Wilson kept using similar language in the latter half of the 1990s, after this exchange of words and moment of self-examination. In keeping up the polarizing theme, Wilson was just putting into practice the neoconservatives' self-imposed 1983 program of explaining to "the people" why they were right and to "the intellectuals" why they were wrong.

Acknowledgments

This book has benefited immensely from the insightful comments of several students of US intellectual history. At the early stages, J. David Hoeveler Jr., an expert on the Scottish intellectual tradition and US conservatism, was persuasive in suggesting that the Scottish philosophical tradition deserved a careful look in my study, even if it was primarily about recent American political and cultural controversies. Andrew Hartman, as an unrivaled expert on the history of the American culture wars, encouraged me to focus on themes such as race that would help the work gain traction in the American historiographical discourse. At the closing stages of the study, Andrew again stepped in and gave me useful comments and much encouragement, for which I owe a special debt of gratitude to him. Daniel Wickberg, very importantly, helped me clarify my argument by encouraging me to be more explicit about how I see the agency of neoconservative thinkers in the shaping of moral and political language. Later he, too, read the entire manuscript and again gave valuable comments. Finally, as an author of two books on neoconservatism, Gary Dorrien helpfully pointed out that my study on the neoconservative culture wars also needs some forest-and-trees explaining to ensure that the entire neoconservative phenomenon, with its different factions, comes clearly into view.

I am also deeply indebted to Markku Peltonen and Petteri Pietikäinen, two vitally important mentors at the early stages of my academic career. For the past decade, they have provided me with both friendship and an excellent model for scholarly inquiry. During this project, they offered invaluable advice and crucial support in innumerable ways.

I am thankful for the contributions and cheerful company of all my colleagues in the history department at the University of Helsinki, my home institution during the writing of this book. Wide-ranging discussions and friendship with Mikko Immanen have been especially important to me through the years. Kari Saastamoinen consistently identified themes that needed more thorough analysis in the drafts of individual chapters and made sophisticated remarks on the parts dealing with eighteenth-century Scottish moral philosophy. Soile Ylivuori, Laura Tarkka-Robinson, Anna Koivusalo, Tupu Ylä-Anttila, Elise Garritzen, Markku Kekäläinen, and Antti Taipale also deserve thanks for giving helpful feedback and for their warm companionship.

My colleague and friend Otto Pipatti also deserves a big thanks. I have enjoyed spending time with him discussing our shared interests—such as the Scottish Enlightenment—while exploring Helsinki's burgeoning public sauna scene. In Finland, there is no better guide to saunas and Adam Smith than Otto.

I began this study while working in a research project on evolutionary theories of morality led by Olli Lagerspetz. I wish to thank him and others in the group for all their support. I also want to thank Ari Helo and Janne Kivivuori for reading individual chapters and giving helpful feedback. My thanks also go to Kevin Drain and Erik Hieta for grammar revision. Naturally, they are not responsible for any remaining errors. I am also grateful to the Kone Foundation, the University of Helsinki Research Foundation, and the Finnish Cultural Foundation for funding my research.

I also wish to thank the readers for the University of Chicago Press for extremely valuable comments. I was very pleased to have my manuscript reviewed by specialists on both twentieth-century American and eighteenth-century Scottish thought. I am grateful to Michael Frazer, an expert on the Scottish Enlightenment, whose generous comments helped me clarify a number of important points. At the press, I want to especially thank Timothy Mennel for all his work on this book as well as his faith and encouragement along the way. My thanks also go to others at the press who helped make this book a reality, including Susannah Engstrom, Rachel Kelly Unger, Elizabeth Ellingboe, Tyler McGaughey, and Levi Stahl. Thanks also to Danny Constantino at Scribe for project management and to Vaneesa Cook for indexing.

I am grateful, too, to the archivists and librarians who aided my work, especially Patrick Kerwin at the Library of Congress Manuscript Division in Washington, DC, Susan Scheiberg at RAND Library in Santa Monica, CA, and Harry Miller at the Wisconsin Historical Society in Madison.

Finally, I want to thank the three people with whom I share my home: my partner, Tuuli, our daughter, Emilia, and our son, Erik. Large parts of this book were written in my own Helsinki apartment, and I was not always particularly happy about the working conditions with our noisy neighbors or (after their relocation) the disturbing silence. Now that I have been a parent for over two years and I write these lines in our new home, hearing these three wonderful people fooling around in the background, I realize that I have finally entered the perfect soundscape. Therefore, I thank my loved ones for creating a joyous atmosphere for writing and for living.

Notes

Introduction

1. Irving Kristol, "Whatever Happened to Common Sense?," *Wall Street Journal*, January, 17, 1984, 30. On the culture wars, see James Davison Hunter, *Culture Wars: The Struggle to Define America* (New York: Basic Books, 1991); Andrew Hartman, *A War for the Soul of America: A History of the Culture Wars* (Chicago: University of Chicago Press, 2015); Irene Taviss Thomson, *Culture Wars and Enduring American Dilemmas* (Ann Arbor: University of Michigan Press, 2010); James Davison Hunter and Alan Wolfe, eds., *Is There a Culture War? A Dialogue on Values and American Public Life* (Washington, DC: Brookings Institution, 2006); and David T. Court-wright, *No Right Turn: Conservative Politics in a Liberal America* (Cambridge, MA: Harvard University Press, 2010). Buchanan is quoted in Morris P. Fiorina, Samuel J. Abrams, and Jeremy C. Pope, *Culture Wars? The Myth of a Polarized America*, 3rd ed. (Boston: Longman, 2011), 1. As Fiorina, Abrams, and Pope point out (pp. 2, 7n21), the divisions over morality, religion, and sexuality seemed new to political commentators whose experiences of political life stretched back to the midcentury, when such issues were relatively muted and economic conflict—capitalism versus socialism—animated politics. Of course, cultural conflict as such was not new in the United States.

2. Kristol, "Whatever Happened to Common Sense?," 30.

3. Irving Kristol, *On the Democratic Idea in America* (New York: Harper & Row, 1972), 11, 14.

4. While the neoconservatives celebrated Hutcheson, Hume, and Smith as philosophers who had high regard for ordinary people and their natural "moral sense" or "moral sentiments," they simply ignored the famed eighteenth-century Scottish "common sense" philosopher Thomas Reid. The neoconservative reference point during the culture wars was typically the human emotional pattern, or the "heart," not reason or the "head." The moral sense concept served this purpose even better than common sense. See the section "The Morality of Ordinary People in Scottish Philosophy" in chapter 1. The significant differences between Hutchesonian "moral sense" and Smithian "moral sentiments" are also discussed in chapter 1.

5. Previously, only two scholars have made serious attempts to explain the significance of the Anglo-Scottish Enlightenment for neoconservatism, and both of these scholars focus solely on Irving Kristol—in fact, solely on Kristol's 1976 essay on Smith, in which Kristol portrayed the tradition of the Anglo-Scottish Enlightenment as a moderate and humane alternative to the collectivistic hubris of the French Enlightenment. See Gary Dorrien, *The Neoconservative Mind:*

Politics, Culture, and the War of Ideology (Philadelphia: Temple University Press, 1993), 104–12; and Nicholas Xenos, "Neoconservatism Kristolized," *Salmagundi* (Spring/Summer 1987): 138–49.

6. On neoconservatism, see Justin Vaïsse, *Neoconservatism: The Biography of a Movement* (Cambridge, MA: Belknap Press of Harvard University Press, 2011); Dorrien, *Neoconservative Mind*; Peter Steinfels, *The Neoconservatives: The Origins of a Movement*, with a new foreword (1979; repr., New York: Simon & Schuster, 2013); Mark Gerson, *The Neoconservative Vision: From the Cold War to the Culture Wars* (Lanham, MD: Madison Books, 1996); Murray Friedman, *The Neoconservative Revolution: Jewish Intellectuals and the Shaping of Public Policy* (New York: Cambridge University Press, 2005); Jean-François Drolet, *American Neoconservatism: The Politics and Culture of a Reactionary Idealism* (New York: Oxford University Press, 2013); Adam L. Fuller, *Taking the Fight to the Enemy: Neoconservatism and the Age of Ideology* (Lanham, MD: Lexington Books, 2012); C. Bradley Thompson, with Yaron Brook, *Neoconservatism: An Obituary for an Idea* (Boulder, CO: Paradigm, 2010); Jacob Heilbrunn, *They Knew They Were Right: The Rise of the Neocons* (New York: Doubleday, 2008); Gary Dorrien, *Imperial Designs: Neoconservatism and the New Pax Americana* (New York: Routledge, 2004); Douglas Murray, *Neoconservatism: Why We Need It* (New York: Encounter Books, 2006); John Ehrman, *The Rise of Neoconservatism: Intellectuals and Foreign Affairs 1945–1994* (New Haven, CT: Yale University Press, 1995); and Stefan Halper and Jonathan Clarke, *America Alone: The Neo-conservatives and the Global Order* (Cambridge: Cambridge University Press, 2004). See also Brandon High, "The Recent Historiography of American Neoconservatism," *Historical Journal* 52, no. 2 (2009): 475–91. Books that focus on neoconservative foreign policy are those by Vaïsse, Ehrman, Heilbrunn, Dorrien (*Imperial Designs*), Murray, Drolet, and Halper and Clarke.

7. The neoconservatives made up an intellectual "movement" only in a loose sense.

8. Gerson, *Neoconservative Vision*, 258.

9. Fuller, *Taking the Fight to the Enemy*, 218. A similar argument about the neoconservative culture wars is made in Vaïsse, *Neoconservatism*, 232. On the neoconservatives' instrumental approach to religion, see, e.g., Friedman, *Neoconservative Revolution*, 218–19, 230–31; Damon Linker, *The Theocons: Secular America under Siege* (New York: Doubleday, 2006), 7; and J. David Hoeveler Jr., *Watch on the Right: Conservative Intellectuals in the Reagan Era* (Madison: University of Wisconsin Press, 1991), 107.

10. Thompson and Brook, *Neoconservatism*, 152–55, 159; see also Drolet, *American Neoconservatism*; Paul Edward Gottfried, *Leo Strauss and the Conservative Movement in America: A Critical Appraisal* (New York: Cambridge University Press, 2012); Shadia B. Drury, *Leo Strauss and the American Right* (New York: St. Martin's, 1997); and Anne Norton, *Leo Strauss and the Politics of American Empire* (New Haven, CT: Yale University Press, 2004).

11. Steinfels, *Neoconservatives*, xiii; Dorrien, *Neoconservative Mind*, 368; Dorrien, *Imperial Designs*, 14–15.

12. Sophia Rosenfeld, *Common Sense: A Political History* (Cambridge, MA: Harvard University Press, 2011); Henry May, *The Enlightenment in America* (New York: Oxford University Press, 1976), 342–44. See also Charles Bradford Bow, ed., *Common Sense in the Scottish Enlightenment* (Oxford: Oxford University Press, 2018).

13. Moral sentimentalism argues that morality originates not in reason alone but at least partly in sentiments. See, e.g., Michael B. Gill, "Moral Rationalism vs. Moral Sentimentalism: Is Morality More like Math or Beauty?," *Philosophy Compass* 2, no. 1 (January 2007): 16–30. In contrast to Kristol's Anglo-Scottish Enlightenment, other neoconservative writers typically spoke of the Scottish Enlightenment or the British Enlightenment. Significantly, though, they all had in

mind, in most cases, the *Scottish* moral sentimentalist philosophers Francis Hutcheson, David Hume, and Adam Smith. The neoconservatives had the tendency to lump these different sentimentalist thinkers together. An English philosopher, Lord Shaftesbury, discussed the notion of moral sense in his works at the turn of the seventeenth century but only casually—he did not develop a theory of the moral sense. Yet Shaftesbury is considered an important influence on later Scottish moral philosophy. See, e.g., D. D. Raphael, *The Impartial Spectator: Adam Smith's Moral Philosophy* (Oxford: Oxford University Press, 2007), 28. In this study, I will use the terms *Anglo-Scottish Enlightenment*, *Scottish Enlightenment*, and *British Enlightenment* interchangeably, following the neoconservative practice.

14. One can find both egalitarian *and* elitist passages and themes in the works of the leading eighteenth-century Scottish moral philosophers (see chapter 1). This is especially true of Smith, the neoconservatives' favorite Scottish thinker. Among experts on eighteenth-century thought, Samuel Fleischacker favors an egalitarian interpretation of Smith and Scottish moral philosophy more generally; see his "The Impact on America: Scottish Philosophy and the American Founding," in *The Cambridge Companion to the Scottish Enlightenment*, ed. Alexander Broadie (Cambridge: Cambridge University Press, 2003), 333; *On Adam Smith's Wealth of Nations* (Princeton, NJ: Princeton University Press, 2004), 75–78; and "Adam Smith on Equality," in *The Oxford Handbook of Adam Smith*, ed. Christopher J. Berry, Maria Pia Paganelli, and Craig Smith (Oxford: Oxford University Press, 2013), 485–500. For a different view, see, e.g., Eric Schliesser, *Adam Smith: Systematic Philosopher and Public Thinker* (New York: Oxford University Press, 2017), 117–18.

15. Irving Kristol, *Reflections of a Neoconservative: Looking Back, Looking Ahead* (New York: Basic Books, 1983), xiv–xv.

16. Wilson to Michael Joyce, August 9, 1994, box 16, folder 18, James Q. Wilson Public Policy Collection, Pardee RAND Graduate School, Santa Monica, California (hereafter Wilson Collection); James Q. Wilson, *The Moral Sense* (New York: Free Press, 1993).

17. James Q. Wilson, "Untitled," outline (with the acronym *TMS*), box 19, folder 8, Wilson Collection. The outline is marked as "untitled" in the Wilson Collection Finding Aid, but actually, it is titled "TMS," which might refer to Smith's *Theory of Moral Sentiments* or else Wilson's own *The Moral Sense*. I have removed underlining from parts of the quote. James Q. Wilson, *Moral Judgment: Does the Abuse Excuse Threaten Our Legal System?* (New York: Basic Books, 1997); James Q. Wilson, "On Abortion," *Commentary* 97, no. 1 (January 1994): 21–29; James Q. Wilson, "Against Homosexual Marriage," *Commentary* 101, no. 3 (March 1996): 34–39.

18. Gertrude Himmelfarb, "Three Paths to Modernity: The British, American, and French Enlightenments" (lecture, American Enterprise Institute Bradley Lecture Series, Washington DC, May 10, 2004), American Enterprise Institute online, http://www.aei.org/publication /three-paths-to-modernity/. See also Gertrude Himmelfarb, "Armut und zweierlei Aufklärung," in *Aufklärung Heute: Castelgandolfo-Gespräche 1996*, ed. Krzysztof Michalski (Stuttgart, Ger.: Klett-Cotta, 1997), 162–201; Gertrude Himmelfarb, "The Idea of Compassion: The British vs. the French Enlightenment," *Public Interest*, no. 145 (Fall 2001): 3–24; Gertrude Himmelfarb, "Two Enlightenments: A Contrast in Social Ethics," *Proceedings of the British Academy* 117 (2001): 297–324; and Gertrude Himmelfarb, *The Roads to Modernity: The British, French, and American Enlightenments* (New York: Alfred A. Knopf, 2004).

19. Francis Fukuyama, "How to Re-moralize America," *Wilson Quarterly* 23, no. 3 (1999): 39.

20. James Q. Wilson, "Foreword," in *The Essential Neoconservative Reader*, ed. Mark Gerson (Reading, MA: Addison-Wesley, 1996), ix.

21. Jefferson Cowie, *Stayin' Alive: The 1970s and the Last Days of the Working Class* (New York: New Press, 2010), 194–95; Stephen R. Duncan, "Social and Cultural—a Historiographical Survey," in *The Routledge History of the Twentieth-Century United States*, ed. Jerald Podair and Darren Dochuk (New York: Routledge, 2018), 141; Michael Kazin, *The Populist Persuasion: An American History*, rev. ed. (Ithaca, NY: Cornell University Press, 1998), 246.

22. For analyses of the white working class (and some liberal misperceptions of it) in the United States, see Joan C. Williams, *White Working Class: Overcoming Class Cluelessness in America* (Boston: Harvard Business Review Press, 2017); and Arlie Russell Hochschild, *Strangers in Their Own Land: Anger and Mourning on the American Right* (New York: New Press, 2016).

23. On moral sentimentalism and the secularization of ethics, see Michael B. Gill, *The British Moralists on Human Nature and the Birth of Secular Ethics* (New York: Cambridge University Press, 2006). On common sense, see Rosenfeld, *Common Sense*.

24. See Rosenfeld, *Common Sense*, esp. 14.

25. For an analysis on how populists use "the people" as a moral rather than a sociological category, see Sophia Rosenfeld, *Democracy and Truth: A Short History* (Philadelphia: University of Pennsylvania Press, 2019), 98–100.

26. See, e.g., Gerson, *Neoconservative Vision*; Dorrien, *Neoconservative Mind*; Steinfels, *Neoconservatives*; Melinda Cooper, *Family Values: Between Neoliberalism and the New Social Conservatism* (New York: Zone Books, 2017); and David Garland, *The Culture of Control: Crime and Social Order in Contemporary Society* (Oxford: Oxford University Press, 2001), esp. 98–102.

27. See, e.g., Vaïsse, *Neoconservatism*; Heilbrunn, *They Knew They Were Right*; Dorrien, *Imperial Designs*; and Drolet, *American Neoconservatism*.

28. Rick Perlstein, "I Thought I Understood the American Right: Trump Proved Me Wrong," *New York Times Magazine*, April 11, 2017, https://www.nytimes.com/2017/04/11/magazine/i -thought-i-understood-the-american-right-trump-proved-me-wrong.html.

29. Famously, during his acceptance speech at the 2016 Republican National Convention, Trump declared that he was "the voice" of America's "forgotten men and women." See David Smith, "Trump's Republican Convention Speech: What He Said and What He Meant," *Guardian*, July 22, 2016, https://www.theguardian.com/us-news/ng-interactive/2016/jul/22/donald-trump -republican-convention-speech-transcript-annotated. As Sophia Rosenfeld notes, Trump "made his name pushing a kind of angry, simplistic common-sense populism." See her "The Only Thing More Dangerous than Trump's Appeal to Common Sense Is His Dismissal of It," *Nation*, March 1, 2017, https://www.thenation.com/article/the-only-thing-more-dangerous-than -trumps-appeal-to-common-sense-is-his-dismissal-of-it/.

30. Wilson, for example, took a course by Strauss (on Kant) at the University of Chicago, but he later told a colleague that he did not understand anything Strauss had to say about Kant, except that Kant was somehow wrong. See Larry Arnhart, "The Death of James Q. Wilson," *Darwinian Conservatism* (blog), March 3, 2012, http://darwinianconservatism.blogspot.fi/2012/03 /death-of-james-q-wilson.html.

31. Most scholarly studies on neoconservatism deny Strauss's role as the mastermind behind the entire movement. In fact, even scholars who (over)emphasize the significance of Strauss admit that it is "certainly true to say that there are different strains in neoconservative thought." See Thompson and Brook, *Neoconservatism*, 9. The majority of neoconservatives never identified themselves as Straussians. The most useful scholarly accounts tend to apply the label of Straussianism quite selectively to the scholars who studied under Strauss at the University of Chicago or else under Strauss's students. For valuable criticisms of the works that highlight

Strauss as an inspiration for neoconservatism, see Catherine Zuckert and Michael Zuckert, *The Truth about Leo Strauss: Political Philosophy and American Democracy* (Chicago: University of Chicago Press, 2006); and Vaïsse, *Neoconservatism*, 271–73. Irving Kristol did identify Strauss as one of those who shaped his intellectual formation in the early postwar years, when Kristol, in the words of Gary Dorrien, "was introduced to the possibility of a nonutopian politics"— namely, Aristotelian prudence instead of ideological preoccupations. See Dorrien, *Neoconservative Mind*, 73. Significantly for our purposes, Kristol wanted to point out in 1995 that "Strauss was respectful of the common sense of the common man when this was guided by tradition," even if he "was contemptuous of the modern demagogic idolatry of the common man." See Irving Kristol, "An Autobiographical Memoir," in *Neoconservatism: The Autobiography of an Idea* (New York: Free Press, 1995), 8.

32. Daniel T. Rodgers, *Age of Fracture* (Cambridge, MA: Belknap Press of Harvard University Press, 2011), 5, 3.

33. William J. Bennett, *The De-valuing of America: The Fight for Our Culture and Our Children* (New York: Summit Books, 1992), 256.

34. William J. Bennett, Chester E. Finn Jr., and John T. E. Cribb Jr., *The Educated Child: A Parent's Guide from Preschool through Eighth Grade* (New York: Free Press, 1999), 92.

35. William J. Bennett, John J. DiIulio Jr., and John P. Walters, *Body Count: Moral Poverty . . . and How to Win America's War against Crime and Drugs* (New York: Simon & Schuster, 1996), 167.

36. Christopher Lasch, *The Revolt of the Elites and the Betrayal of Democracy* (New York: W. W. Norton, 1995), 101, 113, 107–8. Lasch quoted Alan Wolfe's 1989 book *Whose Keeper: Social and Moral Obligation* on "common sense, ordinary emotions, and everyday life."

37. Christopher Lasch, "What's Wrong with the Right," *Tikkun* 1, no. 1 (1986), available at Radical Critique (website), http://www.radicalcritique.org/2013/10/whats-wrong-with-right.html.

38. Wendell Berry, *Citizenship Papers* (Washington, DC: Shoemaker & Hoard, 2003), 81–82.

39. Charles Murray, *Losing Ground: American Social Policy, 1950–1980* (New York: Basic Books, 1984), 146.

40. Discounting the neoconservatives, the most thorough conservative explorations into the implications of the natural "moral sense" in the 1990s and early 2000s were made by political theorist Larry Arnhart. See, e.g., his *Darwinian Natural Right: The Biological Ethics of Human Nature* (Albany: State University of New York Press, 1998). See also Robert Bork, *Slouching towards Gomorrah: Modern Liberalism and American Decline* (New York: Regan Books, 1996), 275–76.

41. Catherine Liu, *American Idyll: Academic Antielitism as Cultural Critique* (Iowa City: University of Iowa Press, 2011), 1.

42. Lawrence Grossberg, *We Gotta Get Out of This Place: Popular Conservatism and Postmodern Culture* (New York: Routledge, 1992), 2, 80.

43. John Fiske, *Understanding Popular Culture* (London: Routledge, 1989), 163.

44. Paleoconservatives, including thinkers such as Thomas Fleming and Paul Gottfried, are known for their opposition to immigration, the welfare state, interventionism, and globalism. See, e.g., George H. Nash, *The Conservative Intellectual Movement in America since 1945*, 30th anniversary ed. (Wilmington, DE: ISI Books, 2006), 567–70, 580.

45. Himmelfarb, *Roads to Modernity*, 26.

46. On eighteenth-century Scottish ideas on the aesthetic sense, see, e.g., Alexander Broadie, *A History of Scottish Philosophy* (Edinburgh, Scot.: Edinburgh University Press, 2009), 126, 270.

47. James Q. Wilson's preference for French wines is evident in a letter from Wilson to Richard J. Herrnstein, August 8, 1994, box 9, folder 48, Wilson Collection. Tellingly, Wilson once noted that "if you give him [a person] freedom of expression he may write *The Marriage of Figaro* or he may sing gangsta rap." See James Q. Wilson, "The Moral Life," *Brigham Young Magazine*, August 1994, 54; see also, e.g., Himmelfarb's comments on vulgar popular culture in "The Other Culture War," in *Is There a Culture War?*, 74–82.

48. Rosenfeld, *Common Sense*, 24.

49. Fiorina, Abrams, and Pope, *Culture Wars?*; Hunter, *Culture Wars*, 43. Fiorina and his cowriters, who rely on public opinion data, suggest that the culture war concept ought not to be used in reference to the American public, since "the great mass of the American people" were "for the most part moderate in their views and tolerant in their manner." Fiorina, Abrams, and Pope, *Culture Wars?*, 8. Yet they argue that the American political class certainly was more polarized in the 1980s and 1990s than it had been in the midcentury decades in the sense that partisans became better integrated within the parties than in past decades and extreme voices came to dominate American politics. This in turn made American voters' *choices* seem more polarized, even if their *positions* were not. An important part in upholding the image and reality of the ongoing culture war was played by the journalistic community, which did much to highlight conflict over consensus, polarization over moderation, due to their "news value." Fiorina, Abrams, and Pope, *Culture Wars?*, 8–9, 3. For similar interpretations of the culture wars, see Hunter and Wolfe, eds., *Is There a Culture War?*; Thomson, *Enduring American Dilemmas*; and Alan Wolfe, *One Nation, after All: What Middle-Class Americans Really Think about God, Country, Family, Racism, Welfare, Immigration, Homosexuality, Work, the Right, the Left, and Each Other* (New York: Viking, 1998). Tellingly, Hunter points out in *Culture Wars* (p. 156) that "both ends of the cultural axis claim to speak for the majority."

50. See, e.g., Arland Thornton and Linda Young-DeMarco, "Four Decades of Trends in Attitudes toward Family Issues in the United States," *Journal of Marriage and Family* 63, no. 4 (November 2001): 1009–37; and "Attitudes on Same-Sex Marriage," May 14, 2019, Pew Research Center, http://www.pewforum.org/fact-sheet/changing-attitudes-on-gay-marriage/.

51. "Word of the Year 2016," Oxford Languages (website), accessed July 14, 2020, https://languages.oup.com/word-of-the-year/2016/.

52. The posttruth phenomenon is analyzed in these terms in Sophia Rosenfeld, "Conspiracies and Common Sense: From Founding to the Trump Era" (lecture at the Chicago Humanities Festival, November 5, 2017), https://www.youtube.com/watch?v=eLJoI_NIMnQ. See also Rosenfeld, *Democracy and Truth*.

53. Mark Lilla, *The Once and Future Liberal: After Identity Politics* (New York: Harper Collins, 2017). The quotation is from the back flap. See also Mark Lilla, "The End of Identity Liberalism," *New York Times*, November 18, 2016, https://www.nytimes.com/2016/11/20/opinion/sunday/the-end-of-identity-liberalism.html; Yascha Mounk, *The People vs. Democracy: Why Our Freedom Is in Danger and How to Save It* (Cambridge, MA: Harvard University Press, 2018), 208, chap. 9; and Jefferson Cowie, "Reclaiming Patriotism for the Left," *New York Times*, August 21, 2018, https://www.nytimes.com/2018/08/21/opinion/nationalism-patriotism-liberals-.html.

54. *Identity politics* refers here to "a type of oppositional cultural politics oriented around concerns of race, ethnicity, gender, sexuality, and a myriad of other identity categories." See Amy E. Ansell, "Identity Politics," in *Race and Ethnicity: The Key Concepts* (London: Routledge, 2013), 84.

55. Sally Robinson, *Marked Men: White Masculinity in Crisis* (New York: Columbia University Press, 2000), 14.

56. Kazin, *Populist Persuasion*, 3.

57. See Jan-Werner Müller, *What Is Populism?* (Philadelphia: University of Pennsylvania Press, 2016), 20; Kazin, *Populist Persuasion*, 1; Margaret Canovan, *The People* (Cambridge, UK: Polity, 2005); and Cas Mudde and Cristóbal Rovira Kaltwasser, *Populism: A Very Short Introduction* (New York: Oxford University Press, 2017). For a classic account on anti-intellectualism in the United States, see Richard Hofstadter, *Anti-intellectualism in American Life* (New York: Alfred A. Knopf, 1963); see also Tim Lacy, "Against and beyond Hofstadter: Revising the Study of Anti-intellectualism," in *American Labyrinth: Intellectual History for Complicated Times*, ed. Raymond Haberski Jr. and Andrew Hartman (Ithaca, NY: Cornell University Press, 2018), 253–70. In the context of my analysis of neoconservatism, *anti-intellectualism* refers above all to opposition to liberal intellectual elites (and their ways of thought) that was expressed as criticism of "intellectuals."

58. Müller, *What Is Populism?*, 20.

59. Kristol, *Reflections of a Neoconservative*, xiv–xv.

60. For an attempt to combine moral sentimentalism with descriptive and prescriptive moral pluralism, see Michael B. Gill and Shaun Nichols, "Sentimentalist Pluralism: Moral Psychology and Philosophical Ethics," *Philosophical Issues* 18 (2008): 143–63.

61. Müller, *What Is Populism?*; William A. Galston, *Anti-pluralism: The Populist Threat to Liberal Democracy* (New Haven, CT: Yale University Press, 2018).

62. Ernesto Laclau, *On Populist Reason* (London: Verso, 2005), 83; Rosenfeld, *Common Sense*, 238; Müller, *What Is Populism?*, 23.

63. Rodgers, *Age of Fracture*, 5.

64. Andrew Hartman, "Age of Fracture v. Age of Culture Wars," *US Intellectual History* (blog), March 11, 2015, https://s-usih.org/2015/03/age-of-fracture-v-age-of-culture-wars/.

65. Of course, there never was a complete national moral consensus based on "bourgeois" or other values before the cultural upheaval of the 1960s. Midcentury modernist thought and culture (perhaps most famously the Beat writers) had attacked bourgeois values on a smaller scale than did the counterculture in the 1960s. Moreover, since the end of the nineteenth century, cultural conservatives had been lamenting the loss of bourgeois virtues in the context of a society committed to expanding consumption, commercial leisure, the breakdown of paternal authority, and the rise of a youth culture. A conflict between producerist values—work, saving, delayed gratification, self-control—and consumerist values—leisure, spending, spontaneity, self-expression—can be seen as an ongoing battle throughout the twentieth century. In this sense, neoconservative writers *imagined* a 1950s past in which a consensus, or near consensus, on bourgeois values existed. (I thank Daniel Wickberg for raising these issues.) Still, this is not to say that the 1960s was not an important watershed. As Andrew Hartman notes, "the sixties universalized fracture. Many Americans prior to the sixties, particularly middle-class white Americans, were largely sheltered from the 'acids of modernity,' those modern ways of thinking that subjected seemingly timeless truths, including truths about America, to a lens of suspicion. . . . The radical political mobilizations of the sixties—civil rights, Black and Chicano Power, feminism, gay liberation, the antiwar movement, the legal push for secularization—destabilized the America that millions knew." Hartman, *War for the Soul*, 4. On midcentury modernist thought and culture, see, e.g., Robert Genter, *Late Modernism: Art, Culture, and Politics in Cold War America* (Philadelphia: University of Pennsylvania Press, 2010); and Alan Petigny, *The Permissive Society: America, 1941–1965* (New York: Cambridge University Press, 2009). On American ideas about the producer and the consumer in the late nineteenth and early twentieth centuries,

see Kathleen G. Donohue, *Freedom from Want: American Liberalism and the Idea of the Consumer* (Baltimore: Johns Hopkins University Press, 2003).

66. My use of the notion "the common man" in this book is not meant to refer to any possible overt masculine tone in the neoconservative use of language. More typically, neoconservatives used nongendered terms such as the "ordinary citizen" (as synonyms for the common man). Neoconservative antifeminism is discussed in chapter 3, but other than that, I do not specifically focus on the gendered nature of neoconservative moral and political language. Neoconservatism in the context of gender has been discussed by, for example, Alison Phipps in *The Politics of the Body: Gender in a Neoliberal and Neoconservative Age* (Cambridge, UK: Polity, 2014).

67. Allan Bloom, *The Closing of the American Mind* (New York: Simon & Schuster, 1987); Michael Zuckert, "On Allan Bloom," *Good Society* 17, no. 2 (2008): 81.

68. While best known for his work as an editor and essayist, Kristol also served as the Henry Luce Professor of Urban Values at New York University from 1969 to 1987.

69. On the conservative rhetoric of "decline" in the 1990s, see, e.g., James T. Patterson, *Restless Giant: The United States from Watergate to Bush v. Gore* (New York: Oxford University Press, 2005), chap. 8.

70. Himmelfarb, "Other Culture War," 80–81, 74.

71. In the 2010s, scholars and commentators disagreed over whether the culture war was over or not and, if it was, when it ended. After Donald Trump's election as president, these questions once again became topical. See, e.g., the new conclusion in Andrew Hartman, *A War for the Soul of America: A History of the Culture Wars*, 2nd ed. (Chicago: University of Chicago Press, 2019); Jeffrey Aaron Snyder, "America Will Never Move beyond the Culture Wars," *New Republic*, April 23, 2015, https://newrepublic.com/article/121627/war-soul-america-history -culture-wars-review; Ross Douthat, "Trump's Empty Culture Wars," *New York Times*, September 27, 2017, https://www.nytimes.com/2017/09/27/opinion/trumps-empty-culture-wars.html; Bill Scher, "The Culture War President," *Politico*, September 27, 2017, https://www.politico.com /magazine/story/2017/09/27/trump-culture-war-215653; Timothy Shenk, "The Culture Wars Aren't Over," *Dissent*, June 2, 2017, https://www.dissentmagazine.org/blog/culture-wars-not -over-american-affairs-debate; and John McGuirk, "The Culture War Is Over, and Conservatives Have Lost," *The Journal*, November 7, 2012, http://www.thejournal.ie/readme/conservatives -lose-the-culture-war-john-mcguirk-665454-Nov2012/. On the online culture wars of the 2010s, see Angela Nagle, *Kill All Normies: Online Culture Wars from 4chan and Tumblr to Trump and the Alt-Right* (Winchester, Eng.: Zero Books, 2017).

Chapter One

1. Gertrude Himmelfarb, "Three Paths to Modernity: The British, American, and French Enlightenments" (lecture, American Enterprise Institute Bradley Lecture Series, Washington DC, May 10, 2004), American Enterprise Institute online, http://www.aei.org/publication/three -paths-to-modernity/.

2. Sophia Rosenfeld, *Common Sense: A Political History* (Cambridge, MA: Harvard University Press, 2011), 15, 24, 25–26, 23.

3. Ibid., 67, 70–71. Reed is quoted in Alexander Broadie, *A History of Scottish Philosophy* (Edinburgh, Scot.: Edinburgh University Press, 2009), 235.

4. Rosenfeld, *Common Sense*, 60, 68. See also, e.g., Heiner R. Klemme, "Scepticism and Common Sense," in *The Cambridge Companion to the Scottish Enlightenment*, ed. Alexander Broadie (Cambridge: Cambridge University Press, 2003), 117–35.

5. Rosenfeld, *Common Sense*, 70–71, 66–67, 77–78.

6. Ibid., 89, 62.

7. Ibid., 142, 147, 149–50. Paine is quoted on p. 150 of Rosenfeld's study.

8. Gary Dorrien, *Social Ethics in the Making: Interpreting an American Tradition* (Chichester, Eng.: Wiley-Blackwell, 2009), 14. On the transition to modern research universities, see J. David Hoeveler Jr., *James McCosh and the Scottish Intellectual Tradition: From Glasgow to Princeton* (Princeton, NJ: Princeton University Press, 1981), 232–33, 249, 348–49. Henry May argues that the Scottish thinkers were themselves moderate progressives—"cautious by instinct." According to him, the Scots were, in general, committed to showing that "culture, science, and urbanity were compatible with morality, religion, and law." See his *The Enlightenment in America* (New York: Oxford University Press, 1976), 343. Samuel Fleischacker points out, however, that the Scottish thinkers were "quite radical" in their own context: "Hutcheson was accused of heresy, Hume, Smith and Kames were all suspected of being atheists, and Reid was a political utopian who supported the French Revolution enthusiastically until 1792." Thus Fleischacker concludes that "the leaders of the American academy looked to the Scottish texts while either ignoring or toning down the Scots' more radical doctrines, especially as regards religion." Samuel Fleischacker, "The Impact on America: Scottish Philosophy and the American Founding," in *Cambridge Companion to the Scottish Enlightenment*, 329. See also Daniel Walker Howe, *The Unitarian Conscience: Harvard Moral Philosophy 1805–61* (Cambridge, MA: Harvard University Press, 1970); Douglas Sloan, *The Scottish Enlightenment and the American College Ideal* (New York: Teachers College Press, Columbia University, 1971); and J. David Hoeveler Jr., *Creating the American Mind: Intellect and Politics in the Colonial Colleges* (New York: Rowman & Littlefield, 2002).

9. Garry Wills, *Inventing America: Jefferson's Declaration of Independence* (Garden City, NY: Doubleday, 1978), 284–92, 207–39, esp. 211. See also Ralph E. Luker, "Garry Wills and the New Debate over the Declaration of Independence," *Virginia Quarterly Review* 56, no. 2 (Spring 1980): 244–61, esp. 254.

10. Wills used the word "communitarian" repeatedly to describe the Scottish ideas. See Wills, *Inventing America*, 169, 184, 232. Earlier, Wills had identified himself as a conservative, but he moved toward the left as he covered the civil rights and antiwar movements of the 1960s and 1970s. Ralph Luker points out that especially right-wing writers were critical of Wills's book: they thought that the left wanted to disengage Jefferson from the individualist tradition. Luker, "Garry Wills." Wills published his book after historians Bernard Bailyn and Gordon Wood had published their respective "republican" readings of the American Revolution, which challenged the ruling conception of the birth of the United States as a triumph of Lockean natural rights theory and individualism. See Bernard Bailyn, *The Ideological Origins of the American Revolution* (Cambridge, MA: Harvard University Press, 1967); and Gordon S. Wood, *The Creation of the American Republic, 1776–1787* (Chapel Hill: University of North Carolina Press, 1969).

11. Justin Vaïsse, *Neoconservatism: The Biography of a Movement* (Cambridge, MA: Belknap Press of Harvard University Press, 2011), 21–22. On the New York intellectuals, see, e.g., Alan M. Wald, *The New York Intellectuals: The Rise and Decline of the Anti-Stalinist Left from the 1930s to the 1980s* (Chapel Hill: University of North Carolina Press, 1987); Neil Jumonville, *Critical Crossings: The New York Intellectuals in Postwar America* (Berkeley: University of California Press,

1991); and Richard Pells, *The Liberal Mind in a Conservative Age: American Intellectuals in the 1940s and 1950s* (New York: Harper & Row, 1985).

12. See, e.g., Vaïsse, *Neoconservatism*, 36, 71–76. On neoconservatism's roots in the Cold War, see Vaïsse, *Neoconservatism*, chap. 1; Gary Dorrien, *The Neoconservative Mind: Politics, Culture, and the War of Ideology* (Philadelphia: Temple University Press, 1993), chap. 1; and Mark Gerson, *The Neoconservative Vision: From the Cold War to the Culture Wars* (Lanham, MD: Madison Books, 1996), chap. 2. On Cold War liberalism, see, e.g., Kevin Mattson, *When America Was Great: The Fighting Faith of Postwar Liberalism* (New York: Routledge, 2004); and Michael W. Flamm and David Steigerwald, eds., *Debating the 1960s: Liberal, Conservative, and Radical Perspectives* (Lanham, MD: Rowman & Littlefield, 2008).

13. Vaïsse, *Neoconservatism*, 35–37; David Steigerwald, "The Liberal-Radical Debates of the 1960s," in *Debating the 1960s*, 4; Mattson, *When America Was Great*, chap. 5.

14. Daniel Bell and Irving Kristol, "What Is the Public Interest?," *Public Interest*, no. 1 (Fall 1965): 4. Daniel Bell, *The End of Ideology: On the Exhaustion of Political Ideas in the Fifties* (Glencoe, IL: Free Press, 1960).

15. See esp. Jean-François Drolet, *American Neoconservatism: The Politics and Culture of a Reactionary Idealism* (New York: Oxford University Press, 2013), 39. See also, e.g., Gerson, *Neoconservative Vision*, 97–98; and Patrick Allitt, *The Conservatives: Ideas and Personalities throughout American History* (New Haven, CT: Yale University Press, 2009), 204.

16. Gerson, *Neoconservative Vision*, 98; see also Drolet, *American Neoconservatism*, 39. Cf. Dorrien, *Neoconservative Mind*; and Peter Steinfels, *The Neoconservatives: The Origins of a Movement*, with a new foreword (1979; repr., New York: Simon & Schuster, 2013). Dorrien and Steinfels, in their respective books, have written chapter-length intellectual biographies of key neoconservative thinkers to account for the differences between individual neoconservative writers. On "civic republicanism" in late twentieth-century political thought, see Will Kymlicka, *Contemporary Political Philosophy: An Introduction*, 2nd ed. (Oxford: Oxford University Press, 2002), 294–99. On the history of the concept of "republicanism," see Daniel Rodgers, "Republicanism: The Career of a Concept," *Journal of American History* 79, no. 1 (June 1992): 11–38.

17. Kevin Mattson, *Rebels All! A Short History of the Conservative Mind in Postwar America* (New Brunswick, NJ: Rutgers University Press, 2008), 83, 85. Historian Mark Hulliung also discusses "republican" neoconservatism in his book on liberal and republican traditions in the United States and France. He notes that the neoconservatives in fact should have called their historical role models "whigs," not "republicans." See his *Citizens and Citoyens: Republicans and Liberals in America and France* (Cambridge, MA: Harvard University Press, 2002), 4, 122, 181.

18. Nathan Glazer, "Neoconservative from the Start," *Public Interest*, no. 159 (Spring 2005): 13.

19. For a brief summary of the white middle-class value system in postwar America, see Andrew Hartman, *A War for the Soul of America: A History of the Culture Wars* (Chicago: University of Chicago Press, 2015), 5.

20. Irving Kristol, "The Best of Intentions, the Worst of Results," *Atlantic*, August 1971, reprinted in Kristol, *Neoconservatism: The Autobiography of an Idea* (New York: Free Press, 1995), 48–49.

21. See, e.g., Vaïsse, *Neoconservatism*, 50–55; Gerson, *Neoconservative Vision*, 93–98; and Hartman, *War for the Soul*, 41–42.

22. Theodore Roszak, "Youth and the Great Refusal," *Nation*, March 25, 1968, quoted by Gertrude Himmelfarb, *One Nation, Two Cultures* (New York: Alfred A. Knopf, 1999), 16.

23. On the 1960s social movements, see, e.g., Van Gosse, *Rethinking the New Left: An Interpretative History* (New York: Palgrave Macmillan, 2005); Van Gosse and Richard Moser, eds., *The World the Sixties Made: Politics and Culture in Recent America* (Philadelphia: Temple University Press, 2003); Howard Brick, *Age of Contradiction: American Thought and Culture in the 1960s* (New York: Twayne, 1998); Vaïsse, *Neoconservatism*, 40–46; and Hartman, *War for the Soul*, 10–14.

24. Irving Kristol, "An Autobiographical Memoir," in *Neoconservatism*, 31.

25. Milovan Djilas, *The New Class: An Analysis of the Communist System* (New York: Praeger, 1957), 38, 3.

26. Neoconservative new class rhetoric has been analyzed, for example, in Hartman, *War for the Soul*, 51–52; Dorrien, *Neoconservative Mind*, esp. 7–8, 13–18, 30–34, 382; and Daniel T. Rodgers, *Age of Fracture* (Cambridge, MA: Belknap Press of Harvard University Press, 2011), 82–85. Trilling had presented a theory about the popularization of the "adversary culture." Avant-garde artists had long sheltered themselves from bourgeois norms, but initially, they did not attempt to transform bourgeois society. By the 1960s, however, the bohemian lifestyle and the adversary culture had spread to the mainstream. Lionel Trilling, *Beyond Culture: Essays on Literature and Learning* (New York: Viking Press, 1965); Hartman, *War for the Soul*, 51.

27. On neoconservative populism in the 1970s, see J. David Hoeveler Jr., *The Postmodernist Turn: American Thought and Culture in the 1970s* (New York: Twayne, 1996), 146, 140; Hartman, *War for the Soul*, 53, 63–64; and Dorrien, *Neoconservative Mind*, 382.

28. Some discussions on Kristol from this perspective do exist, however. See Hulliung, *Citizens and Citoyens*, 122–24.

29. Dorrien, *Neoconservative Mind*, 382; Hoeveler, *Postmodernist Turn*, 146, 140. By suggesting that new class thought was "populist" in nature, Dorrien and Hoeveler imply that 1970s neoconservatism contained a populist element. Elsewhere, Hoeveler examines the neoconservatism of the Reagan era and argues that Irving Kristol was "working toward a conservative acceptance of democracy" in the 1980s. Here, he suggests that the neoconservatives "often moved in a populist direction." I agree with these claims. See J. David Hoeveler Jr., "Conservative Intellectuals and the Reagan Ascendancy," *History Teacher* 23, no. 3 (May 1990): 311–12.

30. Hartman, *War for the Soul*, 64, 53.

31. Jan-Werner Müller, *What Is Populism?* (Philadelphia: University of Pennsylvania Press, 2016), 20.

32. Michael Kazin, *The Populist Persuasion: An American History*, rev. ed. (Ithaca, NY: Cornell University Press, 1998), 1, 3.

33. Müller, *What Is Populism?*, 20; Kazin, *Populist Persuasion*, 1; Margaret Canovan, *The People* (Cambridge, UK: Polity, 2005).

34. See, e.g., Nathan Glazer, "Is Busing Necessary?," *Commentary* 53, no. 3 (March 1972): 39–52. See also James Q. Wilson's sympathetic discussions of public views on urban problems and crime in the streets: "The Urban Unease: Community vs. City," *Public Interest*, no. 12 (Summer 1968): 25–39; "The Urban Mood," coauthored with Harold R. Wilde, *Commentary* 48, no. 4 (October 1969): 52–61; and "Crime and the Liberal Audience," *Commentary* 51, no. 1 (January 1971): 71–78.

35. Irving Kristol, "Republican Virtue versus Servile Institutions," in *The Neoconservative Persuasion: Selected Essays, 1942–2009*, ed. Gertrude Himmelfarb (New York: Basic Books, 2011), 75, 64 (originally delivered at and then reprinted by the Poynter Center at Indiana University, May 1974).

36. Irving Kristol, "Urban Civilization and Its Discontents," in *On the Democratic Idea in America* (New York: Harper & Row, 1972), 14. The essay was originally published in *Commentary*, July 1970.

37. Kristol, "Republican Virtue," 64.

38. Ibid., 64–65.

39. Daniel Bell, *The Coming of Post-industrial Society: A Venture in Social Forecasting* (New York: Basic Books, 1973), 424.

40. Samuel P. Huntington, "The Democratic Distemper," *Public Interest*, no. 41 (Fall 1975): 9, 10, 36.

41. Steinfels, *Neoconservatives*, 261, 263. According to Steinfels (p. 68), neoconservatism's message for the people in the 1970s was quite simple: lower your expectations.

42. Moynihan is quoted in Steinfels, *Neoconservatives*, 273. A similar argument about Moynihan and the neoconservatives is made in Vaïsse, *Neoconservatism*, 58.

43. Daniel Patrick Moynihan, *Maximum Feasible Misunderstanding: Community Action in the War on Poverty* (New York: Free Press, 1969).

44. See, e.g., Bruce J. Schulman, *The Seventies: The Great Shift in American Culture, Society, and Politics* (New York: Free Press, 2001), 129–43.

45. Rodgers, *Age of Fracture*, 49–50.

46. Kristol, "Autobiographical Memoir," 34; Murray Friedman, *The Neoconservative Revolution: Jewish Intellectuals and the Shaping of Public Policy* (New York: Cambridge University Press, 2005), chap. 10; Gerson, *Neoconservative Vision*, chap. 5; Drolet, *American Neoconservatism*, 91–105.

47. Daniel Bell, *The Cultural Contradictions of Capitalism* (New York: Basic Books, 1976); Irving Kristol, *Two Cheers for Capitalism* (New York: Basic Books, 1978); Michael Novak, *The Spirit of Democratic Capitalism* (New York: Simon & Schuster, 1982).

48. Drolet, *American Neoconservatism*, 119–20.

49. Irving Kristol, "Adam Smith and the Spirit of Capitalism," in *Reflections of a Neoconservative: Looking Back, Looking Ahead* (New York: Basic Books, 1983), 139. The essay was originally published in Robert Hutchins and Mortimer Adler, eds., *The Great Ideas Today* (Chicago: Encyclopedia Britannica, 1976).

50. On the Scottish Enlightenment, see Broadie, *Cambridge Companion to the Scottish Enlightenment*; Broadie, *History of Scottish Philosophy*; and Aaron Garrett and James Harris, eds., *Scottish Philosophy in the Eighteenth Century*, vol. 1, *Morals, Politics, Art, Religion* (Oxford: Oxford University Press, 2015).

51. Michael B. Gill, "Moral Rationalism vs. Moral Sentimentalism: Is Morality More like Math or Beauty?," *Philosophy Compass* 2, no. 1 (January 2007): 16–30; D. D. Raphael, *The Impartial Spectator: Adam Smith's Moral Philosophy* (Oxford: Oxford University Press, 2007), 6.

52. Michael B. Gill, *The British Moralists on Human Nature and the Birth of Secular Ethics* (New York: Cambridge University Press, 2006), 2.

53. Gill, *British Moralists on Human Nature*, 2; Raphael, *Impartial Spectator*, 103–4. For a different view of the Scottish Enlightenment, see Thomas Ahnert, *The Moral Culture of the Scottish Enlightenment, 1690–1805* (New Haven, CT: Yale University Press, 2014). Ahnert emphasizes the role of religion in Scottish thought.

54. Gill, *British Moralists on Human Nature*, 1.

55. Philosopher and historian Samuel Fleischacker notes that the dignity and intelligence of ordinary people was one of the few ideas generally shared by the eighteenth-century Scottish philosophers, along with the sociability of human nature and the importance of history to moral

philosophy and social science. Fleischacker, "Impact on America," 333. Fleischacker has dealt extensively with Adam Smith's "strong moral egalitarianism." He argues that "Smith appears to have been committed to a remarkably strong version of the claim that people are essentially equal in abilities." Fleischacker, *On Adam Smith's Wealth of Nations* (Princeton, NJ: Princeton University Press, 2004), 208, 76. See also Fleischacker, "Adam Smith on Equality," in *The Oxford Handbook of Adam Smith*, ed. Christopher J. Berry, Maria Pia Paganelli, and Craig Smith (Oxford: Oxford University Press, 2013), 485–500. D. D. Raphael offers some caveats regarding Smith's egalitarianism. Raphael, *Impartial Spectator*, 122–26. For a more elitist interpretation of Smith, see, e.g., Eric Schliesser, *Adam Smith: Systematic Philosopher and Public Thinker* (New York: Oxford University Press, 2017), 117–18. Schliesser writes (p. 118) that for Smith, "anybody can, in principle, develop properly cultivated ability for moral judgment, but, in practise, few do."

56. Gill, *British Moralists on Human Nature*, 1–2, part 4 (on Hume).

57. Broadie, *History of Scottish Philosophy*, 104, 133–43. Hutcheson's key works were *An Inquiry into the Original of Our Ideas of Beauty and Virtue* (1725) and *An Essay on the Nature and Conduct of the Passions and Affections, with Illustrations on the Moral Sense* (1728).

58. Raphael, *Impartial Spectator*, 28; Broadie, *History of Scottish Philosophy*, 134–35, 139–40.

59. David Hume, *A Treatise of Human Nature*, ed. L. A. Selby-Bigge, 2nd ed. (Oxford: Clarendon Press, 1978), 470; Raphael, *Impartial Spectator*, 6–7.

60. Broadie, *History of Scottish Philosophy*, 202, 173; Raphael, *Impartial Spectator*, 25.

61. Raphael, *Impartial Spectator*, 29.

62. David Hume, *An Enquiry concerning the Principles of Morals*, in *Enquiries concerning Human Understanding and concerning the Principles of Morals*, ed. L. A. Selby-Bigge, 3rd ed. (Oxford: Clarendon Press, 1975), appendix 1, 289.

63. Broadie, *History of Scottish Philosophy*, 179–80.

64. Raphael, *Impartial Spectator*, 7. *The Theory of Moral Sentiments* was first published in 1759, but in the following decades, Smith made significant revisions to the book. The final (6th) edition appeared just before Smith's death in 1790.

65. Raphael, *Impartial Spectator*, 31, 11, 127, chap. 5; Broadie, *History of Scottish Philosophy*, 200.

66. Adam Smith, *The Theory of Moral Sentiments*, ed. D. D. Raphael and A. L. Macfie (Indianapolis: Liberty Fund, 1982), 112.

67. Ibid., 113–34; Raphael, *Impartial Spectator*, 38–40, 128; Broadie, *History of Scottish Philosophy*, 213–14.

68. Reid's key works on common sense are *An Inquiry into the Human Mind on the Principles of Common Sense* (1764), *Essays on the Intellectual Powers of Man* (1785), and *Essays on the Active Powers of the Human Mind* (1788).

69. Broadie, *History of Scottish Philosophy*, 269.

70. Fleischacker, "Impact on America," 329–33.

71. Dorrien, *Neoconservative Mind*, 105; see also Nicholas Xenos, "Neoconservatism Kristolized," *Salmagundi* (Spring/Summer 1987): 138–49.

72. I wish to thank Michael Frazer, one of the press's readers and an expert on the Scottish Enlightenment, for helping me clarify the differences between the moral theories of Hutcheson, Hume and Smith, and Reid. For a comprehensive and authoritative account on the history of Scottish philosophy, see Broadie, *History of Scottish Philosophy*.

73. Hume, *Treatise of Human Nature*, 491, 580–85, 602–4. On sentimentalist educational theory, see Michael L. Frazer, *The Enlightenment of Sympathy: Justice and the Moral Sentiments in the Eighteenth Century and Today* (New York: Oxford University Press, 2010), chap. 2, 180–81;

and Charles L. Griswold Jr., *Adam Smith and the Virtues of Enlightenment* (Cambridge: Cambridge University Press, 1999), 210–17.

74. Smith, *Theory of Moral Sentiments*, 147, 148; Griswold Jr., *Adam Smith*, 211–12.

75. Kristol, "Adam Smith," 141, 160, 176.

76. Ibid., 149, 154–56.

77. Ibid., 155–56.

78. Ibid., 158–59.

79. Ibid., 159, 160.

80. See esp. Ryan Patrick Hanley, *Adam Smith and the Character of Virtue* (New York: Cambridge University Press, 2009); and Griswold Jr., *Adam Smith*. No one, however, denies the descriptive aspects of Smith's *Moral Sentiments*.

81. See the discussion in Raphael, *Impartial Spectator*, 115–20.

82. Kristol, "Adam Smith," 158, 161.

83. Irving Kristol, "The Adversary Culture of Intellectuals," in *Reflections of a Neoconservative: Looking Back, Looking Ahead* (New York: Basic Books, 1983), 27. The essay was originally published in *Encounter*, October 1979.

84. Ibid., 29–30.

85. Ibid., 29.

86. Smith, *Theory of Moral Sentiments*, 61.

87. Ibid., 62.

88. Kristol, "Adam Smith," 173. For other readings of the links between neoconservatism and neoliberalism, see Jacob Hamburger and Daniel Steinmetz-Jenkins, "Why Did Neoconservatives Join Forces with Neoliberals? Irving Kristol from Critic to Ally of Free-Market Economics," *Global Intellectual History* (online), January 9, 2018, https://www.tandfonline.com/doi/10.1080/23801883 .2018.1423740; Melinda Cooper, *Family Values: Between Neoliberalism and the New Social Conservatism* (New York: Zone Books, 2017); and Wendy Brown, "American Nightmare: Neoliberalism, Neoconservatism, and De-democratization," *Political Theory* 34, no. 6 (December 2006): 690–714.

89. On neo-Victorianism and the neoliberal order, see Gary Gerstle, "America's Neoliberal Order," in *Beyond the New Deal Order: U.S. Politics from the Great Depression to the Great Recession*, ed. Gary Gerstle, Nelson Liechtenstein, and Alice O'Connor (Philadelphia: University of Pennsylvania Press, 2019), 272–75. Gerstle's article focuses on the rise of a neoliberal market-based order as the dominant political order in America, but he also briefly discusses how a neo-Victorian moral perspective both complemented neoliberal market fundamentalism and clashed with it. His discussion on neoconservative neo-Victorianism (pp. 272–75) draws on Gertrude Himmelfarb's 1995 book *The De-moralization of Society*.

90. See Gertrude Himmelfarb, *The Idea of Poverty: England in the Early Industrial Age* (London: Faber and Faber, 1984), ix.

91. Ibid.; Kristol, *Neoconservatism*, 34.

92. Himmelfarb, *Idea of Poverty*, 48, 46. Himmelfarb wrote a revised version of the book chapter for her essay collection *The Moral Imagination: From Adam Smith to Lionel Trilling*, 2nd ed. (Lanham, MD: Rowman & Littlefield, 2012).

93. Himmelfarb, *Idea of Poverty*, 50.

94. Ibid., 53.

95. "Declaration of the Rights of Man—1789," Avalon Project: Documents in Law, History and Diplomacy, Lillian Goldman Law Library, Yale Law School (website), accessed October 18, 2018, http://avalon.law.yale.edu/18th_century/rightsof.asp.

96. Smith, *Theory of Moral Sentiments*, 61.

97. Himmelfarb, *Idea of Poverty*, 53. The argument of *Moral Sentiments* was, according to Himmelfarb (p. 48), "subtle, complicated, and not without difficulties," but the book's importance also lay in the fact that it demonstrated that "Smith was hardly the ruthless individualist or amoralist he is sometimes made out to be."

98. The political theorist Michael Frazer includes the Prussians Johann Gottfried von Herder and precritical Kant in his sentimentalist canon, and his colleague Dennis Rasmussen demonstrates the sentimentalism of the French (Montesquieu, Voltaire) in his *The Pragmatic Enlightenment*. See Frazer, *Enlightenment of Sympathy*, 4, 112, chap. 5, chap. 6; and Dennis C. Rasmussen, *The Pragmatic Enlightenment: Recovering the Liberalism of Hume, Smith, Montesquieu, and Voltaire* (Cambridge: Cambridge University Press, 2014), 59, 63–64, 71–72.

99. Himmelfarb, *Idea of Poverty*, 53.

100. Ibid., 53–54. Himmelfarb, in *Idea of Poverty* (p. 54), cited Smith as saying, "The difference between the most dissimilar characters, between a philosopher and a common street porter, for example, seems to arise not so much from nature, as from habit, custom, and education. . . . By nature a philosopher is not in genius and disposition half so different from a street porter, as a mastiff is from a greyhound." This Smith quote is from Adam Smith, *An Inquiry into the Nature and Causes of the Wealth of Nations*, ed. R. H. Campbell, A. S. Skinner, and W. B. Todd (Indianapolis: Liberty Fund, 1981), 1:28–29, 30. Since education thus had a role to play in the development of individual differences, Himmelfarb explained Smith's thinking, it was only natural that "the qualities common to all had been developed in them in different degrees." Himmelfarb, *Idea of Poverty*, 53.

101. Himmelfarb, *Idea of Poverty*, 53, 62–63.

102. "Public Opinion on Civil Rights: Reflections on the Civil Rights Act of 1964," Roper Center for Public Opinion Research at Cornell University (website), July 2, 2014, https://ropercenter .cornell.edu/blog/public-opinion-civil-rights-reflections-civil-rights-act-1964-blog; Kathleen Weldon, "Public Opinion on the Voting Rights Act," *Huffington Post*, August 5, 2015, http://www.huff ingtonpost.com/kathleen-weldon/public-opinion-on-the-voting-rights-act_b_7935836.html.

103. *West's Encyclopedia of American Law*, s.v. "Engel v. Vitale," Encyclopedia.com, accessed August 9, 2019, http://www.encyclopedia.com/law/encyclopedias-almanacs-transcripts -and-maps/engel-v-vitale; *West's Encyclopedia of American Law*, s.v. "Abington School District v. Schempp," Encyclopedia.com, accessed August 9, 2019, http://www.encyclopedia.com/law /encyclopedias-almanacs-transcripts-and-maps/abington-school-district-v-schempp; *Dictionary of American History*, s.v. "Griggs v. Duke Power Company," Encyclopedia.com, accessed August 9, 2019, http://www.encyclopedia.com/history/dictionaries-thesauruses-pictures-and-press -releases/griggs-v-duke-power-company; *Encyclopedia Britannica*, s.v. "Bakke Decision," accessed August 9, 2019, https://www.britannica.com/event/Bakke-decision; *West's Encyclopedia of American Law*, s.v. "Swann v. Charlotte-Mecklenburg Board of Education," Encyclopedia. com, accessed August 9, 2019, http://www.encyclopedia.com/social-sciences-and-law/law/court -cases/swann-v-charlotte-mecklenburg-county-board-education; *West's Encyclopedia of American Law*, s.v. "Roe v. Wade," Encyclopedia.com, accessed August 9, 2019, http://www.ency clopedia.com/social-sciences-and-law/law/court-cases/roe-v-wade; Hartman, *War for the Soul*, 73–74, 104–5, 63, 92–93.

104. Hartman, *War for the Soul*, 74, 201, 207.

105. "Public Opinion on Civil Rights," Roper Center for Public Opinion Research at Cornell University; Charlotte Steeh and Maria Krysan, "Trends: Affirmative Action and the Public,

1970–1995," *Public Opinion Quarterly* 60, no. 1 (Spring 1996): 128–58; Hartman, *War for the Soul,* 63, 114.

106. On the history of quantitative social research and the making of a mass public in the United States, see Sarah E. Igo, *The Averaged American: Surveys, Citizens, and the Making of a Mass Public* (Cambridge, MA: Harvard University Press, 2007).

107. On the populist turn in the Republican Party, see Kazin, *Populist Persuasion,* esp. 246.

108. Rick Perlstein, *Nixonland: The Rise of a President and the Fracturing of America* (New York: Scribner, 2008), 748.

109. Kazin, *Populist Persuasion,* 246, 251.

110. The similarities and differences between Nixon's and neoconservative rhetorics have been touched on in Steinfels, *Neoconservatives,* 261; Mattson, *Rebels All!,* 85–86; and Hartman, *War for the Soul,* 63–64. (These authors do not discuss neoconservative moral sentimentalism or the Scottish Enlightenment.)

111. For Kristol, the year 1972 was a clear turning point: he became a supporter of Nixon (as did Himmelfarb), a fellow of the American Enterprise Institute, and a columnist for the *Wall Street Journal.* Although many neoconservatives continued as Democratic voters, the nomination of George McGovern as the Democratic presidential candidate in 1972 was a turning point of a sort for many of them as well. See, e.g., Gerson, *Neoconservative Vision,* 135; and Hartman, *War for the Soul,* 42–43.

112. Neoconservatives were ultimately disappointed with Reagan. They backed Reagan's tax cuts, but they did not like to see domestic spending increasing dramatically during Reagan's time in power. Moreover, Reagan's impact on important moral issues was slight. (This is why Michael Kazin points out that although Reagan resorted to populist rhetoric, his policies were not populist.) Similarly, a widening gulf emerged in foreign policy issues between hard-core neoconservatives and Reagan after the mid-1980s when Reagan took a more conciliatory line toward the Soviet Union. See Gerson, *Neoconservative Vision,* 249–51; Vaïsse, *Neoconservatism,* 194–97; and Kazin, *Populist Persuasion,* 266.

113. Rosenfeld, *Common Sense,* 254–55.

114. Ronald Reagan, "To Restore America," March 31, 1976, The Patriot Post (website), accessed August 3, 2019, https://patriotpost.us/pages/429-ronald-reagan-to-restore-america.

115. Ronald Reagan, "Farewell Speech," January 11, 1989, The Patriot Post (website), accessed August 3, 2019, https://patriotpost.us/pages/453-ronald-reagan-farewell-speech.

116. Rosenfeld, *Common Sense,* 255–56. In line with Rosenfeld's and Kazin's observations about Reagan's populism, Daniel Rodgers underlines the fact that Reagan put an end to the earlier Cold War presidential rhetoric of "sacrifice." See his *Age of Fracture,* chap. 1.

117. Rosenfeld, *Common Sense,* 255–56.

118. Kristol, *Reflections of a Neoconservative,* xiv.

119. Ibid.

120. Irving Kristol, "The New Populism: Not to Worry," *Wall Street Journal,* July 25, 1985, reprinted in Kristol, *Neoconservatism,* 362.

Chapter Two

1. Irving Kristol, *Reflections of a Neoconservative: Looking Back, Looking Ahead* (New York: Basic Books, 1983), xiv–xv.

2. Kristol to Wilson, December 3, 2002, box 9, folder 13, James Q. Wilson Public Policy Collection, Pardee RAND Graduate School, Santa Monica, California (hereafter Wilson Collection).

3. Kristol to Wilson, July 24, 2002, box 9, folder 13, Wilson Collection; Kristol to Wilson, December 3, 2002, box 9, folder 13, Wilson Collection.

4. Brian Forst, "James Q. Wilson," Oxford Bibliographies, last modified September 30, 2013, http://www.oxfordbibliographies.com/view/document/obo-9780195396607/obo-978019539 6607-0156.xml. See also Henry Ruth and Kevin R. Reitz, *The Challenge of Crime: Rethinking Our Response* (Cambridge, MA: Harvard University Press, 2003), 80–91.

5. Franklin E. Zimring, *The City That Became Safe: New York's Lessons for Urban Crime and Its Control* (New York: Oxford University Press, 2012), 125–31; Ruth and Reitz, *Challenge of Crime*, 140–43.

6. President Bush is quoted in John J. DiIulio, "James Q. Wilson, 1931–2012," Contemporary Thinkers (website), accessed August 9, 2019, http://contemporarythinkers.org/jq-wilson/.

7. Michael Sandel, Sidney Verba, and Harvey Mansfield, "James Q. Wilson," *Harvard Gazette*, February 6, 2013, http://news.harvard.edu/gazette/story/2013/02/james-q-wilson/; George F. Will, "James Q. Wilson, America's Prophet," *Washington Post*, March 2, 2012, https://www .washingtonpost.com/opinions/james-q-wilson-americas-prophet/2012/03/02/gIQAtEWGnR _story.html; The editors of the American Enterprise Institute, "The Sinatra of Social Science," American Enterprise Institute online, January 6, 2012, https://www.aei.org/articles/the-sinatra -of-social-science/. Murray spoke in recognition of Wilson at the American Enterprise Institute's chairman's dinner, where Wilson was present.

8. See, e.g., Wilson to Michael Joyce, August 9, 1994, box 16, folder 18, Wilson Collection.

9. Wilson to Arthur Singer, April 11, 1990, box 16, folder 13, Wilson Collection.

10. Wilson's address "The Habits of the Heart" was published in *On Character: Essays by James Q. Wilson*, expanded ed. (1991; repr., Washington, DC: AEI Press, 1995), 112.

11. Wilson to Arthur Singer (of Sloan Foundation), April 11, 1990, box 16, folder 13, Wilson Collection. On the neoconservatives' links to the Sloan Foundation, see Jason Stahl, *Right Moves: The Conservative Think Tank in American Political Culture since 1945* (Chapel Hill: University of North Carolina Press, 2016), 83–84.

12. James Q. Wilson, "The Moral Sense," outline, n.d., box 18, folder 44, Wilson Collection.

13. Allan Bloom, *The Closing of the American Mind* (New York: Simon & Schuster, 1987), 25; Michael Zuckert, "On Allan Bloom," *Good Society* 17, no. 2 (2008): 81.

14. Wilson to Arthur Singer, April 11, 1990, box 16, folder 13, Wilson Collection.

15. Wilson, "Moral Sense."

16. Wilson to Arthur Singer, April 11, 1990, box 16, folder 13, Wilson Collection.

17. James Q. Wilson, "Untitled," outline (with the acronym *TMS*), box 19, folder 8, Wilson Collection.

18. James Q. Wilson, *The Moral Sense* (New York: Free Press, 1993), 220.

19. See, e.g., Wilson, *Moral Sense*; James Q. Wilson, *Moral Judgment: Does the Abuse Excuse Threaten Our Legal System?* (New York: Basic Books, 1997); and James Q. Wilson, *Moral Intuitions*, with an introduction by Emil Uddhammar (New Brunswick, NJ: Transaction, 2000).

20. Wilson to Richard J. Herrnstein, August 8, 1994, box 9, folder 48, Wilson Collection.

21. Wilson, *Moral Sense*, 31.

22. Wilson, *Moral Intuitions*, 39.

23. Wilson, *Moral Sense*, xiii.

24. Ibid., 237. The argument against any identification of moral properties with natural properties is sometimes referred to as Hume's guillotine. Later, it became known as the naturalistic fallacy.

25. Ibid., 237–38. Wilson quoted Hume's *Enquiry concerning the Principles of Morals* and *Treatise of Human Nature.*

26. Ibid., 238. D. D. Raphael presents a similar reading of the is-ought distinction in his *The Impartial Spectator: Adam Smith's Moral Philosophy* (Oxford: Oxford University Press, 2007), 132–35.

27. Wilson, *Moral Intuitions*, 39.

28. James Q. Wilson, "Moral Sentiments and Public Discourse," outline, n.d., box 18, folder 45, Wilson Collection; Wilson, *Moral Intuitions*, 12.

29. Wilson, *Moral Intuitions*, 11, 12–16. See also James Q. Wilson, "Moral Intuitions," *Proceedings of the American Philosophical Society* 140, no. 1 (March 1996): 65; and James Q. Wilson, "Moral Sentiments and Public Discourse," n.d., box 18, folder 45, Wilson Collection.

30. Wilson, "Moral Sentiments and Public Discourse," n.d., box 18, folder 45, Wilson Collection.

31. James Q. Wilson, "Issues Raised in 'The Moral Sense' by James Q. Wilson," outline, n.d., box 18, folder 33, Wilson Collection.

32. Wilson, "Moral Sentiments and Public Discourse," n.d., box 18, folder 45, Wilson Collection.

33. David Fate Norton, *David Hume: Common-Sense Moralist, Sceptical Metaphysician* (Princeton, NJ: Princeton University Press, 1982).

34. Originally, Wilson planned to title the book *Morality and Human Nature*. See Wilson to Richard J. Herrnstein, August 8, 1994, box 9, folder 48, Wilson Collection.

35. John J. DiIulio Jr., "Moral Sense and Social Science: Reading James Q. Wilson," *Claremont Review of Books* 12, no. 4 (Fall 2012), https://claremontreviewofbooks.com/moral-sense -and-social-science/. See also John J. DiIulio Jr., "Moral Sense and Religious Sensibility: James Q. Wilson's Quest to Understand Human Character and Civic Virtue" (paper presentation, Thinking about Politics: A Conference Dedicated to Explaining and Perpetuating the Political Insights of James Q. Wilson, Harvard University and Boston College, April 4–5, 2013), https://www.you tube.com/watch?v=T3zqa2uPoYk. For a list of Wilson's books, see Contemporary Thinkers website http://contemporarythinkers.org/jq-wilson/bibliography/book/.

36. Adam Smith, *The Theory of Moral Sentiments*, ed. D. D. Raphael and A. L. Macfie (Indianapolis: Liberty Fund, 1982), 324–26.

37. Wilson, *Moral Sense*, 34.

38. Ibid., 29–30. On the history of the concept of sympathy, see Eric Schliesser, ed., *Sympathy: A History* (New York: Oxford University Press, 2015). On sympathy in American thought and culture, see Daniel Wickberg, "The Sympathetic Self in American Culture, 1750–1920," in *Figures in the Carpet: Finding the Human Person in the American Past*, ed. Wilfred M. McClay (Grand Rapids, MI: William B. Eerdmans, 2007), 129–61.

39. Alexander Broadie, *A History of Scottish Philosophy* (Edinburgh, Scot.: Edinburgh University Press, 2009), 204; Raphael, *Impartial Spectator*, 116.

40. These are the terms that Wilson used to describe the content of his book in a letter to Michael Joyce, August 9, 1994, box 16, folder 18, Wilson Collection.

41. Wilson, *Moral Sense*, 32.

42. Ibid.

43. Ibid., 34.

44. Ibid., 33.

45. Ibid., 33–34.

46. Ibid., 90, 107–8.

47. Wilson succeeded in his project of rehabilitating the status of emotions at least in the restricted sense that *The Moral Sense* encouraged several well-known fellow neoconservatives to reassess the moral characteristics of the American people in light of Scottish philosophical ideas on human moral nature. See chapter 6 for an analysis of the case of Francis Fukuyama. The columnist and author David Brooks has continued to praise Wilson in his *New York Times* columns for understanding "that people are moral judgers and moral actors." Brooks describes *The Moral Sense* as a "masterpiece," writing that Wilson "brilliantly investigated the virtuous sentiments we are born with and how they are cultivated by habit." Brooks follows Wilson's approach also in the sense that he claims that modern science essentially confirms that the moralists of the British Enlightenment were right when compared with the French thinkers. The new findings related to the "cognitive revolution of the past thirty years," Brooks argues in his 2011 *New York Times* bestseller *The Social Animal*, "strongly indicate that the British Enlightenment view of human nature is more accurate than the French Enlightenment view. . . . The thinkers from the British Enlightenment were right to depict us as Social Animals." David Brooks, "The Rediscovery of Character," *New York Times*, March 5, 2012, http://www.nytimes.com/2012/03/06/opinion/brooks-the-rediscovery-of-character.html; David Brooks, *The Social Animal* (New York: Random House, 2011), 235–36. See also David Brooks, "A Moral Philosophy for Middle Class America," *New York Times*, October 15, 2006, http://www.nytimes.com/2006/10/15/opinion/15brooks.html.

Chapter Three

1. See, e.g., Seth Dowland, *Family Values and the Rise of the Christian Right* (Philadelphia: University of Pennsylvania Press, 2015); Rhys H. Williams, "From the 'Beloved Community' to 'Family Values': Religious Language, Symbolic Repertoires, and Democratic Culture," in *Social Movements: Identity, Culture, and the State*, ed. David S. Meyer, Nancy Whittier, and Belinda Robnett (New York: Oxford University Press, 2002), 247–65; and Amanda Marcotte, "More Proof That the Religious Right's 'Family Values' Obsession Is Really about Misogyny," *Salon*, August 14, 2014, https://www.salon.com/2014/08/14/more_proof_that_the_religious_rights_family_values_obsession_is_really_about_misogyny_partner/. See also Matthew D. Lassiter, "Inventing Family Values," in *Rightward Bound: Making America Conservative in the 1970s*, ed. Bruce J. Schulman and Julian Zelizer (Cambridge, MA: Harvard University Press, 2008), 13–28.

2. *Commentary* became neoconservative at the turn of the 1970s. Edited by Norman Podhoretz, it focused on anticommunist and Jewish themes. See Murray Friedman, ed., *Commentary in American Life* (Philadelphia: Temple University Press, 2005); Benjamin Balint, *Running Commentary: The Contentious Magazine That Transformed the Jewish Left into the Neoconservative Right* (New York: Public Affairs, 2010); and Thomas L. Jeffers, *Norman Podhoretz: A Biography* (Cambridge: Cambridge University Press, 2010).

3. Daniel Patrick Moynihan, *The Negro Family: The Case for National Action*, in *The Moynihan Report and the Politics of Controversy*, ed. Lee Rainwater and William L. Yancey (Cambridge, MA: MIT Press, 1967), 39–124. See also Daniel Geary, *Beyond Civil Rights: The Moynihan Report and Its Legacy* (Philadelphia: University of Pennsylvania Press, 2015); and James T. Patterson, *Freedom Is Not Enough: The Moynihan Report and America's Struggle over Black Family Life from LBJ to Obama* (New York: Basic Books, 2010).

4. Robert O. Self, *All in the Family: The Realignment of American Democracy since the 1960s* (New York: Hill and Wang, 2012). See also Natasha Zaretsky, *No Direction Home: The American*

Family and the Fear of National Decline, 1968–1980 (Chapel Hill: University of North Carolina Press, 2007); and Marisa Chappell, *The War on Welfare: Family, Poverty, and Politics in Modern America* (Philadelphia: University of Pennsylvania Press, 2010). On second-wave feminism, see, e.g., Ruth Rosen, *The World Split Open: How the Modern Women's Movement Changed America*, rev. ed. (New York: Penguin, 2006); and Alice Echols, *Daring to Be Bad: Radical Feminism in America 1967–1975* (Minneapolis: University of Minnesota Press, 1989).

5. Self, *All in the Family*.

6. See esp. Geary, *Beyond Civil Rights*; and Patterson, *Freedom Is Not Enough*.

7. See, e.g., Gary Dorrien, *The Neoconservative Mind: Politics, Culture, and the War of Ideology* (Philadelphia: Temple University Press, 1993), 352–67; and Andrew Hartman, *A War for the Soul of America: A History of the Culture Wars* (Chicago: University of Chicago Press, 2015), 66–68.

8. Daniel Patrick Moynihan, "Defining Deviancy Down," *American Scholar* 62, no. 1 (Winter 1993): 17–30.

9. As Moynihan remarked in a personal correspondence in April 1994, "Mayor Giuliani cited [Defining Deviancy Down] repeatedly during his mayoral campaign, and more recently President Clinton did in an address to the American Society of Newspaper Editors." Moynihan to the Reverend Stephen P. Bauman, April 29, 1994, Daniel Patrick Moynihan Papers, Manuscript Division, Library of Congress, Washington, DC (hereafter Moynihan Papers), box 4: 6, folder 12. An example of a favorable neoconservative reference to Moynihan's article is Gertrude Himmelfarb, *One Nation, Two Cultures* (New York: Alfred A. Knopf, 1999), 28. Himmelfarb wrote that Moynihan had managed to encapsulate "the social and cultural situation of our time."

10. Murray Friedman, *The Neoconservative Revolution: Jewish Intellectuals and the Shaping of Public Policy* (New York: Cambridge University Press, 2005), 185.

11. Midge Decter, *The Liberated Woman and Other Americans* (New York: Coward, McCann, and Geoghegan, 1971); Midge Decter, *The New Chastity and Other Arguments against Women's Liberation* (1972; repr., London: Wildwood House, 1973). Decter has been married since 1956 to Norman Podhoretz, the longtime editor of *Commentary*.

12. Second-wave feminism achieved many of its key legal victories in the 1970s. The first no-fault divorce law was passed in California in 1969, abortion was legalized in 1973, and the first law against marital rape was passed in 1976 in Nebraska. Title IX (1972) and the Women's Educational Equity Act (1974) in turn improved educational equality, and the Pregnancy Discrimination Act (1978) and sexual harassment legislation made the American workplace friendlier to women in the late 1970s. On the legal victories of second-wave feminism, see Rosen, *World Split Open*, xvii–xlii; and Self, *All in the Family*.

13. Decter, *Arguments against Women's Liberation*, 179.

14. Moynihan, *Negro Family*, 43; Geary, *Beyond Civil Rights*, 2.

15. Moynihan, *Negro Family*, 43, 76–77; Patterson, *Freedom Is Not Enough*, chap. 3, 81–83; William A. Kelso, *Poverty and the Underclass: Changing Perceptions of the Poor in America* (New York: New York University Press, 1994), 22–23; Patrick Allitt, *The Conservatives: Ideas and Personalities throughout American History* (New Haven, CT: Yale University Press, 2009), 207. The concept of "victim blaming" was coined by psychologist William Ryan in his book *Blaming the Victim* (New York: Pantheon, 1971), which specifically attacked the Moynihan Report.

16. See, e.g., Edward C. Banfield, "Welfare: A Crisis without 'Solutions,'" *Public Interest*, no. 16 (Summer 1969): 94; Irving Kristol, "The Best of Intentions, the Worst of Results," *Atlantic*,

August 1971, reprinted in Kristol, *Neoconservatism: The Autobiography of an Idea* (New York: Free Press, 1995), 45; James Q. Wilson and Robert L. DuPont, "The Sick Sixties," *Atlantic Monthly*, October 1973, 92; and James Q. Wilson, *Thinking about Crime* (New York: Basic Books, 1975), 5. On the inconsistencies of the Moynihan Report, see Geary, *Beyond Civil Rights*, 6.

17. Karl Alexander, "The Coleman Report at 50: A Prospectus," Johns Hopkins University, School of Education, accessed May 23, 2017, http://education.jhu.edu/coleman/prospectus.

18. James S. Coleman et al., *Equality of Educational Opportunity* (Washington, DC: US Government Printing Office, 1966); Geary, *Beyond Civil Rights*, 182–84; Katie Pearce, "An Enduring Legacy: The Study That Changed the Conversation on Education Policy," Johns Hopkins University, Hub (news center), September 30, 2016, https://hub.jhu.edu/2016/09/30/coleman-report-at-50-conference/.

19. Daniel Bell, "On Meritocracy and Equality," *Public Interest*, no. 29 (Fall 1972): 46; see also Irving Kristol and Paul Weaver, "Who Knows New York?—and Other Notes on a Mixed-Up City," *Public Interest*, no. 16 (Summer 1969): 50–51; James Q. Wilson, "'Policy Intellectuals' and Public Policy," *Public Interest*, no. 64 (Summer 1981): 39; and James Q. Wilson, "The Rediscovery of Character: Private Virtue and Public Policy," *Public Interest*, no. 81 (Fall 1985): 5–7.

20. Justin Vaïsse, *Neoconservatism: The Biography of a Movement* (Cambridge, MA: Belknap Press of Harvard University Press, 2011), 86–90. The Coalition for a Democratic Majority wanted to reject the newly influential idea (on the political left) that American society was sick and guilty. A new generation of neoconservatives was beginning to emerge around CDM in the mid-1970s that was mainly interested in foreign politics. Still, in 1975, Decter published one more book on family issues, *Liberal Parents, Radical Children* (New York: Coward, McCann, and Geoghegan, 1975).

21. Self, *All in the Family*, 310. See also Chappell, *War on Welfare*, 18, and see chap. 4 for the debate over the crisis of the family in the late 1970s.

22. Hartman, *War for the Soul*, 166; Daniel T. Rodgers, *Age of Fracture* (Cambridge, MA: Belknap Press of Harvard University Press, 2011), 146.

23. Since the early 1980s, the Moynihan Report has been continuously debated. See Geary, *Beyond Civil Rights*, 3.

24. Daniel Patrick Moynihan, *Family and Nation* (San Diego: Harcourt Brace Jovanovich, 1986), 146.

25. Moynihan to James Q. Wilson et al., September 2, 1980, Moynihan Papers, box 2: 2, folder 5.

26. Nathan Glazer to Moynihan, January 19, 1981, Moynihan Papers, box 2: 3, folder 6.

27. James S. Coleman to Moynihan, March 14, 1984, Moynihan Papers, box 2: 8, folder 6.

28. Moynihan, *Family and Nation*, 146.

29. See, e.g., Daniel K. Williams, *God's Own Party: The Making of the Christian Right* (New York: Oxford University Press, 2010), chap. 9.

30. William Julius Wilson, *The Truly Disadvantaged: The Inner City, the Underclass, and Public Policy* (Chicago: University of Chicago Press, 1987), 21, 27; Charles Murray, *Losing Ground: American Social Policy, 1950–1980* (New York: Basic Books, 1984).

31. E. J. Dionne, "Children Emerge as Issue for Democrats," *New York Times*, September 27, 1987.

32. "Left and Right Fight for Custody of 'Family' Issue," *New York Times*, August 20, 1987.

33. Mary McGrory, "Moynihan Was Right 21 Years Ago," *Washington Post*, January 26, 1986; Dennis Wrong, "21 Years Later," *New Republic*, March 17, 1986; "Senator Moynihan and the Children," *New York Times*, April 9, 1985; Geary, *Beyond Civil Rights*, 212.

34. Moynihan to Bill Jovanovich (of Harcourt Brace Jovanovich), February 26, 1986, Moynihan Papers, box 2: 13, folder 8; Moynihan to Bill Jovanovich, March 21, 1986, Moynihan Papers, box 2: 13, folder 9.

35. Irving Kristol, *Reflections of a Neoconservative: Looking Back, Looking Ahead* (New York: Basic Books, 1983), xiv–xv.

36. Irving Kristol, "Whatever Happened to Common Sense?," *Wall Street Journal*, January 17, 1984, 30.

37. Ibid.

38. Adam Smith, *The Theory of Moral Sentiments*, ed. D. D. Raphael and A. L. Macfie (Indianapolis: Liberty Fund, 1982), 220.

39. Kristol, "Whatever Happened to Common Sense?," 30.

40. Irving Kristol, "The New Populism: Not to Worry," *Wall Street Journal*, July 25, 1985, reprinted in Kristol, *Neoconservatism*, 362.

41. Michael Lipka, "South Carolina Valedictorian Reignites Debate on Prayer in School," Pew Research Center, Fact Tank, June 13, 2013, http://www.pewresearch.org/fact-tank/2013/06/13/south-carolina-valedictorian-reignites-debate-on-prayer-in-school/.

42. Kristol, "New Populism," 362.

43. Irving Kristol, "American Universities in Exile," *Wall Street Journal*, June 17, 1986, 28.

44. Irving Kristol, "America's 'Exceptional Conservatism,'" *Wall Street Journal*, April 18, 1995, A20; Irving Kristol, "The New Face of American Politics," *Wall Street Journal*, August 26, 1994, A10.

45. Kristol, "America's 'Exceptional Conservatism,'" A20.

46. Kristol, "New Face of American Politics," A10.

47. On religious populism, see Michael P. Federici, *The Challenge of Populism: The Rise of Right-Wing Democratism in Postwar America* (New York: Praeger, 1991), chap. 5; and Michael Kazin, *The Populist Persuasion: An American History*, rev. ed. (Ithaca, NY: Cornell University Press, 1998). Eventually, the largely secular Jews in the neoconservative movement and the Christian Right came to share material resources, including funding sources and institutional networks. See, e.g., Robert B. Horwitz, *America's Right: Anti-establishment Conservatism from Goldwater to the Tea Party* (Cambridge, UK: Polity, 2013), 123–26.

48. For an analysis of Kristol's attempt to "join the modernism, the practical spirit, and the sociological temper of the neoconservatives to the enduring ideals—traditional, religious, metaphysical—of classical conservatism," see J. David Hoeveler Jr., *Watch on the Right: Conservative Intellectuals in the Reagan Era* (Madison: University of Wisconsin Press, 1991), 113, 107.

49. Kristol is quoted in Friedman, *Neoconservative Revolution*, 218.

50. On the posttruth phenomenon, see Sophia Rosenfeld, "Conspiracies and Common Sense: From Founding to the Trump Era" (lecture at the Chicago Humanities Festival, November 5, 2017), https://www.youtube.com/watch?v=eLJoI_NIMnQ; and Sophia Rosenfeld, *Democracy and Truth: A Short History* (Philadelphia: University of Pennsylvania Press, 2019).

51. Kristol, "America's 'Exceptional Conservatism,'" A20.

52. Sophia Rosenfeld, "The Only Thing More Dangerous than Trump's Appeal to Common Sense Is His Dismissal of It," *Nation*, March 1, 2017, https://www.thenation.com/article/the-only-thing-more-dangerous-than-trumps-appeal-to-common-sense-is-his-dismissal-of-it/; Rosenfeld, "Conspiracies and Common Sense."

53. James Q. Wilson, "The Family-Values Debate," *Commentary* 95, no. 4 (April 1993): 31.

54. Ibid.

55. James Q. Wilson, "Justice versus Humanity in the Family," in *The Neoconservative Imagination*, ed. Christopher Demuth and William Kristol (Washington, DC: AEI Press, 1995), 147.

56. James Q. Wilson, *The Moral Sense* (New York: Free Press, 1993), xi.

57. James Q. Wilson, "A New Approach to Welfare Reform: Humility," *Wall Street Journal*, December 29, 1994, A10.

58. Wilson, "Family-Values Debate," 27.

59. Ibid., 24, 27.

60. Ibid., 27–28.

61. Wilson to Michael Joyce, August 9, 1994, box 16, folder 18, James Q. Wilson Public Policy Collection, Pardee RAND Graduate School, Santa Monica, California (hereafter Wilson Collection).

62. James Q. Wilson, "On Abortion," *Commentary* 97, no. 1 (January 1994): 21, 29, 26.

63. Ibid., 26.

64. Ibid., 29, 22.

65. Ibid., 21–23. Wilson noted (p. 22) correctly that "Americans have made it clear in repeated opinion polls that they oppose both abortion on demand and a prohibition on all abortions. A majority will support abortions under carefully defined circumstances, such as a pregnancy that endangers the mother's life or is the result of rape, particularly (and possibly only) during the first trimester." For an extended argument that "public opinion on abortion does not support militants on either side of the issue," see Morris P. Fiorina, Samuel J. Abrams, and Jeremy C. Pope, *Culture Wars? The Myth of a Polarized America*, 3rd ed. (Boston: Longman, 2011), 93, chap. 5.

66. Wilson to Michael Joyce, August 9, 1994, box 16, folder 18, Wilson Collection.

67. James Q. Wilson, "Against Homosexual Marriage," *Commentary* 101, no. 3 (March 1996): 39. The Defense of Marriage Act was ruled unconstitutional in 2013. Since 2015, same-sex marriage has been legal nationwide.

68. Ibid., 39, 37.

69. Wilson to Michael Joyce, August 9, 1994, box 16, folder 18, Wilson Collection.

70. Wilson, "Against Homosexual Marriage," 36–37, 39.

71. Wilson remarked in "Against Homosexual Marriage" (p. 37) that "though the campaign to aid [homosexuals] has been going on vigorously for about a quarter of a century, it has produced few, if any, gains in public acceptance, and the greatest resistance, I think, has been with respect to homosexual marriages."

72. Wilson, "Against Homosexual Marriage," 39.

73. "Attitudes on Same-Sex Marriage," Pew Research Center, May 14, 2019, http://www.pew forum.org/fact-sheet/changing-attitudes-on-gay-marriage/.

74. Wilson to Herrnstein, August 8, 1994, box 9, folder 48, Wilson Collection; James Q. Wilson and Richard J. Herrnstein, *Crime and Human Nature: The Definite Study of the Causes of Crime* (New York: Simon & Schuster, 1985).

75. At the time Wilson wrote *The Moral Sense*, he was well read in sociobiological literature, and through the years, he discussed related themes with such leading late twentieth-century biologists, sociobiologists, and evolutionary psychologists as Edward O. Wilson, Ernst Mayr, and David Buss. E. O. Wilson and Mayr were Wilson's colleagues at Harvard. Mayr was particularly impressed by Wilson's *The Moral Sense*. See Mayr to Wilson, July 1, 1994, box 14, folder 44, Wilson Collection.

76. "The Free Society Requires a Moral Sense, Social Capital," interview of James Q. Wilson, *Religion and Liberty* 9, no. 4 (July–August 1999), Acton Institute online, https://acton.org/pub /religion-liberty/volume-9-number-4/free-society-requires-moral-sense-social-capital.

77. Wilson, *Moral Sense*, 2.

78. Ibid., 229.

79. Smith, *Theory of Moral Sentiments*, 324–26. On this aspect of Smith's moral theory, see Daniel Wickberg, "The Sympathetic Self in American Culture, 1750–1920," in *Figures in the Carpet: Finding the Human Person in the American Past*, ed. Wilfred M. McClay (Grand Rapids, MI: William B. Eerdmans, 2007), 150, 152; and Charles L. Griswold Jr., *Adam Smith and the Virtues of Enlightenment* (Cambridge: Cambridge University Press, 1999), 115.

80. On Americans' attitudes toward family issues, see, e.g., Arland Thornton and Linda Young-DeMarco, "Four Decades of Trends in Attitudes toward Family Issues in the United States," *Journal of Marriage and Family* 63, no. 4 (November 2001): 1009–37; Susan L. Brown and Matthew R. Wright, "Older Adults' Attitudes toward Cohabitation: Two Decades of Change," *Journals of Gerontology: Series B* 71, 4 (July 2016), https://academic.oup.com/psychsocgeron tology/article/71/4/755/2604978; and Andrew Dugan, "US Divorce Rate Dips, but Moral Acceptability Hits New High," Gallup (website), July 7, 2017, http://news.gallup.com/poll/213677 /divorce-rate-dips-moral-acceptability-hits-new-high.aspx.

81. David Hume, *A Treatise of Human Nature*, ed. L. A. Selby-Bigge, 2nd ed. (Oxford: Clarendon Press, 1978), 486. On the Scottish thinkers and the family, see, e.g., Sebastiano Nerozzi and Pierluigi Nuti, "Adam Smith and the Family," *History of Economic Ideas* 19, no. 2 (2011): 11–41; and Christopher J. Berry, *Social Theory of the Scottish Enlightenment* (Edinburgh, Scot.: Edinburgh University Press, 1997), 27–28.

82. Griswold Jr., *Adam Smith*, 210–11; Nerozzi and Nuti, "Adam Smith and the Family," 20, 24. As Griswold notes, moral education was a "continuous theme" in both *Moral Sentiments* and *Wealth of Nations*, even if Smith never wrote an essay or a book on education and no chapter or part of *Moral Sentiments* is solely devoted to it.

83. Griswold Jr., *Adam Smith*, 210–11.

84. Smith, *Theory of Moral Sentiments*, 145.

85. Ibid., 222.

86. Adam Smith, *Lectures on Jurisprudence*, ed. R. L. Meek, D. D. Raphael, and P. G. Stein (Indianapolis: Liberty Fund, 1982), 142–43; Nerozzi and Nuti, "Adam Smith and the Family," 24.

87. Smith, *Theory of Moral Sentiments*, 222.

88. For Smith's view on parental affection, see *Theory of Moral Sentiments*, 142, 219.

89. Smith, *Lectures on Jurisprudence*, 142.

90. Smith, *Theory of Moral Sentiments*, 219.

91. Ibid., 220.

92. Ibid.

93. James Q. Wilson, *The Marriage Problem: How Our Culture Has Weakened Families* (New York: HarperCollins, 2002), 13.

94. Wilson, *Marriage Problem*, 85; Smith, *Theory of Moral Sentiments*, 222.

95. Wilson, *Moral Sense*, xiii.

96. Wilson discussed Smith's ideas, e.g., in the teaching material (found in the Wilson Collection) for the spring 1992 lecture series "Morality and Human Character," which explored "the nature, development, and expression of the moral sense." Wilson writes in his teaching material that "Aristotle says man is naturally social w[ith] a natural affection for children" and continues,

"How does this lead to moral judgments? Adam Smith (TMS, 1759) provides an answer." "Morality and Human Character," course materials, Spring 1992, box 38, folder 6, Wilson Collection. Wilson to Arthur Singer, April 11, 1990, box 16, folder 13, Wilson Collection.

97. Wilson, *Moral Sense*, 25, 2, chap. 7. On the similarities between Wilson's and Smith's moral theories from the point of view of a philosopher, see James R. Otteson, *Adam Smith's Marketplace of Life* (Cambridge: Cambridge University Press, 2002), 314–20.

98. Wilson, *Moral Sense*, 18.

99. Wilson, *Marriage Problem*, 84–85.

100. On Westermarck as "the first sociobiologist," see Stephen K. Sanderson, "Edward Westermarck: The First Sociobiologist," in *The Oxford Handbook of Evolution, Biology, and Society*, ed. Rosemary L. Hopcroft (New York: Oxford University Press, 2018), Oxford Handbooks Online, http://www.oxfordhandbooks.com/view/10.1093/oxfordhb/9780190299323.001.0001/oxfordhb -9780190299323-e-34. Wilson was hardly alone among late twentieth-century American conservatives in citing Westermarck as an authority on familial emotions. See Antti Lepistö, "Darwinian Conservatives and Westermarck's Ethics," in *Evolution, Human Behaviour and Morality: The Legacy of Westermarck*, ed. Olli Lagerspetz et al. (London: Routledge, 2017), 194–208.

101. See Edward Westermarck, *The Origin and Development of the Moral Ideas*, vols. 1–2 (London: Macmillan, 1906–8); and Edward Westermarck, *The History of Human Marriage* (London: Macmillan, 1891). On Westermarck's intellectual debt to the Scottish moral philosophers and Darwin, see Otto Pipatti, *Morality Made Visible: Edward Westermarck's Moral and Social Theory* (London: Routledge, 2019); and Lagerspetz et al., *Evolution, Human Behaviour and Morality*. Darwin argued that the "moral sense" was a product of human evolutionary history. See, e.g., Greg Priest, "Charles Darwin's Theory of Moral Sentiments: What Darwin's Ethics Really Owes to Adam Smith," *Journal of the History of Ideas* 78, no. 4 (2017): 571–93.

102. In a 1991 interview, Wilson stated that the question "Why are most people decent human beings?" "occurred to me after I finished *Crime and Human Nature*." Neil Miller, "The Prolific Professor," *UCLA Magazine*, Fall 1991, 23.

103. James Q. Wilson, "Raising Kids," *Atlantic Monthly*, October 1983, reprinted in *On Character: Essays by James Q. Wilson*, expanded ed. (1991; repr., Washington, DC: AEI Press, 1995), 61.

104. Wilson, *Moral Sense*, xiv.

105. Ibid., x, xv. See also Lepistö, "Darwinian Conservatives," 197–98.

106. James Q. Wilson, "Bring Back the Orphanage," *Wall Street Journal*, August 22, 1994, A10.

107. James Q. Wilson, "What to Do about Crime," *Commentary* 98, no. 3 (September 1994): 34.

108. Ibid.

109. Wilson, *Marriage Problem*, 85.

110. See, e.g., Mark Gerson, *The Neoconservative Vision: From the Cold War to the Culture Wars* (Lanham, MD: Madison Books, 1996), 337; Mark Gerson, ed., *The Essential Neoconservative Reader* (Reading, MA: Addison-Wesley, 1996), 290; Friedman, *Neoconservative Revolution*, 187; and Hartman, *War for the Soul*, 126.

111. Moynihan to Peter Steinfels, December 28, 1992, Moynihan Papers, box 2: 33, folder 4.

112. Moynihan to Richard T. Gill, July 23, 1992, Moynihan Papers, box 2: 32, folder 4.

113. Moynihan to Peter Steinfels, December 28, 1992, Moynihan Papers, box 2: 33, folder 4.

114. Moynihan to James Q. Wilson, April 13, 1994, Moynihan Papers, box 4: 6, folder 11.

115. Moynihan, "Defining Deviancy Down," 22.

116. On the idea of decline in early 1990s America, see James T. Patterson, *Restless Giant: The United States from Watergate to Bush v. Gore* (New York: Oxford University Press, 2005), chap. 8.

117. Moynihan, "Defining Deviancy Down," 19, 30.

118. James Q. Wilson to Michael Joyce, August 9, 1994, box 16, folder 18, Wilson Collection.

119. Alan Wolfe, *One Nation, after All: What Middle-Class Americans Really Think about God, Country, Family, Racism, Welfare, Immigration, Homosexuality, Work, the Right, the Left, and Each Other* (New York: Viking, 1998), 276, 54.

120. Ibid., 111.

121. Wilson, *Moral Sense*, vii.

122. Himmelfarb, *One Nation, Two Cultures*, 135, 123-26.

123. Ibid., 28-29.

124. Ibid., 128-29, 144-45.

125. Francis Fukuyama, "What Divides America," *Wall Street Journal*, November 15, 2000, A26.

126. Ibid.

127. Francis Fukuyama, *The Great Disruption: Human Nature and the Reconstitution of Social Order* (New York: Free Press, 1999), 90.

128. Irene Taviss Thomson, *Culture Wars and Enduring American Dilemmas* (Ann Arbor: University of Michigan Press, 2010), chap. 3.

129. Fukuyama, *Great Disruption*, esp. 6-8, 271. The quote is from p. 8.

130. Ibid., 272-73.

131. James Q. Wilson, "The 11th Commandment Seems to Be 'Judge Not,'" *Wall Street Journal*, April 5, 2001, A20.

132. Patterson, *Freedom Is Not Enough*, 181-82.

133. Wilson, *Marriage Problem*, 4-5.

Chapter Four

1. James Q. Wilson, "Culture, Incentives, and the Underclass," in *Values and Public Policy*, ed. Henry J. Aaron, Thomas E. Mann, Timothy Taylor (Washington, DC: Brookings Institution, 1994), 54.

2. Herbert J. Gans, *The War against the Poor: The Underclass and Antipoverty Policy* (New York: Basic Books, 1995), 2. On the underclass debate, see also Michael B. Katz, *The Undeserving Poor: America's Enduring Confrontation with Poverty*, 2nd ed. (New York: Oxford University Press, 2013); William A. Kelso, *Poverty and the Underclass: Changing Perceptions of the Poor in America* (New York: New York University Press, 1994); Michael B. Katz, ed., *The "Underclass" Debate: Views from History* (Princeton, NJ: Princeton University Press, 1993); Marisa Chappell, *The War on Welfare: Family, Poverty, and Politics in Modern America* (Philadelphia: University of Pennsylvania Press, 2010), 139-55; and Alice O'Connor, *Poverty Knowledge: Social Science, Social Policy, and the Poor in Twentieth-Century U.S. History* (Princeton, NJ: Princeton University Press, 2001), chap. 10.

3. For analytic purposes, I will thus differentiate between the family wars, which centered on divorce, parenting, abortion, and gay marriage, and the underclass debate, which revolved around poverty, welfare dependency, crime, and punishment. There were, though, significant overlaps between these debates—most importantly, with respect to the questions of nonmarital children and moral education.

4. Martin Gilens, *Why Americans Hate Welfare: Race, Media, and the Politics of Antipoverty Policy* (Chicago: University of Chicago Press, 1999), x. See also Mark Peffley, Jon Hurwitz, and

Paul Sniderman, "Racial Stereotypes and Whites' Political Views of Blacks in the Context of Welfare and Crime," *American Journal of Political Science* 41, no. 1 (1997): 30–60; and Kathlyn Taylor Gaubatz, *Crime in the Public Mind* (Ann Arbor: University of Michigan Press, 1995).

5. Mark Gerson, *The Neoconservative Vision: From the Cold War to the Culture Wars* (Lanham, MD: Madison Books, 1996), 146–57, 8; Andrew Hartman, *A War for the Soul of America: A History of the Culture Wars* (Chicago: University of Chicago Press, 2015), 65. Gerson argues (p. 8) that "neoconservatism insists on the liberal idea that involuntary characteristics such as race, rank, and station should never restrain an individual."

6. Jean-François Drolet, *American Neoconservatism: The Politics and Culture of a Reactionary Idealism* (New York: Oxford University Press, 2013), 119–20, 115; Thomas McCarthy, *Race, Empire and the Idea of Human Development* (Cambridge: Cambridge University Press, 2009), 12.

7. Elizabeth Hinton, *From the War on Poverty to the War on Crime: The Making of Mass Incarceration in America* (Cambridge, MA: Harvard University Press, 2016), 21.

8. On the national discussion about race in the 1980s and 1990s, see Hartman, *War for the Soul*, chap. 4, esp. 126.

9. James T. Patterson, *America's Struggle against Poverty, 1900–1994* (Cambridge, MA: Harvard University Press, 1994), 100; O'Connor, *Poverty Knowledge*, 146.

10. Harrington is quoted in Patterson, *America's Struggle against Poverty*, 99.

11. Patterson, *America's Struggle against Poverty*, 99, 126; Michael Flamm, "The Liberal-Conservative Debates of the 1960s," in *Debating the 1960s: Liberal, Conservative, and Radical Perspectives*, ed. Michael W. Flamm and David Steigerwald (Lanham, MD: Rowman & Littlefield, 2008), 107–15.

12. Godfrey Hodgson, *The Gentleman from New York: Daniel Patrick Moynihan—a Biography* (Boston: Houghton Mifflin, 2000), 130.

13. Daniel T. Rodgers, *Age of Fracture* (Cambridge, MA: Belknap Press of Harvard University Press, 2011), 200.

14. Ibid., 201–2.

15. Patrick Allitt, *The Conservatives: Ideas and Personalities throughout American History* (New Haven, CT: Yale University Press, 2009), 206; Rodgers, *Age of Fracture*, 202; Kelso, *Poverty and the Underclass*, 18.

16. Ken Auletta, *The Underclass*, rev. ed. (Woodstock, NY: Overlook, 1999), 20.

17. Auletta, *Underclass*; James T. Patterson, *Freedom Is Not Enough: The Moynihan Report and America's Struggle over Black Family Life from LBJ to Obama* (New York: Basic Books, 2010), 146.

18. William Julius Wilson, *The Declining Significance of Race: Blacks and Changing American Institutions* (Chicago: University of Chicago Press, 1978), 22, 134, 120. See also Rodgers, *Age of Fracture*, 122–25. Other major works by William Julius Wilson on the subject are *The Truly Disadvantaged: The Inner City, the Underclass, and Public Policy* (Chicago: University of Chicago Press, 1987); and *When Work Disappears: The World of the New Urban Poor* (New York: Alfred A. Knopf, 1996).

19. Orlando Patterson, *The Ordeal of Integration: Progress and Resentment in America's 'Racial' Crisis* (Washington, DC: Civitas/Counterpoint, 1997), 38–40; Patterson, *Freedom Is Not Enough*, 155–57.

20. Kelso, *Poverty and the Underclass*, 293–94.

21. Ibid., 299. Kelso cites Lawrence M. Mead, *Beyond Entitlement: The Social Obligations of Citizenship* (New York: Basic Books, 1986); and *The New Politics of Poverty: The Nonworking Poor*

in America (New York: Free Press, 1992). Kelso identifies market conservatism with such names as Charles Murray and Thomas Sowell.

22. Kelso, *Poverty and the Underclass*, 294, 326.

23. See the biography of Banfield by Wilson: James Q. Wilson, "A Connecticut Yankee in King Arthur's Court: A Biography," in *Edward C. Banfield: An Appreciation*, ed. Charles S. Kesler (Claremont, CA: Henry Salvatori Center for the Study of Individual Freedom in the Modern World, 2002), 31–78, accessed at http://www.scribd.com/doc/49101990/Edward-C-Banfield-An -Appreciation. The title of Wilson's dissertation was "Negro Leaders in Chicago."

24. Edward Banfield, *The Unheavenly City: The Nature and Future of Our Urban Crisis* (Boston: Little, Brown, 1970), 53, 14, 12.

25. Ibid., 14–16.

26. James Q. Wilson, *Thinking about Crime* (New York: Basic Books, 1975), 29. On Wilson's intellectual debt to Banfield, see John J. DiIulio Jr., "Moral Sense and Religious Sensibility: James Q. Wilson's Quest to Understand Human Character and Civic Virtue" (paper presentation, Thinking about Politics: A Conference Dedicated to Explaining and Perpetuating the Political Insights of James Q. Wilson, Harvard University and Boston College, April 4–5, 2013), https://www.you tube.com/watch?v=T3zqa2uPoYk.

27. Wilson and Moynihan met in 1962 when Moynihan came to Harvard University's Joint Center for Urban Studies. Wilson regarded Moynihan as one of his "best friends," one with whom he "met endlessly" until Moynihan's passing in 2003. See James Q. Wilson, "Gentleman, Politician, Scholar," *Public Interest*, no. 152 (Summer 2003): 113; and James Q. Wilson, "Pat Moynihan Thinks about Families," *Annals of the American Academy of Political and Social Science* 621 (January 2009): 28, 30. Wilson was, in general, receptive to Moynihan's notions about "the weakness of the family structure among a large minority of blacks." See Wilson, *Thinking about Crime*, 8. Yet he also noted later that "to the despair of some of his friends, [Moynihan] never explained how the government might halt the weakening of families, black or white." See his "Gentleman, Politician, Scholar," 114.

28. James Q. Wilson, "Entering Criminology through the Back Door," *Criminologist: Official Newsletter of the American Society of Criminology* 13, no. 6 (November–December 1988): 1, 5, 8, 14–15. Within the criminological community, Wilson—a political scientist by training—is typically seen as a theorist of criminal policy or an intellectual who thought about crime, not a criminologist. Personal correspondence with Janne Kivivuori, professor of criminology at the University of Helsinki, October 10, 2017.

29. James Q. Wilson, "The Urban Unease: Community vs. City," *Public Interest*, no. 12 (Summer 1968): 25–26; see also the revised versions of the article in Wilson, *Thinking about Crime*, 21–25; and James Q. Wilson, *Thinking about Crime*, rev. ed. (New York: Basic Books, 1983), 26–28. On "dirty" cities, see Philip Jenkins, *Decade of Nightmares: The End of the Sixties and the Making of Eighties America* (New York: Oxford University Press, 2006), 66.

30. See Wilson, *Thinking about Crime*; and Henry Ruth and Kevin R. Reitz, *The Challenge of Crime: Rethinking Our Response* (Cambridge, MA: Harvard University Press, 2003), 4.

31. James Q. Wilson, *On Character: Essays by James Q. Wilson*, expanded ed. (1991; repr., Washington, DC: AEI Press, 1995), 1.

32. Franklin E. Zimring, *The Great American Crime Decline* (New York: Oxford University Press, 2008), 28–30.

33. Wilson to Kristol, November 19, 1971, Irving Kristol Papers, box 23, folder 46, Wisconsin Historical Society, Madison, Wisconsin.

34. Gertrude Himmelfarb, *The Idea of Poverty: England in the Early Industrial Age* (London: Faber and Faber, 1984); Gertrude Himmelfarb, *Poverty and Compassion: The Moral Imagination of the Late Victorians* (New York: Alfred A. Knopf, 1991).

35. Himmelfarb, *Poverty and Compassion*, 388.

36. James Q. Wilson, "The Rediscovery of Character: Private Virtue and Public Policy," *Public Interest*, no. 81 (Fall 1985): 14–15.

37. Ibid., 15. By "virtue," Wilson meant "habits of moderate action; more specifically, acting with due restraint on one's impulses, due regard for the rights of others, and reasonable concern for distant consequences." This comes very close to Banfield's idea of class culture that was not lower class—that is, pathological. Cf. Banfield, *Unheavenly City*, 47–54.

38. Wilson, "Rediscovery of Character," 9, 14, 6.

39. Ibid., 5, 16.

40. James Q. Wilson, "Incivility and Crime," in *Civility and Citizenship in Liberal Democratic Societies*, ed. Edward C. Banfield (Saint Paul, MN: Paragon House, 1992), 104. See also Wilson, "Crime and American Culture," *Public Interest*, no. 70 (Winter 1983): 22–48.

41. Wilson, "Incivility and Crime," 110.

42. Ibid., 110, 106–7.

43. Himmelfarb, *Poverty and Compassion*, 389.

44. Ibid., 5–6. Perhaps Himmelfarb had in mind Banfield's remarks in *Unheavenly City* about the War on Poverty—namely, his argument that government assistance to the poor, even if it would *lower* the incomes of the poor, would make providers of the aid feel virtuous. Banfield also argued that in America, "doing good is becoming—has already become—a growth industry, like the other forms of mass entertainment, while righteous indignation and uncompromising allegiance to principle are becoming *the* motives of political commitment." See Banfield, *Unheavenly City*, 251, 254.

45. Himmelfarb, *Poverty and Compassion*, 5–6, 190. The last quote ("to create the power of self-help") is from Charity Organisation Society's *Principles of Decision* (1905), which Himmelfarb discusses on p. 190.

46. Ibid., 12–13, 389.

47. Himmelfarb to James Q. Wilson, August 19, 1991, box 14, folder 40, James Q. Wilson Public Policy Collection, Pardee RAND Graduate School, Santa Monica, California (hereafter Wilson Collection).

48. James Q. Wilson, *The Moral Sense* (New York: Free Press, 1993), vii.

49. Ibid., vii–viii.

50. Ibid., 25.

51. Ibid., 32, chap. 2.

52. Ibid., 70, chap. 3.

53. Ibid., 81, 97, chap. 4.

54. Ibid., 100, chap. 5.

55. Ibid., xiv.

56. Ibid., xiii, vii.

57. Wilson to Michael Joyce, August 9, 1994, box 16, folder 18, Wilson Collection.

58. Currently, there is no consensus on how Wilson's book should be viewed. Political scientist John J. DiIulio, a student and colleague of Wilson, holds that for Wilson, understanding the moral sense was the key to understanding human character and defending civic virtue. Writer, social activist, and Jewish historian Murray Friedman, for his part, views *The Moral Sense* as

an attempt to reassert "the validity of morality in an age that lacked religious conviction." Philosophers Joseph Duke Filonowicz and James Otteson focus on Wilson's famous "predecessors": they see *The Moral Sense* as a sort of revival of Enlightenment moral philosophy. Furthermore, sociologist Guido Giacomo Preparata claims that *The Moral Sense* is an "epitomic synthesis," in the field of ethics, of the criminological control theory of the 1990s, which in itself was, with its "fixation with self-control," "an implicit reaffirmation of the inevitability of class division" (Preparata mentions Wilson's *The Moral Sense* only in passing, however). See DiIulio, "Moral Sense and Religious Sensibility"; Murray Friedman, *The Neoconservative Revolution: Jewish Intellectuals and the Shaping of Public Policy* (New York: Cambridge University Press, 2005), 189; Joseph Duke Filonowicz, *Fellow-Feeling and the Moral Life* (Cambridge: Cambridge University Press, 2008), 20, 33, 205–21; James R. Otteson, *Adam Smith's Marketplace of Life* (Cambridge: Cambridge University Press, 2002), 314–20; and Guido Giacomo Preparata, "Suburbia's 'Crime Experts': The Neo-conservatism of Control Theory and the Ethos of Crime," *Critical Criminology* 21, no. 1 (March 2013): 73, 78.

59. Zimring, *Great American Crime Decline*, 5.

60. Ibid., 24.

61. Ibid., 196, 17.

62. Ibid., 23.

63. Wilson, *Moral Sense*, 9–10.

64. Ibid., 174.

65. Ibid., 47.

66. Ibid., 50.

67. Ibid., 161.

68. Ibid., 229–30.

69. Wilson, "Culture, Incentives, and the Underclass," 65.

70. James Q. Wilson, "Crime, Race, and Values," *Society* 30, no. 1 (1992): 91.

71. Wilson, *Moral Sense*, 10.

72. Ibid., 10–11.

73. Wilson, "Culture, Incentives, and the Underclass," 54.

74. Kristol's description of Wilson's book can be found on the back cover of *The Moral Sense*.

75. Wilson referred to the working and middle classes only a couple of times in *The Moral Sense* (mainly with reference to middle-class families) but did refer (p. 221) to the opposition between the "adversary culture" and the "habits and preferences of the working and middle classes." In most cases, he spoke of "ordinary people," "ordinary men and women," and so on. The Kristol quote is from his "The New Populism: Not to Worry," *Wall Street Journal*, July 25, 1985, reprinted in Kristol, *Neoconservatism: The Autobiography of an Idea* (New York: Free Press, 1995), 363.

76. Wilson, *Moral Sense*, 11, xii, x.

77. Ibid., 240–41.

78. Wilson's explanation as to why he wrote *The Moral Sense* is on p. vii.

79. Wilson, *Moral Sense*, 241.

80. Hartman, *War for the Soul*, 5.

81. Wilson, *Moral Sense*, 215.

82. Ibid., xv, 50, 110, 115.

83. Ibid., 251.

84. Ibid., 12.

85. Hinton, *From the War on Poverty*, 21.

86. Elliot Turiel, "Making Sense of Social Experiences and Moral Judgments," *Criminal Justice Ethics* 13, no. 2 (Summer/Fall 1994): 69–70.

87. James Q. Wilson, "Emotions, Reason, and Character," *Criminal Justice Ethics* 13, no. 2 (Summer/Fall 1994): 87.

88. Wilson to Arthur Singer, April 11, 1990, box 16, folder 13, Wilson Collection.

89. Jan-Werner Müller, *What Is Populism?* (Philadelphia: University of Pennsylvania Press, 2016), 3.

90. Ibid.

91. Himmelfarb to Wilson, August 19, 1991, box 14, folder 40, Wilson Collection.

92. See Gertrude Himmelfarb, "The Idea of Compassion: The British vs. the French Enlightenment," *Public Interest*, no. 145 (Fall 2001): 3–24; Gertrude Himmelfarb, *The Roads to Modernity: The British, French, and American Enlightenments* (New York: Alfred A. Knopf, 2004); Gertrude Himmelfarb, "Three Paths to Modernity: The British, American, and French Enlightenments" (lecture, American Enterprise Institute Bradley Lecture Series, Washington DC, May 10, 2004), American Enterprise Institute online, http://www.aei.org/publication/three-paths-to-modernity/; Gertrude Himmelfarb, "Armut und zweierlei Aufklärung," in *Aufklärung Heute: Castelgandalfo-Gespräche 1996*, ed. Krzysztof Michalski (Stuttgart, Ger.: Klett-Cotta, 1997), 162–201; and Gertrude Himmelfarb, "Two Enlightenments: A Contrast in Social Ethics," *Proceedings of the British Academy* 117 (2001): 297–324.

93. Gertrude Himmelfarb, *The De-moralization of Society: From Victorian Virtues to Modern Values* (New York: Alfred A. Knopf, 1995), 244.

94. Gertrude Himmelfarb, "Democratic Remedies for Democratic Disorders," *Public Interest*, no. 131 (Spring 1998): 12–13.

95. Himmelfarb, *De-moralization of Society*, 233, 245.

96. Charles Murray, "The Coming White Underclass," *Wall Street Journal*, October 29, 1993, A14.

97. Himmelfarb, *Poverty and Compassion*, 7–8.

98. Gertrude Himmelfarb, "A Genealogy of Morals: From Clapham to Bloomsbury," in *Marriage and Morals among the Victorians* (New York: Alfred A. Knopf, 1986), 32. The essay was originally published in *Commentary*, February 1985. Himmelfarb was quoting Virginia Woolf.

99. Gertrude Himmelfarb, *One Nation, Two Cultures* (New York: Alfred A. Knopf, 1999), 118–28. See also Himmelfarb, *De-moralization of Society*.

100. Himmelfarb, *One Nation, Two Cultures*, 24. Himmelfarb admitted (p. 21) that some of the statistics relating to "social pathology" of crime, violence, out-of-wedlock births, teenage pregnancy, child abuse, drug addiction, alcoholism, illiteracy, promiscuity, and welfare dependency had "improved in the last few years." Crime had declined "dramatically" since 1990 (e.g., homicides from 9.4 per one hundred thousand to 6.8 per one hundred thousand), and the number of people on welfare "fell by more than a third, from 14.1 million in January 1993 to 7.6 million in December 1998."

101. Himmelfarb, *De-moralization of Society*, 16–17.

102. Himmelfarb, *Roads to Modernity*, 33.

103. Ibid., 21–22.

104. Himmelfarb, "Three Paths to Modernity."

105. Müller, *What Is Populism?*; Michael Kazin, *The Populist Persuasion: An American History*, rev. ed. (Ithaca, NY: Cornell University Press, 1998); Margaret Canovan, *The People* (Cambridge, UK: Polity, 2005).

106. Adam Smith, *The Theory of Moral Sentiments*, ed. D. D. Raphael and A. L. Macfie (Indianapolis: Liberty Fund, 1982), 62.

107. Himmelfarb, *Roads to Modernity*, 129.

108. Ibid., 120.

109. Ibid., 143.

110. Gertrude Himmelfarb, "Compassionate Conservatism Properly Understood," *Weekly Standard*, January 14, 2013, reprinted in Himmelfarb, *Past and Present: The Challenges of Modernity, from the Pre-Victorians to the Postmodernists* (New York: Encounter Books, 2017), 183, 177–78.

111. Himmelfarb, *Roads to Modernity*, 234–35.

112. Himmelfarb, "Compassionate Conservatism Properly Understood," 176–77.

113. Ibid., 183, 178–79, 184.

114. Drolet, *American Neoconservatism*, 115; Cf. McCarthy, *Race, Empire and the Idea*, 12.

115. Drolet, *American Neoconservatism*, 119–20.

116. See esp. Hartman, *War for the Soul*, 65.

117. Nathan Glazer and Daniel Patrick Moynihan, *Beyond the Melting Pot: The Negroes, Puerto Ricans, Jews, Italians, and Irish of New York City*, 2nd ed. (Cambridge, MA: MIT Press, 1970), 84. Glazer was the primary author of *Beyond the Melting Pot*. Moynihan wrote the chapter on the Irish and most of the book's conclusion. On Glazer and Moynihan's book, see Daniel Geary, *Beyond Civil Rights: The Moynihan Report and Its Legacy* (Philadelphia: University of Pennsylvania Press, 2015), 32–33. See also Daniel Patrick Moynihan, *The Negro Family: The Case for National Action*, in *The Moynihan Report and the Politics of Controversy*, ed. Lee Rainwater and William L. Yancey (Cambridge, MA: MIT Press, 1967), 39–124.

118. Irving Kristol, "A Conservative Welfare State," *Wall Street Journal*, June 14, 1993, A14.

119. Adam Smith, *An Inquiry into the Nature and Causes of the Wealth of Nations*, ed. R. H. Campbell, A. S. Skinner, and W. B. Todd (Indianapolis: Liberty Fund, 1981), 2:643–44, 661–62. See also, e.g., Heinz Lubasz, "Adam Smith and the 'Free Market,'" in *Adam Smith's Wealth of Nations: New Interdisciplinary Essays*, ed. Stephen Copley and Kathryn Sutherland (Manchester: Manchester University Press, 1995), 53–54; Eric Schliesser, *Adam Smith: Systematic Philosopher and Public Thinker* (New York: Oxford University Press, 2017), 221, 127; and Warren J. Samuels and Steven G. Medema, "Freeing Smith from the 'Free Market': On the Misperception of Adam Smith on the Economic Role of Government," *History of Political Economy* 37, no. 2 (Summer 2005): 219–26.

Chapter Five

1. My primary aim is not to evaluate whether Wilson's use of social scientific data in his work on crime and criminal justice system was adequate or not; instead, it is to analyze how he used populist language along with the scientific data to persuade his readers to side with him and other neoconservatives on criminal policy.

2. Franklin E. Zimring, *The Great American Crime Decline* (New York: Oxford University Press, 2008), 35.

3. E.g., Henry S. Ruth and Kevin R. Reitz, *The Challenge of Crime: Rethinking Our Response* (Cambridge, MA: Harvard University Press, 2006), 81. See also Philip Jenkins, *Decade of Nightmares: The End of the Sixties and the Making of Eighties America* (New York: Oxford University Press, 2006), 134–35. For Wilson's career as a student of crime, see Matt Delisi, "Conservatism

and Common Sense: The Criminological Career of James Q. Wilson," *Justice Quarterly* 20, no. 3 (September 2003): 661–74. Wilson served on several national commissions concerned with criminal policy: he chaired the White House Task Force on Crime in 1966 and the 1972–73 National Advisory Commission on Drug Abuse Prevention and was a member of the Attorney General's Task Force on Violent Crime in 1981.

4. Zimring, *Great American Crime Decline*, 22.

5. Julian V. Roberts and Loretta J. Stalans, *Public Opinion, Crime, and Criminal Justice* (Boulder, CO: Westview, 1997), 1. There is vast literature now on mass incarceration in America. As numerous activists and scholars have noted, the incarceration rate in the United States quadrupled between 1960 and 1990. By 2000, one in ten black males in their twenties and thirties was imprisoned, which is ten times the rate of their white peers. See, e.g., Michelle Alexander, *The New Jim Crow: Mass Incarceration in the Age of Colorblindness*, rev. ed. (New York: New Press, 2012), 6–9; Elizabeth Hinton, *From the War on Poverty to the War on Crime: The Making of Mass Incarceration in America* (Cambridge, MA: Harvard University Press, 2016), 5–7; and Ta-Nehisi Coates, "The Black Family in the Age of Mass Incarceration," *Atlantic*, October 2015, https://www.theatlantic.com/magazine/archive/2015/10/the-black-family-in-the-age-of-mass -incarceration/403246/. See also David Garland, *The Culture of Control: Crime and Social Order in Contemporary Society* (Oxford: Oxford University Press, 2001), 98–102, 59–60. The neoconservatives, according to Garland (pp. 136–38), were among the most important contributors to one of the most influential criminological frameworks of the late twentieth century: "the criminology of the other" that "functions to demonize the criminal, to act out popular fears and resentments, and to promote support for state punishment."

6. John Pratt, *Penal Populism* (London: Routledge, 2007), 12.

7. Zimring, *Great American Crime Decline*, 5–6, 9, 196.

8. James Q. Wilson, "What to Do about Crime," *Commentary* 98, no. 3 (September 1994): 26.

9. Ibid., 25–26. Wilson cited Alfred Blumstein of Carnegie-Mellon University on the issue. Wilson was not alone in his pessimism about youth violence in the mid-1990s. Zimring notes that the rise of youth violence in the late 1980s and very early 1990s had a great impact on the widespread pessimism of the mid-1990s (he notes that "it takes three or four years to notice trends"). See his *Great American Crime Decline*, 22–23. Correspondingly, in the fall 1994, Wilson pointed out in the *Los Angeles Times* that the falling crime rates were not making Americans feel more secure, because juvenile homicide had increased. See James Q. Wilson, "Why Falling Crime Statistics Don't Make Us Feel More Secure," *Los Angeles Times*, September 25, 1994, http:// articles.latimes.com/1994-09-25/opinion/op-42725_1_crime-rate.

10. Roberts and Stalans, *Public Opinion, Crime, and Criminal Justice*, 26, 30.

11. James Q. Wilson, "To Prevent Riots, Reduce Black Crime," *Wall Street Journal*, May 6, 1992, A16.

12. Wilson, "What to Do about Crime," 26.

13. Alexander, *New Jim Crow*, 56.

14. Zimring, *Great American Crime Decline*, 7–8.

15. Wilson, "What to Do about Crime," 26.

16. Ibid., 28. Reducing the amount of violence on television was a "favorite nostrum" among many people, Wilson noted, but he did not see it as a plausible strategy, since the impact of television violence on criminality was probably not very significant. The establishment of boot camps (as alternatives to jail terms for young offenders) was another proposed remedy, but their effectiveness was not proven at the time, he claimed. "Then, of course, there is gun control," he

pointed out, acknowledging that guns were "almost certainly contributors to the lethality of American violence" but adding dispiritedly that there was "no politically or legally feasible way to reduce the stock of guns now in private possession to the point where their availability to criminals would be much affected." "As for rehabilitating juvenile offenders," Wilson continued, "it has some merit, but there are rather few success stories." Ibid., 28.

17. Ibid., 27.

18. Ibid., 30.

19. Ibid.

20. James T. Patterson, *Restless Giant: The United States from Watergate to Bush v. Gore* (New York: Oxford University Press, 2005), 341–42; Thomas Frank, "Bill Clinton's Crime Bill Destroyed Lives and There Is No Point Denying It," *Guardian*, 15, April, 2016, https://www.the guardian.com/commentisfree/2016/apr/15/bill-clinton-crime-bill-hillary-black-lives-thomas -frank; Peter Beinart, "Hillary Clinton and the Tragic Politics of Crime," *Atlantic*, May 1, 2015, https://www.theatlantic.com/politics/archive/2015/05/the-tragic-politics-of-crime/392114/.

21. Quoted in Alexander, *New Jim Crow*, 56.

22. Wilson, "Falling Crime Statistics."

23. David Johnston with Steven A. Holmes, "Experts Doubt Effectiveness of Crime Bill," *New York Times*, September 14, 1994, https://www.nytimes.com/1994/09/14/us/experts-doubt -effectiveness-of-crime-bill.html.

24. Wilson, "What to Do about Crime," 34, 27–28, 30.

25. Rudolph W. Giuliani, "What New York Owes James Q. Wilson," *City Journal*, Spring 2012, https://www.city-journal.org/html/what-new-york-owes-james-q-wilson-13465.html.

26. Daniel Patrick Moynihan to William Bratton, April 11, 1994, Daniel Patrick Moynihan Papers, Manuscript Division, Library of Congress, Washington, DC (hereafter Moynihan Papers), box 4: 6, folder 11. See also William Bratton, *The Turnaround: How America's Top Cop Reversed the Crime Epidemic* (New York: Random House, 1998). At least some aspects of the broken windows theory were later applied also in other cities, such as Chicago and Los Angeles (where Bratton was appointed as chief of police in 2002). While Giuliani and Bratton have celebrated Wilson as the creator of a theory that helped them reverse the crime epidemic in their city, academics disagree about whether crime rates dropped in New York in the 1990s because of strategy attributed to the broken windows theory or due to other factors, such as changing demographics and the declining crack cocaine trade. See, e.g., Franklin E. Zimring, "How the 'Broken Windows' Strategy Saved Lives in NYC," *New York Post*, August 24, 2014, http://nypost.com/2014/08/24/how-the-broken-windows-strategy-saved-lives-in-nyc/; Bernard E. Harcourt, *Illusion of Order: The False Promise of Broken Windows Policing* (Cambridge, MA: Harvard University Press, 2001); and Bernard E. Harcourt and Jens Ludwig, "Broken Windows: New Evidence from New York City and a Five-City Social Experiment," *University of Chicago Law Review* 73 (2006): 271–320.

27. Wilson, "What to Do about Crime," 28.

28. Wilson, "Falling Crime Statistics."

29. Hinton, *From the War on Poverty*, 317. Smokable crack cocaine arrived in inner-city neighborhoods just as the effects of globalization and deindustrialization hit these neighborhoods, taking away blue-collar jobs from the inner cities. The crack epidemic abated in the 1990s. See Alexander, *New Jim Crow*, 50–55; and Zimring, *Great American Crime Decline*, 81–85.

30. Wilson, "What to Do about Crime," 31.

31. See, e.g., Christina Nifong, "Reformer Calls for a System That Gets Back to the Basics," interview of James Q. Wilson, *Christian Science Monitor*, May 19, 1997, https://www.csmonitor.com/1997/0519/051997.feat.justice.1.html.

32. Patterson, *Restless Giant*, 311.

33. Ibid., 312; Janell Ross, "Two Decades Later, Black and White Americans Finally Agree on O.J. Simpson's Guilt," *Washington Post*, March 4, 2016, https://www.washingtonpost.com/news/the-fix/wp/2015/09/25/black-and-white-americans-can-now-agree-o-j-was-guilty/.

34. Patterson, *Restless Giant*, 284.

35. David Margolick, "Lorena Bobbitt Acquitted in Mutilation of Husband," *New York Times*, January 22, 1994, https://www.nytimes.com/1994/01/22/us/lorena-bobbitt-acquitted-in-mutilation-of-husband.html.

36. Janelle Harris, "Menendez Brothers: Everything You Need to Know," *Rolling Stone*, October 2, 2016, http://www.rollingstone.com/culture/news/menendez-brothers-everything-you-need-to-know-w442897.

37. Tyler is quoted in Alan Abrahamson, "Effects of Menendez Abuse Told," *Los Angeles Times*, October 14, 1993, http://articles.latimes.com/1993-10-14/local/me-45746_1_erik-menendez.

38. James Q. Wilson, *Moral Judgment: Does the Abuse Excuse Threaten Our Legal System?* (New York: Basic Books, 1997), vii.

39. Ibid., 7, 26.

40. Ibid., 7, 20.

41. Ibid., 43.

42. Ibid., 112.

43. Wilson discussed the "habitually criminal" underclass in his "Culture, Incentives, and the Underclass," in *Values and Public Policy*, ed. Henry J. Aaron, Thomas E. Mann, and Timothy Taylor (Washington, DC: Brookings Institution, 1994), 54.

44. Wilson, *Moral Judgment*, 1–2.

45. Ibid., 111.

46. Roberts and Stalans, *Public Opinion, Crime, and Criminal Justice*, 8.

47. Francis T. Cullen, Bonnie S. Fisher, and Brandon K. Applegate, "Public Opinion about Punishment and Corrections," *Crime and Justice* 27 (2000): 8.

48. Roberts and Stalans, *Public Opinion, Crime, and Criminal Justice*, 8.

49. Alexander, *New Jim Crow*, 54.

50. James Q. Wilson, "Reading Jurors' Minds," *Commentary* 101, no. 2 (February 1996): 46.

51. Ibid.

52. Ibid., 47.

53. Wilson, *Moral Judgment*, 1.

54. Ibid., 40.

55. Ibid., 37.

56. Ibid., 27, 112.

57. Ibid., 27–28.

58. Adam Smith, *The Theory of Moral Sentiments*, ed. D. D. Raphael and A. L. Macfie (Indianapolis: Liberty Fund, 1982), 69–70.

59. Adam Smith, *Lectures on Jurisprudence*, ed. R. L. Meek, D. D. Raphael, and P. G. Stein (Indianapolis: Liberty Fund, 1982), 104. See also Richard Stalley, "Adam Smith and the Theory of Punishment," *Journal of Scottish Philosophy* 10, no. 1 (2012): 70.

60. Stalley, "Adam Smith," 73.

61. Smith, *Theory of Moral Sentiments*, 74.

62. Stalley, "Adam Smith," 73–74.

63. Wilson, *Moral Judgment*, 112.

64. Sophia Rosenfeld, *Common Sense: A Political History* (Cambridge, MA: Harvard University Press, 2011), 6.

65. Wilson, *Moral Judgment*, 80–81.

66. Hinton, *From the War on Poverty*, 21.

67. Gerson, *The Neoconservative Vision*, 8, 146–57; Andrew Hartman, *A War for the Soul of America: A History of the Culture Wars* (Chicago: University of Chicago Press, 2015), 65.

68. Amy E. Ansell, "Color-Blindness," in *Race and Ethnicity: The Key Concepts* (London: Routledge, 2013), 42–43.

69. Alexander, *New Jim Crow*; see also Helen A. Neville, Miguel E. Gallardo, and Derald Wing Sue, eds., *The Myth of Racial Color Blindness: Manifestations, Dynamics, and Impact* (Washington, DC: American Psychological Association, 2016); and Michael K. Brown et al., *Whitewashing Race: The Myth of a Color-Blind Society* (Berkeley: University of California Press, 2003).

70. Alexander, *New Jim Crow*, 43, 2.

71. Ibid., 45–52.

72. Ibid., 2, 244.

73. Wilson, *Moral Judgment*, 85.

74. Ibid., 109.

75. Ibid., 111.

76. See, e.g., Daniel Bergner, "Is Stop-and-Frisk Worth It," *Atlantic*, April 2014, https://www.theatlantic.com/magazine/archive/2014/04/is-stop-and-frisk-worth-it/358644/.

77. Mark A. R. Kleiman, "Thinking about Punishment: James Q. Wilson and Mass Incarceration" (working paper no. 11, Marron Institute, New York University, June 26, 2014), http://marroninstitute.nyu.edu/uploads/content/Thinking_About_Punishment.pdf; Mark A. R. Kleiman, "Wilson's Machiavellian Cruelty" (paper presentation, Thinking about Politics: A Conference Dedicated to Explaining and Perpetuating the Political Insights of James Q. Wilson, Harvard University and Boston College, April 4–5, 2013), https://www.youtube.com/watch?v=zKouSgtb2bY.

78. James Q. Wilson, "Foreword: Never Too Early," in *Serious and Violent Juvenile Offenders: Risk Factors and Successful Interventions*, ed. Rolf Loeber and David P. Farrington (Thousand Oaks, CA: Sage, 1998), ix. Wilson never retreated from the idea that incarceration was a significant strategy for reducing crime, especially for serious crimes. See Brandon C. Welsh and David P. Farrington, "Preventing Crime Is Hard Work: Early Intervention, Developmental Criminology, and the Enduring Legacy of James Q. Wilson," *Journal of Criminal Justice* 41, no. 6 (November–December 2013): 448.

79. Roberts and Stalans, *Public Opinion, Crime, and Criminal Justice*, 31.

80. On the public misperceptions, see ibid., 30. *Superpredator* was a term popularized by John J. DiIulio Jr., a student and collaborator of James Q. Wilson. See John DiIulio, "The Coming of Super-Predators," *Weekly Standard*, November 27, 1995, https://www.weeklystandard.com/john-j-dilulio-jr/the-coming-of-the-super-predators.

81. Rosenfeld, *Common Sense*, 15.

82. Ibid., 14.

83. Mark Hulliung, *Citizens and Citoyens: Republicans and Liberals in America and France* (Cambridge, MA: Harvard University Press, 2002), 124.

Chapter Six

1. On the debate over Strauss during the presidency of George W. Bush, see Catherine Zuckert and Michael Zuckert, *The Truth about Leo Strauss: Political Philosophy and American Democracy* (Chicago: University of Chicago Press, 2006), 1–20, esp. 6–8. The political theorist Shadia Drury was an academic pioneer of the claim that there is a strong connection between Strauss and neoconservative politics. See esp. Shadia B. Drury, *Leo Strauss and the American Right* (New York: St. Martin's, 1997).

2. For criticisms of the argument that Strauss promoted mass deception, see Zuckert and Zuckert, *Truth about Leo Strauss*; and Leora Batnitzky, "Leo Strauss," ed. Edward N. Zalta, *Stanford Encyclopedia of Philosophy* (Summer 2016 edition), https://plato.stanford.edu/archives/sum2016/entries/strauss-leo/.

3. Francis Fukuyama, *The End of History and the Last Man* (New York: Free Press, 1992). Fukuyama long regarded himself as a neoconservative, but after becoming critical of his friends' eagerness to use military intervention to promote American values around the globe after the 2003 invasion of Iraq, he distanced himself from the group. See his *America at the Crossroads: Democracy, Power, and the Neoconservative Legacy* (New Haven, CT: Yale University Press, 2006).

4. Earlier analysts of Fukuyama's moral and political thought have largely focused on *End of History*, including Fukuyama's conception of human nature in this book, while his later use of the "moral sense" has been largely ignored. On Fukuyama's use of evolutionary biological concepts such as *kin selection* and *reciprocal altruism* in his late 1990s and early 2000s works, see Carson Holloway, *The Right Darwin? Evolution, Religion, and the Future of Democracy* (Dallas: Spence, 2006).

5. Francis Fukuyama, "The End of History?," *National Interest*, no. 16 (Summer 1989): 3–18.

6. The quote is from Strobe Talbott, "Terminator 2: Gloom on the Right," *Time*, January 27, 1992, 31.

7. This issue is discussed, e.g., in Shadia B. Drury, *Alexandre Kojève: The Roots of Postmodern Politics* (New York: St. Martin's, 1994), 179.

8. Fukuyama, *End of History*, xxi; Jennifer Ratner-Rosenhagen, *American Nietzsche: A History of an Icon and His Ideas* (Chicago: University of Chicago Press, 2011), 272; Jan-Werner Müller, *What Is Populism?* (Philadelphia: University of Pennsylvania Press, 2016), 5–6; Edmund Fawcett, *Liberalism: The Life of an Idea* (Princeton, NJ: Princeton University Press, 2014), 404.

9. See, e.g., Drury, *Alexandre Kojève*, 179–98; Ratner-Rosenhagen, *American Nietzsche*, 272–73; and Stephen Holmes, "The Scowl of Minerva," *New Republic* 206, no. 12 (March 23, 1992): 27–33. Fukuyama himself agreed with one scholar's description of his book as a "most pessimistic of optimistic books." See Francis Fukuyama, "Reflections on *The End of History*, Five Years Later," *History and Theory* 34, no. 2 (1995): 42–43.

10. Will Kymlicka, *Contemporary Political Philosophy: An Introduction*, 2nd ed. (Oxford: Oxford University Press, 2002), 284–85; Jane Lewis, "Fukuyama and Fin de Siècle Anxiety about the Family," *Political Quarterly* 70, no. 4 (October–December 1999): 427.

11. Robert Booth Fowler, *Enduring Liberalism: American Political Thought since the 1960s* (Lawrence: University Press of Kansas, 1999), 149.

12. Daniel Rodgers sums up the discussion on "virtue" by noting that for

those working within the tradition of civic republicanism, virtue's essence was the sacrifice of the self for the public weal. In much of the conservative lexicon, the word "virtue" simply became a synonym for ethical certainty, a slogan with which they set out to inject harder-edged morals into the schools than mere values clarification and to enlist families and teachers in pushing back the moral relativism of the times. But for still others the term "virtue" flagged not commonweal or certainty but smaller, more piecemeal terrains of everyday practice: the common, community-embedded social practices of sympathy, duty, fairness, cooperation, and self-control that James Coleman and others had begun to call "social capital."

See Daniel T. Rodgers, *Age of Fracture* (Cambridge, MA: Belknap Press of Harvard University Press, 2011), 196.

13. James T. Kloppenberg, *The Virtues of Liberalism* (New York: Oxford University Press, 1998), 8.

14. Ibid.

15. Ibid., 10–11.

16. On Fukuyama's connections with the Straussians, see Fukuyama's *America at the Crossroads*, 21–31; and see, e.g., Jacob Heilbrunn, *They Knew They Were Right: The Rise of the Neocons* (New York: Doubleday, 2008), 109–10; and Nicholas Wroe, "History's Pallbearer," *Guardian*, May 11, 2002, https://www.theguardian.com/books/2002/may/11/academicexperts.artsandhumanities. Strauss immigrated to the United States in 1938 and spent the most of his career as a professor of political philosophy at the University of Chicago.

17. Andrew Hartman, *A War for the Soul of America: A History of the Culture Wars* (Chicago: University of Chicago Press, 2015), 236. *The Closing of the American Mind* was the second-best-selling hardback book in the United States in 1987. See Ratner-Rosenhagen, *American Nietzsche*, 308.

18. Allan Bloom, *The Closing of the American Mind* (New York: Simon & Schuster, 1987), 25; Michael Zuckert, "On Allan Bloom," *Good Society* 17, no. 2 (2008): 81.

19. Bloom, *Closing of the American Mind*; Ratner-Rosenhagen, *American Nietzsche*, 271–72.

20. Ratner-Rosenhagen, *American Nietzsche*, 271.

21. Zuckert and Zuckert, *Truth about Leo Strauss*, esp. 66, 178–79; see also Michael P. Zuckert and Catherine H. Zuckert, *Leo Strauss and the Problem of Political Philosophy* (Chicago: University of Chicago Press, 2014), 170.

22. Zuckert and Zuckert, *Truth about Leo Strauss*, 66. In Strauss's account, an important consequence of this democratization of the moral scene was that modernity became characterized by political immoderation, since the lowering of sights raised the hopes for politics. Patience was no longer accepted when the moderns understood that their goals were achievable. Political ambitions were raised to a new level, which signified political idealism without limits, leading to repeated political horrors in the name of highest aspirations. See Zuckert and Zuckert, *Truth about Leo Strauss*, 66–67.

23. Ibid., 66; Zuckert and Zuckert, *Leo Strauss and the Problem of Political Philosophy*, 341.

24. On Fukuyama's and Strauss's Nietzschean ideas, see Haroon Sheikh, "Nietzsche and the Neoconservatives," *Journal of Nietzsche Studies*, nos. 35–36 (Spring–Autumn 2008): esp. 30.

25. Fukuyama, "Reflections on *The End of History*," 27.

26. Fukuyama, *End of History*, xxi.

27. Robert B. Pippin, "Being, Time, and Politics: The Strauss-Kojève Debate," *History and Theory* 32, no. 2 (May 1993): 159.

28. Fukuyama, *End of History*, 162–63. Fukuyama noted (pp. 162–63) that over "the millennia, there has been no consistent word used to refer to [this] psychological phenomenon. . . . Plato

spoke of *thymos*, or 'spiritedness,' Machiavelli of man's desire for glory, Hobbes of his pride or vainglory, Rousseau of his *amour-propre*, Alexander Hamilton of the love of fame and James Madison of ambition, Hegel of recognition, and Nietzsche of man as the 'beast with red cheeks.' All of these terms refer to that part of man which feels the need to place *value* on things— himself in the first instance, but on the people, actions, or things around him as well."

29. Ibid., 165.

30. Ibid., 171.

31. Ibid., 165.

32. Ibid., 172.

33. Ibid., 182.

34. Ibid., 321. See also Drury, *Alexandre Kojève*, chap. 12.

35. Fukuyama discussed Nietzsche's derogatory view of the typical citizen of a liberal democracy as the "last man" on pp. xxii and 301 of *End of History*. Part 5 of Fukuyama's book titled "The Last Man" is, in many ways, congruent with Nietzsche's view; in contemporary liberal democracies, Fukuyama claims (p. 320–21), megalothymia is "driven underground."

36. Fukuyama, *End of History*, 185.

37. Ibid., 305–6. The phrase "Men without Chests" derives from C. S. Lewis's *The Abolition of Man* (1943).

38. Ibid., chap. 13.

39. Ibid., 149.

40. Shadia Drury argues that Fukuyama's "whole book [*End of History*] is a subtle, but unmistakable, celebration of death and violence." See Drury, *Alexandre Kojève*, 196. This is clearly a misconception.

41. Francis Fukuyama, "Political and Legal," review of *The Lucifer Principle: A Scientific Expedition into the Forces of History*, by Howard Bloom, *Foreign Affairs* 74, no. 4 (July/August 1995): 131; Francis Fukuyama, *Trust: The Social Virtues and the Creation of Prosperity* (New York: Free Press, 1995), 41, 370.

42. Fukuyama, *Trust*, 41, 370; Francis Fukuyama, *The End of Order* (London: Profile Books, 1997), 107; Francis Fukuyama, *The Great Disruption: Human Nature and the Reconstitution of Social Order* (New York: Free Press, 1999), 183, 325; Francis Fukuyama, *Our Posthuman Future: Consequences of the Biotechnology Revolution* (New York: Farrar, Straus and Giroux, 2002), 101–2, 142, 175.

43. Fukuyama, *Trust*, 41, 370.

44. Francis Fukuyama, "Is It All in the Genes?," *Commentary* 104, no. 3 (September 1997): 34.

45. Fukuyama notes in Wilson's obituary that he came to know Wilson personally in the early 2000s. He adds, however, that "of course the way I got to really know him was through reading his books, from early ones like *City Politics* to the later volumes like *Crime and Human Nature* . . . and *The Moral Sense*." See Francis Fukuyama, "James Q. Wilson, 1931–2012," *American Interest*, March 4, 2012, http://www.the-american-interest.com/2012/03/04/james-q-wilson -1931-2012/.

46. See the acknowledgments section in Fukuyama, *Great Disruption*, xi–xii.

47. See Fukuyama, *Great Disruption*, 183; Francis Fukuyama, "How to Re-moralize America," *Wilson Quarterly* 23, no. 3 (Summer 1999): 39; Francis Fukuyama, "The Moralist of the Dismal Science," review of *Adam Smith and the Virtues of Enlightenment*, by Charles Griswold, *Public Interest*, no. 136 (Summer 1999): 124–25; and Fukuyama, *Our Posthuman Future*, 101–2, 142, 175. In "Moralist of the Dismal Science," Fukuyama suggested (p. 124–25) that Adam Smith could have

grounded his moral theory on the "moral sense" idea instead of the impartial spectator, which perhaps would have enabled him to establish "natural rules of justice" applicable to all nations.

48. Fukuyama, "How to Re-moralize America," 42, 39.

49. Fukuyama, *Great Disruption*, 272.

50. Ibid., 8; see also 271.

51. Edward Ashbee, "Remoralization: American Society and Politics in the 1990s," *Political Quarterly* 71, no. 2 (April 2000): 200.

52. Konrad Lorenz, *On Aggression*, trans. Marjorie Kerr Wilson (New York: Harcourt, Brace & World, 1966); Robert Ardrey, *The Territorial Imperative: A Personal Inquiry into the Animal Origins of Property and Nations* (New York: Atheneum, 1966). See also Erika Lorraine Milam, *Creatures of Cain: The Hunt for Human Nature in Cold War America* (Princeton, NJ: Princeton University Press, 2019).

53. William D. Hamilton, "The Genetical Evolution of Social Behaviour I–II," *Journal of Theoretical Biology* 7, no. 1 (1964): 1–16, 17–52; Robert L. Trivers, "The Evolution of Reciprocal Altruism," *Quarterly Review of Biology* 46 (1971): 35–57; Edward O. Wilson, *Sociobiology: The New Synthesis* (Cambridge, MA: Harvard University Press, 1975). See also Carl Degler, *In Search of Human Nature: The Decline and Revival of Darwinism in American Social Thought* (New York: Oxford University Press, 1991).

54. See Robin Fox, "Moral Sense and Utopian Sensibility," in *Conjectures and Confrontations: Science, Evolution, Social Concern* (New Brunswick, NJ: Transaction, 1997), 117, 122.

55. Francis Fukuyama and Caroline S. Wagner, *Information and Biological Revolutions: Global Governance Challenges—Summary of a Study Group* (Santa Monica, CA: RAND, 2000), http://www.rand.org/content/dam/rand/pubs/monograph_reports/2007/MR1139.pdf; Fukuyama, *Great Disruption*, xi.

56. On the overlaps between Scottish moral philosophy and Darwinian evolutionary psychology, see, e.g., Kristen Renwick Monroe, Adam Martin, and Priyanka Ghosh, "Politics and an Innate Moral Sense: Scientific Evidence for an Old Theory?," *Political Research Quarterly* 62, no. 3 (September 2009): 614–34; and John Laurent and Geoff Cockfield, "Adam Smith, Charles Darwin and the Moral Sense," in *New Perspectives on Adam Smith's The Theory of Moral Sentiments*, ed. Geoff Cockfield, Ann Firth, and John Laurent (Cheltenham, England: Edward Elgar, 2007), 141–62.

57. Robert D. Putnam, "Bowling Alone: America's Declining Social Capital," *Journal of Democracy* 6, no. 1 (January 1995): 65–78; Kymlicka, *Contemporary Political Philosophy*, 286. See also Robert D. Putnam, *Bowling Alone: The Collapse and Revival of American Community* (New York: Simon & Schuster, 2000). On the history of the concept, see Alejandro Portes, "Social Capital: Its Origins and Applications in Modern Sociology," *Annual Review of Sociology* 24 (1998): 1–24.

58. See, e.g., Everett C. Ladd, "The Data Just Don't Show Erosion of America's 'Social Capital,'" *Public Perspective* 7 (June–July 1996): 5–22; and Michael Schudson, "What If Civic Life Didn't Die?," *American Prospect* 25 (March–April 1996): 17–20.

59. Fukuyama, *Trust*, 309.

60. Fukuyama, *Great Disruption*, 49–55, esp. 54. Fukuyama defined social capital in *Great Disruption* (p. 16) "as a set of informal values or norms shared among members of a group that permits cooperation among them."

61. Fukuyama, *End of History*, 150, chap. 13.

62. Drury, *Alexandre Kojève*, 195.

63. Ibid., 192.

64. Ibid., 198.

65. Fukuyama, "How to Re-moralize America," 39.

66. Political scientist Stephen Holmes is correct to note that Fukuyama, in *End of History*, "sometimes . . . claims that thymos is a permanent feature of the human mind. At other times he claims that it can be extinguished, and perhaps has been extinguished, in bourgeois societies." See his "Scowl of Minerva," 31.

67. Fukuyama, *Trust*, 370.

68. Fukuyama, "How to Re-moralize America," 39. To my knowledge, Fukuyama no longer wrote about the decline of thymos in the late 1990s. In his 2018 book *Identity: The Demand for Dignity and the Politics of Resentment* (New York: Farrar, Straus and Giroux, 2018), 18, Fukuyama presents thymos as "the seat of today's identity politics."

69. Fukuyama, "How to Re-moralize America," 39.

70. Francis Fukuyama, "Immigrants and Family Values," *Commentary* 95, no. 5 (May 1993): 26.

71. Ibid., 26, 29–30.

72. Ibid., 31. As Patrick Allitt writes, the neoconservatives' idea was that "liberal democracy is, potentially, for everyone and that immigration does more good than harm." Famously, paleoconservatives such as Thomas Fleming, Paul Gottfried, and Sam Francis attacked neoconservatives ruthlessly in the 1980s for such democratic universalism and secularism. See Patrick Allitt, *The Conservatives: Ideas and Personalities throughout American History* (New Haven, CT: Yale University Press, 2009), 249. For the neoconservative-paleoconservative rift, see also Mark Gerson, *The Neoconservative Vision: From the Cold War to the Culture Wars* (Lanham, MD: Madison Books, 1996), 309–20; and George H. Nash, *The Conservative Intellectual Movement in America since 1945*, 30th anniversary ed. (Wilmington, DE: ISI Books, 2006), 567–70.

73. Fukuyama, "Immigrants and Family Values," 30.

74. See, e.g., James T. Patterson, *Restless Giant: The United States from Watergate to Bush v. Gore* (New York: Oxford University Press, 2005), 270; and Hartman, *War for the Soul*, 198–99.

75. Fukuyama, "Immigrants and Family Values," 29–30.

76. Ibid., 32.

77. Fukuyama, "How to Re-moralize America," 42. Fukuyama made a similar case in "Cheer Up, Conservatives," *Wall Street Journal*, February 11, 1999, A26.

78. Fukuyama, *Great Disruption*, 8.

79. Fukuyama, "How to Re-moralize America," 41.

80. Ibid., 44.

81. On the libertarian belief in "the self-balancing and natural evolution of a social order," see Michael Freeden, *Ideologies and Political Theory: A Conceptual Approach* (Oxford: Oxford University Press, 1996), 374; see also David Boaz, *The Libertarian Mind: A Manifesto for Freedom* (New York: Simon & Schuster, 2015), 26. Freeden remarks that this idea—whether referred to as spontaneous order or not—is the "*most salient* conservative principle in libertarian thought." Friedrich Hayek referred to this idea as "spontaneous order," which, Freeden notes, "on closer observation referred to a balance independent of human design." Although there are important differences between libertarianism and conservatism, both ideologies tend to warn "against the consequences of human intervention in the social evolutionary process, seemingly an act of rational and volitional control but in fact immensely damaging for its miscomprehension of the forces sustaining society." Freeden notes that libertarians interpret the "balance independent of design" as "a dynamic equilibrium, capable of producing a progressive momentum, and thus

distance themselves from those conservatives whose conception of order tends to the static end of the analytic continuum." Freeden, *Ideologies and Political Theory*, 374.

82. Fukuyama, *Great Disruption*, 274, 218.

83. Ibid., 6.

84. Ibid., 145.

85. Ibid., 159–60.

86. Fukuyama, *Trust*, 362.

87. Ibid., 361, 353.

88. Ibid., 318, 320.

89. Ibid., 318.

90. Fukuyama, *Great Disruption*, 15, chap. 15, chap. 16.

91. Hartman, *War for the Soul*, 5. As noted earlier, these and other "bourgeois" values were not wholly unquestioned in the 1950s, and in this sense, neoconservative writers like Fukuyama *imagined* a 1950s past in which a consensus, or near-consensus, on bourgeois values existed. On midcentury modernist thought and culture, see, e.g., Robert Genter, *Late Modernism: Art, Culture, and Politics in Cold War America* (Philadelphia: University of Pennsylvania Press, 2010); and Alan Petigny, *The Permissive Society: America, 1941–1965* (New York: Cambridge University Press, 2009).

92. Fukuyama discusses Puritan values in *Great Disruption*, 17.

93. Ibid., 231.

94. Ibid., 173.

95. Ibid., 183. In *Great Disruption* (p. 183), Fukuyama identified the "moral sense" with the natural human capacity to "empathize with other people." In *Our Posthuman Future*, he used the term "moral sense" more systematically, speaking of a "natural human moral sense that evolved over time out of the requirements of hominids." He argued that "what is ultimately at stake with biotechnology is . . . the very grounding of the human moral sense, which has been a constant ever since there were human beings." See *Our Posthuman Future*, 101–2, 142.

96. Fukuyama, *Great Disruption*, 177.

97. The quote (on Victorian values) is from ibid., 275.

98. Ibid., 273.

99. Ibid., 273, 120, 276.

100. Ibid., 15–16.

101. Ibid., 275.

102. Ibid., chap. 13.

103. Ibid., 243–44.

104. Daniel Stedman Jones, *Masters of the Universe: Hayek, Friedman, and the Birth of Neoliberal Politics* (Princeton, NJ: Princeton University Press, 2012), 113.

105. Sometimes "libertarianism" is understood as a more radical "laissez-faire" version of free market ideology, while neoliberalism is seen as advocating for somewhat more intervention in the economy and society. Historian Quinn Slobodian argues that early European "neoliberals" such as Friedrich von Hayek, Ludwig von Mises, and Wilhelm Röpke did not advocate laissez-faire but instead wanted to use states and global institutions to protect markets from sovereign states and democratic control. See Quinn Slobodian, *Globalists: The End of Empire and the Birth of Neoliberalism* (Cambridge, MA: Harvard University Press, 2018).

106. On the neoliberal use of Adam Smith, see Stedman Jones, *Masters of the Universe*, 100–116.

107. Milton Friedman is quoted in Stedman Jones, *Masters of the Universe*, 102.

108. Stedman Jones, *Masters of the Universe*, 115.

109. On the history of free market ideology in the United States since the Great Depression, see, e.g., Angus Burgin, *The Great Persuasion: Reinventing Free Markets since the Depression* (Cambridge, MA: Harvard University Press, 2012); and Stedman Jones, *Masters of the Universe*. Stedman Jones, who explicitly focuses on "neoliberalism," defines it (on p. 2) as "the free market ideology based on individual liberty and limited government that connected human freedom to the actions of the rational, self-interested actor in the competitive marketplace."

110. On the "neoliberal order," see Gary Gerstle, "America's Neoliberal Order," in *Beyond the New Deal Order: U.S. Politics from the Great Depression to the Great Recession*, ed. Gary Gerstle, Nelson Liechtenstein, and Alice O'Connor (Philadelphia: University of Pennsylvania Press, 2019), 257–78. My analysis of the links between neoliberalism and neoconservatism draws on and complements the work of Gerstle, who argues (p. 272–75) that the "neo-Victorianism" of neoconservatives such as Gertrude Himmelfarb both buttressed neoliberal market fundamentalism and clashed with it.

111. On these debates, see Daniel Wickberg, "Modernisms Endless: Ironies of the American Mid-century," *Modern Intellectual History* 10, no. 1 (2013): 207–19; and Daniel Wickberg, "Intellectual—a Historiographical Survey," in *The Routledge History of the Twentieth-Century United States*, ed. Jerald Podair and Darren Dochuk (New York: Routledge, 2018), 116–26.

112. Fukuyama, *Great Disruption*, 90.

Epilogue

1. Rick Perlstein, "I Thought I Understood the American Right: Trump Proved Me Wrong," *New York Times Magazine*, April 11, 2017, https://www.nytimes.com/2017/04/11/magazine/i-thought-i-understood-the-american-right-trump-proved-me-wrong.html.

2. Jan-Werner Müller, *What Is Populism?* (Philadelphia: University of Pennsylvania Press, 2016), 3.

3. Yascha Mounk, *The People vs. Democracy: Why Our Freedom Is in Danger and How to Save It* (Cambridge, MA: Harvard University Press, 2018), 42–43.

4. David A. Hollinger, *Postethnic America: Beyond Multiculturalism*, 10th anniversary ed. (1995; repr., New York: Basic Books, 2005), 201.

5. Mounk, *People vs. Democracy*, 205, 203. See also Mark Lilla, *The Once and Future Liberal: After Identity Politics* (New York: HarperCollins, 2017). For leftist arguments against identity politics, see Walter Benn Michaels, *The Trouble with Diversity: How We Learned to Love Identity and Ignore Inequality* (New York: Metropolitan Books, 2006); and Adolph Reed Jr., *Class Notes: Posing as Politics and Other Thoughts on the American Scene* (New York: New Press, 2000).

6. Cf. Mounk, *People vs. Democracy*, part two, especially chap. 4 on social media.

7. Gertrude Himmelfarb, "The Other Culture War," in *Is There a Culture War? A Dialogue on Values and American Public Life*, ed. James Davison Hunter and Alan Wolfe (Washington, DC: Brookings Institution, 2006), 76.

8. James Q. Wilson, *The Moral Sense* (New York: Free Press, 1993), vii. The phrase "contempt machines of social media" is from Arthur C. Brooks, "Our Culture of Contempt," *New York Times*, March 2, 2019, https://www.nytimes.com/2019/03/02/opinion/sunday/political-polarization.html.

9. David Hume, *A Treatise of Human Nature*, ed. L. A. Selby-Bigge, 2nd ed. (Oxford: Clarendon Press, 1978), 491, 580–85, 602–4.

10. Adam Smith, *The Theory of Moral Sentiments*, ed. D. D. Raphael and A. L. Macfie (Indianapolis: Liberty Fund, 1982), 147, 148; Charles L. Griswold Jr., *Adam Smith and the Virtues of Enlightenment* (Cambridge: Cambridge University Press, 1999), 211–12. On the similarities and differences between Hume's and Smith's accounts of the correction of biased moral sentiments, see Michael L. Frazer, *The Enlightenment of Sympathy: Justice and the Moral Sentiments in the Eighteenth Century and Today* (New York: Oxford University Press, 2010), esp. 96.

11. Frazer, *Enlightenment of Sympathy*, 180–81.

12. On "species-centered" and "ethnos-centered" discourse, see Hollinger, *Postethnic America*, chap. 3.

13. Sophia Rosenfeld, *Common Sense: A Political History* (Cambridge, MA: Harvard University Press, 2011), 15.

14. James Q. Wilson, "Emotions, Reason, and Character," *Criminal Justice Ethics* 13, no. 2 (Summer/Fall 1994): 87.

Bibliography

Archival Sources

Daniel P. Moynihan Papers. Manuscript Division. Library of Congress, Washington, DC.
Irving Kristol Papers. Wisconsin Historical Society, Madison, WI.
James Q. Wilson Papers. Pardee RAND Graduate School, Santa Monica, CA.

Published Primary Sources

Abrahamson, Alan. "Effects of Menendez Abuse Told." *Los Angeles Times*, October 14, 1993. http://articles.latimes.com/1993-10-14/local/me-45746_1_erik-menendez.

Ardrey, Robert. *The Territorial Imperative: A Personal Inquiry into the Animal Origins of Property and Nations*. New York: Atheneum, 1966.

Arnhart, Larry. *Darwinian Natural Right: The Biological Ethics of Human Nature*. Albany: State University of New York Press, 1998.

Ashbee, Edward. "Remoralization: American Society and Politics in the 1990s." *Political Quarterly* 71, no. 2 (April 2000): 192–201.

Auletta, Ken. *The Underclass*. Rev. ed. Woodstock, NY: Overlook, 1999.

Banfield, Edward C. *The Unheavenly City: The Nature and Future of Our Urban Crisis*. Boston: Little, Brown, 1970.

———. "Welfare: A Crisis without Solutions." *Public Interest*, no. 16 (Summer 1969): 89–101.

Bell, Daniel. *The Coming of Post-industrial Society: A Venture in Social Forecasting*. New York: Basic Books, 1973.

———. *The Cultural Contradictions of Capitalism*. New York: Basic Books, 1976.

———. *The End of Ideology: On the Exhaustion of Political Ideas in the Fifties*. Glencoe, IL: Free Press, 1960.

———. "On Meritocracy and Equality." *Public Interest*, no. 29 (Fall 1972): 29–68.

Bell, Daniel, and Irving Kristol. "What Is the Public Interest?" *Public Interest*, no. 1 (Fall 1965): 3–5.

Bennett, William J. *The Devaluing of America: The Fight for Our Culture and Our Children*. New York: Summit Books, 1992.

Bennett, William J., John J. DiIulio Jr., and John P. Walters. *Body Count: Moral Poverty . . . and How to Win America's War against Crime and Drugs*. New York: Simon & Schuster, 1996.

Bennett, William J., Chester E. Finn Jr., and John T. E. Cribb Jr. *The Educated Child: A Parent's Guide from Preschool through Eighth Grade*. New York: Free Press, 1999.

Berry, Wendell. *Citizenship Papers: Essays by Wendell Berry*. Washington, DC: Shoemaker & Hoard, 2003.

Bloom, Allan. *The Closing of the American Mind*. New York: Simon & Schuster, 1987.

Bork, Robert. *Slouching towards Gomorrah: Modern Liberalism and American Decline*. New York: Regan Books, 1996.

Brooks, David. "A Moral Philosophy for Middle Class America." *New York Times*, October 15, 2006. http://www.nytimes.com/2006/10/15/opinion/15brooks.html.

———. "The Rediscovery of Character." *New York Times*, March 5, 2012. http://www.nytimes.com/2012/03/06/opinion/brooks-the-rediscovery-of-character.html.

———. *The Social Animal*. New York: Random House, 2011.

Coleman, James S., Ernest Q. Campbell, Carol J. Hobson, James McPartland, Alexander M. Mood, Frederic D. Weinfeld, and Robert L. York. *Equality of Educational Opportunity*. Washington, DC: US Government Printing Office, 1966.

Decter, Midge. *Liberal Parents, Radical Children*. New York: Coward, McCann, and Geoghegan, 1975.

———. *The Liberated Woman and Other Americans*. New York: Coward, McCann, and Geoghegan, 1971.

———. *The New Chastity and Other Arguments against Women's Liberation*. London: Wildwood House, 1973.

DiIulio, John. "The Coming of Super-Predators." *Weekly Standard*, November 27, 1995. https://www.weeklystandard.com/john-j-dilulio-jr/the-coming-of-the-super-predators.

Dionne, E. J. "Children Emerge as Issue for Democrats." *New York Times*, September 27, 1987. https://www.nytimes.com/1987/09/27/us/children-emerge-as-issue-for-democrats.html.

Djilas, Milovan. *The New Class: An Analysis of the Communist System*. New York: Praeger, 1957.

Fiske, John. *Understanding Popular Culture*. London: Routledge, 1989.

Fox, Robin. *Conjectures and Confrontations: Science, Evolution, Social Concern*. New Brunswick, NJ: Transaction, 1997.

Fukuyama, Francis. *America at the Crossroads: Democracy, Power, and the Neoconservative Legacy*. New Haven, CT: Yale University Press, 2006.

———. "Cheer Up, Conservatives." *Wall Street Journal*, February 11, 1999.

———. "The End of History?" *National Interest*, no. 16 (Summer 1989): 3–18.

———. *The End of History and the Last Man*. New York: Free Press, 1992.

———. *The End of Order*. London: Profile Books, 1997.

———. *The Great Disruption: Human Nature and the Reconstitution of Social Order*. New York: Free Press, 1999.

———. "How to Re-moralize America." *Wilson Quarterly* 23, no. 3 (Summer 1999): 32–44.

———. *Identity: The Demand for Dignity and the Politics of Resentment*. New York: Farrar, Strauss and Giroux, 2018.

———. "Immigrants and Family Values." *Commentary* 95, no. 5 (May 1993): 26–32.

———. "Is It All in the Genes?" *Commentary* 104, no. 3 (September 1997): 30–35.

———. "James Q. Wilson, 1931–2012." *American Interest*, March 4, 2012. http://www.the-ameri can-interest.com/2012/03/04/james-q-wilson-1931-2012/.

———. "The Moralist of the Dismal Science." *Public Interest*, no. 136 (Summer 1999): 121–25.

———. *Our Posthuman Future: Consequences of the Biotechnology Revolution.* New York: Farrar, Strauss and Giroux, 2002.

———. "Political and Legal." Review of *The Lucifer Principle*, by Howard Bloom. *Foreign Affairs* 74, no. 4 (July/August 1995): 130–31.

———. "Reflections on *The End of History*, Five Years Later." *History and Theory* 34, no. 2 (May 1995): 27–43.

———. *Trust: The Social Virtues and the Creation of Prosperity.* New York: Free Press, 1995.

———. "What Divides America." *Wall Street Journal*, November 15, 2000.

Fukuyama, Francis, and Caroline S. Wagner. *Information and Biological Revolutions: Global Governance Challenges—Summary of a Study Group.* Santa Monica, CA: RAND, 2000. http://www.rand.org/content/dam/rand/pubs/monograph_reports/2007/MR1139.pdf.

Gerson, Mark, ed. *The Essential Neoconservative Reader.* Reading, MA: Addison-Wesley, 1996.

Glazer, Nathan. "Is Busing Necessary?" *Commentary* 53, no. 3 (March 1972): 39–52.

———. "Neoconservative from the Start." *Public Interest*, no. 159 (Spring 2005): 12–17.

Glazer, Nathan, and Daniel Patrick Moynihan. *Beyond the Melting Pot: The Negroes, Puerto Ricans, Jews, Italians, and Irish of New York City.* 2nd ed. Cambridge, MA: MIT Press, 1970.

Grossberg, Lawrence. *We Gotta Get Out of This Place: Popular Conservatism and Postmodern Culture.* New York: Routledge, 1992.

Hamilton, William D. "The Genetical Evolution of Social Behaviour I–II." *Journal of Theoretical Biology* 7, no. 1 (1964): 1–16, 17–52.

Himmelfarb, Gertrude. "Armut und zweierlei Aufklärung." In *Aufklärung Heute: Castelgandalfo-Gespräche 1996*, edited by Krzysztof Michalski, 162–201. Stuttgart, Ger.: Klett-Cotta, 1997.

———. "Democratic Remedies for Democratic Disorders." *Public Interest*, no. 131 (Spring 1998): 3–24.

———. *The De-moralization of Society: From Victorian Virtues to Modern Values.* New York: Alfred A. Knopf, 1995.

———. "A De-moralized Society: The British/American Experience." *Public Interest*, no. 117 (Fall 1994): 57–80.

———. "The Idea of Compassion: The British vs. the French Enlightenment." *Public Interest*, no. 145 (Fall 2001): 3–24.

———. *The Idea of Poverty: England in the Early Industrial Age.* London: Faber and Faber, 1984.

———. *Marriage and Morals among the Victorians.* New York: Alfred A. Knopf, 1986.

———. *The Moral Imagination: From Adam Smith to Lionel Trilling.* 2nd ed. Lanham, MD: Rowman & Littlefield, 2012.

———, ed. *The Neoconservative Persuasion: Selected Essays, 1942–2009, Irving Kristol.* New York: Basic Books, 2011.

———. *One Nation, Two Cultures.* New York: Alfred A. Knopf, 1999.

———. *Past and Present: The Challenges of Modernity, from the Pre-Victorians to the Postmodernists.* New York: Encounter Books, 2017.

———. *Poverty and Compassion: The Moral Imagination of the Late Victorians.* New York: Alfred A. Knopf, 1991.

———. *The Roads to Modernity: The British, French, and American Enlightenments.* New York: Alfred A. Knopf, 2004.

———. "Three Paths to Modernity: The British, American, and French Enlightenments." Lecture for the American Enterprise Institute Bradley Lecture Series, Washington, DC, May 10, 2004. http://www.aei.org/publication/three-paths-to-modernity/.

———. "Two Enlightenments: A Contrast in Social Ethics." *Proceedings of the British Academy* 117 (2001): 297–324.

Holmes, Stephen. "The Scowl of Minerva." *New Republic* 206, no. 12 (March 23, 1992): 27–33.

Hume, David. *Enquiries concerning Human Understanding and concerning the Principles of Morals.* 1751/77. Edited by L. A. Selby-Bigge. 3rd. ed. Oxford: Clarendon Press, 1975.

———. *A Treatise of Human Nature.* 1739–40. Edited by L. A. Selby-Bigge. 2nd ed. Oxford: Clarendon Press, 1978.

Huntington, Samuel P. "The Democratic Distemper." *Public Interest*, no. 41 (Fall 1975): 9–38.

Hutcheson, Francis. *An Essay on the Nature and Conduct of the Passions and Affections, with Illustrations on the Moral Sense.* 1728. Edited with an introduction by Aaron Garrett. Indianapolis: Liberty Fund, 2002.

———. *An Inquiry into the Original of Our Ideas of Beauty and Virtue.* 1726. Rev. ed. Edited with an introduction by Wolfgang Leidhold. Indianapolis: Liberty Fund, 2004.

Johnston, David, and Steven A. Holmes. "Experts Doubt Effectiveness of Crime Bill." *New York Times*, September 14, 1994. https://www.nytimes.com/1994/09/14/us/experts-doubt-effectiveness-of-crime-bill.html.

Kristol, Irving. "American Universities in Exile." *Wall Street Journal*, June 17, 1986.

———. "America's 'Exceptional Conservatism.'" *Wall Street Journal*, April 18, 1995.

———. "A Conservative Welfare State." *Wall Street Journal*, June 14, 1993.

———. *Neoconservatism: The Autobiography of an Idea.* New York: Free Press, 1995.

———. "The Neoconservative Persuasion." *Weekly Standard*, August 25, 2003. http://www.weeklystandard.com/the-neoconservative-persuasion/article/4246.

———. "The New Face of American Politics." *Wall Street Journal*, August 26, 1994.

———. *On the Democratic Idea in America.* New York: Harper & Row, 1972.

———. *Reflections of a Neoconservative: Looking Back, Looking Ahead.* New York: Basic Books, 1983.

———. *Two Cheers for Capitalism.* New York: Basic Books, 1978.

———. "Urban Civilization and Its Discontents." *Commentary* 50, no. 1 (July 1970): 29–35.

———. "Whatever Happened to Common Sense?" *Wall Street Journal*, January 17, 1984.

Kristol, Irving, and Paul Weaver. "Who Knows New York?—and Other Notes on a Mixed-Up City." *Public Interest*, no. 16 (Summer 1969): 41–59.

Ladd, Everett C. "The Data Just Don't Show Erosion of America's 'Social Capital.'" *Public Perspective* 7 (June–July 1996): 5–22.

Lasch, Christopher. *The Revolt of the Elites and the Betrayal of Democracy.* New York: W. W. Norton, 1995.

———. "What's Wrong with the Right." *Tikkun* 1, no. 1 (1986): 23–29. http://www.radicalcritique.org/2013/10/whats-wrong-with-right.html.

Lorenz, Konrad. *On Aggression.* Translated by Marjorie Kerr Wilson. New York: Harcourt, Brace & World, 1966.

Margolick, David. "Lorena Bobbitt Acquitted in Mutilation of Husband." *New York Times*, January 22, 1994. https://www.nytimes.com/1994/01/22/us/lorena-bobbitt-acquitted-in-mutilation-of-husband.html.

McGrory, Mary. "Moynihan Was Right 21 Years Ago." *Washington Post*, January 26, 1986. https://

www.washingtonpost.com/archive/opinions/1986/01/26/moynihan-was-right-21-years
-ago/04e753db-ba4a-4a0b-9ca3-230b68151b5d/?utm_term=.148122450ae3.

Mead, Lawrence M. *Beyond Entitlement: The Social Obligations of Citizenship*. New York: Free
Press, 1986.

———. *The New Politics of Poverty: The Nonworking Poor in America*. New York: Basic Books,
1992.

Miller, Neil. "The Prolific Professor." *UCLA Magazine*, Fall 1991: 19–23.

Moynihan, Daniel Patrick. "Defining Deviancy Down." *American Scholar* 62, no. 1 (Winter 1993):
17–30.

———. *Family and Nation*. San Diego: Harcourt Brace Jovanovich, 1986.

———. *Maximum Feasible Misunderstanding: Community Action in the War on Poverty*. New
York: Free Press, 1969.

———. *The Negro Family: The Case for National Action*. In *The Moynihan Report and the Politics
of Controversy*, edited by Lee Rainwater and William L. Yancey, 39–124. Cambridge, MA:
MIT Press, 1967 [1965].

Murray, Charles. "The Coming White Underclass." *Wall Street Journal*, October 29, 1993.

———. *Losing Ground: American Social Policy, 1950–1980*. New York: Basic Books, 1984.

New York Times. "Left and Right Fight for Custody of 'Family' Issue." August 20, 1987.

———. "Senator Moynihan and the Children." April 9, 1985. https://www.nytimes.com/1985/04
/09/opinion/senator-moynihan-and-the-children.html.

Nifong, Christina. "Reformer Calls for a System That Gets Back to the Basics." Interview of
James Q. Wilson. *Christian Science Monitor*, May 19, 1997. https://www.csmonitor.com/1997
/0519/051997.feat.justice.1.html.

Novak, Michael. *The Spirit of Democratic Capitalism*. New York: Simon & Schuster, 1982.

Patterson, Orlando. *The Ordeal of Integration: Progress and Resentment in America's 'Racial' Crisis*. Washington, DC: Civitas/Counterpoint, 1997.

Putnam, Robert D. "Bowling Alone: America's Declining Social Capital." *Journal of Democracy*
6, no. 1 (January 1995): 65–78.

———. *Bowling Alone: The Collapse and Revival of American Community*. New York: Simon &
Schuster, 2000.

Reagan, Ronald. "Farewell Speech." January 11, 1989. The Patriot Post. https://patriotpost.us/pages
/453-ronald-reagan-farewell-speech.

———. "To Restore America." March 31, 1976. The Patriot Post. https://patriotpost.us/pages
/429-ronald-reagan-to-restore-america.

Schudson, Michael. "What If Civic Life Didn't Die?" *American Prospect* 25 (March–April 1996):
17–20.

Smith, Adam. *An Inquiry into the Nature and Causes of the Wealth of Nations*. 1776. Edited by
R. H. Campbell, A. S. Skinner, and W. B. Todd. 2 vols. Indianapolis: Liberty Fund, 1981.

———. *Lectures on Jurisprudence*. 1762–63. Edited by R. L. Meek, D. D. Raphael, and P. G. Stein.
Indianapolis: Liberty Fund, 1982.

———. *The Theory of Moral Sentiments*. 1759. Edited by D. D. Raphael and A. L. Macfie. Indianapolis: Liberty Fund, 1982.

Talbott, Strobe. "Terminator 2: Gloom on the Right." *Time*, January 27, 1992.

Trilling, Lionel. *Beyond Culture: Essays on Literature and Learning*. New York: Viking Press, 1965.

Trivers, Robert L. "The Evolution of Reciprocal Altruism." *Quarterly Review of Biology* 46 (1971):
35–57.

Turiel, Elliot. "Making Sense of Social Experiences and Moral Judgments." *Criminal Justice Ethics* 13, no. 2 (Summer/Fall 1994): 69–76.

Westermarck, Edward. *The History of Human Marriage.* London: Macmillan, 1891.

———. *The Origin and Development of the Moral Ideas.* Volumes 1–2. London: Macmillan, 1906–8.

Wills, Garry. *Inventing America: Jefferson's Declaration of Independence.* Garden City, NY: Doubleday, 1978.

Wilson, Edward O. *Sociobiology: The New Synthesis.* Cambridge, MA: Harvard University Press, 1975.

Wilson, James Q. "Against Homosexual Marriage." *Commentary* 101, no. 3 (March 1996): 34–39.

———. "Bring Back the Orphanage." *Wall Street Journal,* August 22, 1994.

———. "A Connecticut Yankee in King Arthur's Court: A Biography." In *Edward C. Banfield: An Appreciation,* edited by Charles S. Kesler, 31–78. Claremont, CA: Henry Salvatori Center for the Study of Individual Freedom in the Modern World, 2002. http://www.scribd.com/doc/49101990/Edward-C-Banfield-An-Appreciation.

———. "Crime and American Culture." *Public Interest,* no. 70 (Winter 1983): 22–48.

———. "Crime and the Liberal Audience." *Commentary* 51, no. 1 (January 1971): 71–78.

———. "Crime, Race, and Values." *Society* 30, no. 1 (1992): 90–93.

———. "Culture, Incentives, and the Underclass." In *Values and Public Policy,* edited by Henry J. Aaron, Thomas E. Mann, and Timothy Taylor, 54–80. Washington, DC: Brookings Institution, 1994.

———. "The 11th Commandment Seems to Be 'Judge Not.'" *Wall Street Journal,* April 5, 2001.

———. "Emotions, Reason, and Character." *Criminal Justice Ethics* 13, no. 2 (Summer/Fall 1994): 83–92.

———. "Entering Criminology through the Back Door." *The Criminologist: Official Newsletter of the American Society of Criminology* 13, no. 6 (November–December 1988): 1, 5, 8, 14–15.

———. "The Family-Values Debate." *Commentary* 95, no. 4 (April 1993): 24–31.

———. "Foreword." In *The Essential Neoconservative Reader,* edited by Mark Gerson, vii–x. Reading, MA: Addison-Wesley, 1996.

———. "Foreword: Never Too Early." In *Serious and Violent Juvenile Offenders: Risk Factors and Successful Interventions,* edited by Rolf Loeber and David P. Farrington, ix–xi. Thousand Oaks, CA: Sage, 1998.

———. "The Free Society Requires a Moral Sense, Social Capital." Interview of James Q. Wilson. *Religion and Liberty* 9, no. 4 (July–August 1999). https://acton.org/pub/religion-liberty/volume-9-number-4/free-society-requires-moral-sense-social-capital.

———. "Gentleman, Politician, Scholar." *Public Interest,* no. 152 (Summer 2003): 113–18.

———. "Incivility and Crime." In *Civility and Citizenship in Liberal Democratic Societies,* edited by Edward C. Banfield, 95–113. Saint Paul, MN: Paragon House, 1992.

———. "Justice versus Humanity in the Family." In *The Neoconservative Imagination,* edited by Christopher Demuth and William Kristol, 147–64. Washington, DC: AEI Press, 1995.

———. *The Marriage Problem: How Our Culture Has Weakened Families.* New York: HarperCollins, 2002.

———. "Moral Intuitions." *Proceedings of the American Philosophical Society* 140, no. 1 (March 1996): 65–76.

———. *Moral Intuitions*. With an introduction by Emil Uddhammar. New Brunswick, NJ: Transaction, 2000.

———. *Moral Judgment: Does the Abuse Excuse Threaten Our Legal System?* New York: Basic Books, 1997.

———. *The Moral Sense*. New York: Free Press, 1993.

———. "Negro Leaders in Chicago." PhD Diss., University of Chicago, 1959.

———. "A New Approach to Welfare Reform: Humility." *Wall Street Journal*, December 29, 1994.

———. "On Abortion." *Commentary* 97, no. 1 (January 1994): 21–29.

———. *On Character: Essays by James Q. Wilson*. Expanded edition. Washington, DC: AEI Press, 1995.

———. "Pat Moynihan Thinks about Families." *Annals of the American Academy of Political and Social Science* 621 (January 2009): 28–33.

———. "Policy Intellectuals and Public Policy." *Public Interest*, no. 64 (Summer 1981): 31–46.

———. "Raising Kids." *Atlantic Monthly*, October 1983.

———. "Reading Jurors' Minds." *Commentary* 101, no. 2 (February 1996): 45–48.

———. "The Rediscovery of Character: Private Virtue and Public Policy." *Public Interest*, no. 81 (Fall 1985): 3–16.

———. *Thinking about Crime*. New York: Basic Books, 1975.

———. *Thinking about Crime*. Rev. ed. New York: Basic Books, 1983.

———. "To Prevent Riots, Reduce Black Crime." *Wall Street Journal*, May 6, 1992.

———. "The Urban Mood." Coauthored with Harold R. Wilde. *Commentary* 48, no. 4 (October 1969): 52–61.

———. "The Urban Unease: Community vs. City." *Public Interest*, no. 12 (Summer 1968): 25–39.

———. "What to Do about Crime." *Commentary* 98, no. 3 (September 1994): 25–34.

———. "Why Falling Crime Statistics Don't Make Us Feel More Secure." *Los Angeles Times*, September 25, 1994.

Wilson, James Q., and Robert L. DuPont. "The Sick Sixties." *Atlantic Monthly*, October 1973.

Wilson, James Q., and Richard J. Herrnstein. *Crime and Human Nature: The Definite Study of the Causes of Crime*. New York: Simon & Schuster, 1985.

Wilson, James Q., and George L. Kelling. "Broken Windows: The Police and Neighborhood Safety." *Atlantic Monthly*, March 1982.

Wilson, William Julius. *The Declining Significance of Race: Blacks and Changing American Institutions*. Chicago: University of Chicago Press, 1978.

———. *The Truly Disadvantaged: The Inner City, the Underclass, and Public Policy*. Chicago: University of Chicago Press, 1987.

———. *When Work Disappears: The World of the New Urban Poor*. New York: Alfred A. Knopf, 1996.

Wolfe, Alan. *One Nation, after All: What Middle-Class Americans Really Think about God, Country, Family, Racism, Welfare, Immigration, Homosexuality, Work, the Right, the Left, and Each Other*. New York: Viking, 1998.

Wrong, Dennis. "21 Years Later." *New Republic* 194, no. 11 (March 17, 1986): 30–33.

Yale Law School, Lillian Goldman Law Library. "Declaration of the Rights of Man—1789." http://avalon.law.yale.edu/18th_century/rightsof.asp.

Secondary Sources

Ahnert, Thomas. *The Moral Culture of the Scottish Enlightenment, 1690–1805*. New Haven, CT: Yale University Press, 2014.

Alexander, Karl. "The Coleman Report at 50: A Prospectus." Johns Hopkins University. http://education.jhu.edu/coleman/prospectus.

Alexander, Michelle. *The New Jim Crow: Mass Incarceration in the Age of Colorblindness*. Rev. edition. New York: New Press, 2012.

Allitt, Patrick. *The Conservatives: Ideas and Personalities throughout American History*. New Haven, CT: Yale University Press, 2009.

Ansell, Amy E. *Race and Ethnicity: The Key Concepts*. London: Routledge, 2013.

Arnhart, Larry. "The Death of James Q. Wilson." *Darwinian Conservatism* (blog), March 3, 2012. http://darwinianconservatism.blogspot.fi/2012/03/death-of-james-q-wilson.html.

Bailyn, Bernard. *The Ideological Origins of the American Revolution*. Cambridge, MA: Harvard University Press, 1967.

Balint, Benjamin. *Running Commentary: The Contentious Magazine That Transformed the Jewish Left into the Neoconservative Right*. New York: PublicAffairs, 2010.

Batnitzky, Leora. "Leo Strauss." In *Stanford Encyclopedia of Philosophy*, edited by Edward N. Zalta. Summer 2016 edition. https://plato.stanford.edu/archives/sum2016/entries/strauss-leo/.

Beinart, Peter. "Hillary Clinton and the Tragic Politics of Crime." *Atlantic*, May 1, 2015. https://www.theatlantic.com/politics/archive/2015/05/the-tragic-politics-of-crime/392114/.

Bergner, Daniel. "Is Stop-and-Frisk Worth It." *Atlantic*, April 2014. https://www.theatlantic.com/magazine/archive/2014/04/is-stop-and-frisk-worth-it/358644/.

Berry, Christopher J. *Social Theory of the Scottish Enlightenment*. Edinburgh, Scot.: Edinburgh University Press, 1997.

Boaz, David. *The Libertarian Mind: A Manifesto for Freedom*. New York: Simon & Schuster, 2015.

Bow, Charles Bradford, ed. *Common Sense in the Scottish Enlightenment*. Oxford: Oxford University Press, 2018.

Bratton, William. *The Turnaround: How America's Top Cop Reversed the Crime Epidemic*. New York: Random House, 1998.

Brick, Howard. *Age of Contradiction: American Thought and Culture in the 1960s*. New York: Twayne, 1998.

Broadie, Alexander, ed. *The Cambridge Companion to the Scottish Enlightenment*. Cambridge: Cambridge University Press, 2003.

———. *A History of Scottish Philosophy*. Edinburgh, Scot.: Edinburgh University Press, 2009.

Brooks, Arthur C. "Our Culture of Contempt." *New York Times*, March 2, 2019. https://www.nytimes.com/2019/03/02/opinion/sunday/political-polarization.html.

Brown, Michael K., Martin Carnoy, Elliott Currie, Troy Duster, David B. Oppenheimer, Marjorie M. Schultz, and David Wellman. *Whitewashing Race: The Myth of a Color-Blind Society*. Berkeley: University of California Press, 2003.

Brown, Susan L., and Matthew R. Wright. "Older Adults' Attitudes toward Cohabitation: Two Decades of Change." *Journals of Gerontology: Series B* 71, no. 4 (July 2016): 755–64.

Brown, Wendy. "American Nightmare: Neoliberalism, Neoconservatism, and De-democratization." *Political Theory* 34, no. 6 (December 2006): 690–714.

Burgin, Angus. *The Great Persuasion: Reinventing Free Markets since the Depression*. Cambridge, MA: Harvard University Press, 2012.

Canovan, Margaret. *The People*. Cambridge: Polity, 2005.

Chappell, Marisa. *The War on Welfare: Family, Poverty, and Politics in Modern America*. Philadelphia: University of Pennsylvania Press, 2010.

Coates, Ta-Nehisi. "The Black Family in the Age of Mass Incarceration." *Atlantic*, October 2015. https://www.theatlantic.com/magazine/archive/2015/10/the-black-family-in-the-age-of -mass-incarceration/403246/.

Cooper, Melinda. *Family Values: Between Neoliberalism and the New Social Conservatism*. New York: Zone Books, 2017.

Courtwright, David T. *No Right Turn: Conservative Politics in a Liberal America*. Cambridge, MA: Harvard University Press, 2010.

Cowie, Jefferson. "Reclaiming Patriotism for the Left." *New York Times*, August 21, 2018. https:// www.nytimes.com/2018/08/21/opinion/nationalism-patriotism-liberals-.html.

———. *Stayin' Alive: The 1970s and the Last Days of the Working Class*. New York: New Press, 2010.

Cullen, Francis T., Bonnie S. Fisher, and Brandon K. Applegate. "Public Opinion about Punishment and Corrections." *Crime and Justice* 27 (2000): 1–79.

Degler, Carl. *In Search of Human Nature: The Decline and Revival of Darwinism in American Social Thought*. New York: Oxford University Press, 1991.

Delisi, Matt. "Conservatism and Common Sense: The Criminological Career of James Q. Wilson." *Justice Quarterly* 20, no. 3 (September 2003): 661–74.

Dictionary of American History. S.v. "Griggs v. Duke Power Company." Accessed August 9, 2019. http://www.encyclopedia.com/history/dictionaries-thesauruses-pictures-and-press-re leases/griggs-v-duke-power-company.

DiIulio, John J., Jr. "James Q. Wilson, 1931–2012." Contemporary Thinkers (website). Accessed August 9, 2019. http://contemporarythinkers.org/jq-wilson/.

———. "Moral Sense and Religious Sensibility: James Q. Wilson's Quest to Understand Human Character and Civic Virtue." Paper presented at Thinking about Politics: A Conference Dedicated to Explaining and Perpetuating the Political Insights of James Q. Wilson, Harvard University and Boston College, April 4–5, 2013. https://www.youtube.com /watch?v=T3zqa2uPoYk.

———. "Moral Sense and Social Science: Reading James Q. Wilson." *Claremont Review of Books* 12, no. 4 (Fall 2012). https://claremontreviewofbooks.com/moral-sense-and-social-science/.

Donohue, Kathleen G. *Freedom from Want: American Liberalism and the Idea of the Consumer*. Baltimore: Johns Hopkins University Press, 2003.

Dorrien, Gary. *Imperial Designs: Neoconservatism and the New Pax Americana*. New York: Routledge, 2004.

———. *The Neoconservative Mind: Politics, Culture, and the War of Ideology*. Philadelphia: Temple University Press, 1993.

———. *Social Ethics in the Making: Interpreting an American Tradition*. Chichester, Eng.: Wiley-Blackwell, 2009.

Douthat, Ross. "Trump's Empty Culture Wars." *New York Times*, September 27, 2017. https:// www.nytimes.com/2017/09/27/opinion/trumps-empty-culture-wars.html.

Dowland, Seth. *Family Values and the Rise of the Christian Right*. Philadelphia: University of Pennsylvania Press, 2015.

Drolet, Jean-François. *American Neoconservatism: The Politics and Culture of a Reactionary Idealism*. New York: Oxford University Press, 2013.

Drury, Shadia B. *Alexandre Kojève: The Roots of Postmodern Politics*. New York: St. Martin's, 1994.

———. *Leo Strauss and the American Right*. New York: St. Martin's, 1997.

Dugan, Andrew. "US Divorce Rate Dips, but Moral Acceptability Hits New High." Gallup (website). July 7, 2017. http://news.gallup.com/poll/213677/divorce-rate-dips-moral-acceptability-hits-new-high.aspx.

Duncan, Stephen R. "Social and Cultural—a Historiographical Survey." In *The Routledge History of the Twentieth-Century United States*, edited by Jerald Podair and Darren Dochuk, 138–48. New York: Routledge, 2018.

Echols, Alice. *Daring to Be Bad: Radical Feminism in America 1967–1975*. Minneapolis: University of Minnesota Press, 1989.

Ehrman, John. *The Rise of Neoconservatism: Intellectuals and Foreign Affairs 1945–1994*. New Haven, CT: Yale University Press, 1995.

Encyclopedia Britannica. S.v. "Bakke Decision." Accessed August 9, 2019. https://www.britannica.com/event/Bakke-decision.

Fawcett, Edmund. *Liberalism: The Life of an Idea*. Princeton, NJ: Princeton University Press, 2014.

Federici, Michael P. *The Challenge of Populism: The Rise of Right-Wing Democratism in Postwar America*. New York: Praeger, 1991.

Filonowicz, Joseph Duke. *Fellow-Feeling and the Moral Life*. Cambridge: Cambridge University Press, 2008.

Fiorina, Morris P., Samuel Abrams, and Jeremy C. Pope. *Culture Wars? The Myth of a Polarized America*. 3rd ed. Boston: Longman, 2011.

Flamm, Michael W. "The Liberal-Conservative Debates of the 1960s." In *Debating the 1960s: Liberal, Conservative, and Radical Perspectives*, edited by Michael W. Flamm and David Steigerwald, 99–165. Lanham, MD: Rowman & Littlefield, 2008.

Fleischacker, Samuel. "Adam Smith on Equality." In *The Oxford Handbook of Adam Smith*, edited by Christopher J. Berry, Maria Pia Paganelli, and Craig Smith, 485–500. Oxford: Oxford University Press, 2013.

———. "The Impact on America: Scottish Philosophy and the American Founding." In *The Cambridge Companion to the Scottish Enlightenment*, edited by Alexander Broadie, 316–37. Cambridge: Cambridge University Press, 2003.

———. *On Adam Smith's Wealth of Nations*. Princeton, NJ: Princeton University Press, 2004.

Forst, Brian. "James Q. Wilson." Oxford Bibliographies. Last modified September 30, 2013. http://www.oxfordbibliographies.com/view/document/obo-9780195396607/obo-9780195396607-0156.xml.

Fowler, Robert Booth. *Enduring Liberalism: American Political Thought since the 1960s*. Lawrence: University Press of Kansas, 1999.

Frank, Thomas. "Bill Clinton's Crime Bill Destroyed Lives and There Is No Point Denying It." *Guardian*, April 15, 2016. https://www.theguardian.com/commentisfree/2016/apr/15/bill-clinton-crime-bill-hillary-black-lives-thomas-frank.

Frazer, Michael L. *The Enlightenment of Sympathy: Justice and the Moral Sentiments in the Eighteenth Century and Today*. New York: Oxford University Press, 2010.

Freeden, Michael. *Ideologies and Political Theory: A Conceptual Approach*. Oxford: Oxford University Press, 1996.

Friedman, Murray, ed. *Commentary in American Life*. Philadelphia: Temple University Press, 2005.

———. *The Neoconservative Revolution: Jewish Intellectuals and the Shaping of Public Policy*. New York: Cambridge University Press, 2005.

Fuller, Adam L. *Taking the Fight to the Enemy: Neoconservatism and the Age of Ideology*. Lanham, MD: Lexington Books, 2012.

Galston, William A. *Anti-pluralism: The Populist Threat to Liberal Democracy*. New Haven, CT: Yale University Press, 2018.

Gans, Herbert J. *The War against the Poor: The Underclass and Antipoverty Policy*. New York: Basic Books, 1995.

Garland, David. *The Culture of Control: Crime and Social Order in Contemporary Society*. Oxford: Oxford University Press, 2001.

Garrett, Aaron, and James Harris, eds. *Scottish Philosophy in the Eighteenth Century*. Vol. 1, *Morals, Politics, Art, Religion*. Oxford: Oxford University Press, 2015.

Gaubatz, Kathlyn Taylor. *Crime in the Public Mind*. Ann Arbor: University of Michigan Press, 1995.

Geary, Daniel. *Beyond Civil Rights: The Moynihan Report and Its Legacy*. Philadelphia: University of Pennsylvania Press, 2015.

Genter, Robert. *Late Modernism: Art, Culture, and Politics in Cold War America*. Philadelphia: University of Pennsylvania Press, 2010.

Gerson, Mark. *The Neoconservative Vision: From the Cold War to the Culture Wars*. Lanham, MD: Madison Books, 1996.

Gerstle, Gary. "America's Neoliberal Order." In *Beyond the New Deal Order: U.S. Politics from the Great Depression to the Great Recession*, edited by Gary Gerstle, Nelson Liechtenstein, and Alice O'Connor, 257–78. Philadelphia: University of Pennsylvania Press, 2019.

Gilens, Martin. *Why Americans Hate Welfare: Race, Media, and the Politics of Antipoverty Policy*. Chicago: University of Chicago Press, 1999.

Gill, Michael B. *The British Moralists on Human Nature and the Birth of Secular Ethics*. New York: Cambridge University Press, 2006.

———. "Moral Rationalism vs. Moral Sentimentalism: Is Morality More like Math or Beauty?" *Philosophy Compass* 2, no. 1 (January 2007): 16–30.

Gill, Michael B., and Shaun Nichols. "Sentimentalist Pluralism: Moral Psychology and Philosophical Ethics." *Philosophical Issues* 18 (2008): 143–63.

Giuliani, Rudolph W. "What New York Owes James Q. Wilson." *City Journal*, Spring 2012. https://www.city-journal.org/html/what-new-york-owes-james-q-wilson-13465.html.

Gosse, Van. *Rethinking the New Left: An Interpretative History*. New York: Palgrave Macmillan, 2005.

Gosse, Van, and Richard Moser, eds. *The World the Sixties Made: Politics and Culture in Recent America*. Philadelphia: Temple University Press, 2003.

Gottfried, Paul Edward. *Leo Strauss and the Conservative Movement in America: A Critical Appraisal*. New York: Cambridge University Press, 2012.

Griswold, Charles L., Jr. *Adam Smith and the Virtues of Enlightenment*. Cambridge: Cambridge University Press, 1999.

Halper, Stefan, and Jonathan Clarke. *America Alone: The Neo-conservatives and the Global Order*. Cambridge: Cambridge University Press, 2004.

Hamburger, Jacob, and Daniel Steinmetz-Jenkins. "Why Did Neoconservatives Join Forces with Neoliberals? Irving Kristol from Critic to Ally of Free-Market Economics." *Global*

Intellectual History, January 9, 2018. https://www.tandfonline.com/doi/10.1080/23801883.20 18.1423740.

Hanley, Ryan Patrick. *Adam Smith and the Character of Virtue*. New York: Cambridge University Press, 2009.

Harcourt, Bernard E. *Illusion of Order: The False Promise of Broken Windows Policing*. Cambridge, MA: Harvard University Press, 2001.

Harcourt, Bernard E., and Jens Ludwig. "Broken Windows: New Evidence from New York City and a Five-City Social Experiment." *University of Chicago Law Review* 73 (2006): 271–320.

Harris, Janelle. "Menendez Brothers: Everything You Need to Know." *Rolling Stone*, October 2, 2016. http://www.rollingstone.com/culture/news/menendez-brothers-everything-you-need -to-know-w442897.

Hartman, Andrew. "Age of Fracture v. Age of Culture Wars." *US Intellectual History* (blog). March 11, 2015. https://s-usih.org/2015/03/age-of-fracture-v-age-of-culture-wars/.

———. *A War for the Soul of America: A History of the Culture Wars*. Chicago: University of Chicago Press, 2015.

———. *A War for the Soul of America: A History of the Culture Wars*. 2nd ed. Chicago: University of Chicago Press, 2019.

Heilbrunn, Jacob. *They Knew They Were Right: The Rise of the Neocons*. New York: Doubleday, 2008.

High, Brandon. "The Recent Historiography of American Neoconservatism." *Historical Journal* 52, no. 2 (2009): 475–91.

Hinton, Elizabeth. *From the War on Poverty to the War on Crime: The Making of Mass Incarceration in America*. Cambridge, MA: Harvard University Press, 2016.

Hochschild, Arlie Russell. *Strangers in Their Own Land: Anger and Mourning on the American Right*. New York: New Press, 2016.

Hodgson, Godfrey. *The Gentleman from New York: Daniel Patrick Moynihan—a Biography*. Boston: Houghton Mifflin, 2000.

Hoeveler, J. David Jr. "Conservative Intellectuals and the Reagan Ascendancy." *History Teacher* 23, no. 3 (May 1990): 305–18.

———. *Creating the American Mind: Intellect and Politics in the Colonial Colleges*. New York: Rowman & Littlefield, 2002.

———. *James McCosh and the Scottish Intellectual Tradition: From Glasgow to Princeton*. Princeton, NJ: Princeton University Press, 1981.

———. *The Postmodernist Turn: American Thought and Culture in the 1970s*. New York: Twayne, 1996.

———. *Watch on the Right: Conservative Intellectuals in the Reagan Era*. Madison: University of Wisconsin Press, 1991.

Hofstadter, Richard. *Anti-intellectualism in American Life*. New York: Alfred A. Knopf, 1963.

Holloway, Carson. *The Right Darwin? Evolution, Religion, and the Future of Democracy*. Dallas: Spence, 2006.

Horwitz, Robert B. *America's Right: Anti-establishment Conservatism from Goldwater to the Tea Party*. Cambridge: Polity, 2013.

Howe, Daniel Walker. *The Unitarian Conscience: Harvard Moral Philosophy 1805–61*. Cambridge, MA: Harvard University Press, 1970.

Hulliung, Mark. *Citizens and Citoyens: Republicans and Liberals in America and France*. Cambridge, MA: Harvard University Press, 2002.

Hunter, James Davison. *Culture Wars: The Struggle to Define America*. New York: Basic Books, 1991.

Hunter, James Davison, and Alan Wolfe, eds. *Is There a Culture War? A Dialogue on Values and American Public Life*. Washington, DC: Brookings Institution, 2006.

Igo, Sarah E. *The Averaged American: Surveys, Citizens, and the Making of a Mass Public*. Cambridge, MA: Harvard University Press, 2007.

Jeffers, Thomas L. *Norman Podhoretz: A Biography*. New York: Cambridge University Press, 2010.

Jenkins, Philip. *Decade of Nightmares: The End of the Sixties and the Making of Eighties America*. New York: Oxford University Press, 2006.

Jumonville, Neil. *Critical Crossings: The New York Intellectuals in Postwar America*. Berkeley: University of California Press, 1991.

Kazin, Michael. *The Populist Persuasion: An American History*. Rev. ed. Ithaca, NY: Cornell University Press, 1998.

Katz. Michael B., ed. *The "Underclass" Debate: Views from History*. Princeton, NJ: Princeton University Press, 1993.

———. *The Undeserving Poor: America's Enduring Confrontation with Poverty*. 2nd ed. New York: Oxford University Press, 2013.

Kleiman, Mark A. R. "Thinking about Punishment: James Q. Wilson and Mass Incarceration." Working paper, Marron Institute, New York University, June 26, 2014. http://marroninsti tute.nyu.edu/uploads/content/Thinking_About_Punishment.pdf.

———. "Wilson's Machiavellian Cruelty." Paper presented at Thinking about Politics: A Conference Dedicated to Explaining and Perpetuating the Political Insights of James Q. Wilson, Harvard University and Boston College, April 4–5, 2013. https://www.youtube.com /watch?v=zKouSgtb2bY.

Kloppenberg, James T. *The Virtues of Liberalism*. New York: Oxford University Press, 1998.

Kymlicka, Will. *Contemporary Political Philosophy: An Introduction*. 2nd ed. Oxford: Oxford University Press, 2002.

Laclau, Ernesto. *On Populist Reason*. London: Verso, 2005.

Lacy, Tim. "Against and beyond Hofstadter: Revising the Study of Anti-intellectualism." In *American Labyrinth: Intellectual History for Complicated Times*, edited by Raymond Haberski Jr. and Andrew Hartman, 253–70. Ithaca, NY: Cornell University Press, 2018.

Lagerspetz, Olli, Jan Antfolk, Ylva Gustafsson, and Camilla Kronkvist, eds. *Evolution, Human Behaviour and Morality: The Legacy of Westermarck*. London: Routledge, 2017.

Lassiter, Matthew D. "Inventing Family Values." In *Rightward Bound: Making America Conservative in the 1970s*, edited by Bruce J. Schulman and Julian Zelizer, 13–28. Cambridge, MA: Harvard University Press, 2008.

Laurent, John, and Geoff Cockfield. "Adam Smith, Charles Darwin and the Moral Sense." In *New Perspectives on Adam Smith's The Theory of Moral Sentiments*, edited by Geoff Cockfield, Ann Firth, and John Laurent, 141–62. Cheltenham, England: Edward Elgar, 2007.

Lepistö, Antti. "Darwinian Conservatives and Westermarck's Ethics." In *Evolution, Human Behaviour and Morality: The Legacy of Westermarck*, edited by Olli Lagerspetz, Jan Antfolk, Ylva Gustafsson, and Camilla Kronkvist, 194–208. London: Routledge, 2017.

Lewis, Jane. "Fukuyama and Fin de Siècle Anxiety about the Family." *Political Quarterly* 70, no. 4 (October–December 1999): 426–34.

Lilla, Mark. "End of Identity Liberalism." *New York Times*, November 18, 2016. https://www
.nytimes.com/2016/11/20/opinion/sunday/the-end-of-identity-liberalism.html.

———. *The Once and Future Liberal: After Identity Politics*. New York: HarperCollins, 2017.

Linker, Damon. *The Theocons: Secular America under Siege*. New York: Doubleday, 2006.

Lipka, Michael. "South Carolina Valedictorian Reignites Debate on Prayer in School." Pew Research Center. June 13, 2013. http://www.pewresearch.org/fact-tank/2013/06/13/south-carolina
-valedictorian-reignites-debate-on-prayer-in-school/.

Liu, Catherine. *American Idyll: Academic Antielitism as Cultural Critique*. Iowa City: University of Iowa Press, 2011.

Lubasz, Heinz. "Adam Smith and the Free Market." In *Adam Smith's Wealth of Nations: New Interdisciplinary Essays*, edited by Stephen Copley and Kathryn Sutherland, 45–69. Manchester: Manchester University Press, 1995.

Luker, Ralph E. "Garry Wills and the New Debate over the Declaration of Independence." *Virginia Quarterly Review* 56, no. 2 (Spring 1980): 244–61.

Marcotte, Amanda. "More Proof That the Religious Right's 'Family Values' Obsession Is Really about Misogyny." *Salon*, August 14, 2014. https://www.salon.com/2014/08/14/more
_proof_that_the_religious_rights_family_values_obsession_is_really_about_misogyny
_partner/.

Mattson, Kevin. *Rebels All! A Short History of the Conservative Mind in Postwar America*. New Brunswick, NJ: Rutgers University Press, 2008.

———. *When America Was Great: The Fighting Faith of Postwar Liberalism*. New York: Routledge, 2004.

May, Henry. *The Enlightenment in America*. New York: Oxford University Press, 1976.

McCarthy, Thomas. *Race, Empire and the Idea of Human Development*. Cambridge: Cambridge University Press, 2009.

McGuirk, John. "The Culture War Is Over, and Conservatives Have Lost." *The Journal*, November 7, 2012. http://www.thejournal.ie/readme/conservatives-lose-the-culture-war-john
-mcguirk-665454-Nov2012/.

Michaels, Walter Benn. *The Trouble with Diversity: How We Learned to Love Identity and Ignore Inequality*. New York: Metropolitan Books, 2006.

Milam, Erika Lorraine. *Creatures of Cain: The Hunt for Human Nature in Cold War America*. Princeton, NJ: Princeton University Press, 2019.

Monroe, Kristen Renwick, Adam Martin, and Priyanka Ghosh. "Politics and an Innate Moral Sense: Scientific Evidence for an Old Theory?" *Political Research Quarterly* 62, no. 3 (September 2009): 614–34.

Mounk, Yascha. *The People vs. Democracy: Why Our Freedom Is in Danger and How to Save It*. Cambridge, MA: Harvard University Press, 2018.

Mudde, Cas, and Cristóbal Rovira Kaltwasser. *Populism: A Very Short Introduction*. New York: Oxford University Press, 2017.

Müller, Jan-Werner. *What Is Populism?* Philadelphia: University of Pennsylvania Press, 2016.

Murray, Douglas. *Neoconservatism: Why We Need It*. New York: Encounter Books, 2006.

Nagle, Angela. *Kill All Normies: Online Culture Wars from 4chan and Tumblr to Trump and the Alt-Right*. Winchester: Zero Books, 2017.

Nash, George H. *The Conservative Intellectual Movement in America since 1945.* 30th anniversary ed. Wilmington, DE: ISI Books, 2006.

Nerozzi, Sebastiano, and Pierluigi Nuti. "Adam Smith and the Family." *History of Economic Ideas* 19, no. 2 (2011): 11–41.

Neville, Helen A., Miguel E. Gallardo, and Derald Wing Sue, eds. *The Myth of Racial Color Blindness: Manifestations, Dynamics, and Impact.* Washington, DC: American Psychological Association, 2016.

Norton, Anne. *Leo Strauss and the Politics of American Empire.* New Haven, CT: Yale University Press, 2004.

Norton, David Fate. *David Hume: Common-Sense Moralist, Sceptical Metaphysician.* Princeton, NJ: Princeton University Press, 1982.

O'Connor, Alice. *Poverty Knowledge: Social Science, Social Policy, and the Poor in Twentieth-Century U.S. History.* Princeton, NJ: Princeton University Press, 2001.

Otteson, James R. *Adam Smith's Marketplace of Life.* Cambridge: Cambridge University Press, 2002.

Oxford Languages. "Word of the Year 2016." Oxford Languages (website). Accessed July 14, 2020. https://languages.oup.com/word-of-the-year/2016/.

Patterson, James T. *America's Struggle against Poverty, 1900–1994.* Cambridge, MA: Harvard University Press, 1994.

———. *Freedom Is Not Enough: The Moynihan Report and America's Struggle over Black Family Life from LBJ to Obama.* New York: Basic Books, 2010.

———. *Restless Giant: The United States from Watergate to Bush v. Gore.* New York: Oxford University Press, 2005.

Pearce, Katie. "An Enduring Legacy: The Study That Changed the Conversation on Education Policy." Johns Hopkins University. September 30, 2016. https://hub.jhu.edu/2016/09/30/coleman-report-at-50-conference/.

Peffley, Mark, Jon Hurwitz, and Paul Sniderman. "Racial Stereotypes and Whites' Political Views of Blacks in the Context of Welfare and Crime." *American Journal of Political Science* 41, no. 1 (1997): 30–60.

Pells, Richard. *The Liberal Mind in a Conservative Age: American Intellectuals in the 1940s and 1950s.* New York: Harper & Row, 1985.

Perlstein, Rick. "I Thought I Understood the American Right: Trump Proved Me Wrong." *New York Times Magazine,* April 11, 2017. https://www.nytimes.com/2017/04/11/magazine/i-thought-i-understood-the-american-right-trump-proved-me-wrong.html.

———. *Nixonland: The Rise of a President and the Fracturing of America.* New York: Scribner, 2008.

Petigny, Alan. *The Permissive Society: America, 1941–1965.* New York: Cambridge University Press, 2009.

Pew Research Center. "Attitudes on Same-Sex Marriage." May 14, 2019. http://www.pewforum.org/fact-sheet/changing-attitudes-on-gay-marriage/.

Phipps, Alison. *The Politics of the Body: Gender in a Neoliberal and Neoconservative Age.* Cambridge: Polity, 2014.

Pipatti, Otto. *Morality Made Visible: Edward Westermarck's Moral and Social Theory.* London: Routledge, 2019.

Pippin, Robert B. "Being, Time, and Politics: The Strauss-Kojève Debate." *History and Theory* 32, no. 2 (May 1993): 138–61.

Portes, Alejandro. "Social Capital: Its Origins and Applications in Modern Sociology." *Annual Review of Sociology* 24 (1998): 1–24.

Pratt, John. *Penal Populism*. London: Routledge, 2007.

Preparata, Guido Giacomo. "Suburbia's 'Crime Experts': The Neo-conservatism of Control Theory and the Ethos of Crime." *Critical Criminology* 21, no. 1 (March 2013): 73–86.

Priest, Greg. "Charles Darwin's Theory of Moral Sentiments: What Darwin's Ethics Really Owes to Adam Smith." *Journal of the History of Ideas* 78, no. 4 (2017): 571–93.

Raphael, D. D. *The Impartial Spectator: Adam Smith's Moral Philosophy*. Oxford: Oxford University Press, 2007.

Rasmussen, Dennis C. *The Pragmatic Enlightenment: Recovering the Liberalism of Hume, Smith, Montesquieu, and Voltaire*. Cambridge: Cambridge University Press, 2014.

Ratner-Rosenhagen, Jennifer. *American Nietzsche: A History of an Icon and His Ideas*. Chicago: University of Chicago Press, 2011.

Reed, Adolph Jr. *Class Notes: Posing as Politics and Other Thoughts on the American Scene*. New York: New Press, 2000.

Roberts, Julian V., and Loretta J. Stalans. *Public Opinion, Crime, and Criminal Justice*. Boulder, CO: Westview, 1997.

Robinson, Sally. *Marked Men: White Masculinity in Crisis*. New York: Columbia University Press, 2000.

Rodgers, Daniel T. *Age of Fracture*. Cambridge, MA: Belknap Press of Harvard University Press, 2011.

———. "Republicanism: The Career of a Concept." *Journal of American History* 79, no. 1 (June 1992): 11–38.

Roper Center for Public Opinion Research at Cornell University. "Public Opinion on Civil Rights: Reflections on the Civil Rights Act of 1964." July 2, 2014. https://ropercenter.cornell.edu/blog/public-opinion-civil-rights-reflections-civil-rights-act-1964-blog.

Rosen, Ruth. *The World Split Open: How the Modern Women's Movement Changed America*. Rev. ed. New York: Penguin, 2006.

Rosenfeld, Sophia. *Common Sense: A Political History*. Cambridge, MA: Harvard University Press, 2011.

———. "Conspiracies and Common Sense: From Founding to the Trump Era." Lecture at the Chicago Humanities Festival, November 5, 2017. YouTube. https://www.youtube.com/watch?v=eLJoI_NIMnQ.

———. *Democracy and Truth: A Short History*. Philadelphia: University of Pennsylvania Press, 2019.

———. "The Only Thing More Dangerous than Trump's Appeal to Common Sense Is His Dismissal of It." *Nation*, March 1, 2017. https://www.thenation.com/article/the-only-thing-more-dangerous-than-trumps-appeal-to-common-sense-is-his-dismissal-of-it/.

Ross, Janell. "Two Decades Later, Black and White Americans Finally Agree on O.J. Simpson's Guilt." *Washington Post*, March 4, 2016. https://www.washingtonpost.com/news/the-fix/wp/2015/09/25/black-and-white-americans-can-now-agree-o-j-was-guilty/?utm_term=.0461c411dc46.

Ruth, Henry, and Kevin R. Reitz. *The Challenge of Crime: Rethinking Our Response*. Cambridge, MA: Harvard University Press, 2003.

Samuels, Warren J., and Steven G. Medema. "Freeing Smith from the 'Free Market': On the Misperception of Adam Smith on the Economic Role of Government." *History of Political Economy* 37, no. 2 (Summer 2005): 219–26.

Sandel, Michael, Sidney Verba, and Harvey Mansfield. "James Q. Wilson." *Harvard Gazette*, February 6, 2013. http://news.harvard.edu/gazette/story/2013/02/james-q-wilson/.

Sanderson, Stephen K. "Edward Westermarck: The First Sociobiologist." In *The Oxford Handbook of Evolution, Biology, and Society*, edited by Rosemary L. Hopcroft, 63–86. New York: Oxford University Press, 2018. http://www.oxfordhandbooks.com/view/10.1093/oxfordhb/9780190299323.001.0001/oxfordhb-9780190299323-e-34.

Scher, Bill. "The Culture War President." *Politico*, September 27, 2017. https://www.politico.com/magazine/story/2017/09/27/trump-culture-war-215653.

Schliesser, Eric. *Adam Smith: Systematic Philosopher and Public Thinker*. New York: Oxford University Press, 2017.

———, ed. *Sympathy: A History*. New York: Oxford University Press, 2015.

Schulman, Bruce J. *The Seventies: The Great Shift in American Culture, Society, and Politics*. New York: Free Press, 2001.

Sheikh, Haroon. "Nietzsche and the Neoconservatives." *Journal of Nietzsche Studies*, nos. 35–36 (Spring–Autumn 2008): 28–47.

Shenk, Timothy. "The Culture Wars Aren't Over." *Dissent*, June 2, 2017. https://www.dissentmagazine.org/blog/culture-wars-not-over-american-affairs-debate.

Self, Robert O. *All in the Family: The Realignment of American Democracy since the 1960s*. New York: Hill and Wang, 2012.

Sloan, Douglas. *The Scottish Enlightenment and the American College Ideal*. New York: Teachers College Press, Columbia University, 1971.

Slobodian, Quinn. *Globalists: The End of Empire and the Birth of Neoliberalism*. Cambridge, MA: Harvard University Press, 2018.

Smith, David. "Trump's Republican Convention Speech: What He Said and What He Meant." *Guardian*, July 22, 2016. https://www.theguardian.com/us-news/ng-interactive/2016/jul/22/donald-trump-republican-convention-speech-transcript-annotated.

Snyder, Jeffrey Aaron. "America Will Never Move beyond the Culture Wars." *New Republic*, April 23, 2015. https://newrepublic.com/article/121627/war-soul-america-history-culture-wars-review.

Stahl, Jason. *Right Moves: The Conservative Think Tank in American Political Culture since 1945*. Chapel Hill: University of North Carolina Press, 2016.

Stalley, Richard. "Adam Smith and the Theory of Punishment." *Journal of Scottish Philosophy* 10, no. 1 (2012): 69–88.

Stedman Jones, Daniel. *Masters of the Universe: Hayek, Friedman, and the Birth of Neoliberal Politics*. Princeton, NJ: Princeton University Press, 2012.

Steeh, Charlotte, and Maria Krysan. "Trends: Affirmative Action and the Public, 1970–1995." *Public Opinion Quarterly* 60, no. 1 (Spring 1996): 128–58.

Steigerwald, David. "The Liberal-Radical Debates of the 1960s." In *Debating the 1960s: Liberal, Conservative, and Radical Perspectives*, edited by Michael W. Flamm and David Steigerwald, 3–71. Lanham: Rowman & Littlefield, 2008.

Steinfels, Peter. *The Neoconservatives: The Origins of a Movement*. With a new foreword. New York: Simon & Schuster, 2013.

The editors of the American Enterprise Institute. "The Sinatra of Social Science." American Enterprise Institute online. January 6, 2012. https://www.aei.org/articles/the-sinatra-of-social-science/.

Thompson, C. Bradley, and Yaron Brook. *Neoconservatism: An Obituary for an Idea.* Boulder, CO: Paradigm, 2010.

Thomson, Irene Taviss. *Culture Wars and Enduring American Dilemmas.* Ann Arbor: University of Michigan Press, 2010.

Thornton, Arland, and Linda Young-DeMarco. "Four Decades of Trends in Attitudes toward Family Issues in the United States." *Journal of Marriage and Family* 63, no. 4 (November 2001): 1009–37.

Vaïsse, Justin. *Neoconservatism: The Biography of a Movement.* Cambridge, MA: Belknap Press of Harvard University Press, 2011.

Wald, Alan M. *The New York Intellectuals: The Rise and Decline of the Anti-Stalinist Left from the 1930s to the 1980s.* Chapel Hill: University of North Carolina Press, 1987.

Weldon, Kathleen. "Public Opinion on the Voting Rights Act." *Huffington Post*, August 5, 2015. http://www.huffingtonpost.com/kathleen-weldon/public-opinion-on-the-voting-rights -act_b_7935836.html.

Welsh, Brandon C., and David P. Farrington. "Preventing Crime Is Hard Work: Early Intervention, Developmental Criminology, and the Enduring Legacy of James Q. Wilson." *Journal of Criminal Justice* 41, no. 6 (November–December 2013): 448–51.

West's Encyclopedia of American Law. S.v. "Abington School District v. Schempp." Accessed August 9, 2019. http://www.encyclopedia.com/law/encyclopedias-almanacs-transcripts-and -maps/abington-school-district-v-schempp.

———. S.v. "Engel v. Vitale." Accessed August 9, 2019. http://www.encyclopedia.com/law/encyclo pedias-almanacs-transcripts-and-maps/engel-v-vitale.

———. S.v. "Roe v. Wade." Accessed August 9, 2019. http://www.encyclopedia.com/social-sciences -and-law/law/court-cases/roe-v-wade.

———. S.v. "Swann v. Charlotte-Mecklenburg Board of Education." Accessed August 9, 2019. http://www.encyclopedia.com/social-sciences-and-law/law/court-cases/swann-v-charlotte -mecklenburg-county-board-education.

Wickberg, Daniel. "Intellectual—a Historiographical Survey." In *The Routledge History of the Twentieth-Century United States*, edited by Jerald Podair and Darren Dochuk, 116–26. New York: Routledge, 2018.

———. "Modernisms Endless: Ironies of the American Mid-century." *Modern Intellectual History* 10, no. 1 (2013): 207–19.

———. "The Sympathetic Self in American Culture, 1750–1920." In *Figures in the Carpet: Finding the Human Person in the American Past*, edited by Wilfred M. McClay, 129–61. Grand Rapids, MI: William B. Eerdmans, 2007.

Will, George F. "James Q. Wilson, America's Prophet." *Washington Post*, March 2, 2012. https:// www.washingtonpost.com/opinions/james-q-wilson-americas-prophet/2012/03/02/gIQA tEWGnR_story.html?utm_term=.6f786cc78e99.

Williams, Daniel K. *God's Own Party: The Making of the Christian Right.* New York: Oxford University Press, 2010.

Williams, Joan C. *White Working Class: Overcoming Class Cluelessness in America.* Boston: Harvard Business Review Press, 2017.

Williams, Rhys H. "From the 'Beloved Community' to 'Family Values': Religious Language, Symbolic Repertoires, and Democratic Culture." In *Social Movements: Identity, Culture, and the State*, edited by David S. Meyer, Nancy Whittier, and Belinda Robnett, 247–65. New York: Oxford University Press, 2002.

Wood, Gordon S. *The Creation of the American Republic, 1776–1787.* Chapel Hill: University of North Carolina Press, 1969.

Wroe, Nicholas. "History's Pallbearer." *Guardian,* May 11, 2002. https://www.theguardian.com /books/2002/may/11/academicexperts.artsandhumanities.

Xenos, Nicholas. "Neoconservatism Kristolized." *Salmagundi* (Spring/Summer 1987): 138–49.

Zaretsky, Natasha. *No Direction Home: The American Family and the Fear of National Decline, 1968–1980.* Chapel Hill: University of North Carolina Press, 2007.

Zimring, Franklin E. *The City That Became Safe: New York's Lessons for Urban Crime and Its Control.* New York: Oxford University Press, 2012.

———. *The Great American Crime Decline.* New York: Oxford University Press, 2008.

———. "How the Broken Windows Strategy Saved Lives in NYC." *New York Post,* August 24, 2014. http://nypost.com/2014/08/24/how-the-broken-windows-strategy-saved-lives-in-nyc/.

Zuckert, Catherine, and Michael Zuckert. *The Truth about Leo Strauss: Political Philosophy and American Democracy.* Chicago: University of Chicago Press, 2006.

Zuckert, Michael. "On Allan Bloom." *Good Society* 17, no. 2 (2008): 81–83.

Zuckert, Michael P., and Catherine H. Zuckert. *Leo Strauss and the Problem of Political Philosophy.* Chicago: University of Chicago Press, 2014.

Index